W9-ADB-080

A Concise Companion to
the Restoration and Eighteenth Century

Edited by Cynthia Wall

Blackwell
Publishing

BLACKWELL PUBLISHING
350 Main Street, Malden, MA 02148-5020, USA
108 Cowley Road, Oxford OX4 1JF, UK
550 Swanston Street, Carlton, Victoria 3053, Australia

First published 2005 by Blackwell Publishing Ltd

Library of Congress Cataloging-in-Publication Data

A concise companion to the Restoration and eighteenth century / edited by Cynthia Wall.
        p. cm. — (Blackwell concise companions to literature and culture)
    Includes bibliographical references and index.
    ISBN 1-4051-0117-2 (hardback : acid-free paper) — ISBN 1-4051-0118-0
(pbk. : acid-free paper)   1. English literature—18th century—History and criticism.
2. English literature—Early modern, 1500–1700—History and criticism.   3. Literature
and history—Great Britain—History—18th century.   4. Literature and history—Great
Britain—History—17th century.   5. Great Britain—History—Restoration, 1660–1688.
6. Great Britain—Civilization—18th century.   7. Great Britain—Civilization—17th
century.   I. Wall, Cynthia, 1959–   II. Series.
PR441.C665 2005
820.9′005—dc22

                                                                        2004012930

A catalogue record for this title is available from the British Library.

Set in 9.75/12.25pt Meridien
by Graphicraft Limited, Hong Kong
Printed and bound in the United Kingdom
by MPG Books Ltd, Bodmin, Cornwall

The publisher's policy is to use permanent paper from mills that operate a sustainable forestry policy, and which has been manufactured from pulp processed using acid-free and elementary chlorine-free practices. Furthermore, the publisher ensures that the text paper and cover board used have met acceptable environmental accreditation standards.

For further information on Blackwell Publishing,
visit our website:
www.blackwellpublishing.com

Contents

List of illustrations vii
Notes on Contributors viii

Introduction 1
Cynthia Wall

1 **Travel, Trade, and Empire**: Knowing other Places,
1660–1800 13
Miles Ogborn and Charles W. J. Withers

2 **Scientific Investigations**: Experimentalism and
Paradisal Return 36
Joanna Picciotto

3 **Public and Private**: The Myth of the Bourgeois
Public Sphere 58
J. A. Downie

4 **The Streets**: Literary Beggars and the Realities of
Eighteenth-Century London 80
Tim Hitchcock

5 **The Sewers:** Ordure, Effluence, and Excess in the
Eighteenth Century 101
Sophie Gee

Contents

6 **The Novel**: Novels in the World of Moving Goods   121
   Deidre Shauna Lynch

7 **The Gothic**: Moving in the World of Novels   144
   Mark R. Blackwell

8 **Gendering Texts**: "The Abuse of Title Pages":
   Men Writing as Women   162
   Susan Staves

9 **Drama**: Genre, Gender, Theater   183
   John O'Brien

10 **Poetry**: The Poetry of Occasions   202
   J. Paul Hunter

11 **Forms of Sublimity**: The Garden, the Georgic,
   and the Nation   226
   Rachel Crawford

12 **Criticism**: Literary History and Literary Historicism   247
   Mark Salber Phillips

Index   266

Illustrations

Figure 1   London to Oxford from John Ogilby's *Britannia*
(1675)   5

Figure 1.1 The title page to John Seller's *The Coasting Pilot*
(1671)   17

Figure 1.2 The map of Lilliput from Jonathan Swift's
Gulliver's Travels (1726)   31

Figure 6.1 Page 40 from the first edition of Daniel Defoe's
A Journal of the Plague Year (1722)   133

Figure 6.2 Frontispiece and title-page to the first Irish edition
of Francis Coventry's *History of Pompey the Little*
(1751)   139

Figure 9.1 "A Just View of the British Stage," by
William Hogarth (1724)   184

Figure 11.1 "Burlington House in Pickadilly" from Kip and
Knyff's *Britannia Illustrata* (1714)   230

Figure 11.2 "Frontispiece," from John Philips's, *Cyder* (1708)   233

Figure 11.3 "Design of an Elegant Kitchen Garden" from
Batty Langley's *New Principles of Gardening* (1728)   240

Notes on Contributors

Mark R. Blackwell is Associate Professor of English at the University of Hartford. His essays on Cleland's *Memoirs of a Woman of Pleasure* and on live-tooth transplantation have recently appeared in *Eighteenth-Century Novel* and *Eighteenth-Century Life*, and an article on allusion in Austen's *Sense and Sensibility* is forthcoming in *Eighteenth-Century Fiction*. He is currently editing a collection of essays on it-narratives.

Rachel Crawford is the author of *Poetry, Enclosure, and the Vernacular Landscape 1700–1830* (2002) and has published articles in *Journal of English Literary History, The Huntington Quarterly, Studies in Romanticism, Romanticism,* and *Romantic Science: The Literary Forms of Natural History*. Her current project investigates the literary placing of Southeast Asia in Britain's eighteenth century. She teaches at the University of San Francisco.

J. A. Downie is Professor of English at Goldsmiths College, University of London. His books include *Robert Harley and the Press: Propaganda and Public Opinion in the Age of Swift and Defoe* (1979), *Jonathan Swift, Political Writer* (1984), and *To Settle the Succession of the State: Literature and Politics, 1678–1750* (1994). He edited the "Party Politics" volume of *The Complete Works of Daniel Defoe* (2000) for Pickering and Chatto. He is currently working on a book entitled *The Making of the English Novel*.

Sophie Gee is an Assistant Professor in the Department of English at Princeton University. Her forthcoming publications include essays on

Dryden, Pope, and Milton. She is currently working on a book about waste in the eighteenth century, exploring the figurative and historical significance of material remnants in writing from Milton to Defoe.

Tim Hitchcock is Professor of Eighteenth-Century History at the University of Hertfordshire. He has published widely on the histories of eighteenth-century British poverty, gender, and sex. He is author of *English Sexualities, 1700–1800* (1997) and *Down and Out in Eighteenth-Century London* (2004). He is also co-director of "The Old Bailey Online" (www.oldbaileyonline.org).

J. Paul Hunter is Professor of English at the University of Virginia (and Barbara E. and Richard J. Franke Professor Emeritus at the University of Chicago). He is the author of several books on the eighteenth-century novel, including *Before Novels* (1990), which won the Louis Gottshalk Prize in 1991. He is now working on a book on the cultural history of the Anglophone couplet.

Deidre Shauna Lynch is Associate Professor of English at Indiana University. She is the author of *The Economy of Character: Novels, Market Culture, and the Business of Inner Meaning* (1998), editor of *Janeites: Austen's Disciples and Devotees* (2000), and co-editor, with William B. Warner, of *Cultural Institutions of the Novel* (1996).

John O'Brien is Associate Professor of English at the University of Virginia. He is the author of *Harlequin Britain: Pantomime and Entertainment, 1690–1760* (2004) and has recently published an edition of Susanna Centlivre's *The Wonder: A Woman Keeps a Secret* (2004).

Miles Ogborn is Reader in Geography at Queen Mary College, University of London. He is author of *Spaces of Modernity: London's Geographies, 1680–1780* (1998) and co-editor with Charles W. J. Withers of *Georgian Geographies: Essays on Space, Place and Landscape in the Eighteenth Century* (2004). He is currently working on the writing practices of the English East India Company in the seventeenth and eighteenth centuries.

Mark Salber Phillips is Professor of History at Carleton University. He is the author of *Society and Sentiment: Genres of Historical Writing in Britain, 1740–1820* (2000), as well as earlier studies of historical and political thought in the Italian Renaissance. His chapter is part of a new examination of the idea of historical distance.

Joanna Picciotto is Assistant Professor of English at the University of California, Berkeley. She is currently working on a book about literary and scientific experimentalism in seventeenth- and eighteenth-century England.

Susan Staves's scholarly interests center on English literature and history in the Restoration and eighteenth century, She is the author of *Players' Scepters: Fictions of Authority in the Restoration* (1979) and *Married Women's Separate Property in England, 1660–1833* (1990). With John Brewer, she has edited and contributed to *Early Modern Conceptions of Property* (1995). Her current book project is a literary history of women's writing in Britain from 1660 to 1789.

Cynthia Wall is Associate Professor of English at the University of Virginia. She is the author of *The Literary and Cultural Spaces of Restoration London* (1998) and an editor of Pope and Defoe.

Charles W. J. Withers is Professor of Historical Geography at the University of Edinburgh. Recent publications include *Geography and Enlightenment* (1999), *Science and Medicine in the Scottish Enlightenment* (2002), and *Georgian Geographies: Essays on Space, Place and Landscape in the Eighteenth Century* (2004), all as co-editor, and, as author, *Geography, Science and National Identity: Scotland Since 1520*. He is currently working on geographies of the Enlightenment and on the connections between geography and the scientific revolution.

Introduction

Cynthia Wall

I would like to introduce this volume of essays on the eighteenth century by introducing The Eighteenth Century, as captured by various voices at various times. It was not difficult to come up with mildly inconsistent to violently competing perspectives, not only from different generations but within the same decade:

> To the first and second generation after this revolution in taste, the classical species of poetry seemed no poetry at all. Dryden and Pope, who had been enthroned so long in secure promise of immortality, felt their shrines shaken as by an earthquake. It became the fashion to say that these men were no poets at all. (Edmund Gosse, *From Shakespeare to Pope*, 1885)

> We are to regard Dryden as the puissant and glorious founder, Pope as the splendid high priest, of our age of prose and reason, of our excellent and indispensable eighteenth century. (Matthew Arnold, "The Study of Poetry," 1888)

> Sir Leslie Stephen said that the Century began in 1688 and ended in 1832, and surely he was right; Revolution and Reform are its natural boundaries. . . . And yet, in a sense, the deaths of Pitt and Fox marked the close of the era; for with them – except that Sheridan still lived – ended the race of the great men, the Giants of the Century. Nor has England since seen their like. (O. F. Christie, *England in the Eighteenth Century: Essays in Verse*, 1921)

To many of us the eighteenth is perhaps the dullest and drabbest of modern centuries. (The Bishop of Clifton's Foreword to Robert Bracey, *Eighteenth Century Studies*, 1925)

Why is it that the eighteenth century so particularly delights us? Are we perhaps simply reacting against a reaction? Is the twentieth century so fond of the eighteenth because the nineteenth disliked it so intensely? . . . There is a divine elegance everywhere, giving a grace to pomposity, a significance to frivolity, and a shape to emptiness. (Lytton Strachey, "The Eighteenth Century," 1926)

There was never a century which did less harm than the eighteenth in England. (George Saintsbury, *The Peace of the Augustans*, 1916)

In the most general sense of progressive thought, the Enlightenment has always aimed at liberating men from fear and establishing their sovereignty. Yet the fully enlightened earth radiates disaster triumphant. (Max Horkheimer and Theodor W. Adorno, *Dialectic of Enlightenment*, 1947)

Not surprisingly, every critic as well as every reader has his or her own personal Eighteenth Century, and critics, like readers, employ a vocabulary of praise or distaste according to (or pushing against) the events and attitudes shaping their historical moment. The Eighteenth Century has been seen as a "place of rest and refreshment" (during the First World War); as the source of totalitarianism (after the Second World War); as a distinctly unpoetic time (said the Romantics); as a highpoint of poetic achievement (said themselves). Throw in the Restoration and we have once again the best of times, the worst of times: women on stage freed by new roles, and women on stage newly objectified by the male gaze; sexual equality in wit and sex, but marriages of convenience and sexual profligacy; women in trade, country houses for tradesmen – but the looming specter of the Angel in the House (Elizabeth Bennet disdained for "dirty ancles"); companionate marriage, but subordinated sexuality and increased prostitution; increasing wealth, literacy, and opportunity, but enclosure acts and industrialization. The twentieth century has devised its own characterizations of the period, from a "providence of wit" (Battestin 1974) to "intercultural collision, institutionalized racism, class tension" (Brown 1993: 7). In graduate school I was genially introduced to "Dr Johnson and his Circle" by one professor, and wittily to Grub Street by another. We've seen the rise of the novel, the idea of the bourgeois public sphere, the clamp of colonialism, the explosion of consumerism; various Marxist, deconstructionist, feminist, psychoanalytic, postcolonial, new historicist, and cultural studies approaches shape our perceptions of and assumptions about "our" eighteenth century. It's a bewildering cluster of worlds for any of us, and perhaps we can never have too many "companions" to help us negotiate them.

The original title for this series, under which I was approached to commission and edit essays, was *New Perspectives*, and that has been my operating principle. This collection of essays is not an introduction or a standard companion in the sense of laying out the basic territory to the novice pilgrim. To some extent it presumes enough prior knowledge to recognize the "new" in these perspectives. Each of these essays, to a greater or lesser degree, takes on certain widely held assumptions about eighteenth-century cultural contexts or literary practices, and pokes, prods, or overturns them. Each essay is by a scholar – whether well established in or relatively new to the profession – who makes a habit of shaping theses out of thorough research rather than driving research by a thesis. Each of these authors has been for me at one time or another a model for scholarship, textual analysis, conceptual argument, and good writing. This collection will be a companion of new perspectives for the eighteenth-century student and scholar.

My original desire for a dust jacket image was something from John Ogilby's 1675 *Britannia* – an utterly exquisite and historically influential roadmap (among other things it replaced the old British mile of 2428 yards with the statute mile of 1760 yards, "thus effecting a revolution in customary measurements" (Fordham 1925: 157)). (This desire has been translated into Figure 1.) In the Preface, Ogilby explains how to read the map: "We have Projected [the roads] upon imaginary Scrolls, the *Initial City* or *Town* being always at the Bottom of the outmost Scroll on the Left Hand; whence your *Road* ascends to the Top of the said Scroll; then from the Bottom of the next Scroll ascends again." It's a bird's-eye view, a self-reflexively cartographic enterprise: "the *Capital Towns* are describ'd *Ichnographically*, according to their Form and Extent; but the *Lesser Towns* and *Villages*, with the *Mansion Houses, Castles, Churches, Mills, Beacons, Woods, &c. Scenographically*, or in *Prospect*." Thus in the first scroll we see London figured as a two-dimensional survey, an upended plan, but as we follow some of the main roads up (west), through Hyde Park and Acton, we cross a "Brick Bridge & Rill," trees dot the landscape in Buckinghamshire, and hills rise round Oxford. Each scroll has its own compass relating the vertical presentation to the geographic reality. The whole is an art form of perspectives generally, employing several at once, continually reorienting itself, combining large prospects with close detail. In short, it captures *my* image of this collection of some of the best new work in eighteenth-century studies.

The first five chapters cover geographical and conceptual territories of the eighteenth century in Britain – what places were explored, how things were observed, the social, political, and religious realities versus their intellectual representations. The next six range over generic territory and our various assumptions about the author, the novel, drama, and poetry. The final chapter returns to conceptual geography: the critical perception of texts in historical contexts.

The collection opens with a large prospect and a mention of Ogilby in yet another of his roles, as Master of the King's Revels organizing the pageant for the celebration of the restoration of Charles II around a "display of geography and regal authority" (p. 13). In TRAVEL, TRADE AND EMPIRE: KNOWING OTHER PLACES 1600–1800, Charles Withers and Miles Ogborn explore the various written forms of "earth writing" and the influence of geographical discoveries and writings on the literature of the period in its peculiar fascination with negotiating between fact and fiction. Ogborn and Withers look at the complexity of "world writing," the competing interests of mercantile lobbyists, politicians, and explorers. They note that "the relationship between geographical knowledge and imperial power should not be drawn too tightly" because "the production of geographical knowledge was part of many different processes, and what was produced was far from being a coherent body of facts, theories or genres" (p. 16). What is often lost in some postcolonial stereotypes of eighteenth-century geographical practice is the possibility of *good* faith, of intellectual engagement and humanitarian principles as something other than a disingenuous front for capitalist and imperialist agendas. Captain Bligh, Captain Cook, and Captain Gulliver had quite different and quite individualized journals for their journeys.

From geography to micrography. Joanna Picciotto looks at scientific experimentalism and its relationship to literature and theology, pointing out that the "one-sided emphasis in recent scholarship on the gentlemanly character of experimental science obscures the extent to which the practice, rather than the mere theory, of mechanical philosophy – widely and correctly viewed as the philosophy of 'mechanicks' – required as much social as intellectual experimentation, forcing gentlemen virtuosi into behavior that was, to say the least, unusual for members of their class" (p. 43). She traces the trajectory from the New Jerusalem of Bacon's Eden as the site of innocence as *insight* rather than ignorance, and the Royal Society's microscopes and telescopes as "prosthetic replacements for lost parts of the first man's body" (p. 38), to the machines of the end of the eighteenth century as the "prosthetic extensions of the industrialist's power" (p. 54). Hooke, Sprat, Newton,

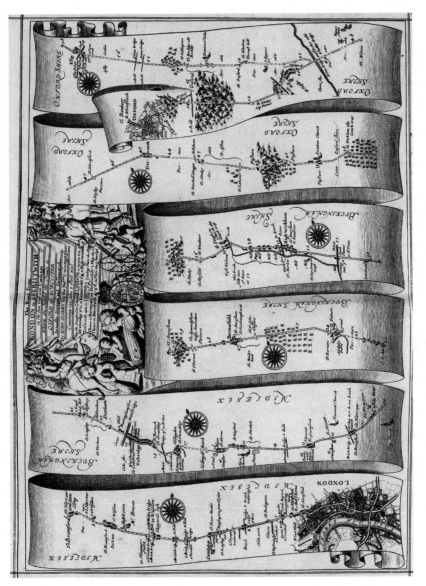

Figure 1 John Ogilby, *Britannia, Volume the First: Or, An Illustration of the Kingdom of England and Dominion of Wales: By A Geographical and Historical Description of the Principal Roads thereof* (London, 1675). Courtesy of the British Library, London.

Milton, Pope, and Swift intersect in their techniques of observation, their fascination with scale, their perceptions and representations of the favorite trope of *concordia discors*.

Harmony in discord? A geography of the social world emerges next, as J. A. Downie confronts the Habermasian "myth of the bourgeois public sphere." Habermas, he argues, didn't really know what he was talking about, at least when it came to English political and social life. On the issues of censorship, social inclusiveness, the Bank of England, cabinet government, the definition of an English "bourgeoisie," and the "literary" public sphere, Habermas historically misplaces events and influences too early, too late, or too iconoclastically. And "he clearly did not undertake any original research of his own on seventeenth- and eighteenth-century English history", relying instead on outdated secondary sources (p. 75). Downie then goes on to analyze why we have been so smitten with this idea, and how we might adjust our assumptions to reflect not an appealing thesis but a more accurate perception of Restoration and eighteenth-century England. A number of the following essays will continue to demonstrate the more recent pattern of critical breakdowns of the post-Habermasian separation between public and private spheres.

Discrepancies between literary and historical perceptions drive Tim Hitchcock's analysis of the realities of eighteenth-century street life in London. "Literary" beggars – in the works of Gay, Ward, Mackenzie, Addison and Steele, Defoe, Carew, Barker, and others – often inhabit a romantically free and ingenious underworld, with "lives of adventure, travel, and freedom of movement" (p. 89), and they are very rarely female. In the real streets, women dominated the numbers of beggarly poverty, and "although single, physically fit, adult male beggars could be found, they represent the tiniest minority of the whole" (p. 89). This much may not be surprising; literary scholars aren't much in the habit of thinking that their texts necessarily correspond to some social reality. But Hitchcock pushes against other assumptions. His careful archival analysis shows a surprising ingenuity and power that these beggarly women exerted on the institutional networks, arguing for "a legacy of pauper agency" such that "by the end of the eighteenth century there was an almost uniform carpet of health and social welfare provision that even the exigencies of war and dearth could not overturn" (p. 98). Hitchcock in effect uses literary stereotypes to dislodge our historical ones about the oppressed-therefore-powerless poor.

Sophie Gee continues the exploration of the streets in their literal and literary spaces. "The eighteenth century did its best to appear polite"

(p. 101), she begins, and that is certainly one of its most common self-presentations as well as a common mid-twentieth-century assumption. But Gee contextualizes the ways that and reasons why the poetry and prose of "towering Augustans" traded so happily in "seeping sewage, brimming chamber pots, vomit, filth, and domestic squalor" – presumably more a milieu for the hack writers of Grub Street than the self-styled culture monitors Dryden, Swift, and Pope (p. 102). She argues the centrality of waste metaphor is grounded in its paradoxical relation to production and recuperation – the etymological, historical, and economic connection between "effluence" and "affluence." The "excremental vision" of the Augustans in some sense derived literally from the filth of sewers and streets (which Gee details), and has an imaginative precedent in the political representations of the civil war and the interregnum. Through historical contextualizations and close readings of a variety of political writings and the works of Dryden, Swift, and Pope, Gee brings to the surface the rich literary and cultural possibilities in the paradox that on the one hand "remainders are symptomatic of decay and degradation, and on the other hand they maintain a perverse affinity with abundance, with the valuable plenitude to which remnants always provide a shadow" (p. 119).

Deidre Shauna Lynch's essay, NOVELS IN THE WORLD OF MOVING GOODS, looks at the novel from a new perspective – not so much its *rise* as its *motion*, contextualizing its "Englishness" in terms of Georg Christoph Lichtenberg's 1775 claim that England's system of roads, mail, and coaches practically *delivered* the possibilities of plot and character interaction. "(He complains that, given the state of the German roads, a German father could overtake a runaway daughter and forestall a would-be novelists's narrative altogether)" (p. 121). Lynch looks at bodies in motion, identities in circulation, the mobility of property, portable books, French and German influences, cultural interconnectedness and intersubjectivity, and – like Downie, Hitchcock, and Staves – institutional systems and public spaces, as forces in the novel's implications for cultural change. She reads Manley, Behn, Haywood, Defoe, Barker, Richardson, Gildon, Brooke, and others, considering novelistic characters "not so much as *individuals*" in the traditional history led by Ian Watt, but rather, "first and foremost, as transients who are either shuttled themselves from one location to another or whose correspondence is" (p. 123). She concludes that this novelistic penchant for worlds and modes of transport is "testimony to the gusto with which the novel throughout the eighteenth century defined itself as a machine for social interconnection and reflected on the marketability permitting it to fill that role" (p. 140).

The substructure of streets and motion carries through in Mark Blackwell's essay on the physiology of gothic in Radcliffe's fiction in MOVING IN THE WORLD OF NOVELS. He analyzes the sublimity of terror as a "healthful tonic" in Edmund Burke's terms, corroborated by a host of medical authorities and accompanied by various mechanisms from swings to chamber horses designed to produce those therapeutic effects. Its literary manifestation, the Gothic novel, became "a narrative vehicle with an unprecedented power to move its readers" (p. 145). Radcliffe perfected the arts of tension and suspense that "hurr[ied] the reader along," as Sir Walter Scott declared. Blackwell looks at reading practices, aesthetic philosophy, contemporary criticism, and pays a close attention to the rhetorical strategies of Radcliffe's novels (in connection with other gothic fiction), to dissect exactly how and why gothic novels are able (then and now) "to move us without making us leave our seats" (p. 159).

Most of the essays in this *Companion* have at least an indirect bearing on issues of gender, in continuing to record where women appeared and where they disappeared, where literary strategies targeted gendered readers or employed gendered topoi. In "THE ABUSE OF TITLE PAGES": MEN WRITING AS WOMEN, Susan Staves confronts a particular instance of gender manipulation in the book world – in its underworld of spurious authorship in general, and at men posing as women authors in particular. The eighteenth century liked to play with identity for a number of reasons. Men might want to pretend to be women on title pages because as gender differences became increasingly emphasized, "women's experience seemed to have a specific authority that could tempt male writers to appropriate it" (p. 164). Or for commercial purposes: appealing to the growing market of female readers, for novelty or celebrity value. Or educative purposes: introducing or reinforcing modes of conduct. Or for plain flat-out attacks (p. 166). Sometimes the pose was collaborative or at least consensual, but other times it became an act of textual theft or textual rape. Staves concludes her essay by calling for a more stringent methodological and analytical approach to the concept of "authentic" texts generally – within and also beyond eighteenth-century studies: "That we still share the enlightenment concern about the relation between authors and title pages is evident in current controversies over the supposed memoirs of Asian women and Native Americans written by white men and the supposed holocaust memoirs not written by survivors" (p. 181).

John O'Brien similarly tests the connections between gender, culture, and form in his chapter on GENRE, GENDER, THEATER and counters the traditional charge that theater declined in the eighteenth century, showing instead its "continuous adaptation to a culture that was changing more quickly than its inhabitants could easily comprehend" (p. 186). He argues that genre and gender seemed to provide "permanent, seemingly natural categories through which these changes could be managed" (p. 186). Generically, the newly reopened theaters to some extent filled themselves with Renaissance repertoire, but those had a musty smell, so the English theater also washed and aired the classical poetics *à la française*. O'Brien shows the redrawing of the lines, and the various steppings-over-them, in tragedy, in comedy, and in theories of spectatorial relations in terms of gender as well as genre. This chapter reveals how politics can be subsumed in and naturalized by gendered spectacle – which paradoxically signalled lines of divergence from neoclassical models: "For although spectators were surely encouraged to admire and learn from virtue and fortitude in the face of suffering expressed by the heroines of these plays, they were not necessarily being held up as models to emulate" (p. 198). Theater was watching and assessing *itself*, its transition from moral instructor to entertainer, its separation from church and state, its changing position in and importance to eighteenth-century life and culture.

J. Paul Hunter works against the Big Historical Generalizations that we tend to make about eighteenth-century poetry: its fetish for the past, its alleged lack of lyric, its predilection for generalities, its preference for the public over the private. This chapter focuses on "occasional poems," an under-discussed category in the first place, and a tag which summons up the idea of the political or military or courtly event – *public* occasions of "wars, battles, treaties, activities of the royals, deaths of the famous, births in prominent families, anniversaries or memorials of some earlier major event that still stirs loyalty or dread" (p. 207). But Hunter argues that thousands of contemporary poems dwell emphatically in the private, the local, the ordinary – "moments of shared experience that two or more people need to remember together" (p. 207). He examines the reasons for the critical devaluing and neglect of occasional poems, including genre permeability (conceptually contiguous with Staves's and O'Brien's chapters here, in that we tend to rely too much on the integrity of title-pages defining themselves), Romanticism-seeded suspicion of events themselves as worthy subjects of poetry, the whiff of *requirement* about it all – the kinds of things that made Matthew Arnold label Dryden and Pope the founders and priests of *prose and reason* rather than poetry and spirit. In pulling out the rich textures and colors of both public and private occasional poems from behind the reputation of a coerced, charmless, or offhanded genre, Hunter wants to bring back the *pleasures* of eighteenth-century poetry.

Rachel Crawford's essay adjoins Blackwell's on the sublime and Hunter's on poetic practices. THE GARDEN, THE GEORGIC, AND THE NATION looks at estate plans, architectural prefaces, horticultural and agricultural treatises, and the transformation of the georgic to "articulate a distinctive notion of the sublime that is simultaneously subjective and practical, aesthetic and political" (p. 226), and which challenges Burke's careful partition between the beautiful and the sublime in the actual usage of gardeners, aestheticians, and poets. Birmingham industries, the British kitchen garden, the ideas of prospect and enclosure, the innovations in the lyric and the ode, all inform the reappearance of the georgic and shape its position in private, public, and nationalistic domains as the physical idea of "containment" is transformed into "a sign of vastness and power" (p. 243).

We swing back to a bird's-eye-view, as well as to the opening epigraphs of this introduction, to close the volume. Mark Salber Phillips, like Hunter, wants to pull us away from overemphasizing the public nature of eighteenth-century writing; in this case, he reminds us that historical writing is not a monolithic recording of the events of a political nation, but "a cluster of overlapping and competing genres that collectively make up a family of historiographical forms" (p. 249). Literary history in particular began to develop an interest in "the thoughts and feelings of another time" and "often of the most everyday sort" (pp. 249, 250). Phillips notes that the trajectory of English literary history began to interest itself in the possibilities for "wholesale revision" of the Elizabethan and Augustan ages. Literary historians became interested in *why* poetic tastes change, speculating on, among other things, the success of programs of improvements in manners; the influence of other cultures, languages, and literatures; the patriotic invention of a national literature against the rebellions of the French and Americans. Phillips concludes by suggesting that "if we want to understand how contemporary readers thought about books and authors as historical objects, it would be fruitful to consider the kinds of historical descriptions literary texts made possible – including the various forms of affective and ideological engagement to which literature, more than histories of public life, promised access" (p. 263).

Phillips quotes Anna Laetitia Barbauld on the association between literature and culture: "Books make a silent and gradual, but a sure change in our ideas and opinions; and as new authors are continually taking possession of the public mind, and old ones falling into disuse, new associations insensibly take place, and shed their influence unperceived over our taste, our manners, and our morals" (p. 262). In 1987, Felicity Nussbaum and Laura Brown published *The New Eighteenth Century*, in which a number of eminent scholars challenged various mid-twentieth century notions of the eighteenth century as a time and place of order, decorum, design, and Enlightenment. (Not that any of the really eminent mid-century scholars appear quite so simplistic or naive on good rereading, and any good new scholar should of course become familiar with *all* the standard critical repertoire – of all centuries.) The late twentieth-century trilogy of race, class, and gender entered the discourse with essays such as Laura Brown's "The Romance of Empire," John Richetti's "Representing an Under Class," and Jill Campbell's " 'When Men Women Turn.' " For 15 years this collection has very perceptibly influenced our critical tastes and shaped many of our new critical assumptions. But it's been 15 years, and the critical discourse has taken new trajectories and reabsorbed in new ways some older interests – making more "silent [or not so silent] and gradual, but sure change[s] in our ideas and opinions." The essays in Nussbaum and Brown "consistently question issues of literary pleasure, aesthetic unity, and coherence" (1987: 3) because of their "historical" (literary critical) collaboration with the dominant, the elite, the agenda of "the preservation and elucidation of canonical masterpieces of cultural stability" (p. 5). The editors declared: "The most important work . . . always insists on the relations between ideology, gender, race, and class, and on the functions of the oppressed and excluded in texts and cultural formations" (p. 20).

The essays in this volume are all unmistakably informed by the issues of ideology, gender, race, and class. But they are also in many cases unabashedly interested in revisiting issues of literary pleasure, aesthetic unity, and coherence. The early twentieth-century's interest in formalism and historicism have combined into a renewed and theoretically informed interest in the relationship between form and culture, formalism and history. "In the beginning," says David Bromwich, "literature was just books" (quoted in Phillips, p. 248); the later eighteenth century critical process started separating out the literary sheep from the nonliterary goats. We've been gradually herding things back together, learning from new historicists to apply close readings to all kinds of texts, to thicken our literary approach with archival thoroughness, to recognize how cultural contexts can in fact better contextualize and refine an interpretation, how a culture shapes (but perhaps never overdetermines) a form. These essays represent just a few of the latest and soundest examples of yet another critical Eighteenth Century – another set of *Houses*,

Castles, Churches, Mills, Beacons, Woods, &c. seen from new perspectives, in new *Prospect.*

References and further reading

Arnold, M. (1888) "The study of poetry," in *Essays in Criticism*. London: Macmillan.

Battestin, M. (1974) *The Providence of Wit: Aspects of Form in Augustan Literature and the Arts*. Oxford: Oxford University Press.

Bracey, R. (1925) *Eighteenth Century Studies and Other Papers*. Oxford: Blackwell.

Brown, L. (1993) *Ends of Empire: Women and Ideology in Early Eighteenth-Century English Literature*. Ithaca: Cornell University Press.

Brown, L. and Nussbaum, F. (eds.) (1987) *The New Eighteenth Century: Theory, Politics, English Literature*. New York and London: Methuen.

Christie, O. F. (1921) *England in the Eighteenth Century: Essays in Verse*. Oxford: Blackwell.

Eliot, T. S. (1930) "Poetry in the eighteenth century," in B. Ford (ed.) *The Pelican Guide to English Literature: From Dryden to Johnson* (pp. 271–8). Harmondsworth: Penguin, 1970.

Fordham, H. G. (1925) *John Ogilby (1600–1676), His Britannia, and the British Itineraries of the Eighteenth Century*. London: Oxford University Press.

Gosse, E. (1885) *From Shakespeare to Pope: An Inquiry into the Causes and Phenomena of the Rise of Classical Poetry in England*. Cambridge: At the University Press.

Horkheimer, M. and Adorno, T. W. (1947) *Dialectic of Enlightenment*, trans. John Cumming. New York: Continuum, repr. 1998.

Hunter, J. P. (1990) *Before Novels: The Cultural Contexts of Eighteenth-Century English Fiction*. New York: W. W. Norton.

Ogilby, J. (1675) *Britannia, Volume the First: Or, an Illustration of the Kingdom of England and Dominion of Wales: By a Geographical and Historical Description of the Principal Roads Thereof*. London: Printed by the Author at his House in White-Fryers.

Saintsbury, G. (1916) *The Peace of the Augustans: A Survey of Eighteenth-Century Literature as a Place of Rest and Refreshment*. London: G. Bell.

Strachey, L. (1926) "The eighteenth century," in *Biographical Essays*. New York: Harcourt Brace Jovanovich (repr. n.d.).

Chapter 1

Travel, Trade, and Empire

Knowing other Places, 1660–1800

Miles Ogborn and Charles W. J. Withers

In his 1661 pageant for the restoration of Charles II, the geographer John Ogilby, who was also Master of the King's Revels, organized the ceremony as a living display of geography and regal authority. The display centered upon four triumphal arches and the themes of nationhood, monarchical power, travel, trade and empire. The first arch symbolized a united Britain, the second Charles's command over the oceans. The third arch offered an animated tableaux of four continents:

> [Pedestals] were adorn'd with living Figures, representing *Europe, Asia, Africa,* and *America,* with Escutcheons and Pendents, bearing the Arms of the Companies Trading Into those parts. *Europe* a Woman arm'd antique. . . . *Asia,* on her head a Glory, a Stole of Silk, with several forms of Wild Beasts wrought upon it. *Africa,* a woman, in her Hand a Pomegranate, on her head a Crown of Ivory and Ears of Wheat, at her Feet two Ships laden with Corn. *America,* Crown'd with Feathers of divers Colours; on her Stole a Golden River, and in her hand a Silver Mountain.

On the final arch, Charles II was portrayed between "two Celestial Hemispheres an *Atlas* bearing a Terrestrial Glob, and on it a Ship under Sail," and, in the niches of the arch, four women represented "Arithmetick, Geometry, Astronomy and Navigation" (Ogilby 1661: 2–5). Taken as a whole, Ogilby's pageant performed late seventeenth-century British ideas of *imperium* and of the world as Britain's emporium. Its figurative displays used geographical knowledge to make manifest a set of claims about political and commercial power. Ogilby's depiction of arithmetic, geometry, astronomy, and navigation also symbolized that crucial shift in emphasis during the seventeenth century away from emblematic display and Aristotelian scholasticism towards new rational and mathematical techniques of global investigation.

Our aim in this chapter is to use diverse and changing forms of geographical knowledge, such as those produced by Ogilby, to explore how the world of the Restoration and the eighteenth century was the subject of geography in its literal sense as "earth writing." We want to show that geographical inquiries into the extent and nature of the globe took different written forms, and did so to reflect different intentions and the demands of different audiences keen to know about other places. Our principal concern is with what we have called "world writing," that is, with geographical knowledge's role in travel, trade, and the politics and economics of empire between about 1660 and 1800. We consider some of the different modes of writing that were produced to deal with that expanding world: travel accounts and narratives of a voyage; descriptions of newly encountered lands and peoples; maps; geographical grammars, gazetteers and dictionaries; and works of political arithmetic, political economy, and statistical description. This is not to claim that these types of geographical literature, which all increased in prevalence and popularity in the period, were either ever wholly separate one from another, unchanging over time, or that certain types were more or less "important" than others. It is, rather, to trace in them the different ways in which the world was ordered and written about through geography. Our aim is to show how these different modes of "world writing" – and, in particular, the representational conventions of these forms of inscription and depiction – tried to negotiate the shifting boundaries between fact and fiction. In a final section, "writing worlds," we conclude by briefly considering the way attention to these forms of writing also shaped the powerful novelistic fictions of travel, trade, and empire presented by Jonathan Swift and Daniel Defoe in *Gulliver's Travels* and *Robinson Crusoe*.

World Writing

Europeans' experience of travel, trade, and empire changed dramatically in the period from 1660 to 1800, as did the nature of geographical knowledge, the ways in which it was presented, and the audiences that it reached. Travel from Britain became more extensive and took many forms, from the young aristocrat's Grand Tour of Europe, to the indentured servant's passage to the North American colonies, or the fortune-seeking of English artists in Bengal. The myriad forms of travel, impossible to classify and describe, were all shaped by the geographical networks, connections, and forms of governance established by commerce, trade, and imperial expansion. These were changing in important ways too. Over the course of the eighteenth century, and especially after 1750, the volume of Britain's overseas trade with the Americas increased dramatically. The triangular trade – in manufactured goods from Britain's workshops, enslaved people from Africa, and tropical agricultural produce from the Americas – dispatched thousands of ships and their crews to bind together merchants, clerks, warehouse keepers, plantation owners, overseers, and enslaved workers across the Atlantic world. The East India Company, with its monopoly on trade to the Indies around the Cape of Good Hope, entered a period of extraordinary profitability in the late seventeenth century based on the exchange of gold and silver for the Indian calicoes and muslins which became the object of demand among London's fashion-conscious consumers. In both sets of trades there was a need for knowledge about the worlds that were being encountered and the new forms of economy and exchange that were being created. Commercial directories; merchants' guides to trades, commodities, and exchange rates; printed maps and gazetteers; and instruction books on accounting and writing letters and bills of exchange, all sought to codify knowledge as a way of ordering this new world. At the same time, the advocates of different trades and industries, those for or against free trade, mercantilism, or other forms of protectionism, went into print to argue their case to the public and to parliament.

The arguments that the mercantile lobbyists made were, in large part, about how what was understood as an "Empire of Trade" should be organized. Britain's imperial reach both grew and changed shape over the course of the century and a half from the Restoration. Between Oliver Cromwell's capture of Jamaica in 1655 and the end of the Seven Years War in 1763 there was a fivefold increase in the extent of Britain's empire. Through a series of increasingly global military conflicts with Holland, Spain, and France, Britain added territories in North America, India, and the Caribbean to its overseas possessions. By the mid-1760s control extended from Labrador to Florida, across a substantial selection of the Caribbean islands, and over large portions of northern India. This geography was, however, far from static. Islands and territories changed hands. The American War of Independence marked the end of one imperial phase and shifted attention to India and to the Pacific where European navigators were assiduously naming and claiming islands and coastal territories for the crowned heads of Europe.

Geographical knowledge was intimately connected with making and keeping this empire. Cartography and hydrography enabled the organization and administration of territories for taxation and warfare, and of shipping routes for naval and merchant vessels. This conjunction of commerce, navigation and of knowing one's bounds through geography is apparent in works that sought to make geographical inquiry practically useful (see Figure 1.1). Imperial utility was also evident in the collection of information about peoples, plants, and minerals that was used for the "improvement" of empire through a global redistribution of human and natural "resources" (Drayton 2000). This was a world order built on new ways of knowing other places.

Yet while the publication and popularity in the eighteenth century of maps, geography books, works of travel, and narratives of a voyage reflected the developing global geographies of European empires, the relationship between geographical knowledge and imperial power should not be drawn too tightly. The production of geographical knowledge was part of many different processes, and what was produced was far from being a coherent body of facts, theories, or genres. This is readily apparent in the works of John Ogilby, the geographer with whom we started this chapter. Ogilby's geographical activities and writings are illustrative of the diverse forms and changing uses of early modern geography. His *Britannia* (1675), a geographical description of England and Wales, was one part of his intended but never-realized "A Geographical Description of the Whole World." *Britannia* was a road book, a chorographical or regional description, and Ogilby was a key member of that circle of *virtuosi* who helped plan and map London after the Great Fire of 1666. Outside of his British-based mapping work, Ogilby traveled little. His other works – *Embassy to China* (1669), *Atlas Japannensis* (1670), *Africa* (1670), *America* (1671), *Atlas Chinensis* (1671), and *Asia* (1673) – were, largely, compiled from others' writings. Yet, in incorporating the latest travel accounts and using lavish illustrations, Ogilby provided for better-off audiences geography books that helped to describe and depict if not always to define their fast-enlarging world (Chambers 1996: 23–5).

The diversity of forms of geographical knowledge may also be illustrated for the late eighteenth century by the ventures which opened up the new worlds of the Pacific to European audiences. Best known are the three voyages of James Cook, which were represented in Europe through exhibitions of artifacts, contributions to debates in natural science and moral philosophy, theatrical performances, and the publication of the journals of the participants to eager and critical audiences. This variety reflected the mixture of motives that underlay the voyages.

Figure 1.1 The title page to John Seller's *The Coasting Pilot* (1671) illustrates the importance of the "experience and practice of diverse Able and Expert Navigators" in promoting geographical knowledge as a basis to commercial and political empires. Reproduced by permission of the Trustees of the National Library of Scotland.

They were exercises in humanitarian and Enlightenment science promoted by the Royal Society and, simultaneously, they were part of the pursuit of imperial territories and trades sponsored by the Admiralty. The voyages continued an intellectual engagement with new worlds characteristic of writers such as Diderot, who, drawing upon the geographical discoveries of the French navigators Bougainville and Lapérouse, saw the Pacific as, at once, paradisal, part of European theories of social difference, and a world of hitherto unheralded natural richness (Lamb et al. 2000). The voyages also carried on commercial and imperial considerations – of global knowledge rooted in trade in goods rather than in the good of natural philosophy – that were evident in the early eighteenth century. In his *An Essay on the South-Sea Trade* (1712), for example, Daniel Defoe had emphasized Britain's Pacific markets as "capable of being the Greatest, most Valuable, most Profitable, and most Encreasing Branch of Trade in our whole British Commerce" (Defoe 1712: 17). Like Africa, the South Seas were to be incorporated into precisely wrought networks of trade, empire and geographical accounting (Schaffer 2002). Overall, in enterprises like the search for the Great Southern Continent, the Northwest Passage, or the mapping of New Zealand, science and commerce could not be separated.

As a result, the works of geographical knowledge produced by these voyages into the Pacific varied in terms of form, content, and audience. Alongside the new and accurate maps of New Zealand or Vancouver Island produced using specialized scientific instruments and meticulous engraving were the official narratives of the voyages commissioned by the Admiralty and commercially published. There was also a plethora of other publications, plays, pictures, and stories that emerged from these and other accounts, variously criticizing and celebrating the voyages and their participants. Each genre of travel writing, or of geographical knowledge more generally, had its different purposes and audiences (Elsner and Rubiés 1999; Leask 2002). It is clear that the knowledge produced about the Pacific was not simply framed by a logic of commercial accumulation or a politicized rhetoric of conquest so much as it was also characterized by the languages of difference and confusion, even of anxiety. In many instances it was that which made these works compelling and popular (Lamb 2001).

There was, therefore, a demand for maps, travel accounts, images and descriptions of other places which was limited neither to the places of empire and trade, nor to their direct administrators or beneficiaries. Just as the empire was enormously varied in the range of interests that it brought together, so was the geographical knowledge that sprang from and surrounded it. What was required by a surveyor in Calcutta was very different from what was wanted by a Glasgow tobacco merchant, a shopkeeper in Boston, or an anti-slavery campaigner in London. There was a huge market for printed texts and images fed by a vast range of products. Many of these were dubious in their credibility, either outdated, plagiarized, or simply fictional. More importantly, perhaps, there was a vast production of geographical knowledge because no one could be sure what was useful, or what would sell. Geographical knowledge was produced for many reasons, and its forms and content exceeded the boundaries of imperial power. By 1800 shifts in scientific method, geological theory, and map-making meant that the world was bigger, older, and better mapped than in Ogilby's day. Yet it was no less an object of wonder or of curiosity and uncertainty.

There is another reason why geography's writings – in travel accounts, in maps, in books of geography – cannot simply be taken as straightforward factual accounts of the world that could be used unproblematically for economic and political ends by merchants and empire-builders. Those who sought to produce new, empirically grounded knowledge about the world operated on the basis that travel made truth. They were concerned to challenge or confirm the geographical knowledge that came from classical works, medieval travelers, or contemporary voyagers. For those charting the Australian coastline, for example, or documenting African natives, or for the first time recording in European classificatory terms the botanical richness of the Amazonian tropics, geographical knowledge was reliable and truthful precisely because it was determined by direct experience, direct observation, and direct recording. For those, however, who did not or could not directly engage with other parts of the world through mapping, travel, or trade, what was recounted to them by others was only a presumed geographical truth that had to be taken on trust. They were like the overseas merchants in their London counting houses whose profits, credit, and futures were dependent upon the information about events and situations in distant places – in this case sales, prices, and investment opportunities – sent by factors, agents, foreign merchants, and other intermediaries, whose word they could not simply assume was the truth.

The problem of knowing the truth – of what you are told (or read) about things you have not seen by persons you do not know – was especially crucial from the later seventeenth century in relation to the rise of the "experimental philosophy" (see also Chapter 2 Sᴄɪᴇɴᴛɪꜰɪᴄ Iɴᴠᴇsᴛɪɢᴀ-ᴛɪᴏɴs). The truth claims of scientific knowledge depended, we are told, upon personal credibility, upon the gentlemanly status of practitioners and of those who witnessed their experiments. Such social warrants of credibility cannot so easily apply to claims about far away places as re-counted, for example, in travel narratives. The problem with crediting travelers' tales was twofold. First, if the tale provided new information about the world – and that was their purpose for both science and the market – it potentially conflicted with what was already securely known. Second, tales "were commonly told by people about whom one knew little or nothing, by people to whom one might legitimately impute an interest . . . in fabricating testimony or embroidering the truth, or by people whose reliability was accounted suspect or compromised in the general culture which related integrity and truth-telling" (Shapin 1994: 247). Even in the Enlightenment, much geographical information was produced by persons whose credibility could not always be sanctioned, depended upon the testimony of native "others," and was consumed by metropolitan audiences distant from the sites of know-ledge making and the producers of it (Adams 1962; Stagl 1995).

There was, of course, no way to resolve this problem once and for all, but there were ways to try and manage it. These can be illustrated by thinking about how merchants dealt with trust and truth. First, they chose *whom* to trust. Merchants' dealings in the Atlantic world were based on the extension of credit (trusting people to pay) and on the delega-tion of decision making to agents or factors in other places (trusting peo-ple to act). Overseas merchants built extensive transatlantic networks based on family members, friends, and co-religionists (Hancock 1995). These social and cultural relationships offered a basis for extending trust, even though the expectation was frequently disappointed. Second, they chose *what* to trust. Trust and truth were not simply vested in people, but in writing. Each trade was inscribed in and surrounded by a net-work of writing – bills of lading, bills of exchange, charterparties, con-tracts, and double-entry bookkeeping – that, because it could be checked and double-checked, was depended upon to secure trade and to form a basis for truth. What was important, in accounting and in legal documentation, was strict adherence to the prescribed form. It was adherence to the rigidities of form more than the content that formed a basis for believing what the documents contained, for trusting them as truth, and for using them as the basis of action in further investments or in the courts.

These ideas about writing, trust, and truth can be extended into the world of travel writing. Many narratives of sea-voyages, in both manu-script and print, took the form of a daily journal recounting the events of the voyage, describing people, places, and events along with sequential information on location, weather, and on ship, sailing directions. This format is partly a matter of geographical knowledge. It is derived from the requirements of deep-sea navigation. Once out of sight of land, at a time when longitude was not easily determined, the only practical way for those on board ship to know where they were with any tolerable degree of accuracy was to know where they had been and the direction and speed in which they were moving. This produced a series of sequential observations, each one dependent on the last. These were recorded in a logbook (the name derived from the use of log and line to determine speed in the water), and then written up into a journal. Such writing positioned both the author and the reader. This format was also a matter of power. Both the Admiralty and merchant companies required their officers to keep journals on board ship so that there would be a record of the voyage which could be used to judge outcomes against expectations (had the ship gone where it was supposed to have gone? had the captain and crew done what they were supposed to have done? if not, why not?), and as the basis for amending maps or making future voyages. The combination of sequential narrative and the "eye-witness" description of places or events was produced in part by the demands of powerful readers, and in part by writing in situations where the author was never sure what would become significant later. As with accounting for purchases and sales, credit and debt, the format of the journal (the term was also used for the strictly chronological record of incomings and outgoings used in double-entry book-keeping) formed a basis for trust and some guarantee of truth-telling.

Even so, such journals were produced in many forms and were reproduced in different ways with varying consequences for their credibility. The records of Pacific voyages are again instructive. British naval officers were trained in the disciplines of what to record in their journals and how to record it, in words, numbers, and images. Their status as officers, and the judgments made of their conduct, depended upon their writings as much as their other actions. These writing practices should be seen in opposition to the tall stories, or yarns, spun by the common sailors in the foc'sle, and to the quite different "economy of truth" evident in traders' journals (Clayton 2000: 84). Captain Bligh, for example, cast adrift in an open boat after the mutiny on the *Bounty*, and facing the constant dangers of starvation and capsize, continued to maintain a meticulous journal, including sketched surveys and coastal profiles. He ensured, moreover, that his record was the only record, refusing John Fryer a pencil or piece of paper to keep his own account. As Greg Dening notes, "Bligh had always a sense of the power of archives" (Dening 1992:

102). The Admiralty certainly had a keen appreciation of the importance of such records. Cook's instructions for the first voyage ordered: "Before leaving the vessel on his return he is to collect all logs, books and journals which any of the officers many have kept, and enjoin secrecy about the voyage on the whole ship's company" (quoted in Edwards 1994: 83). Yet these journals would also have been rewritten, amended, and annotated as the voyage progressed. Cook himself assiduously rewrote and edited elements of his account, such as his involvement in the killing of Maori at Poverty Bay, to refine the presentation of himself, his actions, and his interpretation of them. Finally, of course, the journals might make it into print. In doing so they usually retained their form, but much else could change. John Marra, on Cook's second voyage, asked his bookseller, "What name is my journal of the voyage to come out in?" (quoted in Edwards 1994: 221). William Wales, also on Cook's second voyage, was more pessimistic:

> I cannot avoid remarking the unfortunate situation of every man of real knowledge and integrity, whose works . . . must pass through so many hands before they can reach the eye of the Public thereby giving an opportunity to every piratical pretender, either through interest or bribery, to purloin and publish them as his own, sometimes before the real author has been able to do it. (Quoted in Lamb 2001: 97)

Cook knew all about such problems. The Admiralty appointed the periodical essayist Dr John Hawkesworth to prepare the journals of the first voyage for publication, for which he reportedly received the huge sum of £6,000 from his publishers. The result was an account of the voyages which maintained the form of the journal's first-person narrative, but which rewrote them through Hawkesworth's own "sentiments and observations" (quoted in Lamb 2001: 100). They were disowned by Cook and Joseph Banks, and caused considerable public controversy.

This is not to suggest that geographical writing between 1660 and 1800, if not always wholly factually accurate, was as wholly fictitious. It is to note that the geographical description of the earth presented problems – of perception, of rhetorical style, of distance, of authorial credibility and of audiences' credulousness – which cannot be ignored. Indeed, it is to argue that facts, or what are taken as facts, are not self-evident. Instead, they are dependent upon particular fictions, in the sense of fiction as "something made." This attempt to make facts by careful presentation and adherence to certain representational conventions is evident in the journal of a voyage in its recording of location, climatic conditions, its first-person witnessing, its plain descriptive language, and its strict chronology. These questions of form all made truth claims. They could not guarantee the truth and ensure trust but they made claims to it that were recognizable to readers.

There were parallels in other forms of geographical writing, not least in its close connection with natural history. The need for precision in the language of geographical collection prompted the Royal Society after 1660 to emphasize a plain and simple style for the conduct and reporting of scientific inquiry. John Woodward's 1696 *Brief Instructions for Making Observations in All Parts of the World*, subtitled *An Attempt to settle an Universal Correspondence for the Advancement of Knowledge both Natural and Civil*, was one such manual of practice. Under three principal headings – "At Sea," "Upon the Sea-shores," and "At Land" – Woodward's instructional language emphasized observation, recording, and detail. The trade in knowledge of nature's empire had itself to travel securely and it was for this reason that he entitled a section "Directions for the Collecting, Preserving, and Sending over Natural things, from Foreign Countries" (Woodward 1696: 10–16). The rehabilitation of curiosity through a more precise language was a crucial element in the objectification of scientific knowledge after 1660, and, in turn, of geographical inquiry. Through such standardized textual forms knowledge might be brought back to London, evaluated, and collated. These accurate eye-witness accounts were valued over other forms of knowledge. The editors of one early eighteenth-century collection of travels marked the distance between themselves and Richard Hakluyt's *Principall Navigations*, the classic text of the Elizabethan "Age of Discovery":

> The Collection is scarce and valuable for the good there is to be pick'd out; but it might be wish'd the Author had been less voluminous, delivering what was really authentick and useful, and not stuffing his Work with so many Stories taken upon trust, so many trading Voyages that have nothing new in them, so many Warlike Exploits not at all pertinent to his Undertaking, and such a multitude of Articles, Charters, Privileges, Letters, Relations, and other things little to the purpose of Travels and Discoveries. (Churchill and Churchill 1704: xciii)

Similar processes can be detected in cartography. The map is a key form of geographical inscription, one central to the acquisition and depiction of world knowledge through a rhetoric that is a powerful combination of measurement, visualization, and narration. Mapping is a creative process, designed to put the world to order through its scaled representation. Each map is a spatialized embodiment of geographical knowledge designed for a particular context – traders and navigators, for example, required maps with more dependable notions of accuracy than was necessary in the topographic portrayal of an individual's travels or for display on the parlor wall. Because they serve particular and different interests, are naturalized but not natural objects, and embody human agency, maps are ideological and political documents invested with social and epistemological authority through their conventions of representation (Cosgrove 1999).

By the mid-seventeenth century, four interrelated groups of map makers may be identified: mariners (a category which includes merchant traders as well as global navigators); practicing geographers; commercial publishers; and land measurers. From the later seventeenth century, we can note the rise of a fifth group we might term "professional geographers," specifically military and state surveyors whose work was undertaken as a means to state authority. The leader in Europe in this respect was France which, as a result of the first and second "Cassini Surveys" from 1680 to 1744 and 1747 to 1789 respectively, was thoroughly mapped. The Cassini surveys prompted similar ventures in Denmark, the German and the Italian states. In Britain, the regulatory cartographic language that was to be embodied in the Ordnance Survey has its origins in the 1747–54 Military Survey of Scotland, itself a project of geographical state surveillance following the Jacobite Rebellion of 1745. In India, North America and in the Pacific, the British empire took shape in the eighteenth century through the map and in associated textual memoirs which sought, through the rhetoric of accuracy, to reduce global difference to a common and recognizable geographical language (Edney 1998).

It is for these reasons that the eighteenth century has been commonly regarded as the formative period for modern cartography, one in which map making was stripped of its "artistic" elements and reduced to a strictly "scientific" practice. The increasing plainness of formal maps during the eighteenth century and the interpretative association between plainness and factuality lends this view some credence. But beneath the truth claims made by their surface rhetoric, Enlightenment maps embody statements of ideology and power which reflect the views of map makers rather more than they do the views of the mapped. In North American maps, for example, native peoples are effaced through cartography. In the French cartographic depiction of late eighteenth-century Egypt, ancient "otherness" is shown as an extension of contemporary Europe, and maps of India, produced through compilation and partial survey, claim total coverage and observational accuracy (Edney 1999).

Mapping in the eighteenth century was also a metaphorical practice. Enlightenment geographical discovery and common styles of mapping effectively brought the whole world into view. This was a world in which social difference was measured in geographical distance: in terms of theories of social development, what was "before Europe" was also "beyond Europe." This is what Edmund Burke meant when he noted in 1791 how "the Great Map of Mankind is unroll'd at once; and there is no state or Gradation of barbarism, and no mode of refinement which we have not at the same instant under our view." For Diderot and d'Alembert, their monumental *Encyclopédie* (1751–65) was also a chart of world knowledge, "a kind of world map which is to show the principal countries, their position and their mutual dependence, the road that lies directly from one to the other" (quoted in Withers and Livingstone 1999: 5, 14).

For travelers and traders, however, the map had a more exact practical function, a utility established in part by Ogilby's *Britannia* which, in depicting Britain in the form of 100 strip maps – a form much imitated in the eighteenth century – was the first major development in British cartography since the Tudor period. Maps were crucial to trade at local, national, and global scales. As has been shown of Defoe's *A Tour thro' the Whole Island of Great Britain* (1724–6), his itinerary was also an exercise in national mapping. In paying attention to road networks, Defoe portrayed actual historical space and topographical difference as conceptual space, geographically and economically meaningful because it was bound together into a useable system of intersecting lines (Parkes 1995: 402–3).

This multiplicity of forms of representation of geographical knowledge meant that geography was a key element of the emergent public sphere from the later seventeenth century in two interrelated respects. First, geography as a subject and as a practice was written about. As the terraqueous globe was more and more revealed, so books of geography and a developing trade in them flourished. Geography was taught in universities and military academies and was the subject of public lectures and private tuition aimed at promoting politeness as a civic discourse (Withers 2001: 119–33). Second, we may consider that the literate eighteenth-century public sphere itself had geographical expression. It was located in national cities where international trading networks came together and it was constituted locally in certain social spaces such as coffee houses, Halls of Exchange and societies' meeting rooms. Networks of global knowledge were everywhere underlain by local geographies of trade in information, domestic exchanges over imperial news, and by the circulation of books, newspapers, and journals and the audiences who read them.

One genre of geography book that was prominent in this period, especially in Britain, was the special geography. Special geographies purported to describe all the countries in the world and to do so under a more or less standard set of headings: the limits of a country, its principal features, and so on. Such works reflected a concern with the prevailing philosophy of utility. It is also possible to see both in individual books and in changes over time the different ways in which new information or current concerns were realized. Patrick Gordon's *Geography anatomiz'd: or, a compleat geographical grammar* (1693) claimed in its preface to have "reduc'd the whole body of modern geography to a true grammatical method." In this claim, the work – as with others of the time – reflected in its formal organization and factual claims both the Baconian interest in particulars and that emphasis given to the languages of descriptive order by men like John Woodward (Sitwell 1993).

Geography's books did not simply reflect the world, partly, of course, because the volume of geographical information being accumulated after 1660 worked against such universalizing intentions. The problem of keeping up to date with new information and the costs of mapping new geographies is one reason why so many geographical books were plagiarized from others. Different geographical genres were apparent, especially in the eighteenth century, between the geographical gazetteer or dictionary, which organized material alphabetically under place names, and the geographical grammar which arranged the world according to continent and nation under standard headings. In Georgian Britain, geography books engaged with political life in several ways. Thomas Salmon's *Modern Gazetteer* (1746) and his *New Geographical and Historical Grammar* (1749) discuss political patronage and the nature of constitutional democracy. William Guthrie's *New Geographical, Historical and Commercial Grammar* (1770) – intended by its author as the lineal successor to Salmon's 1749 work and in its eighteenth edition by 1800 – argued that a comparative geographical analysis of the nations of the world aided the political interpretation of national development. In these works and in others' accounts, geographical description of Britain's colonies facilitated the running of the empire and of later eighteenth-century Britain as a fiscal-military state. British geographical writing was thoroughly implicated in the languages of politics and of territorial governance not just of terrestrial enumeration (Mayhew 2000; 2004). In the United States, Jedidiah Morse's *American Universal Geography* (1789) emphasized geography as part of the languages of post-Revolutionary American political unity (Brückner 1999).

The claims that were made by the concise and seemingly neutral and objective depictions of territory in geographical grammars and gazetteers run parallel to many of the claims made by late seventeenth-century political arithmetic. This also involved the tabulated description of places, and of the value of different trades, to aid comparison, action, and political and economic administration. Political arithmetic set itself up as an antidote to explicitly factional and rhetorical argument about the state and finance, offering as an alternative the truth claims of numerical representation. As William Petty, its foremost proponent, argued:

> The Method I take to do this is not very usual; for instead of using only comparative and superlative Words, and intellectual Arguments, I have taken the course (as a Specimen of the Political Arithmetick I have long aimed at) to express myself in Terms of *Number, Weight,* or *Measure*; To use only arguments of Sense, and to consider only such Causes, as have visible Foundations in Nature; leaving those that depend upon the mutable Minds, Opinions, Appetites, and Passions of particular Men, to the consideration of others. (Quoted in Poovey 1998: 132)

Petty's claims for the objectivity of numerical representation were partly the intellectual product of his education by Thomas Hobbes and his position as a founder member of the Royal Society together with his contacts at Oxford and in the Hartlib circle of natural philosophers. They were also a result of his previous attempts to produce knowledge about other places under very specific political conditions. In 1651 he had left his position of Chair of Music at Gresham College in London (he had formerly been Professor of Anatomy at Oxford University) to go to Ireland as medical officer and personal physician to the Lieutenant General and his family. He was, therefore, part of Cromwell's military campaign, which had been pursued since 1641, to put down the Irish insurrection and colonize that country. He was to play a crucial role in this process since he was appointed to make a topographical survey and compile detailed maps of parts of Ireland – the so-called "Down Survey" – in order to allocate confiscated lands to Cromwell's soldiers and English settlers. In all its uses William Petty's political arithmetic offered the certainty and objectivity of numerical representation in the service of particular political interests.

There is no simple historical continuity between the political arithmetic of men like William Petty or Charles Davenant – who called it "the art of reasoning by figures on things relating to government" (quoted in Ogborn 1998: 163) – and the later collection and use of statistical information in the service of politics or the economy. Mary Poovey (1998) has traced the development of what she calls "the modern fact" – best represented by a numerical value which is simultaneously both an accurate objective and independent factual statement and the evidence to support or destroy a theoretical position or system – through accounting to political arithmetic, moral philosophy and political economy. Yet in all these instances there is evidence of numerical or statistical representation, often in the form of tables of figures, being used to describe either other places (population counts, taxation totals, or numbers of acres or livestock) or the relationships between places (numbers of migrants, the value of imports and exports, numbers of ships employed in a trade). On the basis of these abstractions – often involving guesswork, estimation and extrapolation rather than direct observation – a particular picture of the workings of an economy or polity was produced and argued over.

It has been argued, indeed, that it was "[t]hrough published writings [that] a conception of a commercial economy took shape" (Appleby 1978: 18). And this is as true of later political economists such as Adam Smith and of population theorists such as Thomas Malthus as it was of the seventeenth-century pamphleteers. In Appleby's argument these writings were not simply a response to economic changes or a set of class-based ideological positions. They were, instead, actively implicated in the process of understanding, and thereby of shaping, the emergent social relations and subjectivities of the global market economy. Through these writings, and the responses that they provoked, abstractions like the market, the national economy or the balance of trade between nations came to seem real and to be real. It was often through numerical representation of these abstractions – ideas like "national wealth" or the "value of the East India trade" – usually in monetary terms, that these entities had most reality and effect. The truth claims made by the geographical representations involved in political arithmetic and political economy, and set out in tables of statistics or the computations based upon them, were more often grounded in the fact that the reasoning was pursued in numerical and mathematical terms than upon what those numbers were.

Writing Worlds

It is, of course, unremarkable either that eighteenth-century novelists drew on these forms of geographical writing in order to construct their fictions, or that it was not easy to tell the difference between fictional and factual narratives. Robert Drury's journal of his shipwreck and captivity on Madagascar, for example, has slipped between the categories of fact and fiction several times since it was published in 1729 (Adams 1962; Edwards 1994). In concluding, we examine how the authors of fictional travel narratives deployed and toyed with the formal conventions of the modes of geographical writing and representation outlined here in order to destabilize, but not simply to dismantle, their truth claims. What they wrote served to reveal the work of representation that went into the making of the facts of geographical knowledge. We do so by briefly considering Gulliver's maps and Crusoe's journal.

In *Gulliver's Travels* (1726) Jonathan Swift used his extensive reading of travel narratives, and the public demand for them, as a vehicle for social and political satire. This depended upon the problematic truth claims of such geographical works, particularly those which were set, as *Gulliver* was, in the "never-never land" of the South Seas (Williams 1997: 210). Swift has his eponymous narrator signal both to the desire for truth from printed travel narratives and the impossibility of establishing it. Gulliver wishes that "a law were enacted, that every traveller, before he was permitted to publish his voyages, should be obliged to make an oath before the Lord High Chancellor that all he intended to print was absolutely true to the best of his knowledge" (Swift 1726/1985: 340). Yet at the outset he also issued a warning that the printer has "confound[ed] the times, and mistakes the dates" (p. 39), and, since the manuscript has been destroyed and no copy kept, they cannot be rectified.

Gulliver's maps play a similar game (see Figure 1.2). The book's confident depiction of a new geography of exotic lands was enough, one of Swift's correspondents reported, to send "an old Gentleman" to whom the book was lent "immediately to his Map to search for Lilly putt" (Williams 1963 vol. 3: 180). The island's outline was confidently engraved on the map, and its "discovery" by Gulliver in 1699 declared in print. The map, based on Herman Moll's "New & Correct Map of the Whole World" (1719), located these fantasy islands in relation to Sumatra and to a portion of coastline identified as "Dimen's Land" (Tasmania). Yet this is an uncertain geography. There is the presence of only a portion of the southern coast of van Dieman's land, its full extent remaining unknown. Moreover, the absence of the bulk of New Holland (Australia) whose western coast had been mapped by Abel Tasman on the same voyage as the island which now bears his name, meant that a comparison with most other maps would put Lilliput at the heart of the Australian land mass. Without a scale or lines of

latitude or longitude its spaces are confounded and suggest that cartographic modes of representation are in themselves no guarantee of truth.

Daniel Defoe's *Robinson Crusoe* (1719) has been called a "prophecy of
empire" (McLeod 1999: 177). Its account of one Englishman's subdu-
ing of a hostile environment through work and reason, of himself through
the Protestant faith, and of other people through either force or guile to
make a society ordered by race and class, is a powerful story of empire-
building. Yet it is just that – a story – and a story whose crucial first
stages are told and retold several times for the reader. Importantly, the
mechanism for these retellings is "The Journal."

Crusoe begins with a narrative, related some time after the event, of
what happened in the shipwreck on September 30, 1659 and in his first
few weeks on the island. It is a tale of hopelessness and anguish being
displaced through overlapping accounts of his actions; first by the work
of salvaging what he can from the ship and of building a "habitation"
(Defoe 1719/1985: 84), and second by the work of putting things in
order. He devises a calendar; considers the writing materials, books, mathematical instruments, and charts that he has rescued from the wreck;
builds shelves "to separate every thing at large in their places" (p. 86);
constructs a table and chair; and most important of all he begins to write.
First he "drew up the state of my affairs in writing . . . and I stated it
very impartially, like debtor and creditor" (p. 83). This moral accounting of what was "good" and "evil" in his situation, and the work that
writing it all out did to distance himself from his passions "as my reason began now to master my despondency" (p. 83), was paralleled in
his journal. This is a journal he only begins to write when his world
has been put in order.

Crusoe retells his day of arrival twice more in order to establish the
principles on which his journal is based. He first argues that he did not
keep a journal from the outset because "I was in too much hurry, and
not only hurry as to labour, but in too much discomposure of mind"
(p. 86). He then shows the reader what an entry would have been like
if written on "Sept. the 30th," a passion-filled and bodily account of the
immediacy and despair of the castaway: "I ran about the shore, wringing my hand and beating my head and face, exclaiming at my misery,
and crying out, I was undone, undone, till tyred and faint I was forced
to lye down on the ground to repose, but durst not sleep for fear of
being devoured" (p. 86). Only after having made "all as handsome about
me as I could" (p. 86) did he begin the journal. Crusoe provides "a copy"
(p. 86) of what he had written until his ink ran out. It begins on
"September 30, 1659" with the wreck:

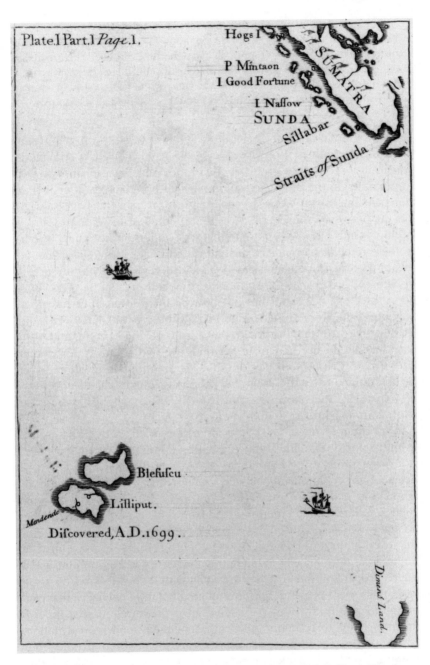

Figure 1.2 The map of Lilliput from Jonathan Swift's (1726) *Gulliver's Travels* combines existing geographical knowledge and fictional representations of space in the same frame. Reproduced by permission of the British Library: C.59.e.11.

> All the rest of the day I spent afflicting myself at the dismal circumstances I was brought to, viz. I had neither food, house, clothes, weapon, or place to fly to, and in despair of any relief, saw nothing but death before me, either that I should be devoured by wild beasts, murthered by savages, or starved to death for want of food. At the approach of night, I slept in a tree for fear of wild creatures, but slept soundly tho' it rained all night. (p. 87)

The final journal account establishes a series of distances: it is a looking-back in time, but it also distances Crusoe from himself. It emphasizes practicality, even in the enumeration of the dangers faced, and, as such, runs parallel to the moral accounting in which metaphysical evils (I am alone in the world) were set against practical goods (I have salvaged lots of "necessary things" (p. 84)). It also emphasizes solutions, and its ending sounds like the beginning that it is, and its author knew it to be. In these retellings, organized around the journal's form, Defoe demonstrates that the same events can be, and are, recounted very differently in different circumstances. Although Crusoe tells us that he "kept things very exact" (p. 82), and that by showing his journal after having already told the story "in it will be told all those particulars over again" (p. 86), there are significant differences in tone and content, and in the dates, which do not match up between the two accounts. Eventually, after a year, Crusoe's ink ran out, but the account barely falters. While he determined to "write down only the most remarkable events of my life" (p. 117), the narrative spun from them, supposedly many years later, continues in full and vivid "factual" detail.

In all these forms of geographical writing, then, both those aspiring to the status of fact and those presenting themselves as fictions, there is a negotiation of the boundaries of fact and fiction which lay at the heart of the relationship between geographical knowledge and the world that it depicted. As Defoe well knew, the new natural philosophy, commercial reputations, and authorial claims to geographical accuracy each depended on the writer's credit rating (Schaffer 1989). From the Restoration to the end of the eighteenth century, in a world whose limits were dramatically extended by travel, trade and empire and in which people found themselves engaging with far away places on a daily basis, there were demands for forms of geographical knowledge that could bring order to this world. We have argued that bringing that order by making claims to certainty and truth depended upon representational conventions which were necessarily carefully crafted fictions. Both literature and the works of geographical knowledge explored these borderlands in representing this new world.

Acknowledgments

We thank Cynthia Wall, J. Paul Hunter and, particularly, David Livingstone, Robert Mayhew, and Paul Wood for their critical reading and comments upon an earlier draft, and the staff of the British Library and the National Library of Scotland for assistance with sources and the illustrations. Miles Ogborn's work on this chapter was made possible by the award of a Philip Leverhulme Prize by the Leverhulme Trust. Charles Withers undertook the work whilst in receipt of a British Academy Research Readership and gratefully acknowledges this support.

References and further reading

Adams, P. G. (1962) *Travelers and Travel Liars 1660–1800*. Berkeley: University of California Press.

Appleby, J. O. (1978) *Economic Thought and Ideology in Seventeenth-Century England*. Princeton: Princeton University Press.

Brückner, M. (1999) "Lessons in geography: maps, spellers, and other grammars of nationalism in the early republic," *American Quarterly* 51: 311–43.

Chambers, D. (1996) *The Reinvention of the World: English Writing 1650–1750*. London: Edward Arnold.

Churchill, A. and Churchill, J. (1704) *A Collection of Voyages and Travels*, 4 vols. London: Churchill and Churchill.

Clayton, D. W. (2000) *Islands of Truth: The Imperial Fashioning of Vancouver Island*. Vancouver: University of British Columbia Press.

Cosgrove, D. E. (1999) "Introduction: mapping meaning," in D. E. Cosgrove (ed.) *Mappings* (pp. 1–23). London: Reaktion Books.

Defoe, D. (1712) *An Essay on the South Sea-Trade. With an Enquiry into the Grounds and Reasons of the Present Dislike and Complaint against the Settlement of a South-Sea Company*. London: Printed for J. Baker.

—— (1719) *The Life and Adventures of Robinson Crusoe*, ed. with an introduction by Angus Ross. Harmondsworth: Penguin, 1985.

Dening, G. (1992) *Mr Bligh's Bad Language: Passion, Power and Theatre on the Bounty*. Cambridge: Cambridge University Press.

Drayton, R. (2000) *Nature's Government: Science, Imperial Britain, and the "Improvement" of the World*. New Haven: Yale University Press.

Edney, M. H. (1998) "Cartography: disciplinary history," in G. A. Good (ed.) *Sciences of the Earth: An Encyclopedia of Events, People, and Phenomena*, 2 vols. (vol. I: pp. 81–5). New York: Garland.

Edney, M. J. (1999) "Reconsidering Enlightenment geography and map making: reconnaissance, mapping, archive," in D. N. Livingstone and C. W. J. Withers (eds.) *Geography and Enlightenment* (pp. 165–98). Chicago: University of Chicago Press.

Edwards, P. (1994) *The Story of the Voyage: Sea-Narratives in Eighteenth-Century England*. Cambridge: Cambridge University Press.

Elsner, J., and Rubiés, J.-P. (eds.) (1999) *Voyages and Visions: Towards a Cultural History of Travel*. London: Reaktion Books.

Gordon, P. (1693) *Geography Anatomiz'd: or, A Compleat Geographical Grammar*. London: Printed by J. R. for Robert Morden and Thomas Cockerid.

Guthrie, W. (1770) *New Geographical, Historical and Commercial Grammar*. London: J. Knox.

Hancock, D. (1995) *Citizens of the World: London Merchants and the Integration of the British Atlantic Community, 1735–1785*. Cambridge: Cambridge University Press.

Lamb, J. (2001) *Preserving the Self in the South Seas, 1680–1840*. Chicago: University of Chicago Press.

Lamb, J., Smith, V., and Thomas, N. (eds.) (2000) *Exploration and Exchange: A South Seas Anthology, 1680–1900*. Chicago: University of Chicago Press.

Leask, N. (2002) *Curiosity and the Aesthetics of Travel Writing 1770–1840*. Oxford: Oxford University Press.

Mayhew, R. J. (2000) *Enlightenment Geography: The Political Languages of British Geography, 1650–1850*. London and New York: Macmillan and St Martin's Press.

—— (2004) "Geography books and the character of Georgian politics," in M. Ogborn and C. W. J. Withers (eds.) *Georgian Geographies: Essays on Space, Place and Landscape in the Eighteenth Century* (pp. 192–211). Manchester: Manchester University Press.

McLeod, B. (1999) *The Geography of Empire in English Literature 1580–1745*. Cambridge: Cambridge University Press.

Ogborn, M. (1998) *Spaces of Modernity: London's Geographies, 1680–1780*. New York: Guilford Press.

Ogilby, J. (1661) *The Relation of His Majestie's Entertainment passing through the City of London, to His Coronation*. London: T. Roycroft for R. Marriott.

Parkes, C. (1995) "'A True Survey of the Ground': Defoe's *Tour* and the rise of thematic cartography," *Philological Quarterly* 74: 395–414.

Poovey, M. (1998) *A History of the Modern Fact: Problems of Knowledge in the Sciences of Wealth and Society*. Chicago: Chicago University Press.

Salmon, T. (1746) *Modern Gazetteer*. London: Printed for S. and E. Ballard.

—— (1749) *New Geographical and Historical Grammar*. London: Printed for William Johnston.

Schaffer, S. (1989) "Defoe's natural philosophy and the worlds of credit," in J. Christie and S. Shuttleworth (eds.) *Nature Transfigured: Science and Literature, 1700–1900* (pp. 13–44). Manchester: Manchester University Press.

—— (2002) "Golden means: assay instruments and the geography of precision in the Guinea trade," in M.-N. Bourguet, C. Licoppe, and H. O. Sibum (eds.) *Instruments, Travel and Science: Itineraries of Precision from the Seventeenth to the Twentieth Century* (pp. 20–50). London: Routledge.

Shapin, S. (1994) *A Social History of Truth: Civility and Science in Seventeenth-Century England*. Chicago: University of Chicago Press.

Sitwell, O. F. G. (1993) *Four Centuries of Special Geography*. Vancouver: University of British Columbia Press.

Stagl, J. (1995) *A History of Curiosity: The Theory of Travel, 1550–1800*. Chur, Switzerland: Harwood Academic.

Swift, J. (1726) *Gulliver's Travels*, ed. and with an introduction by P. Dixon and J. Chalker. Harmondsworth: Penguin, 1985.

Williams, G. (1997) *The Great South Sea: English Voyages and Encounters, 1570–1750*. New Haven: Yale University Press.

Williams, H. (ed.) (1963) *The Correspondence of Jonathan Swift*, 5 vols. Oxford: Clarendon Press.

Withers, C. (2001) *Geography, Science and National Identity: Scotland since 1520*. Cambridge: Cambridge University Press.

Withers, C. and Livingstone, D. (1999) "Introduction: on geography and enlightenment," in D. N. Livingstone and C. W. J. Withers (eds.) *Geography and Enlightenment* (pp. 1–28). Chicago: University of Chicago Press.

Woodward, J. (1696) *Brief Instructions for Making Observations in All Parts of the World*. London: Richard Wilkin.

Chapter 2

Scientific Investigations

Experimentalism and Paradisal Return

Joanna Picciotto

Experimentalism challenged traditional forms of literacy and divinity by extending the Protestant call of *sola scriptura* to the first book God wrote: nature. Experimentalists took as their model the first philosopher, who with "no Study but Reflection . . . no book, but the volume of the world," named the animals according to their natures (Genesis 2:19; South 1663: 15). Musing on "the first service, that Adam perform'd to his *Creator*, when he obey'd him in mustring, and naming, and looking into the *Nature* of all the *Creatures*," Thomas Sprat grew wistful: "This had bin the only *Religion*, if men had continued innocent in *Paradise*" (1667: 349–50). Sprat's Adam did not just survey the creatures before naming them, he penetrated their very natures; through techniques like dissection and the use of optical instruments, modern experimentalists did the same. In doing so, they reenacted the first act of obedience, perhaps the first divine service.

Sprat's fantasy of a primitive religion based on natural investigation took as its point of departure Francis Bacon's celebrated account of Eden as a place of knowledge and discovery. Identifying innocence not with ignorance but with insight, Bacon's description of Eden as an epistemological paradise provided a theodicy for the recently "fallen" senses at the start of the seventeenth century. The mortification of Copernicanism, the epiphany of a microworld beneath the threshold of visibility, and the resurrection of the ancient atomists' distinction between primary and secondary qualities (which redefined the bulk of our sensory experience as several steps removed from things themselves) had all revealed the extent of humanity's blindness to the creation over which it was supposed to be sovereign (see Blumenberg 1991). Bacon traced this apparent design flaw to original sin and redescribed the curse as a contract stipulating that, through exertion, humanity could recover its original rational command over creation. The curse of labor was not a punishment to be borne but an opportunity to be seized.

The doctrine of original sin made identification with Adam compulsory at the moment of the first disobedience; Baconians like Sprat turned this identification to account, using the innocent Adam to designate the expression of human potential under ideal conditions, conditions they worked hard to recreate. The intellectual hunger and restlessness once identified with the fall now characterized a regimen of self-exertion whose aim was to *reverse* the fall. A theodicy had become a research program. "The end then of learning," Milton wrote in his Baconian treatise *Of Education*, "is to repair the ruins of our first Parents"; its means, experimental: "conning over the visible and inferior creature" (1644: 2).

During the Interregnum, Baconians pursued this program at Gresham College, the progressive London center for practical adult education founded by a relative of Bacon's, and at Cromwell's "Greshamized" Oxford (see Hill 1968). After the Restoration, under the guidance of men like John Evelyn and Sir Robert Moray, this community of experimentalists adopted a name calculated to ingratiate itself with the restored king: the Royal Society. But although Charles granted the Society a charter in 1662, he never gave it money; the Society remained a self-supporting institution, a vulnerable *hortus conclusus* within Restoration culture.

Innocent Curiosity

Like Milton's Eden, the new space of the laboratory held "in narrow room Natures whole wealth" (*Paradise Lost* (hereafter *PL*): 4.207). Here, experimentalists like Robert Hooke attempted to break down the phenomenological boundary that separated corrupted humanity from created humanity, to answer the question: what is creation *before* the fallen body and mind experience it? Rather than delight in creation as revealed to the senses, experimentalists sought to excavate the *causes* of sensory experience. The subjective conflict between body and soul, for centuries the source of the vicissitudes of the Christian ego, was reprised in the laboratory as a dialectical tension between the fallen body with which the investigator was saddled and an ideal spectatorial body towards which he strove. In practice, this ideal body was recovered as his own body, subject to rational control, directed towards spiritual ends, and artificially enhanced by new investigative technologies.

Revealing to readers of the *Micrographia* the "stupendious Mechanisms and contrivances" that characterize "the smallest and most despicable Fly" when viewed under the microscope, Hooke wondered, "Who knows but Adam might from some such contemplation, give [sic] names to all creatures?" (1665: 154). Hooke's slide into the present tense is telling. What he called the "artificial Organs" of the microscope and telescope were prosthetic replacements for lost parts of the first man's body; by "disciplining" the senses with such instruments of restoration, fallen humanity as a whole was regaining that body's powers. To claim, as Joseph Glanvill did, that Adam had not needed "*Galileo's* tube" in order to contemplate distant planets, and that "he had as clear a perception of the earths motion, as we think we have of its quiescence" was really to celebrate *contemporary* technologies and discoveries (1661: 5). As originary longings were reconciled to progress, "Adam" became a laboring collective and innocence was reborn as objectivity: paradise began its journey into future time.

The first step in regaining innocence, de-education, was a daunting one: as Glanvill put it, "we must endeavour to estrange our assent from every thing . . . we must unlive our former lives" (pp. 108, 72). The experimentalist guarded what Walter Charleton called a "virgin Mind" by maintaining a provisional relationship to belief (1654: 99). Demurring from expressions of certainty and the furious clashes of opinion identified with "the schools," the Christian virtuoso toiled humbly in the sphere of probability. The "relations" he penned were short on conclusive opinions, long on "real Experiments and Observation[s]" susceptible to open-ended use (Power 1664: sig. c3v–4).

Abjuring the philosopher's traditional diet of pure theory freed experimentalists to indulge their ontological hunger for knowledge of "things themselves," a phrase they obsessively repeated. Even as they disdained the sacred relics of the old religion, they cultivated a well-nigh idolatrous fascination with apparent trifles such as roots, fossils, and teeth. Clearly, a reverse snobbery governed their proud susceptibility to such "wonders" as "a piece of a BONE voided by Sir W. Throgmorton with his Urine. Given by Thomas Cox Esq"; "A TOOTH taken out of the Testicle or Ovary of a Woman, and given by Dr. Edward Tyson" (Grew 1681: 8–9). On display in the Society's repository alongside these mundane anomalies produced by human bodies was the virtuoso's ability to *see through* traditional hierarchies of value, discerning the wondrous variety of creation where "sons of Sense" could see only a kidney stone (Power

1664: sig. a3v). The care the virtuoso lavished on the contemplation of things beneath notice – literally, in the case of microscopic specimens – revealed his awareness that the distinction between the trivial and the "curious" was not visible to the naked, or fallen, eye.

Such overturning of conventional hierarchies established new canons of value. The experimentalist was interested in "rare" objects; this meant he was interested in weird ones. To the virtuoso, a thing seemed most rare – most like a thing itself – when it thwarted assumptions, forcing a priori knowledge to submit to the pressure of brute facts: the leg of a deformed or "monstrous" calf was rarer, in this sense, than a precious stone (see Park and Daston 1981). Experiments, contrived experiences of nature taken out of its regular course, were another way to produce singular facts. Like a petrified piece of wood, the spectacle of a suffocating bird in an exhausted air receiver offered a *denaturalized* view of nature. Natural histories composed in the manner of a Boylean "relation," eschewing peremptory conclusions in favor of circumstantial detail, were another avenue into the world of things themselves. The Royal Society's journal, the *Philosophical Transactions*, teems with reports on strange events and things that were the object of someone's direct sensory acquaintance: a lightning storm, a dissected opossum, an unexplained noise. The investigator schooled in these lessons of estrangement became an innocent observer, qualified to discern the strange in the familiar and render it visible to others.

The attempt to discern and harness the processes that governed creation demanded more from the observer than reposeful contemplation. Simply to see the "small letters" of nature's book one had to slice specimens open, pin them down, and observe them under various lighting conditions, gently coaxing the things within "things themselves" into visibility. Experimentalist observation could not be separated from intervention. Experimentalists leaned heavily on the etymon *cura*, care, to suggest that, far from breeding pride, curiosity promoted a humble willingness to invest *care* and take pains in the production of knowledge: the Adamic investigator of nature got his hands dirty in it. As Hooke, the Society's "Curator of Experiments," declared, the pains and drudgery of experimentalist's labor could not finally be distinguished from his "high *rapture* and *delight*" (1665: sig. d2). When Boyle built his first laboratory – literally a workroom – on his estate, he felt as if he had escaped into "Elysium": "painful digging, and toiling in *Nature*" was, it turned out, the very stuff of paradise (Boyle 1772/1966: vol. 6: 49–50; Sprat 1667: 94). As the experimentalists' laborious program of *imitatio Adami* rendered paradise an attribute, not of a lost place or time, but of a collective subject engaged in the progressive work of discovery, the means and end of paradisal return became hard to distinguish.

This processual vision of paradise was shared by a man who was both a close friend of the Society's first secretary, Henry Oldenburg, and the tutor of Boyle's nephew: John Milton. *Paradise Lost* (1667) and *Paradise Regained* (1671) both seek to cleanse originary desire of any attachment to a privileged time or place. They assimilate paradise to the process of trial, of cultivating and inhabiting "a paradise within," one "happier farr" than a mere pleasure garden could ever be (*PL* 12.587). Contemporary experimentalists could recognize their idealized self-reflections in Milton's Adam, whose physical exertions on creation keep pace with his labors to understand it. He is actually relieved by the curse, reassured that he won't be, as he puts it, "unimploid" after the expulsion: "What harm? Idleness had bin worse" (*PL* 4.617; 10.1055).

Experimentalism's originary obsession went beyond an idolatrous attachment to the figure of the first man to animate its key words. *Curiosity*'s constant companion word *ingenuity*, for example, denotes innocence and innovation simultaneously, making one the sign of the other. Even the word *revolution* was systematically ambiguous, referring at once to a return to the starting point, a "rolling back," and to the forward movement such rolling back enabled. In Protestant England, the vocabulary that expressed fidelity to origins *was* the vocabulary of progress. Isaac Newton never doubted that his discoveries were recoveries of an original philosophy of nature, a *prisca theologica*, that had been passed down, in progressively corrupted form, through figures such as Noah, Orpheus, Hermes Trismegistus, Pythagoras, and Plato.

Although this originary ideology could be abstracted from the image repertoire of paradise, that imagery retained a strong grip on the experimentalist imagination. Boyle's essay *"Upon his paring of a rare summer apple"* in the *Occasional Reflections* (1665), for example, shows him face to face with the fruit that "inveigled our first parents." "How prettily has curious nature painted this gaudy fruit?" Boyle asks, as if he had caught out nature being curious, investing care in fashioning a tempting object. He remarks that the fruit's beauty, which "delights me strangely," is so great as to "justify her pride"; imputing feminine pride to the apple itself, he lumps the object of temptation together with its first victim, then defines himself against both. With the assistance of a paring knife, Boyle puts the source of temptation on trial, to "know whether it performs to the taste what it promises to the sight." As the agency of curiosity migrates from the apple to Boyle, idle curiosity yields to innocent *cura*, and the first sin is reformed into the first virtue. Eve's "sad experiment" (*PL* 10.977) was an attempt to consume knowledge; Boyle *produces* knowledge by investing labor in the object of temptation. By working to "strip and divest" bodies of their "cheating disguises . . . which so often conceal or misrepresent their true and genuine nature," Boyle gains carnal knowledge without submitting to carnal temptation and manages to transform even the eating of the apple into a form of innocent inquiry. The scene of temptation morphs into the scene of naming. As "all this gay outside is cut and thrown away" the apple takes its place in the creation mustered and looked into by "the severer scrutiny of reason" (1772/1966 vol. 2: 364–5).

Newton employed some stagecraft when retailing his own apple story to William Stukeley, bringing his young admirer to the scene of his famous epiphany where "the notion of gravitation came into his mind . . . occasion'd by the fall of an apple, as he sat in a contemplative mood" (1752/1936: 19–20). Like Boyle, Newton uses the apple to contain the threat it once represented: an apple occasioned the fall, but here the fall of an *apple* occasions the solitary garden dweller's insight into the omnipresent attractive force of gravity, through which, as we will see, Newton believed he could discern the hand of the Creator Himself. These two fables of paradise regained – one stressing active physical intervention and the other a purely rational penetration – may model the difference between Restoration natural history and eighteenth-century Newtonianism, but both provide the same lesson in Adamic self-invention: the virtuoso defines himself against the (frequently feminized) *subject* of temptation by transforming the *object* of temptation into an "occasion" for rational labor.

The Sovereign Worker

Adam's nominative and material powers over creation were intertwined: in a world where names correspond to natures, language is knowledge, but in a world where natures can be forced to correspond to names, it is power, or "maker's knowledge" (see Perez-Ramos 1998). Such knowledge could not be assimilated to the classical understanding of intellectual pursuits as an extension of gentlemanly leisure. Aristotle had identified the mechanical arts (*artes serviles*) with the slave and the liberal arts with the freeborn; by redefining trustworthy knowledge as the product of combined physical and intellectual fitness, experimentalists collapsed this distinction. Uniting the fallen antinomies of action and contemplation, *negotium* and *otium*, body and mind, the worker and the thinker, the figure of Adam provided the basis for the distinctly modern concept of intellectual labor.

The first man, for whom the concerted discipline of hand, eye, and brain was a source of knowledge, power, and bliss, conjured up his fallen opposite: the scholastic philosopher or "schoolman," a grotesque, belated figure in bondage to useless study, at once physically and mentally inert and crazed by uncontrolled speculation about imaginary metaphysical entities such as essences and substantial forms. As his mastery of learned languages, refusal to work, reverence for tradition, and haughty indifference to things themselves suggest, the schoolman was a covert caricature of the idle aristocrat. Through this figure experimentalists lamented the existence of an entire class of people to whom labor was as alien as paradise. As an object of the experimentalist's ritual abuse, the schoolman embodied the intellectual deprivations sustained by aristocratic privilege. Deploring the fragile constitutions and ignorance of "the better sort," John Locke argued that if the blessing of labor were distributed more equally, "there would be more knowledge, peace, health and plenty in it than now there is. And mankind be much more happy than now it is" (1997: 328). Experimental labor promoted precisely this brand of happiness: Sprat excitedly informed his readers that "Of our *Nobility*, and *Gentry*, the most *Noble* and *Illustrious* have condescended, to labour here with their hands" (1667: 131). Such men distinguished themselves from the "learned ignorance" of textual authorities by their exemplary willingness to slum (Locke 1690: 243).

The faith that one can gain access to an idealized past by imitating social inferiors is what creates Arcadias. By locating the power to recover innocent habits of investigation in their social inferiors, experimentalists embraced what William Empson called "pastoral logic" unironically. Experimentalism was an exercise in applied pastoral, with philosophers attempting not only to speak the language of their social inferiors, but to make use of their knowledge. Like the simple herdsmen of pastoral who live in nature's bosom and have an insight into nature that their refined betters lack, working-class practitioners could lend their betters the power to repair a terrible loss. But among experimentalists, what Empson describes as the quintessentially pastoral sentiment of the high regarding the low – "I am in one way better, in another not so good" – lost its disingenuous character; rueful condescension succumbed to straightforward reverence and envy (1960: 15).

Alongside the drive to restore humanity's original synthesis of faculties – divided in the fallen world between those who worked with words and those who worked with things – was the dream of uniting the noble and the common in the collective subject of science. Adam, the first sovereign who was also the first worker, modeled this collective subject in which "the minds, and labours of men of all Conditions, are join'd" (Sprat 1667: 6). In this collectivist sense, worker's knowledge was itself the fruit of Adam's labor, the product of the collective subject of humanity in traffic with nature. By virtue of their necessary immersion in "things themselves" in order to make a living, artisans and working-class practitioners had produced valuable reports of trial and error experimentation, condensed in craft secrets and folk wisdom. The product of centuries of discourse and experience that had traveled over vast distances, this body of knowledge was much like the *prisca theologica*. In fact, "wisefolk" arrested for magical offenses often boasted that they inherited their knowledge from such figures as Moses, the Archangel Raphael (the natural philosophy instructor of Milton's Adam) and Adam himself (Thomas 1971: 271–2, 248).

The Royal Society's vaunted "Histories of Trades" thus merely registered age-old "discoveries" already made in fields such as tanning, iron-making, refining, and fermentation; the Society hoped to produce from these a series of descriptions of nature under constraint that could be applied across "arts" (see Ochs 1985). The phenomenal culture of rustics and commoners had evolved for centuries in isolation from the Latinate culture of the universities; by declaring the Society's preference for "the language of Artizans, Countrymen, and Merchants, before that, of Wits, or Scholars," Sprat acknowledged that this technical jargon bound up with physical actions could not be translated into conventional scholarly terms: scholars really did need to learn a new language (1667: 113). With a mixture of diffidence and optimism, Henry Oldenburg touted the Society's publications as language aids to "enable Gentlemen and Schollars to converse with Tradesmen . . . at least it will qualify them to ask questions of men that converse with things; and sometimes to exchange Experiments with them" (quoted in Ochs 1985: 148). The one-sided emphasis in recent scholarship on the gentlemanly character of experimental science obscures the extent to which the practice, rather than the mere theory, of mechanical philosophy – widely viewed as the philosophy of "mechanicks" – required as much social as intellectual experimentation, forcing gentlemen virtuosi into behavior that was, to say the least, unusual for members of their class.

In the *Sceptical Chymist* Boyle spoke openly of his "good fortune" in having been instructed in chemical operations by "illiterate Persons," who viewed them "with lesse prejudice, and consequently with other Eyes" than educated philosophers. Following their example, Boyle was able to "take notice of divers Phaenomena, overlook'ed by prepossest Persons." This was not just propaganda: Boyle's discovery that acids and bases differ in their effect on vegetable juices, for example, was based on the knowledge of dyers (Boyle 1661: A8; Eamon 1980: 206–7). To prove their own ability to "take notice," experimentalists often strove to present themselves as virtual illiterates. Modest illiteracy was an extension of epistemological "innocence," and it offered the same rewards. Richard Waller's hagiography of Hooke portrays him as almost untouched by literate culture: the more Hooke applied himself to his books as a child, the more he became "subject to the Head-ach," with the result that his father soon "laid aside all Thoughts of breeding him a Scholar and . . . wholly neglected his farther Education" (Hooke 1705: 2). Though the Honorable Robert Boyle could hardly pretend to such credentials, he represented his entrance into literacy as an unmitigated trauma. He "hated the Study of Bare words, naturally," finding it "much nobler . . . to learne to do things" than to learn "the Gowne-men's Language" (Boyle 1992: 10).

The revolutionary assault on textual knowledge in favor of experiential knowledge ultimately forced the university to remake itself in the image of "the flourishing Universitie of Eden," accommodating disciplines that just a few decades before "were scarce looked upon as *Academical Studies*, but rather *Mechanical*; as the business of *Traders, Merchants, Carpenters, Surveyors of Lands*, or the like" (Sturtevant 1602: 7; Allen 1949: 228–9). The overthrow of the book by the thing is dramatically evident in Robert Plot's praise of Ashmole for donating to the University of Oxford "the best History of Nature, Arts, and Antiquities . . . not in print . . . but in a generous donation of the real things themselves." When the Ashmolean Museum was finally completed, university finances were so exhausted that for years afterwards the Bodleian was unable to purchase any books at all (Swann 2001: 53, 50). One could hardly ask for a more concise emblem of the shuffling of elite priorities experimentalism promoted.

The detested "schoolmen" had had good reasons to identify natural philosophy with textual commentary rather than physical investigation. The real object of the scholastic's investigation was form, the invisible source of all essential qualities and changes in natural bodies. To understand the essential nature of a thing such as an acorn one had to look to general cases and the "experience" recorded in authoritative texts, not at any particular acorn (see Dear 1995). Form theory had survived in the Paracelsian and hermetic practice of reading signatures, marks of interior invisible forms: the walnut rind, for example, bore "an entire Signature" of the human brain and was therefore good for headaches

(Croll 1670: 1, 2nd pagination). Wresting the topos of nature's book from its most self-assured practitioners, experimentalists denied nature's legibility to those who relied on their fallen intuition and undisciplined perception instead of on the proper reading aids. The lens had revealed that the powers and perceptible properties of natural substances depended on the actions of material particles beneath the threshold of normal perception; the supposedly invisible operations of "form" were merely invisible to the unassisted human eye. Drawing on Lucretius's famous analogy, experimentalists atomized signatures into individual letters, atoms: its scriptural unity dissolved, the book of nature became an on-going process of decomposition and reassemblage – textuality, or a book in the making. Hooke looked forward to excavating the *"Orthography, Etymologia, Syntaxis,* and *Prosodia* of Nature's Grammar,"* which would empower the "Literatus in the Language and Sense of Nature" to scramble and recompose its letters, words, and sentences (1705: 338). Just as virtuosi conflated Adam's nominative power with creative power, so they employed the topos of nature's book to promote authorial intervention: to read was to write.

Labors of Looking

By describing and then imitating the subject of innocence, experiment-alists invented the figure of the intellectual laborer, in whom authors eager to unite mimesis to discovery and intervention began, in turn, to recognize themselves. In particular, the mythology surrounding the new optical technologies made the lens almost irresistible to writers as an emblem for their own undertakings, for it suggested that one who contemplates the world also acts upon it. In violation of the dictum that the literary sign is to be looked *at* rather than *through*, authors reinvented themselves as interventionist spectators by presenting their texts as lenses. Milton presented *Paradise Lost* as the literary equivalent of the telescope of Galileo (the only named contemporary in the poem); it was the first English epic to explore the infinite interstellar space opened up by the telescope as well as the world of atoms suggested by the microscope. Milton's access to the experience of innocence was an extension of this ability to "see and tell / Of things invisible to mortal sight" (*PL* 3.54–5). The most important satire of the first decade of the Restoration, Andrew Marvell's *Last Instructions to a Painter* (1689, written 1667) turns the lens from nature to "the world" in order to expose the hidden causes of the Medway debacle. Penetrating appearances that the hapless state

45

painter, subjected throughout to Marvell's raillery and mock instruction, can only reproduce, the poem begins by putting Lord Clifford under the microscope and ends by aiming the telescope at, and exposing the "spots" on, Charles himself.

What Hooke referred to with *sprezzatura* as the "rude Draughts" of *Micrographia* – most famously, its magnificent fold-out louse – imprinted themselves more deeply on the consciousness of the public than any other book illustrations of the period; Pepys stayed up until two in the morning with it and called it "the most ingenious book that ever I read in my life" (Hooke 1667: sig. A2v; Pepys 1970–83 vol. 6: 18). The microworld to which Hooke's illustrations gave such precise and inspired expression launched a native tradition of literary experimentation with scale. English literature would certainly have developed very differently without this book; Jonathan Swift's *Gulliver's Travels* (1726) is unimaginable without the technology of the lens to which it is testimony. Its mockery of scientists as crazed projectors in the third book can only be read as a blatant symptom of an anxiety of influence. We are supposed to find the foil to the projectors of Lagado in the commonsensical King of Brobdignag, who declares that "whoever could make two Ears of Corn, or two Blades of Grass to grow upon a Spot of Ground where only one grew before; would deserve better of Mankind, and do more essential Service to his Country, than the whole Race of Politicians put together" (1726/1959 vol. 11: 119–20). Bacon could not have said it better.

Paradoxically, the virtuosi's elevation of experiential over textual literacy fostered the emergence of a new literary type: the professional observer. Tom Brown introduces his observations of London life with the declaration that "those that have no other knowledge of the world but what they collect from books . . . are not fit to give instructions to others." To become "literate" in the world, Brown asserts, one has to become fit indeed, by taking the physical pains to "travel through it" (1927: 3–4, 10). In obedience to this mandate, Ned Ward metamorphoses into the London Spy when he abandons his library to roam through "the living library" of the world. In an epiphanic moment, he realizes he has been transformed by years of sedentary study into "Aristotle's sumpter-horse." It is then that he decides to leave his "old calf-skin companions" for London, armed with a new goal: "observation" (1709/1993: 11). No longer a schoolman, he has become an empiricist. Like the virtuosi, Ward refers to his activities as his labor, stressing the physical demands and frequently sordid conditions of empirical investigation. Using and exhibiting his body as an instrument of reason, the professional observer's acquisition of literacy originated in physical expenditure – "a great deal of elbow-labour and much sweating," as Ward puts it (p. 132) – but ended in corporeal transcendence, tracing a progress from "traveling through" to *seeing* through.

The public was inducted into the mysteries of looking "thro' Nature, up to Nature's God," as Pope put it in *Essay on Man* (1733–4), by books and lectures on "physico-theology," which instructed the public in how to observe God in every limb of an insect and drop of dew. This strain of Christian apologetics, institutionalized in 1693 by the Boyle lectures and later reinvigorated in 1829 by the patronage of the Earl of Bridgewater, has an unmistakably Arian odor; its God is emphatically the Creator rather than the Redeemer. Like a good trade history, a work of physico-theology conveyed lessons in "knowing how" rather than "knowing that": rather than a set of axioms, it represented a time splice in an ongoing process of "taking notice."

The union of professional observation and physico-theology spawned a new genre: loco-descriptive or excursion poetry, whose literal and figurative expatiations (the animating pun of *Essay on Man*, announced in its fifth line) are at once demonstrations of physical hustle and acts of rational penetration. Rather than ostentatiously wielding the lens as an emblem, however, the wanderer silently assumes its powers, rendering visible the "soft Inhabitants" of each "flowery leaf" (Thomson *Summer*, ll. 296–7) and "the green myriads in the peopled grass" (Pope *Essay on Man* epistle 1: l. 210). What we may think of as the stock phrases of this verse were attempts to produce an effect of precision; rather than referring to animals or plants using their conventional names, periphrastic phrases like "the mineral kinds" provided a nomenclature that divulged the circumstances of their being (see Arthos 1940). If their wealth of circumstantial detail qualified these poems as Boylean relations, their descriptive phrases allowed readers to become "virtual witnesses" to acts of Adamic naming (on virtual witnessing see Shapin and Schaffer 1985).

God's Invisible Hand

As science became an acceptable gentlemanly undertaking, aristocratic privilege lost its compulsory identification with ignorance of "things themselves." Intellectuals who looked to the new philosophy (now not so new) as a model for interventionist power soon saw a very different image of that power. The spectatorial metaphors through which the concept of intellectual labor first came into its own endured, but the image of the intellectual as a privileged observer became identified with performances of a more rarefied sort. The hardy emphasis on things themselves and on the grinding labor required to transform them into testimonials ebbed as spectatorial privilege passed back into the realm of innate gifts. In contrast to Ward's "rambles," Joseph Addison and Richard Steele's Mr. Spectator refers to his "Rambles, or rather Speculations," around London, using the nouns interchangeably (1711–12/1965 vol. 1: 14; *The Spectator* no. 3); Samuel Johnson's later *Rambler* papers (1750) are *purely* intellectual journeys. Released from the identification with the artisanal laborer, experimentalist-identified intellectuals now defined themselves in relation to an icon of otherworldly genius – Isaac Newton.

A reclusive figure throughout the 1660s and 1670s, Newton was a lecturer of mathematics at Cambridge who "for want of Hearers, read to ye Walls" and whose dealings with the Society and its Curator were uniformly traumatic. In 1672, he sent the Society "my poore & solitary endeavours" from his darkened chamber at Trinity only to withdraw the paper when Hooke challenged its claims to certainty. In January 1680, Hooke shared with Newton his hypothesis that the force of gravity was inversely proportional to the square of the distance measured from the center of a gravitating mass; and although Newton provided the quantitative and experimental support to make this hypothesis a theory, his refusal to give Hooke any credit led to lasting animosity. The Society loyally declined to publish the *Principia Mathematica* (1687), spending their publishing funds on Willoughby's *Historia Piscium* instead. But in 1703, Robert Hooke died; Newton was quickly elected President of the Royal Society. This "poor & solitary" scholar now set about becoming an international celebrity. Before becoming Master of the Royal Mint, he sat as a member of Parliament – and for over 20 portraits and busts, of which thousands of copies were sold. Attaching his name to anything boosted its value on the market: Newton became a brand (Fara 2002: 5, 17).

Temperamentally unsuited to the collective nature of experimentalist labor and always averse to sharing credit (as evinced by his dispute with Leibniz over the calculus or "fluxions"), Newton also had little sympathy for curiosity-collecting and descriptive natural history in general. His effort to reduce surface complexity to what Thomson called "laws sublimely simple" (*Summer*, l. 1562) was fundamentally opposed to the omnivorous spirit of Baconian induction. Uniting an apple with a heavenly body, Newton's theory of physical nature embraced all phenomena of matter in motion; in contrast, John Ray's monumental *Historia Generalis Plantarum*, published in the same year as the *Opticks* (1704), provided exhaustive morphological descriptions of over 18,500 plants. And though the *Opticks* was a "relation," describing particular experiments performed, it was a mathematical text, with definitions, axioms, and theorems. Newton did not require conversation with the humbler sort – or, he implied, anyone at all – in order to proceed with this work.

Gravitational attraction could not be reduced to the mutual action and reaction of material surface areas of collision mechanics; it was a non-mechanical force, acting on and through the entire bulk of bodies. Newton found the proposition that gravity was a property inherent in matter appalling: "no man who has in philosophical matters a competent faculty of thinking" could imagine that action at a distance could have its source in "brute matter" (1958: 302–3). Some contemporaries argued that Newton's action at a distance resurrected the occult forces from which science had just been liberated. As Roger North put it, gravity was "a Simile or rather a Cover for Ignorance . . . If one asks why one thing draws another – It is answered by a certain drawingness it hath": in other words, it was as tautological as the old scholastic concept of form (Fara 2002: 18). Newton's refusal to hypothesize a cause or mechanism was actually a source of his power: "to us it is enough that gravity does really exist, and act according to the laws which we have explained" (1962 vol. 2: 547). Reduced pretensions, it appeared, could elevate a theory above the modest realm of probability – even beyond the realm of debate.

The awful simplicity of the inverse square law and the mystery surrounding its central concept accrued to the figure of Newton himself. Through Newton, it seemed, the mechanical world was born again, its spirit resurrected. Then, in the *Opticks*, Newton untwisted the rainbow, recovering from the differently refrangible rays that made up the symbol of God's covenant a beam of pure white light. If physico-theology made natural philosophers into priests of nature, Newton as a "second Adam" virtually replaced the Son (whose divinity Newton denied): in "The Ecstasy" John Hughes imagined Newton's soul soaring through heaven, like Milton's Christ at the moment of creation (1735); Francis Fawkes's "Elogy [*sic*] on Sir Isaac Newton" (a translation of Halley's ode) concludes by describing Newton as a mediating term between God and man, having "reach'd th'insuperable line, / The nice barrier 'twixt human and divine" (1761: 136 ll. 63–4). The topos of light as a manifestation of the divine animates Pope's famous epitaph: "Nature, and Nature's Laws lay hid in Night. / God said, *Let Newton Be!* And All was *light*" (1950–67 vol. 6: 317).

In Richard Bentley's Boyle lectures on the Newtonian system, the boundary between God and his universe became as porous as that between Newton and God. Not only did the nonmechanical operation of gravity provide an "invincible Argument for the Being of God," it was hardly to be distinguished from that being. The vacuum within which gravity operated was suffused with the Creator's "immaterial living Mind"; gravity itself was "the immediate Fiat & Finger of God," a direct manifestation of divine power (Newton 1958: 342, 347). Although he did not burden his theories with them, Newton did make hypotheses, clearly flagged as scholia or queries, which enhanced Bentley's suggestions. The General Scholium described God as "omnipresent, not *virtually* only, but also *substantially* . . . In him are all things contained and moved" (1962 vol. 2: 545). In the *Opticks* he asked,

> [D]oes it not appear from Phaenomena that there is a Being incorporeal, living, intelligent, omnipresent, who in infinite Space, as it were in his Sensory, sees the things themselves intimately . . . Of which things the Images only carried through the Organs of Sense into our little Sensoriums, are there seen and beheld by that which in us perceives and thinks. (1704/1952: 370)

Few readers could follow Newton's equations, but, reduced to window dressing for revelations like these, such evidence of mathematical genius seemed to confer certainty on a vision of a world not only created but actively maintained by an omnipresent, omniscient God. The secrets of creation no longer needed to be pieced together by Sprat's "vulgar hands"; they had been revealed to a man whose sensorium seemed uniquely continuous with the creator's. Newton's big and little sensoria reprised the Biblical proverb "The spirit of man is the candle of the Lord," providing scientific evidence that the human mind was, as the Cambridge Platonists had imagined, an attribute of the divine (Patrides 1969: 11–13). The magical character of the Adamic investigator's "names" seemed confirmed; the language of nature was the language of mathematics, and Newton spoke it fluently.

To conceive of space as God's sensorium emphasized God's direct comprehension and superintendence of the workings of the universe, even our internal worlds. The immediate dominion of Newton's God over the physical, moral, and political worlds at once offered supporters of the Glorious Revolution the highest justification for flouting divine right – divine providence. Described as God's invisible hand, the operation of gravity was soon expanded into a model of mixed-government and laissez-faire society (see Dobbs and Jacob 1995). In his poem celebrating the coronation of George II, the *Newtonian System of the World the Best*

Pattern of Government (1728) Jean Theophilus Desaguliers used gravity as a metaphor for the "loose" attraction that linked members of a commonwealth. England's mixed government recapitulated the dynamic balance struck by the attraction between the celestial bodies and the inertial momentum of their own independent movement. In contrast, the Cartesian scheme, like the tyrannical French monarchy, subjected all motion to the dead hand of mechanical necessity.

The quibble on "Democrit-al" and "democratic" had been an organizing pun of Restoration philosophy; atomism described a world without natural hierarchy or transcendent order. The ubiquitous analogy between the collisions of "embryon atoms" and civil war led Hobbes to identify the counterpart of inertial motion in the political world as a perpetual desire for power that generated chaos: the state of nature (see Spragens 1973). The Newtonian system retained the democratic character of this world while reducing it to order; the subjection of all bodies to the inverse square law paralleled the subjection of all subjects to the same political laws. The attractive forces that bonded every particle of the universe together were analogous to the ties of sympathy in the moral world that disposed political subjects to cooperation. Gravitation embodied the politically resonant trope of *concordia discors*, suggesting the happy coexistence of sociability and autonomy in nature and in England.

Mr Spectator sees the invisible hand and "immaterial living Mind" at work during his weepy visit to the stock exchange, where the moral expression of gravitational attraction, sociability, is the surplus created by mutually beneficial self-interested exchanges (Addison and Steele 1711–12/1965 vol. 1: 292–4; *The Spectator* no. 69). While these bodies go about pursuing their private interests, sociability is, as it were, spontaneously generated, visible only to Mr Spectator, elevated above the human swarm. The grim object lesson in human selfishness delivered by Mandeville's *Fable of the Bees* (1714) becomes an occasion for sentimental reflection and tears. If Mr Spectator prefigures the lonely sociability of the sentimental author, the spectacle he uncovers is similarly lonely; the bonds of human sympathy are not forged or even directly experienced by any of the participants, only generated from their interactions. This sociability is a subjective feeling without a subjective center; that center is ultimately identified with the "sensorium" of the Author – and the author who understands His ways.

Mr Spectator's "rambles, or speculations" correspond to the itinerant narrative perspective of the novel that, penetrating the barriers of separate subjectivities, finally broke free of subjectivity itself. Free indirect discourse, defined by Ann Banfield (1987) as originating in a deictic center without a subject, is the product of the author's invisible mind and hand – the narrative expression of the interpenetration of the great sensorium and little sensoria. Indirect discourse permits the omniscient view of the author and the limited views of his creatures to come together in the view from everywhere.

The elegant symmetry of the Newtonian universe was not available to direct perception; poets who testified to its beauty expatiated on the limited perspective of humanity as though from a vantage point far above it. Like Newton who could "see" the perceiver's complicity in creating the rainbow he perceived, poets like Thomson defended the "Creative Wisdom" that "Exceeds the narrow vision" of the human mind (*Summer*, ll. 319–23). The author able to record experiences incommensurate with human scale could easily transfer his spectatorial privilege from the cosmos to "the world": we have to see the dunces through Pope's *Dunciad* (1728–42) in order to distinguish them from the successful writers, actors, and public figures they seem to be. Just as Newton became identified with the nonmechanical forces he alone seemed to understand, so in Young's *Night Thoughts* (1743) the grandeur of absolute space has become a property of the self: the night sky is a "Pasture of the *Mind*" where Young "expatiates, strengthens, and exults" (Young 1989 intro. p. 6; *Night the Ninth* ll. 1039–40).

While authors instrumentalized Newton in spectatorial performances of unparalleled grandiosity, scientists were left to cope with the difficulty of redefining their disciplines mathematically. Physicians floundered in the attempt to produce a "Principia Medicinae Theoreticae Mathematica"; Dr Thomas Morgan quantified the imagination using the Newtonian equation $f = ma$ as applied to animal spirits: imagination (force) is the product of nerves (mass) and animal spirits (acceleration). Of course, there were no ready means to calculate these variables. Yet if the elevation of theoretical physics over descriptive natural history did not serve the practical needs of the life sciences, pioneers of what G. S. Rousseau has called "the nervous revolution" were emboldened by Newton's success with gravity to employ vague concepts without shame – almost, indeed, with pride (1969: 123–4). The scholastic elevation of words over things, once abhorred, was now justified by the Newtonian slogan "hypothesis non fingo." Robert Whytt defended his use of the concept of animal spirits he could not define by analogy with Newton's gravitational force; one could explain madness as the result of a disorder of animal spirits relative to their speed of flow or density which (in principle, at least) one might calculate without being able to explain (see Brown 1987).

This audacity proved useful to the study of electricity. By midcentury, this mysterious force was relocated in the body. Rather than hollow tubes through which a vital liquid coursed, the nerves were electrical conductors that, by transmitting impulses from cell to cell, mysteriously mediated between the realms of spirit and matter. The notion of electrical attraction among the ultimate particles of matter blended with the idea of gravitational attraction. Joseph Priestley, the defender of phlogiston who first isolated oxygen, speculated that the attraction of electricity was subject to the same laws as that of gravitation. The proof of the inverse square law for electrical repulsion was finally arrived at in 1784, exactly a century after the *Principia*. The union of electricity and the nerves produced the explosion of "sensibility." The charge given off by the heroes of sentimental fiction, from the irritable spasms of Matthew Bramble in Tobias Smollett's *Humphry Clinker* (1771) to the shudderings of Henry Mackenzie's *Man of Feeling* (1771), acted at a distance – through the medium of print – to produce tremors in the sensible reader.

It is fashionable to insist that, as the scientific revolution yielded to the industrial revolution, the Royal Society became a joke; in fact its membership increased fivefold from 1700 to 1800 (see Sorrenson 1996). That most of its members were not scientists represents no great deviation from its early years; the Society existed largely to enable laymen who wished to experiment with the observant life to sustain the research of its devotees. As the stalled careers of gifted scientists like Nehemiah Grew suggest, such support was finally no substitute for state backing. But it is a mark of the Society's success that it ceased to be the only institution in England to support such work; The British Museum was created by Act of Parliament in 1753; the Society of Arts, founded a year later, provided incentive for discoveries by offering cash prizes for them. Just as experimentalist ideology survived the Adamolatry from which it drew its initial inspiration, so English science thrived outside the incubator of the Royal Society.

It was industry, however, that in the final decades of the century drove research into the chemistry of gases and applied mechanics, the advances in textile machinery and steam engines. The increased number of trades-related articles in the Society's *Transactions*, which had declined after 1688, was due to the work of industrialists, many of them members of smaller voluntary associations such as the Lunar Society of Birmingham. Priestley declared that "the English hierarchy (if there be anything unsound in its constitution) has . . . reason to tremble even at an air-pump or an electrical machine," but, as those who participated in machine-breaking were well aware, these machines posed the harshest threat to the men, women, and children who operated them (Russell 1983: 150). Such machines were really prosthetic extensions of the industrialist's power, as were the workers themselves; a process that had begun with the aristocrat's search for craftsmen's secrets had culminated in the transfer of "maker's knowledge" to the industrial manager.

Early experimentalists had often portrayed themselves as laboring bodies untouched by the corrupting influence of thought: the Society was a "a *union* of *eyes*, and *hands*" Through such strategic metonymies they had tried to articulate their ideal of a collective intellectual life in which body and mind, worker and thinker, both participated. The "Mechanical Hand" was also what Hooke called "a *sincere Hand*," the token of "a *faithful Eye*" and "philosophical mind." By the end of the eighteenth century, however, this ideal was overwhelmed by industrial England's faith in the invisible hand (Sprat 1667: 85; Hooke 1667: a2v, g2v). The labor offered to the mechanical hands of the factory required no corresponding intellectual exertion; the threat to England's New Jerusalem was no longer aristocratic alienation from labor but alienated labor itself.

References and further reading

Addison, J. and Steele, R. (1711–12) *The Spectator*, 5 vols., ed. D. F. Bond. London and Oxford: Oxford University Press, 1965.

Arthos, J. (1940) "Poetic diction and scientific language," *Isis* 32(2): 324–38.

Bacon, F. (1640) *The Twoo Bookes of Francis Bacon. Of the Proficiencie and Advancement and of Learning, Divine and Humane. To the King.* London: for Henrie Tomes.

Banfield, A. (1987) "Describing the unobserved: events grouped around an empty centre," in N. Fabb (ed.) *The Linguistics of Writing: Arguments between Language and Literature* (pp. 265–85). Manchester: Manchester University Press.

Blumenberg, H. (1991) *The Legitimacy of the Modern Age*, trans. R. M. Wallace. Cambridge, Mass. and London: MIT Press.

Boyle, R. (1661) *The Sceptical Chymist: Or, Chymico-Physical Doubts and Paradoxes.* London: J. Cadwell for J. Crooke.

—— (1690) *The Christian Virtuoso: Shewing, That by being Addicted to Experimental Philosophy, a Man is rather Assisted, than Indisposed, to be a good Christian.* London: Edw. Jones for John Taylor.

—— (1772) *The Works of the Honourable Robert Boyle*, 6 vols., ed. T. Birch. London. Repr. Hildesheim: G. Olms Verlagsbuchhandlung, 1966.

—— (1992) "An account of Philaretus during his minority," in M. Hunter (ed.) *Robert Boyle by Himself and His Friends.* London: William Pickering.

Brown, T. (1927) *Amusements Serious and Comical and Other Works*, ed. A. L. Hayward. London: Routledge.

Brown, T. M. (1987) "Medicine in the shadow of the *Principia*," *Journal of the History of Ideas* 48(4): 629–48.

Charleton, W. (1654) *Physiologia Epicuro-Gassendo-Charletoniana, Or a Fabrick of Science Natural, Upon the Hypothesis of Atoms, Founded by Epicurus, Repaired by Petrus Gassendi, Augmented by Walter Charleton*. London: Tho. Newcomb for Thomas Heach.

Croll, O. (1670) *Basilica Chymica, & Praxis Chymiatricae, or, Royal and Practical Chymistry in Three Treatises*. London: John Starkey and Thomas Passinger.

Daston, L. (1995) "The moral economy of science," *Osiris*, 2nd ser., 10: 2–24.

Dear, P. (1995) *Discipline and Experience: The Mathematical Way in the Scientific Revolution*. Chicago: University of Chicago Press.

Desaguliers, J. T. (1728) *The Newtonian System of the World, The Best Model of Government: An Allegorical Poem*. Westminster: A. Campbell for J. Roberts.

Dobbs, B. J. T. and Jacob, M. C. (1995) *Newton and the Culture of Newtonianism*. Atlantic Highlands, NJ: Humanities Press.

Eamon, W. (1980) "New light on Robert Boyle and the discovery of color indicators," *Ambix* 27: 206–7.

Empson, W. (1960) *Some Versions of Pastoral*, Norfolk, Conn.: New Directions.

Evelyn, J. (1656) *Essay on the First Book of T. Lucretius Carus De Rerum Natura. Interpreted and Made English Verse*. London: Gabriel Bedle and Thomas Collins.

Fara, P. (2002) *Newton: The Making of Genius*. New York: Columbia University Press.

Fawkes, F. (1761) *Original Poems and Translations*. London: Printed for the author.

Glanvill, J. (1661) *The Vanity of Dogmatizing. Or Confidence in Opinions Manifested in a Discourse of the Shortness and Uncertainty of our Knowledge, and its Causes*. London: E. C. for Henry Eversden.

Grew, N. (1681) *Musaeum Regalis Societatis. Or a Catalogue & Description of the Natural and Artificial Rarities Belonging to the Royal Society and Preserved at Gresham College*. London: W. Rawlins.

Hill, C. (1968) "The intellectual origins of the Royal Society, London or Oxford?" *Notes and Records of the Royal Society of London* 23(2): 144–56.

—— (1997) *Intellectual Origins of the English Revolution Revisited*. Oxford: Clarendon Press.

Hooke, R. (1665) *Micrographia, or some Physiological Descriptions of Minute Bodies made by Magnifying Glasses with Observations and Inquiries Thereupon*. London: J. Martyn and J. Allestry.

—— (1705) *The Posthumous Works of Robert Hooke, M.D.S.R.S. Geom. Prof. Gresh. &c. Containing his Cutlerian Lectures, and Other Discourses*, ed. R. Waller. London: Sam. Smith and Benj. Walford.

Hughes, J. (1735) *Poems*. London.

Hunter, M. (1982) "Early problems in professionalizing scientific research: Nehemiah Grew and the Royal Society, with an unpublished letter to Henry Oldenburg," *Notes and Records* 36(2): 189–209.

Locke, J. (1690) *An Essay Concerning Humane Understanding*. London: Eliz. Holt for Thomas Basset.

—— (1997) *Locke: Political Essays*, ed. M. Goldie. Cambridge and New York: Cambridge University Press.

Marvell, A. (1927) *The Poems and Letters of Andrew Marvell*, ed. H. M. Margoliouth. Oxford: Clarendon Press.

Milton, J. (1644) *Of Education. To Master Samuel Hartlib*. London: for Thomas Underhill.

—— (1931) *Works of John Milton*, ed. F. A. Patterson, A. Abbott, et al. New York: Columbia University Press.

Newton, I. (1704) *Opticks*. New York: Dover Publications, 1952.

—— (1958) *Isaac Newton's Papers and Letters on Natural Philosophy*, ed. I. Bernard Cohen. Cambridge, Mass.: Harvard University Press, 1952.

—— (1962) *Newton's Principia: Motte's Translation Revised*, 2 vols., ed. and trans. F. Cajori. Berkeley: University of California Press.

Nicolson, M. (1935) "Milton and the telescope," *English Literary History* 2(1): 1–32.

Ochs, K. H. (1985) "The Royal Society of London's history of trades programme: an early episode in applied science," *Notes and Records* 39(2): 129–58.

Park, K. and Daston, L. (1981) "Unnatural conceptions: the study of monsters in sixteenth- and seventeenth-century France and England," *Past and Present* 92: 20–54.

Patrides, C. A. (1969) *The Cambridge Platonists*. Cambridge and London: Cambridge University Press.

Pepys, S. (1970–83) *The Diary of Samuel Pepys*, ed. R. Latham and W. Matthews. Berkeley and Los Angeles: University of California Press.

Perez-Ramos, A. (1988) *Francis Bacon's Idea of Science and the Maker's Knowledge Tradition*. Oxford: Clarendon Press.

Pope, A. (1950–67) *Poems of Alexander Pope*, 6 vols., ed. J. Butt; vol. 3, ed. Maynard Mack; vol. 6, ed. Norman Ault and John Butt. London and New Haven: Yale University Press.

Power, H. (1664) *Experimental Philosophy. Containing New Experiments Microscopical, Mercurial, Magnetical*. London: T. Roycroft for John Martin and James Allestry.

Rousseau, G. S. (1969) "Science and the discovery of the imagination in Enlightened England," *Eighteenth-Century Studies* 3(1): 108–35.

Russell, C. A. (1983) *Science and Social Change in Britain and Europe 1700–1900*. New York: St Martin's Press.

Sailor, D. B. (1964) "Moses and atomism," *Journal of the History of Ideas* 25(1): 3–16.

Shapin, S. and Schaffer, S. (1985) *The Leviathan and the Air Pump: Hobbes, Boyle, and the Experimental Life*. Princeton: Princeton University Press.

Shapiro, B. (2000) *A Culture of Fact: England, 1500–1720*. Ithaca: Cornell University Press.

Sorrenson, R. (1996) "Towards a history of the Royal Society in the eighteenth century," *Notes and Records* 50(1): 29–46.

South, R. (1663) *A Sermon Preached at the Cathedral Church of St. Paul.* London: J. G. for Tho. Robinson.

Spragens, T. (1973) *The Politics of Motion: The World of Thomas Hobbes.* Lexington: University Press of Kentucky.

Sprat, T. (1667) *The History of the Royal Society of London for the Improving of Natural Knowledge.* London: T. R. for J. Martyn.

Starr, G. A. (1985) "Sentimental de-education," in D. L. Patey and T. Keegan (eds.) *Augustan Studies.* Newark: University of Delaware Press.

Stukeley, W. (1752) *Memoirs of Sir Isaac Newton's Life*, ed. A. H. White. London: Taylor and Francis, 1936.

Sturtevant, S. (1602) *Dibre Adam, Or Adam's Hebrew Dictionarie: A Rare and New Invention.* London.

Swann, M. (2001) *Curiosities and Texts: The Culture of Collecting in Early Modern England.* Philadelphia: University of Pennsylvania Press.

Swift, J. (1726) *Gulliver's Travels*, in *Prose Works of Jonathan Swift*, 14 vols., ed. Herbert Davis (1939–68); vol. 11, ed. Harold Williams. Oxford: Blackwell, 1959.

Terry, R. (1992) "Transitions and digressions in the eighteenth-century long poem," *Studies in English Literature* 32(3): 495–510.

Thomas, K. (1971) *Religion and the Decline of Magic: Studies in Popular Belief in Sixteenth- and Seventeenth-Century England.* London: Weidenfeld and Nicolson.

Thomson, J. (1971) *James Thomson: Poetical Works*, ed. J. L. Robertson. London: Oxford University Press.

Ward, N. (1709) *The London Spy*, ed. P. Hyland. East Lansing: Colleagues Press, 1993.

Webster, C. (1975) *The Great Instauration: Science, Medicine, and Reform 1626–1660.* London: Duckworth.

Young, E. (1989) *Night Thoughts*, ed. S. Cornford. Cambridge and New York: Cambridge University Press.

Chapter 3

Public and Private

The Myth of the Bourgeois Public Sphere

J. A. Downie

State censorship of the press in England ended in 1695 with the expiry of the Printing or Licensing Act. Although after that date publications were still subject to the laws relating to blasphemous, seditious, and treasonous libel, writings no longer had to be submitted to an official licenser for approval prior to printing. The end of pre-printing censorship coincided with what has been aptly described as "the first age of party" – an era characterized by conflict within society of such virulence that the nation was divided both at the center of power and in the constituencies. As an unrivalled medium of communication, the press was exploited by Whigs and Tories as they sought to influence political proceedings. Pamphlets and poems on affairs of state, as well as newspapers and essay journals, were published in huge numbers in an unprecedented appeal to what would now be called public opinion.

The most influential recent model of the rise of public opinion as a political and social force in the state is Jürgen Habermas's *The Structural Transformation of the Public Sphere: An Inquiry into a Category of Bourgeois Society* (originally published in German in 1962; translated into English in 1989). While Habermas's thesis actually concerns the way in which the space for public debate was allegedly transformed into an instrument of state manipulation of the public in the course of the nineteenth and twentieth centuries, his assertion that "[a] public sphere that functioned in the political realm arose first in Great Britain at the turn of the eighteenth century" (Habermas 1989: 57) has been seized upon by literary critics eager to claim that "[a] powerful convention had come into being: the convention that ideas are equally accessible to educated men and that, in the realms of public discussion, men are judged by the degree of their information and the quality of their ideas, not by rank, office, or wealth" (Bender 1996: xxi).

It is essential to bear in mind, however, that Habermas's inquiry into the category of bourgeois society that he calls "the public sphere" seeks to account not for a sociological ideal-type, but for the emergence and decline of a phenomenon "that is typical of an epoch." The public sphere, according to Habermas, is the space which emerged in early modern Europe between the "sphere of public authority" and the "private realm"; "a forum in which the private people, come together to form a public, readied themselves to compel public authority to legitimate itself before public opinion." Drawing attention to the party conflict between Whig and Tory which, as he rightly points out, "penetrated . . . even into the disenfranchised segment of the population," as instrumental in originating the appeal to public opinion in an attempt to influence political decisions, Habermas focuses on the years 1694 and 1695 because of certain social and political developments which he regards as crucial – the founding of the Bank of England, the "elimination of the institution of censorship," and the introduction of cabinet government. There are, however, difficulties with each of the examples he gives, especially with his contention that the end of censorship not only allowed the consideration of "rational-critical arguments" in print, but actually made it possible for public opinion to scrutinize political decisions.

The licensing system that came to an end in 1695 had a long history, going back to the middle of the sixteenth century when it became a requirement that all books be submitted for scrutiny prior to printing, and their titles entered in the Stationers' Register. Although the system broke down on the outbreak of civil war, it was reintroduced on the passing of the Printing Act in 1662 which, apart from a lapse between 1679 and 1685, remained in force until 1695 when it was allowed to expire. However, it would be wrong to assume that the end of pre-printing censorship was the consequence of a change in attitude on the part of either executive or legislature. During the 1680s, those in authority had been increasingly concerned about the spread of seditious material, not only in London, but also in the provinces (Bell 2000). No theory of liberty of the press was articulated either during the Revolution of 1688, or in 1695. Indeed, one of the principal reasons for the Printing Act's expiry was that it was thought to be ineffective, and a committee was set up "to prepare and bring in a Bill for better regulating of Printing and Printing Presses." Numerous bills for the regulation of the press were introduced between 1695 and the passing of the Stamp Act in 1712, many proposing the re-introduction of licensing. None became law. Yet it would be imprudent to assume that the political nation, at the turn of the eighteenth century, was in favor of a free press. Only after a number of years, and for particular political ends, was press freedom proclaimed to be a "bulwark of our liberty" (Downie 1981).

On its own, of course, this does not invalidate Habermas's thesis about the emergence of the bourgeois public sphere. It scarcely matters whether the end of censorship came about by accident or design provided that the conditions obtained through which an appeal to public opinion could be made. However, it does indicate a reluctance on the part of those in authority to countenance the free discussion of affairs of state which, in turn, would appear to have been a precondition for the sort of "rational-critical" discourse Habermas suggests was characteristic of the public sphere. Moreover, it is far from clear why it was the breakdown of control in 1695 which was crucial, rather than the breakdowns which occurred in 1642 and in 1679. Many more pamphlets and newsbooks or newspapers were published year on year in the early 1640s, and between 1679 and 1685, than in the final years of the seventeenth century. As these publications were certainly *intended* to appeal to public opinion, Habermas's contention that a public sphere first emerged around 1700 appears to be a conclusion driven by a thesis rather than one drawn from the available evidence.

This inference is strengthened by the consideration that Habermas fails to take into account that the most important precondition for the rise of a political press was not simply the breakdown of the apparatus of state control or the end of censorship, but the development of an effective system of distribution. This was established during the 1640s after the outbreak of civil war. Although Cromwell rigorously reintroduced controls, the distribution network was readily reassembled after his death and record numbers of titles were published in 1659 and 1660. What the authorities wanted to achieve after the Restoration, above all, was control of distribution. As its title indicates, "An act for preventing the frequent abuses in printing seditious, treasonable, and unlicensed books and pamphlets, and for regulating of printing and printing-presses" (14 Charles II, c.33) sought not only to restrict printing to London, Oxford, Cambridge, and the archiepiscopal see of York, but the actual number of printing houses and printing presses in London. This intention was undermined, however, by the retail distribution network that had been set up. "Pedlars, hawkers, carriers, county booksellers, balladmongers at fairs, provincial coffee-house keepers, individual recipients of manuscript newsletters with their printed enclosures were all, so it seemed, irritating agents in the spread of sedition across the nation" (Bell 2000: 94).

It is also important to stress that state control of the press did not cease with the expiry of the licensing system. "To be sure," Habermas acknowledges, "the press continued to be subject to the strict Law of Libel and to the restrictions connected with numerous privileges of Crown and Parliament" (1989: 59). This fails to register the full extent of government intervention in the eighteenth century. The prosecution of Defoe for seditious libel for writing and publishing *The Shortest Way with the Dissenters* (1702) is simply the best-known example of the policy of arrest and harassment favored by the governments of the day. In 1706 the Secretary of State, Robert Harley, attempted "to make examples of the libellers and printers" in the belief that the prosecution of a "few" would "cure, in great measure, this abominable vice." Similarly, in 1711, another Secretary, Henry St John, arrested 14 booksellers and printers in order "to stop a little this madness and folly of the press" (Downie 1979: 92, 151–2). Prosecutions followed a similar pattern under Walpole, while the conviction and imprisonment of John Wilkes for seditious and obscene libel on account of *North Briton No. 45* and the *Essay on Woman* indicates that government attitudes had not changed by the 1760s. Treasonous libel was treated much more severely, however, as John Matthews found to his cost when he was executed in 1719 for printing a Jacobite pamphlet with the significant title (for our purposes) *Vox Populi, Vox Dei*.

Therefore, despite Habermas's contention that the elimination of censorship in 1695 "made the influx of rational-critical arguments into the press possible and allowed the latter to evolve into an instrument with whose aid political decisions could be brought before the new forum of the public," the extent to which governments were convinced of the wisdom of allowing "the voice of the people" an unrestrained hearing in the eighteenth century must remain a question. Habermas quotes Charles James Fox's speech in Parliament in 1791 in which he not only maintained that "[i]t is right and prudent to consult the public opinion," but that "the public" ought to be given "the means of forming an opinion," and it can indeed be argued that government attitudes towards the press became increasingly relaxed as the century wore on (Downie 1981). However, the conservative reaction to the events of the 1790s – the treason trials, the proscription of Paine's *Rights of Man*, and the silencing of radical dissent – is scarcely indicative of an attitude of absolute confidence in the free expression and circulation of political opinion, and a historiographical tradition survives according to which a more or less polite and gentlemanly debate about the merits of Gallic "new modelling" gave way, by late 1792, to an increasingly desperate contest for the nation's political conscience. The battle of wits became a battle of wills as reasoned debate was forced roughly aside by exhortation and intimidation; and then, on the loyalist side, legal repression and legally condoned violence. Eventually the reformers were crushed and silenced, arrested and exiled. During the second half of the 1790s, free debate about the [French] Revolution was almost non-existent. (Claeys 1995 vol. 1: xviii)

Historians differ over the seriousness of "Pitt's reign of terror." Yet it is significant that a century after the "elimination of the institution of censorship" in 1695 – the event which, according to Habermas, "marked a new stage in the development of the public sphere" – the Seditious Societies Act of 1799 (39 George III, c.79) included within its provisions the compulsory registration of all printing presses.

The "People"

Habermas conceives the bourgeois public sphere as "the sphere of private people come together as a public" through "people's public use of their reason" – a phenomenon which was, allegedly, "without historical precedent" (1989: 27). Only when this has taken place, Habermas insists, is it possible to speak of the public sphere. In theory, everyone has to be able to participate, at least in principle, because the deciding factor in "rational-critical" debate is not status, wealth or rank, but the use of reason. "The public sphere of civil society stood or fell with the principle of universal access," Habermas explains. "A public sphere from which specific groups would be *eo ipso* excluded was less than merely incomplete, it was not a public sphere at all" (p. 85).

Does it matter, then, that the bourgeois public sphere as conceived by Habermas did not materialize at the turn of the eighteenth century? The very phrase, "the people's public use of their reason," begs an important question. Who *were* "the people"? While it is true that propagandists often appealed to public opinion in the form of "the voice of the people" for rhetorical purposes, the mass of the population tended to be automatically excluded from participation in political processes. "When we speak of the people," Marchamont Needham explained in 1652, "we do not mean the confused promiscuous body of the people." John Toland explains why. At the very end of the seventeenth century he followed the first order of James Harrington's "Modell of The

Common-Wealth of Oceana" in dividing "the people" into "freemen" and "servants" depending on whether they were "Men of Property, or Persons that are able to live of themselves." If they were unable to "subsist in this Independence," they were clearly servants and therefore unable to bear arms or serve in the militia. The reasons given by Toland in *The Militia Reform'd* (1698) are telling:

> For besides that all the Endowments which Nature has made common to both are improv'd in FREEMEN, the very Temper of their Bodies being much stronger and livelier by better feeding, which is no little Ingredient to Courage, they fight also for their Liberty and Property; whereas the other have nothing to lose but their Lives, which are likewise infinitely dearer to those whose Circumstances render 'em more agreeable and easy. (pp. 18–19)

The rhetoric employed by Trenchard and Gordon in 1721 in *Cato's Letters* belongs to this tradition, and reeks of a society in which the possession of real estate distinguishes those who have a voice in state affairs from those who have not:

> What Briton, blessed with any sense of virtue, or with common sense; what Englishman, animated with a publick spirit, or with any spirit, but must burn with rage and shame, to behold the nobles and gentry of a great kingdom; men of magnanimity; men of breeding; men of understanding, and of letters; to see such men bowing down, like Joseph's sheaves, before the face of a dirty *stock-jobber*, and receiving laws from men bred behind counters, and the decision of their fortunes from hands still dirty with sweeping shops! (1721/1995 vol. 1: 53)

The terms used by Trenchard and Gordon are crucial to a true understanding of the social structure of eighteenth-century England. The English aristocracy comprised both the nobility *and* the gentry, and the peerage were the most important members of the gentry. "Depending on the context, therefore, the terms noble and gentle are either complementary, as in the phrase 'nobility and gentry', or interchangeable" (Sayer 1979: 4). The vital distinction was not between those who were titled and those who were not, but between the aristocracy and the rest. Thus Darcy in *Pride and Prejudice*, although untitled, owns one of the largest estates in the country, and even the frightful Lady Catherine de Bourgh is forced to admit that Mr Bennet, whose property "consisted almost entirely in an estate of two thousand a year" (Austen 1813/1970: 23), is indeed a gentleman, and therefore of equal rank. Trenchard and

Gordon's usage is echoed by numerous writers of the period, and historians have followed suit. Even Lawrence Stone, whose terminology tends to be inconsistent, draws a clear distinction between the aristocracy and the rest in referring to "[t]hose classes below the nobility and gentry, who for convenience may be subsumed under the status category of 'plebs', [and who] comprised the vast bulk of the population, most of whom were resident in villages or small towns" (Stone 1977: 91).

My point is that those who were in positions of authority and influence were, understandably, reluctant to surrender their privileges to the great unwashed: instead of enthusiastically embracing an intellectual egalitarianism based on the appeal to reason, the nobility and gentry sought to perpetuate their hold on power. It is curious that the years identified by Habermas as marking the emergence of the bourgeois public sphere are identical to those during which, according to some modern historians, the English ruling class was consolidating its political position (Speck 1977). "In the eighteenth century the landed interest was at the height of its power," G. E. Mingay remarks. "The outcome of the civil wars and the limitations placed on the crown at the Glorious Revolution put the landowners firmly in the saddle, and their political power was to remain virtually unchallenged for at least the next one hundred years" (Mingay 1963: 10). According to the historian of the English aristocracy, "the aristocratic domination of political life, which had grown since 1688, and more particularly since 1714, was at its strongest" in 1760 (Cannon 1978: xxi). Not all historians agree, of course, and the emergence of "a polite and commercial people" in the mid-eighteenth century has been strongly asserted (Brewer 1982; Langford 1989). Yet even left-wing historians like E. P. Thompson agree that the "class" which "gained the day in 1688" was not the bourgeoisie but the gentry, and he goes on to argue that the "purposive, cohesive, growing middle class of professional men and of the manufacturing middle classes" discernible in the middle of the eighteenth century "fell far short of a class with its own institutions and objectives." "Such a class did not begin to discover itself (except, perhaps, in London)," he maintains, "until the last three decades of the century" (Thompson 1991: 31–2).

Why, then, does Habermas maintain that the years immediately following the Revolution of 1688 witnessed not the triumph of the English aristocracy, but the ascendancy of the bourgeoisie? The answer lies in his Marxist interpretation of English history, according to which it is essential that England became a bourgeois state by the end of the seventeenth century. Thus both the Civil Wars and the Glorious Revolution have been represented as "bourgeois" revolutions in which the old feudal order is finally overcome. Unfortunately, as we have seen, the century after 1688 was dominated not by the urban middle class but by the aristocracy. "The most straightforward Marxist response," Norma Landau wittily explains, "is to declare that the social structure is other than it appears, that the dominant order in the eighteenth century – the landed elite – is actually the bourgeoisie in fancy dress" (Landau 1988/9: 210–11). That this is the position adopted by Habermas is revealed by his assertions that, although the "bourgeois were private persons; as such they did not 'rule,'" nevertheless "the seventeenth-century British gentry [were] becoming more bourgeois in orientation" (Habermas 1989: 28, 44).

There are two major problems with this attempt to explain away a situation in which it is apparent that the ruling class is actually aristocratic rather than bourgeois. Although it is true that the younger sons of the gentry (as distinct from the younger sons of the peerage) often went into trade, this was not a new phenomenon. Similarly, there was nothing new about successful merchants (interestingly, Habermas refers to them as "the high bourgeoisie") using the wealth they had accumulated to buy landed estates. This is the situation in which Bingley finds himself in *Pride and Prejudice*: he has inherited a fortune of £100,000 acquired by trade from his father, "who had intended to purchase an estate, but did not live to do it" (Austen 1813/1970: 12). Were we to inquire into the origins of many of the country's "ancient" families, sooner or later – and quite often sooner rather than later – we would come across an ancestor who had founded the family fortune through trade. Habermas's thesis about the ascendancy of the bourgeoisie is tenable only by representing the landed elite, who, at the turn of the *nineteenth* century, inhabit the imagined worlds of Austen and her contemporaries, as an "agrarian bourgeoisie," or, in other words, as "the bourgeoisie in fancy dress."

The second difficulty for anyone wishing to argue that the English gentry were becoming "more bourgeois in orientation" in the course of the seventeenth century is that there is compelling evidence to the contrary. In support of his assertion, Habermas draws on Trevelyan's survey of English social history from Chaucer to Victoria to argue that the "privatization of life can be observed in a change of architectural style" (1989: 44). This is a particularly unfortunate example to choose, as it is precisely in this period that the plan for the formal country house, imported from the continent, was introduced into England, and which "grew in popularity after the Restoration, until by 1700 it had become more or less obligatory for anyone wanting to be in the fashion"

(Girouard 1978: 129). True, in the course of the eighteenth century it became increasingly important for servants to be unobtrusive if not actually invisible. Yet one of the consequences of axial planning giving way to circular planning in the architecture of houses, both in the country and in London, was that residents and guests spent more time in common dining and drawing rooms and less time in their own private apartments (or *cabinets*). Commenting on the "growing gap between the polite world of the gentry and the impolite world of servants, farmers and smallholders," Mark Girouard explains that "[in] terms of the country house this meant an increasing split between gentry upstairs and non-gentry downstairs" (p. 184). In this context, what should be emphasized is not the removal of the medieval halls and the decline of "old hospitality" but the deliberate exclusion from the country house, *except as servants*, of all those who were not of equal rank with the landowner.

Given that the golden age of the country house followed on from the making of the English ruling class after the Revolution, this is scarcely surprising. Whether in art or in architecture, in gardens or in music, aristocratic taste was increasingly imitated by the upwardly mobile in the century after 1688. Even that new literary phenomenon, the novel, offers significant evidence of the prevailing taste. Despite its alleged "middle-class" readership, a significant number of novels published in the final decades of the eighteenth century, preoccupied with the affairs of the nobility and gentry, are centered on life in the English country house. The increasing popularity of the novel in the final decades of the eighteenth century is powerful testimony to the social aspirations of its readers, and it appears that they preferred to read about the nobility and the gentry rather than the "middling sort." Indeed, "[p]opular fiction cultivated hostile portraits of traders and manufacturers" (Raven 1992: 13).

As evidence of the gentry's burgeoning bourgeois taste, on the other hand, Habermas asserts that "the 'great' public that formed in the theatres, museums, and concerts was bourgeois in its social origin" (1989: 43). While this may have been the case on the continent, there is very little evidence for it as far as Great Britain is concerned. Habermas's brief account of the Restoration theatre world, once again drawn mainly from Trevelyan's *English Social History* (1944: 260), is misleading on several counts. In attempting to explain the "abrupt" change from a "court" theatre to a "public" theatre, he fails in particular to appreciate that neither before nor after the Restoration was there a "court" theatre in England, nor does he take into account the complaints (from Pepys and others) about the attendance of "ordinary prentices and mean people" (Pepys 1970–6 vol. 9: 2) at the London theatres in the 1660s. True, theatre historians have referred to "the rise of a new, bourgeois audience around the end of the [seventeenth] century," but as Robert D. Hume notes, "the old cliché" is "a little too neat." "To put complex matters very simply," Hume continues, "one can say that seventeenth-century drama had come to rely heavily on support from the court, and that when it was substantially deprived of that support, the theatres were in serious trouble" (1976: 8–9, 13). At the turn of the eighteenth century, the two London patent theatres were in considerable financial difficulties. In sum, there is very little evidence of the London theatre around 1700 being patronized by a "great" public of bourgeois origin.

The evolution of London concert life also presents difficulties for Habermas's thesis. True, the first public concerts in Europe took place in London in the later seventeenth century. But the events organized by John Banister and Thomas Britton, the "musical small-coal man," were pretty informal affairs, while the public concerts at York Buildings and Hickford's Room were not much better. Interestingly, private societies like the Academy of Ancient Music founded in 1726 were strictly for gentlemen. The performers were drawn from the members, supplemented by "some of the most eminent masters of the time," and although "auditors" were admitted as members on payment of a two-guinea subscription, women were excluded. Even after the "sudden explosion of concert activity" which took place after 1750, leading to the 1790s when the " 'rage for music' was at its height," there was a clear social stratification as far as the various types of musical entertainment on offer were concerned, as is indicated by the following from *The Morning Post* for 21 January 1789: "The HANOVER-SQUARE [Professional Concert] – QUALITY. The TOTTENHAM-STREET [Concert of Ancient Music] – GENTRY. The FREEMASONS'-HALL [Academy of Ancient Music] – PEOPLE. And the ANACREONTIC [Society] – FOLKS" (McVeigh 1993: xiv, 4, 11).

What we appear to be left with, then, are unsubstantiated assertions that a public sphere which was accessible to all existed in England by 1700, that "a certain parity of the educated" meant that participation in this public sphere was not dependent on status, and that the bourgeoisie were taking the lead in art, literature, music and the theatre. Against these assertions should be set compelling evidence that English society after the Revolution of 1688 was, if anything, more exclusive than it had ever been, that participation in political processes depended on the possession of property, particularly real estate, and that, until at least the second half of the eighteenth century, membership of the various clubs and societies, including those concerned in promoting art, literature and music, was largely restricted to the nobility and the gentry. At the turn of the eighteenth century, financial independence – the ability to pay one's way – was the price of admission to the political public sphere.

Women and the "Private" Sphere

Hitherto, in my discussion of those likely to have been excluded from Habermas's paradigm of the bourgeois public sphere, I have failed to mention the most problematic instance of all. For Habermas's principle of participation to hold, it is essential that women also have access to the public sphere. Interestingly, both Trenchard and Gordon writing in 1721 and John Bender writing in 1996 refer quite specifically to men rather than women. It is obvious why they do so. "Under common law a woman's legal identity during marriage was eclipsed – literally covered – by her husband. . . . The property a woman brought to marriage – her dowry or portion – all came under the immediate control of her husband" (Erickson 1993: 24). Only unmarried women of property – widows or heiresses – enjoyed rights comparable to those of men, and even then they were unable to vote or to stand for any kind of office. The vast majority of women had little or no freedom of action. Although women writers increasingly wrote on political and social topics as the eighteenth century wore on, even Mary Wollstonecraft fought shy of campaigning for votes for women. Despite the publication of Paine's *Rights of Man* and other more radical arguments for parliamentary reform, Charles James Fox was still able to state without fear of contradiction in 1797 that "[i]n all the theories and projects of the most absurd speculation, it has never been suggested that it would be advisable to extend the elective suffrage to the female sex" (Dickinson 1977: 253).

The concept of a "public" sphere implies a separate "private" sphere. The mere notion of a public/private dichotomy is a major issue in feminist theory; in fact it has been suggested that it "is, ultimately, what the feminist movement is about" (Pateman 1989: 118). In such theories, women are invariably restricted to the private sphere, at the core of which, according to Habermas, is the family. Feminist theorists have recognized that, in linking the public/private distinction to the concept of separate spheres, Habermas's thesis about the emergence and development of the bourgeois public sphere is *ideological* – that is, in privileging the (male) public over the (female) private, it obscures and mystifies the inequality of the sexes in the very act of excluding women from participation in the public sphere. Some feminists, citing the growing numbers of publications written by women, have insisted on an extension of women's role into the public sphere in the eighteenth century. Feminist critics have gone further, maintaining that, as women writers were increasingly working within a new discourse which was significantly different from men's, writing was a liberating force. On the other hand, it has also been argued that, on the contrary, the imaginative literature of the period, especially the novel, is highly suggestive that women were increasingly restricted to a domestic setting both in theory and in practice.

According to this latter view, the public sphere becomes primarily a masculine preserve as a consequence of a powerful cultural construct which confines women to an inferior "private" sphere to which they are not necessarily "naturally" adapted, while men, at the same time, "properly inhabit, and rule within, both spheres" (Pateman 1989: 118). Indeed it could be argued that, in insinuating that social and sexual distinctions were elided in the public sphere, Habermas makes the same assumptions about exclusion as Locke's *Two Treatises of Government* (Locke 1690/1990: 287–9). Thus while Locke generously allows that "every Man has a *Property* in his own *Person*" which "no Body has any Right to but himself," servants are implicitly excluded from this right in that "the Turfs my Servant has cut . . . become my Property." Tellingly, Locke does not seem to think that, in this context, the property rights of women are even worth mentioning.

Coffee Houses and Clubs: the "Literary" Sphere

It is scarcely surprising that Habermas himself recognizes the difficulties inherent in his notion of universal accessibility. The way in which he attempts to get round the problem is of interest. According to Habermas, the public sphere which first functioned in the political realm in Great Britain around the turn of the eighteenth century "evolved from the public sphere in the world of letters; through the vehicle of public opinion it put the state in touch with the needs of society." Paradoxically, although "[w]omen and dependents were factually and legally excluded from the political public sphere . . . female readers as well as apprentices and servants often took a more active part in the literary public sphere than the owners of private property and family heads themselves" (1989: 31–2, 56). Habermas, in other words, at once posits the principle of universal accessibility as the sine qua non of the bourgeois public sphere, acknowledges that, *in practice*, women and servants were excluded, yet maintains that they were actively involved in a *literary* public sphere which was in some sense "apolitical."

Not only is this deeply unconvincing, his account of the emergence of the literary public sphere presents further problems. Arguing that, during "their golden age between 1680 and 1730," the coffee houses took over social functions previously associated with the Court, Habermas suggests that non-hierarchical "rational-critical" discourse first emerged "between aristocratic society and bourgeois intellectuals" within their walls (1989: 32). Although some historians have accepted that "a public sphere in the Habermasian sense did emerge in later seventeenth-century England, precipitated largely by a thirst for political discussion and a desire to preserve English liberties" (Pincus 1995: 811), they do not appear sufficiently to have appreciated the important distinction drawn by Habermas between the *political* public sphere and the "apolitical" literary public sphere, nor to have addressed the elision of rank, status and wealth which is central to his thesis. It is not enough simply to assert that the mere existence of coffee houses proves the existence of the bourgeois public sphere. As Swift, himself a frequenter of coffee houses, memorably remarks in *The Conduct of the Allies* (1711): "[i]t is the Folly of too many, to mistake the Eccho of a *London* Coffee-house for the Voice of the Kingdom" (1711/1939–74 vol. 6: 53). First it must be demonstrated that apprentices, servants, and women (to cite the three examples offered by Habermas) actually frequented such places in numbers, that their views were accorded equal status with those of the nobility and gentry, and that the elision of social distinctions meant that public opinion was actually influenced by their views.

The main evidence for the coffee house as a site of social interaction regardless of sex or status reflects official unease at what was perceived to be a dangerous tendency among the disaffected to discuss affairs of state. Habermas quotes a royal proclamation of 1672 which observes: "Men have assumed to themselves a liberty, not only in coffee-houses, but in other places and meetings, both public and private, to censure and defame the proceedings of the State, by speaking evill of things they understand not, and endeavouring to create and nourish universal jealousie and dissatisfaction in the minds of all His Majesties good subjects"

(1989: 59). Not only is the proclamation redolent of official anxiety about the free circulation and discussion of affairs of state during the later seventeenth century to which I have already drawn attention, once again it is gender specific ("men have assumed to themselves a Liberty") and, significantly, it speaks of places and meetings both public *and* private.

That men of different ranks met at coffee houses during the Restoration, both in London and in the provinces, appears uncontentious. As a pamphlet called *The Coffee-Houses Vindicated* (1675) put it: "where can young Gentlemen, or Shop-keepers, more innocently and advantageously spend an Hour or two in the Evening, than at a Coffee-house?" What is less clear is whether the "parity of the educated," through which "bourgeois intellectuals" could influence the ideas of "aristocratic society," is anything other than a polite fiction invented by Habermas upon which subsequent commentators have elaborated. Against the numerous contemporary references to coffee houses as places frequented by various ranks of society in which dangerous, subversive opinions were aired should be set evidence such as that to be found in *A Word without-Doors, Concerning the Bill for Succession* (1680), which relates a conversation the narrator strikes up in a coffee house with "two ingenious Gentlemen" who "hapned to sit at the same Table with [him]," and "who according to the frankness of Conversation now used in the Town, began a Discourse [on the Exclusion Bill]" (p. 2). Up to this point, the pamphlet might be taken as supporting evidence for the sort of coffee-house culture envisaged by Habermas. However, as one of the "ingenious Gentlemen" felt "That the place we were in, was a little too publick for discourses of this nature," he suggested moving to "the next Tavern" where "he would undertake to give me juster measures," over "a Bottle of Wine." What are we to make of this exchange, and what are the implications for Habermas's thesis? It seems to suggest that the coffee house was deemed to be too public a space for private conversation, and recalls the older practice to which Richard Cust has drawn attention: "Letter-writers and local politicians – at least before 1640 – tended to reserve their opinions for the relative security of private conversation or an entry in their 'news-diary' "(Cust 1986: 89).

Attention has been drawn to the growth of clubs and societies in England in the later seventeenth and early eighteenth centuries as an indication of the emergent public sphere. As an early issue of *The Spectator* put it: "When a Sett of Men find themselves agree in any Particular, tho' never so trivial, they establish themselves into a kind of Fraternity, and meet once or twice a Week" (Addison and Steele 1711–12/1965 vol. 1: 39; *The Spectator* no. 9). Contrasting the "proliferation of clubs and societies . . . in provincial towns in the decades after 1720" with "the famous aristocratic and gentlemen's political clubs of Anne's reign," however, Kathleen Wilson notes that "[p]rior to 1740, political societies and associations tended to be thinner on the ground than they would be thereafter, and to be organized under the wing of political elites" (1995: 61, 63). Far from being open to all regardless of rank, they appear, like gentlemen's clubs until the late twentieth century, to have been exclusively male preserves. Although Sir Andrew Freeport, "a Merchant of great Eminence in the City of *London*," is a member, even *The Spectator*'s fictitious Club is for gentlemen only.

This corresponds with what we know about real-life organizations such as the Rota and the Kit-Kat Club. Habermas cites the former as an example of coffee-house culture, yet it is clear from the account offered by Pepys not only that the Rota was "a free and open society of ingenious *gentlemen*," but that one had to pay a subscription of eighteen pence "to be entered of the Club"(Pepys 1970–6 vol. 1: 13). Interestingly, the "republican" ideas to which Habermas refers are founded on a vision in which the ability to participate in political processes is dependent on the ownership of land. Harrington's political ideology, in other words, is aristocratic rather than bourgeois. Similar conclusions are to be drawn from the composition of the Kit-Kat Club. Although much has been made of the alleged elision of hierarchy which permitted dukes, earls and marquesses to mingle on equal social terms with the rank and file, this fails to take into account the fact that, as John Macky put it in *A Journey through England* (1714), the members of the Kit-Kat Club were "all Men of the first Rank, for Quality, or Learning." Admitting "none but are Gentlemen of the greatest Distinction in some way or other," with the sole exception of "their Ingenious *Secretary*, Mr. Tonson" (Macky 1714 vol. 1: 188), it was exclusive not only in political but in social terms. This is borne out by comparing the Rota and the Kit-Kat Club with the London Corresponding Society, founded early in 1792. The first of the "leading rules" of the LCS was, quite simply: "That the numbers of our members be unlimited." As the penny subscription makes clear, the LCS, unlike the earlier political associations to which I have drawn attention, was *not* exclusive.

Even at the turn of the nineteenth century, however, gender was a bar to membership of political clubs and societies. While it has been asserted that women were habituées of coffee houses during their "golden age between 1680 and 1730," the extensive pamphlet literature suggests firstly that although they were frequented by "Animals of every Sort, from the precise diminutive Bard, to the hectoring Cravat and Cuffs in *Folio*" (*The Character of a Coffee-House* 1673) the clientele was almost exclusively male, and second, that women complained about the very existence of coffee and coffee houses. Thus we find titles like *The Women's Petition against Coffee* (1663), *The Maiden's Complaint against Coffee* [1663?], and *The Ale-Wives Complaint Against the Coffee house* (1675). Therefore although there may be "little warrant for the claim that women were excluded" (Pincus 1995: 815), there is equally little evidence to suggest that, unless they provided certain services – including sexual services – women would have been welcome in coffee houses. As *The Grand Concern of England Explained* put it in 1673: "These Houses being many of them professed Bawdy Houses, more expensive than other houses, are become scandalous for a man to be seen in them" (p. 24).

Apparently undismayed, Habermas represents women as participants in the public sphere *as readers* (Habermas 1989: 56). Given the spatial metaphor employed by Habermas, some overlapping between the public and the private spheres would appear to be inevitable. It should also be acknowledged that reading is not necessarily a merely passive activity. However, it seems confusing to suggest that, despite being confined to the "core of the private sphere," the home, women could participate in the public sphere simply by taking the opportunity to read the writings of others. If such reading subsequently were to lead to active intervention in the public sphere – as a writer, say – then perhaps it would be a different matter. As it stands, though, Habermas's suggestion cannot avoid appearing like an attempt to sustain a thesis which requires the public sphere to be accessible to women in order for it to exist.

Even if, for the sake of argument, we were to concede that apprentices, servants, and women were frequenters of coffee houses and members of clubs and societies at the turn of the eighteenth century, it remains to be demonstrated that their views effectively informed the "public opinion" of the day. Habermas's thesis about rational-critical discourse in a public sphere consisting of private individuals coming together as a public seems touchingly naive about the part played by reason in informing opinion. It not only fails to take into account the immense, indeed insuperable, difficulty of disentangling genuinely disinterested, principled action or argument from the sort of *ex post facto* rationalization which seeks to obscure party prejudice or self-interest, it also fails to appreciate that, in an unrepresentative and undemocratic political system, entrenched interest groups were virtually fireproof.

As any analysis of eighteenth-century political writing quickly demonstrates, what purports to be straightforward argument based on fact may be nothing of the sort. As it seeks to manipulate its readers' political perceptions, the political essay does not necessarily seek to persuade through reason. Wilkes and Junius freely used abuse and invective to score their points, while the most successful political pamphlets of the period, Swift's *Conduct of the Allies*, say, or Burke's *Reflections on the Revolution in France*, were carefully slanted towards preconceived audiences and written with their prejudices in mind. Thus Swift articulated a fictitious conspiracy thesis to defraud the wealth of the landed interest, while Burke not only employed the language of sentiment in his apostrophe to Marie Antoinette, his notorious reference to the "swinish multitude" successfully denoted his identification with men of status, wealth and rank. It was not, in short, the appeal to the (male) reader's reason which was crucial in political writing, but the appeal to his emotions and his self-interest.

Habermas and the Nature of English Society

It seems, then, that even Habermas's representation of the *literary* public sphere must be scrutinized, if it requires the active participation of those women and dependents who were excluded, "factually and legally," from the public sphere in the political realm. Indeed, it is difficult not to conclude that, like the "fiction of the *one* public" comprising the literary and the political public spheres which, according to Habermas, allowed "the educated classes" to speak of public opinion per se, the supposed elision of social distinction is nothing more than – in both senses of the term – a polite fiction. In consequence, we must ask ourselves how useful Habermas's paradigm of the bourgeois public sphere can be, given that it did not – and could not – exist in Great Britain at the turn of the eighteenth century in the terms in which it is conceived.

The events occurring in 1694 and 1695 which Habermas regards as marking the beginning of "the weaker party" carrying the debate "into the public sphere," particularly the expiry of the Printing Act, do not stand up to scrutiny. To return briefly to the example of the end of censorship, Habermas contrives both to antedate and to postdate the most important developments. Government control had broken down on two earlier occasions, and a distribution network had been set up during the 1640s. Yet the notion that the liberty of the press was an important constitutional freedom was not articulated until well after the end of pre-printing censorship, and as late as the 1790s – a full century after the emergence of the public sphere according to Habermas – rational-critical debate in print was threatened by the official machinery of the state.

The other events cited by Habermas can be dealt with equally briefly. For Habermas, the Bank of England is intimately linked to "a capitalistically revolutionized mode of production" (1989: 58) which, in turn, is linked to an imaginary expansion in industrial manufacturing in the late seventeenth century. This antedates the arrival of the "industrial revolution" (if there was one) by up to a century, and is palpable nonsense. The most important product of the 1690s as far as the financial revolution is concerned was not the founding of the Bank of England, which was originally no more than a device to raise £1.2 million in credit so that the government could prosecute the war with France in defense of the Revolution Settlement, but the emergence of the stock market. It was this which "signaled a new stage in the development of capitalism" (1989: 58).

As for Habermas's assertions about cabinet government, it is misleading not only to suggest that the ministry appointed by William III between 1695 and 1698 was in some way an innovation, but that the period from the Revolution to the Hanoverian Succession was transitional as far the monarch's ability to choose his own ministers was concerned (Habermas 1989: 262). Contemporaries such as Trenchard noted with dismay that Charles II "was the first who broke the most excellent Part of our Constitution, by settling a Cabal or Cabinet Council, where all Matters of Consequence were debated and resolved" (1698: vii–viii) whereas it had formerly been the Privy Council. William followed his predecessor's example, while retaining power in his own hands, especially over diplomatic affairs. The main innovation was William's decision actually to attend cabinet meetings himself, almost certainly because of the war he was waging with France. Queen Anne began by holding a regular cabinet meeting each Sunday as William had done, before it became apparent that further meetings would be necessary while the country was at war.

As the point about cabinet government illustrates, one of the major problems with Habermas's thesis is that he clearly did not undertake any original research of his own on seventeenth- and eighteenth-century English history. Instead, he relied on outdated secondary sources. Sometimes, as in the case of cabinet government, he used old German monographs – in this case Hasbach's *Die parlamentarische Kabinettsregierung* (1919) (see Habermas 1989: 262) – and sometimes he made do with surveys such as Trevelyan's *English Social History*. As Markman Ellis shrewdly observes, Habermas's representation of the conviviality of the London coffee house is based on nineteenth-century reconstructions congenial to his thesis (Ellis 2000: 44). Habermas was doubly unfortunate in that he was researching and writing his *Habilitationsschrift* during a period which witnessed the publication of a series of monographs by historians of English political, economic, and social history which have transformed our understanding of the period. Interestingly, Habermas made use of Ian Watt's quasi-Marxist "triple-rise" thesis in *The Rise of the Novel* (1957) that the rise of the middle class in England led to the rise of the reading public which, in turn, led to the rise of the novel. Unfortunately, even had he wanted to, he would have been unable to consult G. E. Mingay's *English Landed Society in the Eighteenth Century* (1963) or Geoffrey Holmes's *British Politics in the Age of Anne* (1967) or P. G. M. Dickson's *The Financial Revolution* (1967), let alone the numerous studies of the press and the English book trade which have appeared during the past three decades.

At the heart of Habermas's thesis about the emergence of the bourgeois public sphere is a simple misunderstanding of the nature of English society. While most Marxist historians, following E. P. Thompson's lead, focus not on the bourgeoisie, but on relations between the patricians and the plebeians – the elite and the rest of the population – Habermas's unreconstructed Marxist interpretation of English history requires a bourgeois revolution to have taken place during the seventeenth century, even though the dominance of the nobility and gentry in the century after the Revolution of 1688 can be convincingly documented. As a consequence, those who find the paradigm of a bourgeois public sphere useful are forced to grapple with the uncomfortable fact that, as the example of its ideal of open access makes plain, it was not realized at the turn of the eighteenth century. I suspect it is for this reason that literary critics and cultural historians pick and choose features of the paradigm which suit their own scholarly purposes. The danger is that those who are unaware either of the full extent of the theoretical implications of Habermas's "bourgeois public sphere" or of its fictitious rather than factual nature can be misled into bald statements such as "a public sphere in the Habermasian sense did emerge in later seventeenth-century England" (Pincus 1995: 811) or "[i]n the mean time Britain had witnessed the emergence of a 'bourgeois public sphere'" (Solkin 1993: 27). As the arguments and evidence used in this essay have attempted to show, if "[a] public sphere from which specific groups would be *eo ipso* excluded . . . was not a public sphere at all," then not only is it misleading to write of a "bourgeois" public sphere at the turn of the eighteenth century in England, it is misleading to write of a public sphere *tout court*.

Why, then, have literary critics and cultural historians found the concept of the public sphere so attractive? There are, I think, several principal reasons. First, the notion of a public sphere privileges literature and the arts, and there is something heady about the way in which "bourgeois intellectuals" are depicted as first infiltrating, then being tolerated by, and finally dictating taste to aristocratic society in those "centers of criticism," the coffee houses where, doubtless, people spoke of things that matter, with words that must be said. We have long sought an explanation for the dissemination of the ideas of Enlightenment thinkers and, especially in its over-riding appeal to reason, Habermas's thesis seems to offer one. Yet if we are required to jettison most of the assumptions which accompany the concept before it can be used with safety, then perhaps it would be simpler – and certainly more accurate – to construct a different model for the emergence of public opinion as a force in the state. Such a model might not be as superficially attractive as Habermas's. It might not be all-inclusive, and it might emphasize not "the people's public use of their reason" but the manipulation of "public opinion" by competent political writers. It would, however, have the advantage of being driven not by a thesis, but by our knowledge of Restoration and eighteenth-century England.

References and further reading

Addison, J. and Steele, R. (1711–12) *The Spectator*, 5 vols., ed. D. F. Bond. London and Oxford: Oxford University Press, 1965.

Austen, J. (1813) *Pride and Prejudice*, ed. J. Kinsley and F. Bradbrook. Oxford: Oxford University Press, 1970.

Barry, J. and Brookes, C. (eds.) (1994) *The Middling Sort of People: Culture, Society and Politics in England, 1550–1800*. Basingstoke: Macmillan.

Bell, M. (2000) "Sturdy rogues and vagabonds: Restoration control of pedlars and hawkers," in P. Isaac and B. McKay (eds.) *The Mighty Engine: The Printing Press and its Impact* (pp. 89–96). Winchester: St Paul's Bibliographies.

Bender, J. (1996) "Introduction," in J. Bender and S. Stern (eds.) *Tom Jones*, by Henry Fielding, (pp. ix–xxxiv). Oxford and New York: Oxford University Press.

Brewer, J. (1982) "Commercialization and politics," in N. McKendrick, J. Brewer, and J. H. Plumb, *The Birth of a Consumer Society: The Commercialization of Eighteenth-Century England* (pp. 197–262). London: Europa Publications Limited.

—— (1995) "This, that and the other: public, social and private in the seventeenth and eighteenth centuries," in D. Castiglione and L. Sharpe (eds.) *Shifting the Boundaries: Transformation of the Languages of Public and Private in the Eighteenth Century* (pp. 1–21). Exeter: University of Exeter Press.

Calhoun, C. (ed.) (1992) *Habermas and the Public Sphere*. Cambridge, Mass.: MIT Press.

Cannon, J. (ed.) (1978) *The Letters of Junius*. Oxford: Clarendon Press.

Claeys, G. (1995) "Introduction," in G. Claeys (ed.) *Political Writings of the 1790s*, 6 vols. London: Pickering and Chatto.

Clark, J. C. D. (1985) *English Society, 1688–1832: Ideology, Social Structure and Political Practice during the Ancien Regime*. Cambridge: Cambridge University Press.

Corfield, P. (ed.) (1991) *Language, History and Class*. Oxford and Cambridge, Mass.: Blackwell.

Cust, R. (1986) "News and politics in early seventeenth-century England," *Past and Present* 112 (August): 60–90.

Dickinson, H. T. (1977) *Liberty and Property: Political Ideology in Eighteenth-Century Britain*. London: Weidenfeld and Nicolson.

Dickson, P. G. M. (1967) *The Financial Revolution: A Study in the Development of Public Credit, 1688–1756*. London: Macmillan.

Downie, A. (1981) "The growth of government tolerance of the press to 1790," in R. Myers and M. Harris (eds.) *Development of the English Book Trade, 1700–1899* (pp. 36–65). Oxford: Oxford Polytechnic Press.

Downie, J. A. (1979) *Robert Harley and the Press: Propaganda and Public Opinion in the Age of Swift and Defoe*. Cambridge: Cambridge University Press.

Ellis, M. (2000) "Coffee-women, *The Spectator* and the public sphere in the early eighteenth century," in E. Eger, C. Grant, C. Ó. Gallchoir and P. Warburton (eds.) *Women, Writing and the Public Sphere, 1700–1830* (pp. 27–52). Cambridge: Cambridge University Press.

Erickson, A. L. (1993) *Women and Property in Early Modern England*. London: Routledge.

Girouard, M. (1978) *Life in the English Country House: A Social and Architectural History*. New Haven and London: Yale University Press.

Habermas, J. (1989) *The Structural Transformation of the Public Sphere: An Inquiry into a Category of Bourgeois Society*, trans. T. Burger. Cambridge: Polity Press. (Original work published 1962.)

Holmes, G. (1967) *British Politics in the Age of Anne*. London: Macmillan.

Hume, R. D. (1976) *The Development of English Drama in the Late Seventeenth Century*. Oxford: Clarendon Press.

Landau, N. (1988/9) "Eighteenth-century England: tales historians tell," *Eighteenth-Century Studies* 22: 208–18.

Landes, J. B. (1998) "The public and the private sphere: a feminist reconsideration," in J. B. Landes (ed.) *Feminism, the Public and the Private* (pp. 135–63). Oxford: Oxford University Press.

Langford, P. (1989) *A Polite and Commercial People: England 1727–1783*. Oxford: Clarendon Press.

Locke, J. (1690) *Two Treatises of Government*, ed. P. Laslett. Cambridge: Cambridge University Press, 1990.

Macky, J. (1714) *A Journey Through England*, 2 vols. London.

McVeigh, S. (1993) *Concert Life in London from Mozart to Haydn*. Cambridge: Cambridge University Press.

Mingay, G. E. (1963) *English Landed Society in the Eighteenth Century*. London: Routledge and Kegan Paul.

Pateman, C. (1989) "Feminist critique of the public/private dichotomy," in C. Pateman, *The Disorder of Women: Democracy, Feminism and Political Theory* (pp. 118–40). Cambridge: Polity Press.

Pepys, S. (1970–6) *The Diary of Samuel Pepys*, 11 vols., ed. R. Latham and W. Matthews. London: G. Bell.

Pincus, S. (1995) " 'Coffee politicians does create': coffeehouses and Restoration political culture," *Journal of Modern History* 67: 807–34.

Raven, J. (1992) *Judging New Wealth: Popular Publishing and Responses to Commerce in England, 1750–1800*. Oxford: Clarendon Press.

Raymond, J. (1999) "The newspaper, public opinion, and the public sphere in the seventeenth century," in J. Raymond (ed.) *News, Newspapers, and Society in Early Modern Britain* (pp. 109–40). London and Portland, Ore.: Frank Cass.

Sayer, M. J. (1979) *English Nobility: The Gentry, the Heralds and the Continental Context*. Fakenham: Norfolk Heraldry Society.

Solkin, D. (1993) *Painting for Money: The Visual Arts and the Public Sphere in Eighteenth-Century England*. New Haven and London: Published for the Paul Mellon Centre for Studies in British Art by Yale University Press.

Speck, W. A. (1977) *Stability and Strife: England 1714–1760*. London: Edward Arnold.

Stone, L. (1977) *The Family, Sex and Marriage in England 1500–1800*. London: Weidenfeld and Nicolson.

Swift, J. (1939–74) *The Works of Jonathan Swift*, 16 vols., ed. H. Davis. Oxford: Oxford University Press.

Thompson, E. P. (1991) *Customs in Common*. London: Merlin Press.

Toland, J. (1698) *The Militia Reform'd*. London.

Trenchard, J. (1698) *A Short History of Standing Armies in England*. London.

Trenchard, J. and Gordon, T. (1721) *Cato's Letters*, ed. R. Hamowy. Indianapolis: Liberty Fund, 1995.

Trevelyan, G. M. (1944) *English Social History: A Survey of Six Centuries. Chaucer to Queen Victoria*. London, New York and Toronto: Longmans, Green and Co.

Watt, I. (1957) *The Rise of the Novel: Studies in Defoe, Richardson and Fielding*. London: Chatto and Windus.

Wilson, K. (1995) *The Sense of the People: Politics, Culture and Imperialism in England, 1715–1785*. Cambridge: Cambridge University Press.

Chapter 4

The Streets

Literary Beggars and the Realities of Eighteenth-Century London

Tim Hitchcock

In late February 1765 Jane Austin found herself in a terrible situation. She had lost her lodging in White Hart Yard when the man she was living with, John Duggin, beat her and threw her out. She was homeless and friendless on the streets of London and was suffering from both the beating and a long-standing chest complaint. Her first response was to apply to the overseers of the poor of the parish of St Martin in the Fields for admission to their workhouse. Her settlement was inquired into and she was found to possess none, and as a result was turned back onto the street. For three days she begged about the parish, up and down the Strand and in Covent Garden, sleeping in doorways at night, but by the third day she had become desperate. She was starving and the wound in her side from the beating continued to plague her. At noon on the third day she knocked at the door of Elizabeth Stewart's apartment in a low lodging house belonging to Ann James in New Bedford Court, a tiny enclave off the Strand. Several women were working in the room and Jane begged to be allowed to sit by the fire. She was invited in, and sat for the rest of the afternoon, while more fortunate women – poor but employed – worked around her. In the evening she shared a pint of purl – hot beer and gin mixed together – and at ten, when Elizabeth Stewart returned from an errand, she asked to be allowed to sleep in front of the fire for the night.

In the morning, after long hours punctuated by Jane's groans, Elizabeth Stewart had grown tired of charity. She asked the lodger upstairs, a black man named Michael Reading, to escort Jane out of the house. He took her by the arm and led her to the door and down the stairs. She fell, and he grabbed her around the waist, and together they ended up on the doorstep in confusion. According to the coroner's inquest later held on her body Jane was dead within minutes, the victim of a beating, or hunger, or cold, or her final tumble down stairs.

The point is that Jane's was the reality of eighteenth-century London street life. There were violence and desperation, drink and charity, hard work and hard hearts. There was conflict with parish officers, and limited if casual support from those around you. It was also a world made up substantially of women, and one in which everyone was forced to negotiate a complex set of systems and resources, individual relations, and public attitudes, in order to survive. And yet, if we look at many of the literary depictions of beggars – from John Gay, Henry Fielding, Daniel Defoe, Jonathan Swift, Addison and Steele, Jane Barker, Francis Coventry and Henry Mackenzie – the image of beggarly poverty is distinctly different. And even if we step beyond this canon of authors to the less well known writings of poets such as William King and the criminally inventive editors of Bampfylda Carew, our image of London street life and beggarly poverty is distinctly skew-whiff.

This chapter is an attempt to make two related but free-standing arguments at once. First, it will compare these poles of historical depiction, to juxtapose the literary beggar with the reality of the lives of people like the unfortunately named Jane Austin as reflected in sources that at least purport to describe individual experiences. In the process, this chapter will argue that the differences between the literary and the lived formed a significant boundary that had a real historical impact. It will suggest that eighteenth-century social policy was bound up with literary beggars, and that it was at least in part a literary vision that determined the design and public face of the period's workhouses and hospitals. Second, this chapter will argue that the tension created between the demands and culture of the poor and the literature-informed social policy of the period provides one of the main forces which drove the internal development of eighteenth-century institutions. Everyone, whether pauper or projector, may have been trapped by the languages of poverty and charity, but the administrators and staff of eighteenth-century institutions needed to negotiate the substantial conflict (whether expressed as language or action) that arose every time a real pauper wanted access to an institution founded on a stereotype. This chapter will suggest that it was the impact of this conflict on the people charged with running the system that helped drive an internal evolutionary process that gradually transformed London's institutions. From being a set of disorganized services for a narrowly drawn body of stereotypes, London's network of resources became a flexible and relevant system of relief available to a surprising variety of individuals, in a surprising variety of situations. This outcome was a result of both the power of literature and the demands, agency and authority of the poor.

Literary Beggars

Perhaps the most famous literary beggar of the period is John Gay's narrator in the *Beggar's Opera*. He may not figure in the story, but he does represent beggars in general, and his life and attributes are typical of literary creations of the day. He lives in the crowded back alleys of St Giles's, and makes money by writing ballads, but perhaps most indicative of his stereotypical role, is the character's claim that he attends "weekly festivals" of beggars, in the "great room" of an alehouse. What Gay's character reflects is the powerful literary tradition of a separate and ordered society of beggars. The sixteenth and seventeenth centuries had witnessed the rise of a whole genre of rogue literature in which the canting language and despicable tricks of beggars were supposedly laid out for a wary, if amused, audience. Many historians have noted the decline of this literature in the late seventeenth and eighteenth century, but the point here is that many of its assumptions remained in place, even while the generic conventions of rogue literature disappeared (see Beier 1983; Kinney 1990; Salgado 1992; Carol 1996). Ned Ward, for example, included a "beggars club" in his *History of London Clubs* (1709):

> This society of old bearded hypocrites, wooden legg'd implorers of charity, strolling clapperdugeons, limping dissemblers, sham-disabled seamen, blind gun powder blasted mummers and old broken limb'd labourers, hold their weekly meeting at a famous boozing ken in the midst of Old Street [a site that fits perfectly Gay's suggestion of an ale house in St. Giles], where by the vertue of sound tipple, the pretenders to the dark are restor'd instantly to their sight, those afflicted with feign'd sickness, recover perfect health, and others that halt before they are lame, stretch their legs without their crutches [when] . . . they sing this song, which is call'd the beggars new ballad.

Tho' Begging is an honest trade
That wealthy knaves despise
Yet rich men may be beggars made
And we that beg may rise
The greatest king may be betray'd
And lose his sovereign power
But we that stoops to ask our bread
Can never fall much lower. . . .
What tho' we make the world believe
That we are sick and lame
'Tis now a virtue to deceive,
The Righteous do the same
In trade dissembling is no crime
And we shall live to see
That begging in a little time,
A common trade will be. (Ward 1709: 7)

In this piece, four aspects of literary begging are highlighted: first, it is a trade; second, it is a dishonest one; third, it is highly organized; and fourth it is fun, or at least funny. One could similarly point to the blind beggar who becomes the temporary master to the lap-dog hero of Francis Coventry's eponymous *Pompey the Little* (1752). The beggar is a hardened professional, a charlatan, and father of two of the most rapscallion characters literary Bath has ever seen (1752/1974: 76–105).

These writings reflect a specific and time-honored stereotype. But the point is not to deny the existence of professionally successful beggars on the streets of London. Indeed, one can easily find examples. Nicholas Randall, for instance, was an old man and "a beggar" who regularly stationed himself at the "pissing place going to Brentford." His success as a professional is reflected in his house. Despite being a beggar he lived by himself in a small house with a garden at Turnham Green. By the side of the highway he "[had] a little house . . . and a garden a little distance from it," with "two pear-trees, a damson tree, and two or three apple trees in it" (OBP September 12, 1759, t17590912-22). The point, instead, is that literary depictions of beggars overemphasize their professionalism, and take a tiny minority as the norm. Nor need we assume that the literary stereotype is inevitably as two-dimensional as the examples already mentioned. The barefoot beggar encountered by Harley, the hero of Henry Mackenzie's *The Man of Feeling* (1771), is anything but a cardboard villain. The beggar in this instance was a healthy man, who had been brought down by illness, and forced to beg for a living in difficult circumstances, only to find that the tricks and props of the professional, a trained dog and ragged clothes, were necessary to the role (Mackenzie 1771: 15–18). Rather, the point is that eighteenth-century authors chose to depict a certain variety of beggar, rather than beggars in general. They chose healthy, adult male mendicants to represent a much more varied crew.

In a similar vein, Addison and Steele in *The Spectator* appeal to many of the same conventions. In no. 430, a correspondent complained how he

> looked out of my window the other morning earlier than ordinary, and saw a blind beggar, an hour before the passage he stands in is frequented, with a needle and thread, thriftily mending his stockings: My astonishment was still greater, when I beheld a lame fellow, whose legs were too big to walk within an hour after, bring him a pot of ale.

For Ward, Addison and Steele, Coventry and Gay, beggars were charlatans who practiced their deceits on an unwary urban audience.

Nor were these assumptions about the nature of begging and the character of beggars restricted to these highpoints of eighteenth-century literature. On September 19, 1705, Robert Cunningham was taken into the London Workhouse, and brought before the Court of Governors. He had been begging about the streets, pretending to be deaf and dumb. In a self-congratulatory minute, the governors record how they discover his ruse. At the next meeting the beadle who had originally arrested Robert Cunningham was given a reward, and an advertisement telling the world about the discovery was placed in the *Postman* (Corporation of London Record Office, 1702–5: fol. 242). The story was also picked up by a range of other papers, and repeated regularly in print over the next few years, every time the subject of beggars came up. Some 15 years later, the story received an even greater literary imprimatur by its inclusion in John Strype's magisterial *Survey of the Cities of London and Westminster* (1720 vol. 1: 197) – the point being that Cunningham was lifted from among the thousands of beggars who passed through the London Workhouse in the early eighteenth century, and his unusual experience and behavior was given a normality through publication and repetition. He was chosen for this treatment precisely because he fitted a stereotype. An example of a dissembling beggar was used to reinforce and inform a predetermined idea of who beggars were, and what they were really up to.

But there was more to eighteenth-century stereotypes than this. Beggars were also possessed of a powerfully attractive freedom and romance. Daniel Defoe, in his *Compleat Mendicant: Or Unhappy Beggar* (1699) depicts a free and easy world of the road, in which every house is an opportunity, every community open to the blandishments of a well-schooled beggar with a ready pen. Defoe's hero is educated in the art of begging by a knowing old reprobate whose fortunes are lavishly charted over much of the South of England. And while the hero is eventually saved from the house of correction by a sympathetic, if perhaps gullible, magistrate, it is clear that Defoe is depicting a life possessed of many charms. As is usual with Defoe, the allure of crime and disorder is thinly justified by a last-minute conversion to respectability, but the attractions of disorder are fully chronicled.

Twenty years later Defoe took up the theme of the beggarly poor again in *Colonel Jack* (1722) but this time he chose a rather different stereotype. The eponymous hero of this novel was the bastard child of a gentleman abandoned to his fate on the death of the London nurse charged with his care. Jack became a member of the Black Guard, that quasi-fictional, but also very real group of homeless children who slept under the arches of the annealing yards of London's glasshouses. Loitering and running errands, begging for food and clothing, Jack eventually fell into crime, was kidnapped and indentured as a servant to North America. The Black Guard had been the stuff of newspaper scare stories for a generation, and its existence had in part motivated the re-establishment of the London Workhouse in 1698 (Macfarlane 1986: 263). The Black Guard was most definitely not an entirely fictional group. One young woman, Mary Pewterer, clearly saw herself as a member of the Black Guard. She "us'd to lie in the Glass-house in the Minories, (as many more in the Winter-time use to do) and was call'd the Queen of the Glass-house" (OBP September 6, 1716, t17160906-24). Her behavior also reflects the more unpleasant side of Black Guard life. In 1716 she enticed a nine or ten year old girl, Phillis Delpeck, to an alehouse. Once there, Mary Pewterer, this "Queen of the Glass-house," held Phillis down while a man raped her, giving her venereal disease in the process. Two nurses at St Thomas's Hospital later testified that "they never saw a Person more afflicted with that Disease than she had been" (OBP September 6, 1716, t17160906-24). Defoe does more than anyone else to bring the real world into the fictional, to give a face and form to the nebulous, ever changing, group of young boys and girls who filled this role of underworld myth for Londoners (1722/1970: 1–84).

Similarly, Isaac Bickerstaff could turn an honest penny by recounting *The Life, Strange Voyages and Uncommon Adventures of Ambrose Gwinett* (1771), who, after adventures and mishaps in Spain, the West Indies, among pirates and in Algeria, ended his days as a sweep at Mew's Gate in Charing Cross. For Bickerstaff's readers, it was as if a life of high adventure was to be found hidden beneath the rags and labors of every beggar.

The quintessential example of how writers of fiction took real lives and turned them in to fictional social problems, however, must be Bampfylda Carew, whose autobiography went through tens of editions over the middle decades of the eighteenth century, and was almost continually in print throughout the nineteenth. The son of a minor gentleman, Carew fell in to a life of itinerant begging in the West Country, and eventually ended up travelling through North America, before returning to Somerset. In the first edition, the details of Carew's life were laid out in an essentially factual manner, but later the text was adapted by Robert Goadby and fundamentally amended under the explicit influence of the recently published *Tom Jones*. By the third edition Carew was depicted as a distinctly picaresque figure, falling in with a group of gypsies, rising through their ranks and eventually achieving the sobriquet of "King of the Beggars." What had been an essentially believable story, even a working-class autobiography, was amended to enhance all the stereotypes of beggars the eighteenth century had inherited from the seventeenth.

In its long afterlife of regular editions, Carew's text became increasingly amphibious, partaking both of the solid, if wet and slippery nature of fact, and the life-giving air of fiction. But many better writers than Robert Goadby made use of the trope of the gypsy in their discussions of beggars. Jane Barker, for instance, includes just such a tale in *The Lining of the Patchwork Screen* (1726). Here, as with Carew, thoughtless members of the upper classes, both a man and a woman, are seduced into beggary by freedom and ease (see in particular "The History of the Lady Gypsie," Barker 1726/1997: 227–38). What one is left with after this very brief and partial run through of literary figures is an image of the eighteenth-century beggar comprising a number of common features. He is healthy, he is organized, he is entrepreneurial, he is literate and smart, and he is a charlatan free from the constraints of civil society. But, perhaps most obvious of all, he is a he. With a couple of exceptions female beggars are thin on the ground – or at least between the covers of eighteenth-century literature. With the possible exception of one of Swift's beggars in Brobdingnag, "a woman with a cancer in her breast, swelled to a monstrous size, full of holes" (Swift 1726: 112–13), who is a tragic exemplar of his misanthropic vision of the world, and Jane Barker's narrator alluded to above, beggarly women are seldom allowed into books. The few examples of women to be found among this begging crew are almost universally depicted as sexually attractive and sexually available, although like the men, they are given to tricks and lies. William King, in his *The Beggar Woman* (1709), is a perfect, if rare, example. In the poem he tells the story of a gentleman out riding, who comes across a woman with an infant tied to her back:

> A beggar by her trade; yet not so mean
> But that her cheeks were fresh and linen clean. . . .
> She needed not much courtship to be kind

The beggar leads the gentleman into the woods in search of a secluded spot for a sexual encounter. Before he can satisfy his desires, however, our heroine manages to foist her infant on the gentleman, truss him up in a cloth with the child, and run off, crying:

> Sir, goodbye; be not angry that we part,
> I trust the child to you with all my heart:
> But, ere you get another, 'ti'n't not amiss
> To try a year or two how you'll keep this. (Lonsdale 1984: 79–80)

Even the few female beggars of eighteenth-century literature are healthy and entrepreneurial.

Street Beggars

If we turn now to the actual lives of street beggars, the extent to which these literary figures are at least highly selective if not totally disconnected from reality, becomes more evident. At the very end of the eighteenth century, in perhaps the single most impressive piece of social science undertaken during the eighteenth century, Matthew Martin surveyed the street beggars of London. In 1796 he set up the Mendicity Enquiry Office at no. 190 Piccadilly in the center of the West End. He described his methodology in a *Letter to the Right Hon. Lord Pelham on the State of Mendicity in the Metropolis* (1803):

> Caused tickets to be printed, and about 6000 were disposed of to myself and others, at the price of 3d. each, [in packets of ten, twenty or thirty (Martin 1812: 14)] for the purpose of being distributed to beggars, who were admitted to the office in consequence of their shewing such tickets, and received the value and frequently more. Thus a small fund was raised of which the paupers had the benefit in return for the accounts of them-

selves; and the tickets being lettered and numbered, and registered when disposed of, served as clues in particular cases where required, to assist the donors in tracing the history of the parties on whom they were bestowed . . . (Martin 1803: 6)

Over the next few years some 40 volumes of examinations of street beggars were accumulated, detailing the life histories of some 2,000 adults and over 3,000 dependant children. Statistical tables of the content of these examinations were then drawn up, and published. The result is the most comprehensive survey of street beggars produced prior to the late nineteenth century – and in methodological terms, a more robust source of information than many later surveys. What Martin discovered was a world much closer to that of Jane Austin, than to that of the literary beggars common in fiction.

Of the 2,000 adults found begging, 192 of them were men, of whom 45 were single, 100 were married, and 47 widowed. Among these were 21 military men and 14 seamen. The most striking thing, however, was the number of women and children. There were 1,808 women in this sample – 127 of whom were single, 1,100 married and 581 widowed. Of this number some 240 had a military connection as the wife or widow of a soldier or sailor. And with these women came a further 3,096 children.

In other words, the most obvious characteristic of this sample is the overwhelming preponderance of women, and married or widowed women at that. The male figure of literature is almost entirely absent.

But Martin's figures tell us more than this simple fact, because he also broke down his sample according to the settlement status of each individual interviewed. Every English and Welsh person had a parish of settlement, either by birth, or marriage, or through apprenticeship, or a period in service, or as a result of renting a tenement of over £10 per year in value. For most paupers their settlement was closely guarded and frequently discussed. It was a "right" which the English and Welsh poor felt gave them a claim on their parish of origin (or else the parish of origin of their parent or husband). It was also an issue that struck at the root of class relations in the eighteenth century. Parish worthies and social policy commentators continually sought to undermine the right to a settlement (see Taylor 1976; Snell 1991; Rogers 1991, 1994; Lees 1998). At the same time, the poor knew that their right to a settlement was the closest thing they were ever likely to have to an old age pension and unemployment insurance.

The statistics that Martin collected on the settlement of his examinees suggest that as well as being female, as well as being encumbered with children, the beggars of London were also largely Londoners. Of his beggars, 750 had a settlement in London and Middlesex, while only 336 were from distant English parishes. Only 65 were from Scotland, and 30 from abroad. Indeed there was only one category of beggar who matched the homegrown variety in numbers. Martin noted down 679 Irish beggars among his 2,000 (Martin 1803: 6).

If we go back to our literary beggars for a moment, with their lives of adventure, travel, and freedom of movement, there is an obvious disjuncture. With the possible exception of Irish migrants, the vast majority of the beggarly poor whose lives were recorded by Martin were soliciting alms on their own doorsteps. They were not, in other words the entrepreneurial travelers of myth.

Of course, we could dismiss these figures on the grounds that they come from a slightly later period than most of our literary beggars, and a period characterized by the disruption of war. But earlier evidence suggests that Martin's statistics represent an older and long-lived pattern. Between 1738 and 1742 the Lord Mayor of London decided to crack down on beggars, creating in the process a comprehensive file on vagrancy still held in the Corporation of the London Record Office. Of a sample of 153 individuals apprehended for begging and loitering in the City of London between 1738 and 1742 over half were adult women, and a further eight percent were children. Adult men made up only around 40 percent of the total. And if we look at the settlement of these people, almost half, 75, had a legal settlement in the metropolitan London area. Only 18 were identified as having a settlement elsewhere in the country; while no legal settlement was identified for the other 60 examinees. A full two thirds of the 76 women examined had a London settlement, and three quarters of the children. In other words, whether we look to the early or late eighteenth century, local, adult women continue to dominate the reality of beggarly poverty in the capital. And although single, physically fit, adult male beggars could be found, they represent the tiniest minority of the whole.

The lives of the people represented by these statistics is at odds with the literary stereotype. And if we look at just a couple of examples of this class of individuals, the nature of the difference becomes even more striking.

In 1763 a prospective buyer was looking over a house in Stonecutters Street, which runs between Fleet Market and Shoe Lane, just north of Fleet Street. London was full of abandoned and half-completed houses at this time, and squatting was commonplace. In this instance the buyer found the emaciated bodies of three almost naked women on the ground floor, while in the garret he found two women and a girl, alive, but on the verge of starvation. Two of the bodies were of women who had worked as casual porters in Fleet Market, just a few feet down the road, both of whom were known by the name of "Bet." In the garret, a woman named Pattent had established herself over a long period. She was an out of place servant, who had gone to the Fleet Market to look for casual labor, and had been told by one of the "Bets" that the house on Stonecutters street was empty. In the succeeding months, she lived in the garret as best she could taking what employment she could – sleeping in the house at night, and working in a cook-shop in King Street, Westminster, in exchange for food, during the day. The girl, Elizabeth Surman, was only 16. An orphan, and daughter of a jeweler in Bell Alley, Coleman Street, she had been employed to wind silk in Spitalfields, before working for six years for a washerwoman and children's nurse. When she fell ill, her mistress discharged her and with nowhere to go, she slept on the streets for weeks, before finding a bit of shelter in the house. When she was strong enough she went out begging, coming back to Stonecutters Street at night. A couple of days before they were discovered, Pattent had pawned her apron for six pence, which they spent on food (George 1965: 173–4).

Essentially, these women were beggars. And their situation was typical of eighteenth-century urban beggarly poverty. Equally typical was the experience of Thomas Shaw. He had been a porter at the Kings Arms Inn, near Holborn Bridge, for almost ten years, when he fell ill. For the next two years he haunted the neighborhood of Holborn as a vagrant, begging about the streets. At night he went back to his old place of employment and slept in the stables among the horses. At 11 o'clock at night, in mid January 1792, Richard Hughes found him "lying upon the pavement . . . in a passage leading to the street," appearing very weak and sickly. Hughes gave him some gin, and took him along to the New Compter – the local holding prison – where he stayed the night, the intention being that he would be sent to the workhouse belonging to St Sepulchre's first thing the next day, having recently secured a settlement in the parish by virtue of wringing some relief from the overseers. At the prison, Shaw was sat down before a good fire and covered with a rug. According to the coroner's inquest he died in that position at 4 the following morning.

Like Elizabeth Surman and the other inhabitants of Stonecutters Street, Shaw was forced to live an amphibious life – a life of insecurity and uncertainty, that only occasionally rose into the light and warmth of a more settled existence. Illness was perhaps the one thing that most beggars shared. They were cut down by the innumerable little plagues that ravaged this pre-modern and profoundly unhealthy population. What they also shared was a lack of place, of settled accommodation, of substantial social networks, of "Friends," to use the eighteenth-century term. And perhaps most importantly, they shared an urgent need to access and make use of the complex system of social policy gradually evolving around them.

It is a rather banal observation that fiction is indeed fiction, and that it does not clearly reflect the realities of the society or even the author that creates it. But in this instance there is an important message in the apparent discontinuity between the fictional beggars of Addison, Steele et al., and the more prosaic realities of individual lives and deaths. And if we look for a moment at the assumptions which underpin the development of eighteenth-century, and particularly, London social policy, the importance of this disjuncture will become clear.

If any single development is typical of the period it is the move to an institutional response to the poor, the ill, and the simply inconvenient. Workhouses, hospitals, foundling hospitals, and mad houses, are all characteristics of the carceral archipelago of the eighteenth-century metropolis. The Corporation of the Poor, re-established in 1698, the Westminster Hospital in 1716, and the Foundling Hospital in 1741 are well known highlights in this development (see Macfarlane 1986; Andrew 1989). But the meat and gristle of the system can be found in the parochial workhouses of the capital. By 1776, there were 86 parochial workhouses within the bounds of London, Westminster and Middlesex, housing 15,180 individuals – perhaps 2 per cent of the population of the capital. Nicholas Hawksmoor designed them, Matthew Marriott ran them, and the Society for the Promotion of Christian Knowledge provided the rules and the intellectual underpinnings that determined how they were meant to work (see Hitchcock 1992; Morrison 1999).

What is clear in the very bricks and mortar of these developments is that the pauper that glistened in the mind's eye of every workhouse projector and administrator was a fictional one. Nicholas Hawksmoor, when he created the model for the workhouse at St George Hanover Square in 1724 – a design that was published and widely copied – divided his workhouse clearly down the middle, with half being given over to adult men. Indeed, the assumption of a gendered symmetry is a common aspect of almost all eighteenth-century workhouse and hospital designs. Without research or enquiry, the founders of these institutions simply assumed that the population they were catering for was equally divided between men and women, with children added on as an extra. This despite the fact that at least two thirds of parish pensioners were in fact women – something every householder and overseer knew simply as a result of handing out the money. And while it is impossible to demonstrate that Hawksmoor had recently read Defoe's *The Compleat Mendicant* (1699), or Ned Ward's *History of London Clubs* (1709), it is clear that the stereotypes presented in works such as these, with their emphasis on male poverty, contributed to a situation in which inappropriate buildings could be designed by and built by people who should have known better.

But it was not simply in relation to the sleeping quarters that the influence of the literary stereotype could be found. While many institutions included small infirmaries and lying-in wards, the preponderance of space was always given over to work. There was an underlying assumption that just like the literary beggar, the workhouse inmate would be healthy and able to work. Some early projectors took this even further, and assumed that workhouse inmates would form a natural military resource for the growing demands of the state. Lawrence Braddon, in his *Regular-Government and Judicious Employment of the Poor* (1721), was certain that his own workhouse panacea would result in

> all those poor . . . men . . . [being] judiciously instructed in both martial and naval discipline, according to the best rules of instruction . . . for those necessary and excellent purposes of defending their religion, their king, their liberties and laws against all traitorous attempts or foreign invasions. (pp. 12, 13)

In other words, the kingdom would be insured against the pretender (among others) through the courageous actions of largely fictional beggars.

And while workhouses and healthy male beggars are perhaps at the core of this relationship between social policy and literary invention, we should not forget the equally important literary origins of a range of other social policy initiatives. The Magdalen Hospital established at mid-century has frequently been associated with the rise of a more sentimental version of womanhood by historians of prostitution and the working class (see Nash 1984; Lloyd 1996). The Foundling Hospital and the Marine Society have been implicated in an essentially literary sentimentalization of childhood, combined with the heroic tradition of mercantilism and exploration. The Marine Society in particular combined an increasingly romantic notion of the child with a hard-headed notion of the uses to which child flesh might be put, tied together with high adventure and glory (see Taylor 1985). (For the Foundling Hospital see McClure 1981; Wilson 1989; Outhwaite 1999; for voluntary charities see Andrew 1989.)

In other words, while the direct impact of literature on social policy is impossible to demonstrate, the shape of London's institutional infrastructure suggests that literature did play a significant role. Each type of institution was to some extent informed by its own version of literary poverty. Indeed, many of the voluntary and specialized institutions of mid-century could only flourish while middling sort and elite patrons maintained a sentimental interest in the supposed objects of their charity. Literature and a broader print culture played a central role in maintaining such an interest. From mid-century onwards, in particular, there developed a growing specialization of institutional provision that mapped easily onto a gradually changing literary landscape, but which apparently responded to the letters page of middling sort journals, rather than the demands of the poor. At the same time, however, the realities of poverty, the needs of the poor, their gender and their circumstances remained largely unchanged, and disassociated from the language used to describe them as a class.

To relate this image to our now standard meta-narrative of institutional development, one would have to say that Michel Foucault's vision of a set of institutions governed by discursive constructions and directed at controlling the internal emotional lives of their inhabitants would seem to apply (Foucault 1977). At least in relation to the external shape of the institutions involved, there is a coherent, perhaps anti-Enlightenment, narrative to be told about the design of eighteenth-century social policy and the desires of social policy reformers. The only problem is that if you then look at these same institutions as they are seen in the behavior of the poor themselves, they cease to resemble in any meaningful way the architectural plans from which they were built, or the easy platitudes of their founders.

What looks rigid and well-demarcated, governed by expressed prejudice and legal precept, when viewed from the printed books collection of the British Library, looks very different through the eyes of Elizabeth Surman or Jane Austin's better-informed contemporaries. For them, what emerged in the flurry of foundations was a system of relief that for all of its failings still seemed to promise the resources and care people needed. The way paupers used workhouses, for instance, had only the slightest connection to how the designers thought they should be used. Workhouse populations were dominated by women, children, and the ill (as were the poor of London). The vast majority of the population of the workhouse of St Luke's Chelsea, for instance, was made up of people seeking some kind of medical treatment. As a result the medical provisions available in London's workhouses rapidly increased in both importance and cost (Hitchcock 1997). More than this, it is clear that these same institutions soon took on roles for which they had never been designed. They became crèches for working mothers, lying-in hospitals, and geriatric wards. They quickly became short stay hostels for domestic servants out of work, and one facet of a more complex urban economy of makeshift that included hawking, selling, service, and casual labor. Even the apparently insuperable issue of settlement did not allow institutions to filter out those who failed to fit the stereotype. At the same time, the pressures of their variegated population of clients ensured that the administrators of workhouses developed new relationships with other specialized institutions. The recent work of Kevin Siena on the treatment of venereal disease in London, and Lisa Cody's and Tanya Evan's work on lying-in hospitals and the Foundling Hospital, has made clear that the parishes and parish workhouses in particular quickly developed strong relationships with a wide range of alternative institutions (Cody 1993; Evans 2001; Siena 2001).

In a similar, if more direct way, the Foundling Hospital became a safe repository for illegitimate babies (frequently referred there by parishes at the behest of parents) while the Magdalen quickly realized that none of the prostitutes of London were particularly interested in its brand of reformation, forcing it instead to concentrate on the children of the ne'er-do-well middling sort (Levene 2002; Lloyd 1996; Nash 1984). These changes were the result of hard-pressed administrators and parochial officers finding that the demands of the poor contradicted the rules of their institutions. In every vestry room, at the door of every workhouse and hospital, individuals were faced with a constant stream of demands from the clearly needy. And while the poor quickly learned the type of story they needed to tell in order to gain admission, the gate-keepers of charity were forced to reassign resources to meet real needs (Hitchcock 1997; Outhwaite 1999).

But what is even more impressive is the extent to which the poor wove these disparate institutions into a largely accessible and inter-related system. A clear measure of this process can be found in the City Cash Books for London. Year by year, the amounts spent on capturing and processing vagrants was recorded. Money was spent to keep them alive during their prison sentences, and to pay for their whipping and their removal. But money was also paid to support them through illness. Gradually, over the course of the second half of the eighteenth century, the City of London was forced to refer a higher and higher proportion of its vagrants to hospital for medical care. By the 1790s, the cost of these referrals had risen to an average of £756. 14s. 1d per year for vagrants clothed and supported in St Bartholomew's Hospital, and up to £1,057. 9s. 3d. for those referred to St Thomas's. Almost £2,000 per year was being spent giving vagrants and beggars the best hospital care available in the capital. But from our perspective, what is important here is that the individual vagrants involved were able to use even the apparently unlikely pathway of arrest and imprisonment to gain access to a comprehensive medical service. I think our assumption must be that the vagrants involved were quite self-conscious about the strategy they were adopting.

When Mary Brown, a seventeen-year-old prostitute and orphan, went into labor, she asked the advice of her landlady and bawd, Mrs Davies. A long discussion ensued in the house in Jackson's Alley, off Bow Street, where Mary had entertained men for several years. The question on everyone's lips was, "Which is the best casualty parish?," or in other words, where is the best casualty department in town? One young woman suggested St Martin in the Fields, but was answered, "No, no, St Clement is the best casualty parish – send her there!" Mary was hustled into a coach, and presented herself at the door of the workhouse. And while the workhouse mistress vainly attempted to restrict her access by insisting that the overseer be summoned before she would be admitted, the demands of nature ensured that Mary soon found herself in the well-appointed lying-in ward, giving birth to a healthy boy. She was later examined as to her settlement, giving perhaps the one story that would allow her to stay. She claimed to have been born on shipboard between Ireland and England, and hence completely outside the system of settlement. As a result both Mary and her little boy stayed put and St Clement Danes reinforced its reputation as the best "casualty parish" in London (Westminster Archives Centre, MS. B1187, fols. 147–50).

This story nicely illustrates the extent to which the poor subverted and used institutions in ways that were not intended by the parish worthies who established them. But it only touches the surface of a larger sense of the possible solutions to poverty available.

The case of Paul Patrick Kearney, a uniquely verbose, pedantic, and literate London beggar, makes this second point more clearly. A neat file of correspondence survives in the records of the parish of St Dionis Backchurch, where he had gained a settlement in the 1740s. According to his own account, by the late 1760s he was in dire straits, and in danger of perishing on the winter streets. He was ragged and begging, and on applying to the churchwardens he was eventually relieved with a shilling. During 1766 and 1767, he received a course of balsalmic tincture and balsamic Lohock for his ills. He was also given a cap, a hat, shoes, hose, breeches, a waistcoat and great coat. On medicines and clothing for Kearney, the parish spent £4. 16s. 1d. It also arranged, at his request, for treatment as an outpatient by Westminster Hospital and for him to be taken in to the hospital at the first opportunity. On his discharge from Westminster he was placed in a contract workhouse in Rose Lane in Spitalfields run by a Mr Birch. Kearney was disgusted by the conditions and the idea that he would be required to work regularly at jobs he considered demeaning and within seven weeks he was once again outside the workhouse, under the treatment of an "eminent physician." From here he was sent, again at his own request, and at parochial expense, to Guy's Hospital, where he continued for a couple of months, before finally falling into dispute about the quality of his "body linen" and the hospital's charges for cleaning it.

Having been discharged from Guy's he was lodged at the Ipswich Arms in Cullum Street for several weeks and the parish paid to allow him to advertise for a position. He later tried to take employment as a secretary to a Captain Scott. At this point, after years of frustration and grumbling on the part of the parish officers, they finally concluded that he was mentally ill – a conclusion shared by the house doctor at Guys among others – and he was placed in a private mad house in Hoxton.

The point is that Kearney moved several times through a range of London institutions. He was able to force his parish, over the frustrated whining of generations of parish officers, to give him the care he desired, and while not all the accommodation he was offered was of the quality he wanted, he was transferred between institutions largely at his own request.

If you begin to piece together the lives of London's paupers, what emerges is the extent to which the various institutions of the capital were forced to interrelate with each other as a result of the requests of the poor themselves. There is a constant stream of letters and notes from the administrators of parish workhouses and charitable institutions organizing the transfer of paupers and the repayment of fees. Women went from the lying-in hospitals to the workhouses to the infirmaries and back. Their children (often at their request and always with their permission) were delivered to the Foundling Hospital and the Marine Society. The elderly were constantly moving from workhouses to almshouses, or on to their relatives. In the process, what had been a disparate set of institutions informed by a set of narrow and unrealistic stereotypes, became an increasingly integrated system of social services. For the poor, access to this system was available through the parochial workhouses for those who could claim a settlement, and through the complex prison system for those who could not. This integration was not created by design, but rather by the demands of the poor themselves.

Peter Mandler has recently pointed out that it is the poor, much more than their betters, who need to know how social policy works (Mandler 1990). In eighteenth-century London paupers knew how the system worked, and it was through their collective actions, the force of their collective demands and behaviors, that an incoherent system was forced to evolve into one that could cope with their difficult and disparate needs.

To return momentarily to literary beggars, they did not stand still, nor did their role remain the same. Writers such as Goldsmith, Wordsworth, and Blake gradually humanized and sentimentalized the figure of the beggar. (On romanticism and poverty, see Sampson 1984; Stoddard 1988; Friedman 1989; Rzepka 1989; Benis 2000.) He, and now more frequently she, became the talisman of tragedy. Their stories were gradually re-written, with the occasional dollop of spice and spoonful of sugar. By the nineteenth century, in the works of Dickens and Thackeray, beggars became part and parcel of an apparently realistic cast of characters in a surprisingly realistic landscape. But at the same time, the role of the literary beggar in the formation of social policy was itself transformed. With the rise of political economy, and as importantly, political arithmetic, with the transcendent authority of blue books and verbose reports, the role of the literary beggar in the formation of social policy became increasingly and necessarily limited. During the same period the patchwork quilt of institutions that had done so much to ameliorate the lives of the desperately needy, and that had been created in part from misleading literary stereotypes, was gradually torn apart. It was replaced by the perhaps better-researched but also less charitable institutions of the new Poor Law.

What this chapter has attempted to argue is that while powerful literary stereotypes helped to inform eighteenth-century social policy, ensuring that an unsuitable and ill-organized set of institutions were established, this was not the end of the story. Because the London poor were women, because they had a variety of needs, and a variety of claims to relief, because, in other words, they did not fit the stereotypes, they were able to force the system to evolve in a particular and well-defined way. It was the real demands of the actual poor – beggarly women and children in particular – that forced the institutions of London to evolve into a more coherent and structured form. As a result, by the end of the eighteenth century there was an almost uniform carpet of health and social welfare provision that even the exigencies of war and dearth could not overturn. This was a legacy of pauper agency, just as much as the self-serving and patronizing pamphlets of social policy reformers are the legacy of selective literary stereotypes. In turn this suggests that if we are looking for the origins and meaning of institutional development we need to take seriously the agency and authority, the power and actions, of the apparently least powerful. We also need to be more sensitive than we have been of late to the conflict and competing demands that shaped the historical process.

References and further reading

Andrew, D. T. (1989) *Philanthropy and Police: London Charity in the Eighteenth Century*. Princeton: Princeton University Press.

Barker, J. (1726) *The Lining of the Patch Work Screen; Design'd for the Farther Entertainment of Ladies*, in Carol Shiner Wilson (ed.) *The Galesia Trilogy and Selected Manuscript Poems of Jane Barker*. Oxford: Oxford University Press, 1997.

Beier, A. L. (1983) *The Problem of the Poor in Tudor and Early Stuart England*. London: Methuen.

Benis, T. R. (2000) *Romanticism on the Road: The Marginal Gains of Wordsworth's Homeless*. New York: St Martin's Press.

[Bickerstaff, I.] (1771) *The Life, Strange Voyages and Uncommon Adventures of Abrose Gwinett*. London: printed for and sold by the booksellers in town and country.

Braddon, L. (1721) *The Regular-Government and Judicious Employment of the Poor, the Most Probable Means of Raising and Securing Public Credit* . . . London: Printed and sold by T. Warner and J. Fox.

Carew, B. (1745, 1749) *The King of the Beggars: Bampfylde-Moore Carew*, ed. C. H. Wilkinson. Oxford: Oxford University Press, 1931.

Carol, W. S. (1996) *Fat King, Lean Beggar: Representations of Poverty in the Age of Shakespeare*. Ithaca: Cornell University Press.

City of London Records Office (CLRO)

Cody, L. F. (1993) "The politics of body contact: disciplines of reproduction in Britain, 1688–1834," University of California at Berkeley PhD thesis.

Coventry, F. (1752) *The History of Pompey the Little: Or The Life and Adventures of a Lap-Dog*, ed. R. A. Day. Oxford: Oxford University Press, 1974.

[Defoe, D.] (1699) *The Compleat Mendicant: or, Unhappy Beggar*. London: For E. Harris.

Defoe, D. (1722) *The History and Remarkable Life of the Truly Honourable Col. Jacque, Commonly Call'd Col. Jack*, ed. S. H. Monk. Oxford: Oxford University Press, 1970.

Evans, T. (2001) "Unmarried motherhood in eighteenth-century London," University of London PhD thesis.

Foucault, M. (1977) *Discipline and Punish: The Birth of the Prison*, trans. A. Sheridan. New York: Pantheon Books. (Original work published 1975.)

Friedman, G. (1989) "History in the background of Wordsworth's blind beggar," *English Literary History* 56(1): 125–48.

George, M. D. (1965) *London Life in the Eighteenth Century*, 2nd edn. Harmondsworth: Penguin.

Hitchcock, T. (1992) "Paupers and preachers: the SPCK and the parochial workhouse movement," in L. Davison, T. Hitchcock, T. Kiern, and R. Shoemaker (eds.) *Stilling the Grumbling Hive: The Response to Social and Economic Problems in England, 1689–1750* (pp. 145–66). Stroud, Glos.: Alan Sutton.

—— (1997) "Demography and the culture of sex in the long eighteenth century," in J. Black (ed.) *Culture and Society in Britain, 1660–1800* (pp. 69–84). Manchester: Manchester University Press.

—— (1997) "'Unlawfully begotten on her body': illegitimacy and parish poor in St Luke Chelsea," in T. Hitchcock, P. King, and P. Sharpe (eds.) *Chronicling Poverty: The Voices and Strategies of the English Poor, 1640–1840* (pp. 70–86). London: Macmillan Press.

Kinney, A. F. (ed.) (1990) *Rogues, Vagabonds & Sturdy Beggars: A New Gallery of Tudor and Early Stuart Rogue Literature*. Boston: University of Massachusetts Press.

Lees, L. H. (1998) *The Solidarities of Strangers: the English Poor Laws and the People, 1700–1948*. Cambridge: Cambridge University Press.

Levene, A. (2002) "Health and survival chances at the London Foundling Hospital and the Spedale Degli Innocenti of Florence, 1741–99," University of Cambridge PhD thesis.

Lloyd, S. (1996) "'Pleasure's golden bait': prostitution, poverty and the Magdalen Hospital in eighteenth-century London," *History Workshop Journal* 41: 50–70.

Lonsdale, R. (1984) *Eighteenth-Century Verse*. Oxford: Oxford University Press.

Macfarlane, S. (1986) "Social policy and the poor in the later seventeenth century," in A. L. Beier and R. Finlay, *The Making of the Metropolis, London, 1500–1700* (pp. 252–77). London: Longman.

Mackenzie, H. (1771) *The Man of Feeling*, ed. B. Vickers. Oxford: Oxford University Press 2001.

Mandler, P. (ed.) (1990) *The Uses of Charity: The Poor on Relief in the Nineteenth-Century Metropolis*. Philadelphia: University of Pennsylvania Press.

Martin, M. (1803) *Letter to the Right Hon. Lord Pelham on the State of Mendicity in the Metropolis*. London.

—— (1812) *An Appeal to Public Benevolence for the Relief of Beggars; With a View to a Plan for the Suppression of Beggary*. London: printed for the Philanthropic Society.

McClure, R. K. (1981) *Coram's Children: the London Foundling Hospital in the Eighteenth Century*. New Haven: Yale University Press.

Morrison, K. (1999) *The Workhouse: A Study of Poor-Law Buildings in England*. Swindon: English Heritage.

Nash, S. D. (1984) "Prostitution and charity: the Magdalen Hospital, a case study," *Journal of Social History* 17: 617–28.

Old Bailey Sessions Proceedings (OBSP); www.oldbaileyonline.org.

Outhwaite, R. B. (1999) " 'Objects of charity': petitions to the London Foundling Hospital, 1768–72," *Eighteenth-Century Studies* 32(4): 497–510.

Rogers, N. S. (1991) "Policing the poor in eighteenth-century London: the vagrancy laws and their administration," *Histoire Sociale / Social History* 24: 127–47.

—— (1994) "Vagrancy, impressment and the regulation of labour in eighteenth-century Britain," *Slavery & Abolition* 15:2: 102–13.

Rzepka, C. J. (1989) " 'A gift that complicates employ': poetry and poverty in 'Resolution and Independence,' " *Studies in Romanticism* 28: 225–47.

Salgado, G. (1992) *The Elizabethan Underworld*, 2nd edn. Stroud, Glos.: Alan Sutton.

Sampson, D. (1984) "Wordsworth and the poor: the poetry of survival," *Studies in Romanticism* 23: 31–59.

Siena, K. (2001) "Poverty and the pox: venereal disease in London hospitals, 1600–1800," University of Toronto PhD thesis.

Snell, K. D. M. (1991) "Pauper settlement and the right to poor relief in England and Wales," *Continuity and Change* 6: 375–415.

Stoddard, E. W. (1988) " 'All Freaks of Nature': the human grotesque in Wordsworth's city," *Philological Quarterly* 67(1): 37–61.

Strype, J. (1720) *A Survey of the Cities of London and Westminster*. London.

Swift, J. (1726) *Gulliver's Travels*, ed. H. Davis. Oxford: Oxford University Press, 1965.

Taylor, J. S. (1976) "The impact of pauper settlement 1691–1834," *Past and Present* 73: 42–74.

—— (1985) *Jonas Hanway, Founder of the Marine Society: Charity and Policy in 18th Century Britain*. London: Scolar Press.

Ward, N. (1709) *History of London Clubs; Or the Citizens Pastime . . .* London: Printed for F. Bagnall near Fleetstreet.

Wilson, A. (1989) "Illegitimacy and its implications in mid-18th century London: the evidence of the Foundling Hospital," *Continuity and Change* 4: 103–64.

Chapter 5

The Sewers

Ordure, Effluence, and Excess in the Eighteenth Century

Sophie Gee

The eighteenth century did its best to appear polite. Its literature, art, and music announce their commitment to good manners, good taste, careful judgment, and steady reason. Samuel Johnson, the greatest prose-stylist of the period, summed it all up beautifully when he described the poet Dryden: "What was said of Rome, adorned by Augustus, may be applied by an easy metaphor to English poetry embellished by Dryden: *lateritiam invenit, marmoream reliquit*; he found it brick and he left it marble" (1781/1905).

Johnson's epigram seems to capture the feeling of the early century – classical, grand, enduring. But there is an underside to the grandeur of the Augustan age in England, a contrary literary mode that relied on the expressive possibilities of filth, decay, and unregulated waste. This chapter is about texts that resist the good taste and good manners of the eighteenth century – depending instead for their literary effects on the symbolic resonance of filthy remainders.

In 1678, Dryden himself established an "excremental vision," in Norman O. Brown's sense, in his satirical poem *MacFlecknoe* – a text that attempts to convert a literary enemy into disgusting human effluent. Dryden's trick sneaks up on the reader; when we read the opening line of *MacFlecknoe*: "All human things are subject to decay," we brace ourselves for a somber neo-Augustan historical narrative. But the opening turns out to be a joke – the "thing" subject to decay is Dryden's rival poet Thomas

Shadwell, who putrefies in his own writing and eventually becomes a gigantic turd. At the climax of *MacFlecknoe* Shadwell makes a stately progress along the River Thames in a barge, where he is celebrated on both banks by admirers of his poetry. Even the river's stock of fish flocks to Shadwell's presence: "About thy boat the little Fishes throng, / As at the Morning Toast that floats along" (ll. 49–50). How quaint a phrase is "morning toast" – and how many people know that it is the human refuse thrown into the Thames after people's bowel-movements during the night? The fish are swimming up to nibble at Shadwell and his poems because they think they are excrement. We realize that the ridiculous Shadwell's progress along the river enables a poetic progress for Dryden: from a classical to a mock-classical mode; from a literary to a literal idiom.

Later in the poem, when Dryden scathingly imagines his rival's "coronation" as poet laureate, he jokes that London's streets will be lined not in Persian carpets (a conventional mark of the procession), but with superfluous copies of Shadwell's writings. The manuscripts render the streets virtually impassable: "But loads of Shadwell almost choakt the way," Dryden quips. He prints Shadwell as "Sh—" (l. 103), and readers who remember the morning toasts won't be in any doubt about the true nature of the substance choking London's thoroughfares. The filthy, over-crowded, insanitary aspects of contemporary London are what make Dryden's satirical devices possible. He uses them to manipulate classical poetics, creating a contemporary satirical mode that takes its metaphors from the grim reality of urban life.

This chapter will explain why some of the towering early Augustans – Dryden, Pope, Swift – worked through the degraded and transient imagery of human remainders. It was a subject matter that would normally be expected of hacks, balladeers, and scribblers: seeping sewage, brimming chamber pots, vomit, filth, and domestic squalor (see Manley 1995). I will investigate the paradoxical centrality of waste matter to the great canonical writings of the period.

One explanation is offered by the fact that more people were living in cities (particularly in London), and that English life was becoming more cosmopolitan and sophisticated (Earle 1994). So the old-fashioned filth of Tudor and Stuart London (animals, human waste, garbage) started to seem more jarring, out of place beside the pretensions of bourgeois prosperity. Another explanation is offered by the convention in satirical writing of drawing on scatological imagery (see Rawson 1985; Elias 1994). The filth of London was used to mock the enthusiasm, vigor, and optimism of the Whig government and their supporters who constantly proclaimed the prosperity and magnificence of England's capital city. But accounts of this kind don't explore the particular imaginative effects achieved in the representation of filthy remainders. Why did Pope and Swift want to write about objects that were unwanted – with such virtuosity as to preserve them forever?

We can conceptualize the problem in this way. There is a paradox inherent in the literary representation of waste-matter: it enables the recuperation of matter that is ostensibly without value. So there is a tension in writing that deals in filthy remnants, as these texts do: the attempt to discard or dismiss them is attended simultaneously by the competing desire for their recovery. Remnants exert an allure that belies their status as unwanted objects. The allure is generated by the fact that waste is simultaneously a kind of surplus. Unexpectedly, there is similarity between abundance and decay – a proximity between descriptions of effluence and affluence. For this reason waste has a perversely exhilarating power in narrative because the kind of over-supply that characterizes waste can be reconfigured in the literary text to reflect meaningful or valuable plenitude. The opposition between filth and surplus comes into closer and closer contact in literary texts – making waste oscillate continuously with value and to numb the reader's sense of their distinctness.

Political and Cultural Contexts

But the morning toasts and the loads of sh– haven't just been invented to make fun of Shadwell. They would have been familiar sights from the filthy landscape of eighteenth-century London, only slightly exaggerated for poetic effect. Sanitation came to London relatively late in the day. At the beginning of the eighteenth century it was still the custom to empty chamber-pots into the public street, where excrement would run off into a central "kennel" or open gutter. In his celebrated poem *Trivia* (1716), with its account of London's street culture, John Gay warns visitors against standing too close to the middle of the street, lest they be sprayed with putrid mud. Piles of human excrement were collected by nightmen and stored in "laystalls," or dungheaps in the city, but these were badly managed, often overfull, and emptied all too infrequently. As late as 1721 a pamphlet was still being reprinted from the Great Plague in 1665, describing very primitive strategies for keeping a city free of infection and decay: a prohibition on allowing cattle and swine to wander through the city streets and a caution against the perennial problem of wandering "rogues and beggars" who spread infection and disease. Dead animals were alarmingly common in public passageways – on fair-days and public occasions the overexcited crowd would throw animal entrails at one another. In his collection of essays entitled *The London Spy*, Ned Ward describes how, on a pageant day, the "industrious rabble"

> had procured a dead cat, whose reeking puddings hung dangling from her torn belly, covered all over with dirt, blood and nastiness, in which pickle she was handed about by the babes of grace as an innocent diversion, every now and then being tossed into the face of some gaping booby or another . . . (Ward, in Allen 1998)

And Dryden's "morning toasts" are vividly real: rubbish, ashes, dirt, and excrement washed regularly from the kennels into the Thames, turning it into the filthy canal of the poem. The so-called sewers were crude drains that carried effluence from the streets into a series of filthy tributaries (such as the Fleet River), which then disgorged their contents into the Thames at the "Fleet Ditch." A series of acts of Parliament were passed throughout the century to advance the effective cleaning of the streets and sewers, but to little avail – as Pope indicates in the *Dunciad*, his Dunces dive eagerly into the brown stagnated waters of the Fleet.

An obscure document from 1756 tells the story of the perils of waste-disposal in a world before proper sewage. A man called Charles Harper invented "machines for night-work": carts for carrying "nightsoil" away from dungheaps in the city that could measure the volume of the excrement contained. Apparently a long-standing fraud plagued the waste-removal business: the "nightmen" would charge for carrying away more waste than they actually did remove. The business of taking excrement away from the city was costly, and the authorities were always on the lookout for a way of turning waste-matter back into something more valuable. Hence the Act of Parliament in 1758 that allowed a "certain quantity of dung, compost, earth or soil to be yearly shipped as ballast from the laystalls in London on board any collier or coasting vessel."

It wasn't just effluence that clogged the streets of London. Contemporary commentators describe a class of waste-*people* who fill the passageway like garbage:

> [T]wo persons cannot come together in the Streets but they are instantly encircled with a crew of Beggars, and a Man that hath occasion to pass in haste had need to hire a lusty fellow to go before him with a truncheon to clear the way of those vast Bodies of them that obstruct the Passengers with Brooms, Brushes and crutches. (Anon [Erasmus Jones] 1736)

The beggars and their brooms literally block the way of the men-of-business – implying that waste-matter, especially when it takes the form of leftover people, inhibits commercial prosperity. No wonder that the champions of London's new finance economy argued for the cleaning up of the city. But as readers we are simultaneously aware that beggars, brushes, and crutches are the inevitable fall-out from increased wealth, industry and commerce. Even though affluence and effluence take up their cudgels against each other in the passage, they reach a stalemate: it seems that one is ineluctably the cost of the other.

Civic texts of the period establish a radical opposition between effluence and affluence that the satirical narratives of Dryden, Swift, and Pope set out to collapse. Dryden's description of the insanitary conditions of London trade in the same imagery of excess and abundance as those celebrations of London's prosperity and success he claims to despise. Shadwell, for example, was a successful and highly regarded writer – one of many figures lampooned by the Augustan satirists who in reality belonged to a thriving and prosperous literary marketplace. But Dryden and his followers wanted to show that prosperity and proliferation in London's literary culture were not necessarily signs of value: abundance could equally signal valueless surplus. By folding a mimetic description of London's effluence into their satires, Dryden and others showed that the narrative techniques used to describe commercial and cultural prosperity could equally be used to describe decay and desolation. Effluence and affluence were much closer to one another than people were willing to acknowledge.

Even before Dryden wrote *MacFlecknoe*, the imagery of discarded matter already had a claim on England's political imagination in the seventeenth century. During the civil war and the inter-regnum, pamphlets and ballads campaigned for the political exclusion of Royalists, Republicans, Catholics, and Puritans alike through the imagery of purged waste-matter or discarded effluence. Remaindered matter acquired a politicized resonance as demands for radical change were framed as fantasies about the elimination of human waste. When the period of Republican government finally drew to a close in 1660, Royalists clamored for the violent expulsion of the Republicans – imagining their adversaries as excrement that the diseased body of England was trying to purge. The ballads of the period would establish the trope of effluence and its disposal for the much more sophisticated literary skirmishes in which Swift and Pope were engaged.

Alexander Brome's ballad *Bumm-Fodder* (c.1659) is a particularly boisterous example from the Restoration, proclaiming the defeat of the

Republic by lampooning the last of its parliaments, the "Rump." Predictably enough, Brome's coarse rhymes describe the Rump parliament as an ass that defecates the Republic out of existence:

> There's a Proverb come to my mind not unfit,
> When the head shall see the RUMP all be-shit,
> Sure this must prove a most lucky hit:
>> Which nobody can deny.
>
> There's another Proverb which every Noddy
> Will jeer the RUMP with and cry Hoddy Doddy,
> Here's a Parliament all Arse and no Body.
>> Which nobody can deny.
>
> 'Tis a likely matter the world will mend
> When so much blood and treasure we spend,
> And yet begin again at the wrong End.
>> Which nobody can deny. (&c,&c)

The conceit at work in these lines is that all the money and blood spent during the civil wars has been digested by the Republican government, which has now excreted it out of an enormous rear-end (the Rump). For its pains, England is left with a gigantic rump that has defecated its most valuable institutions – producing "a parliament all arse and no body." Brome's confusing barrage of scatological puns manages to convey an apocalypse: all of England, even the English language, has disintegrated into an all-consuming heap of excrement. The ballad actually succeeds in quite a neat rhetorical move, for the lines "when the head shall see the Rump all be-shit" and "here's a Parliament all arse and no body" stage a crude avenging of the regicide. By forcing a linguistic transformation of the Rump Parliament into a real arse, Brome brings about his own beheading of the Republic.

Bumm-Fodder achieves its rhetorical effect by representing an act of political exclusion and defeat – the dissolution of the Rump and the imminent failure of the Republic – through the image of digestive evacuation. The republican government is so loathsome that it purges itself – an inevitable consequence for its diseased political body. Bodily discharge thus offered an image of a naturally occurring, systemic expulsion that could disguise the ideological conflicts determining political exclusion. The discharge of effluence became a powerful political trope because it made the system that expelled it seem putrid.

The imagery of expelled filth became iconic in the eighteenth century. The pamphlets, poems, and essays of the period, in which political and literary conflicts rage furiously, inherit the excrement of their seventeenth-century predecessors. But in the hands of Pope, Swift, and their contemporaries, the crudeness of *Bumm-Fodder*'s filthy discharge modulates into something disarmingly subtle. Excrement becomes malleable. At one moment it looks like filth; at another, like pleasurable abundance. Augustan writers realized that filth was powerful not as the antithesis of valuable matter, but because the two could be made to look the same.

It wasn't only the satirists of the period for whom such an insight was crucial. In his preface to the *Fable of the Bees* (1714), Bernard Mandeville urged readers to recognize the interdependence of refuse and prosperity. In the Preface to his long text, Mandeville argues that the production of commercial value has its corollary in the discharge of debris:

> There are, I believe, few People in London, of those that are at any time forc'd to go a-foot, but what could wish the Streets of it much cleaner than generally they are . . . [But] if we mind the Materials of all Sorts that must supply such an infinite number of Trades and Handicrafts, as are always going forward; the vast quantity of Victuals, Drink and Fewel that are daily consum'd in it, the Waste and Superfluities that must be produced from them; the multitudes of Horses and other Cattle that are always dawbing the Streets, the Carts, Coaches and more heavy Carriages that are perpetually wearing and breaking the Pavement of them, and above all the numberless swarms of People that are continually harassing and trampling through every part of them: If, I say, we mind all these, we shall find that every Moment must produce new Filth; and . . . it is impossible London should be more cleanly before it is less flourishing. (1724 vol. 1: 11–12)

The technique Mandeville uses to make his case is important: he overlaps the language of superfluity with that of prosperity. The parallel phrases "vast quantity of victuals . . . consum'd" and "waste and superfluities . . . produced" negotiate an equivalence between vast and waste, quantity and superfluity, consumption and production – implying affinity among ostensibly unlike terms. The "infinite number," the "multitude," the "numberless swarms," simultaneously describe an abundance of waste and plenitude – it is impossible to separate one from the other – and the "supply" of materials generates an excess not only of products, but of pollutants. This happy equilibrium enables Mandeville to praise modern commerce while admitting the vices of modern life. But the fantasy of reciprocity between filth and prosperity would have very dark implications for Jonathan Swift, writing at the same time about Ireland.

Swift would argue that the English government was far too sanguine about the visible signs of Irish poverty and degradation – *precisely because* they showed that English commerce and English exports must be prospering in exchange.

Swift: Sex, Sonnets, Cities

Swift is the preeminent figure in eighteenth-century effluence. His writings are filled up with grubby remainders – with excrement, garbage, sweat, false hair, false teeth, prosthetic limbs, dead dogs and cats. Often obsessively, Swift's writing rehabilitates matter that has been left discarded by the polite worlds of eighteenth-century London and Dublin. He brings a world of discarded objects into circulation by paying meticulous attention to their repellent physical properties, which become perverse surrogates for those beautiful and desirable objects that more commonly preoccupy the eighteenth-century gaze. In his famous anti-erotic poem "The Lady's Dressing Room" (1732) Swift aestheticizes filth, describing, as though it were matter of great worth, the grime caught in a lady's comb: "A Paste of Composition rare, / Sweat, Dandruff, Powder, Lead and Hair" (ll. 23–4).

Waste-matter in Swift's writing is characterized by an abundance that also marks it out as degraded. The celebratory energy of his poems often derives from the fact that the kind of over-supply that characterizes filth can be reconfigured in the literary text to reflect meaningful or valuable plenitude.

This overlap between the descriptive language of filth and luxury generates the dark tone and unsettling mood of "The Lady's Dressing Room." Probably the most notorious of all Swift's poems, this is the one in which his hero Strephon cries out, "Celia, Celia, Celia shits!" The sight of his beloved's excrement stimulates Strephon's horrified recoil from Celia – even though he is also compulsively attracted to her brimming chamber pot. For Strephon – and Swift (at least according to some critics) – erotic desire comes perilously close in feeling to sexual disgust (Brown 1964). Swift conveys that discomforting proximity by using the language of a courtly lyric to describe Celia's putrefying waste-matter. "The Lady's Dressing Room" is in fact a parody of courtly love lyrics – and their claim that a work of art can preserve the beloved from decay. Swift fills his poem up with literal waste-matter to burlesque the lyric speaker's traditional anxiety about the effects of time and decay upon physical beauty. The conventional lyric lament that beauty is doomed to decline – the regret "that thou amongst the wastes of time must go" (Shakespeare, sonnet 12) – is thus absurdly literalized in "A Lady's Dressing Room." A glut of discarded matter surrounds the speaker and his beloved, who languish among waste of all descriptions. In substituting a catalogue of the beloved's effluence for a catalogue of her beauties, Swift reveals that the language of lyric invention readily permits the substitution of decay for perfection – much as it appears to insist on their opposition. Swift's parody reveals that the imagery of abundance, of excess, applies equally to waste and plenitude, making them both antitheses and substitutes.

Swift embeds phrases into the poem that establish an association with the expressive register of the courtly sonnet, emphasizing its likeness to a mode that it seems to parody. Swift appropriates Shakespearean imagery to describe the by-products of Celia's toilet:

> The Basin takes whatever comes
> The Scrapings of her Teeth and Gums,
> A nasty Compound of all Hues,
> For here she spits, and here she spews.
> But oh! it turn'd poor Strephon's Bowels,
> When he beheld and smelt the Towels,
> Begumm'd, bematter'd, and beslim'd
> With Dirt, and Sweat, and Ear-Wax grim'd.
> No Object Strephon's Eye escapes,
> Here Pettycoats in frowzy Heaps;
> Nor be the Handkerchiefs forgot
> All varnish'd o'er with Snuff and Snot.
> The Stockings, why shou'd I expose,
> Stain'd with the Marks of stinking Toes; (ll. 58–71)

Strephon sees Celia's bodily discharge through an artist's eyes, observantly attuned to its arrangement, texture and appearance. The words "compound," "counterfeit," "varnished," "stained," and later "disguise," reveal that Strephon's catalogue of filth has been carefully composed for artistic effect. His gaze actively preserves what has been discarded ("nor be the handkerchiefs forgot"), collecting and framing the picture into an aesthetic whole ("no object Strephon's eye escapes"). Thus, the "paste of composition rare" that clogs her combs, the "nasty compound of all hues" in her basin, handkerchiefs "all varnished o'er with snuff and snot," and the "rings and hinges counterfeit" on the chamber pot (later in the poem), all explicitly invoke the imagery of Shakespeare's sonnets, memorializing effluence as though it formed part of the beloved's charms. (Think, for example, of the "sable curls all silver'd o'er with white," or the phrases "sweet hue," "compound sweet," and "painted counterfeit" in the sonnets.)

The most poem's famous lines substitute Strephon's discovery of Celia's excrement for the anticipated lyric climax of rapturous praise at the sight of the beloved's body. Strephon displays his disgust at the climax moment at which the lyric speaker should confess his desire. As Strephon peers excitedly into Celia's chamber pot, Swift's parody makes it clear that one can be all too readily substituted for the other.

> Thus finishing his grand Survey,
> Disgusted Strephon stole away
> Repeating in his amorous Fits
> "Oh! Celia, Celia, Celia shits!" (ll. 115–18)

"Amorous fits" meshes perfectly with "Celia shits" – suggesting that amorous desire is as much at ease with the discovery of excrement as it would be with the unveiling of Celia's physical charms. His rapture trips along just as metrically whether it is filthy refuse or sensual delight under the speaker's gaze. And ghastly as the conclusion of Strephon's survey is, it hardly comes as a surprise, either to us or to the hero himself. After all, what else would follow from the word "fits" than the rhyme "shits"?

The idealizations of courtly lyric – the superfluities of praise, the excesses of rapture, the overwrought exclamations of delight – are ironically preserved in Swift's anti-erotic poem. In other words, Strephon's discovery of Celia's excretions does not block or forestall the language of courtly lyric, but can be incorporated very comfortably into the mode. This tells us something very interesting about effluence and excrement in literature: that it can be inflected with the same characteristics, and can have the same literary effect as the precious and desirable surpluses to which it is ostensibly opposed.

Crucially, Swift's brutal parody of an amorous lyric retains the style and structure of the implied original. The famous final couplet stabilizes Swift's dark poem through a resolution that glibly exchanges desirable and degraded matter: "Such Order from Confusion sprung, / Such gaudy Tulips rais'd from Dung" (ll. 143–4).

The substitution of disgust for enchantment, of bodily discharge for bodily perfection, reveals that literary representation has the peculiar capacity to make them exchangeable – and that this is precisely the danger of the literary mode. Swift's poem is disturbing because the language of admiration collaborates *too readily* with the imagery of human filth. He aligns desire and disgust with such ease that we recoil from the implications of so ready an affinity.

Swift investigates further the exchangeable relationship between effluence and abundance in his political satires to articulate anger, anxiety and disenchantment with the political and literary culture of contemporary London and Dublin. We often think of Swift as a London writer, but he lived there for only four years – the greatest part of his life was spent as an Anglican cleric in Ireland, and in 1713 he was appointed Dean of St Patrick's, Dublin. Swift vacillated between attacking and defending Ireland – defense would always be tempered by the resentment he felt towards his countrymen (Rawson 2001).

The literal piles of filth and excrement that fill the streets in Swift's pamphlets are symbols of Ireland's deep economic and social degradation brought about through English abuse. His pamphlet *An Examination of Certain Abuses, Corruptions and Enormities, in the City of Dublin* was first published anonymously in 1732, and written in the assumed voice of a paranoid Whig pamphleteer. (Swift was a sworn enemy of Walpole's Whig government in Westminster, blaming it for the neglect and abuse suffered by Ireland.) In this pamphlet, Swift's ridiculous speaker warns that the poor who inhabit Dublin's streets – the vendors, muck-rakers, and street criers – are Tory and Jacobite propagandists, seeking to overthrow the Whigs and incite Catholic rebellion.

The speaker rants about the filth and effluence filling the passages, but determinedly refuses to accept them as symptoms of English neglect. Instead, he imagines that the dustmen who walk through Dublin shouting "dirt to carry out" are malignant Tories, baying for the eradication of filthy Whigs. The speaker goes so far as to speculate that the cry is no longer heard in London because "the true political Dirt [that is, the Tory government] is wholly removed and thrown on its proper dunghills, there to corrupt, and be no more heard of." In other words, the speaker is determined to allegorize the disposal of dirt, converting it into a narrative of political conflict and exclusion. So the cry "dirt to carry out," signals a Tory assault, a demand that the Whigs be eradicated. We realize, of course, that Swift's deranged Whig pamphleteer has not really exposed the "disposal tactics" of a covert band of Irish Tories in Dublin. And Swift is making a more barbed point, too: the speaker blithely overlooks the grim realities of the scene that he describes. Dublin is still plagued with filth and decay – while London is modernized and efficient. Swift's underlying suggestion here is that his speaker's paranoid obsession with the symbolic significance of filth evades his true political responsibility towards Ireland – to address its disintegration. The speaker ignores, in other words, the Irish deprivations that should really be the subject of polemical writing.

Swift's pamphleteer escalates in his manic detection of Tory plotting by asserting that the piles of sewage in Dublin's streets are signs of sedition:

> Every Person who walks the streets, must needs observe an immense number of human Excrements at the Doors and Steps of waste Houses, and at the sides of every dead Wall; for which the disaffected Party hath assigned a very false and malicious cause. They would have it that these Heaps were laid there privately by *British Fundamentalists*, to make the World believe, that our *Irish* vulgar do daily eat and drink; and, consequently, that the Clamour of Poverty among us, must be false; proceeding only from *Jacobites* and *Papists*. They would confirm this, by pretending to observe, that a *British Anus* being more narrowly perforated than one of our own Country; and many of these Excrements, upon a strict View appearing Copple-crowned, with a Point like a Cone or Pyramid, are easily distinguished from the *Hibernian*, which lie much flatter, and with less Continuity. I communicated this Conjecture to an eminent physician, who is well versed in such profound Speculations; and at my Request was pleased to make Trial with each of his fingers, by thrusting them into the Anus of several Persons of both Nations; and professed he could find no such Difference between them as those ill-disposed People allege. (pp. 167–8)

This is actually a very complex passage. The Whig speaker claims that the human excrement in the streets of Dublin is used by the Tories to undermine the Government. The Tories are said to *claim* that piles of English excrement are imported into Dublin by the Whigs to make it appear that rumors of Irish poverty are mere fabrication. Dung in the streets is a Whig tactic to dispel opposition to their government – so the Tories would have it, says the speaker. But, he assures us, these *really are* Irish excrements. His friend, a doctor, has proven it. The speaker damns himself with his own absurd narrative as he lampoons the insanity of the Tories who imagine that Whig conspirators would bring human excrement all the way from England. He indicts himself by confessing to having consulted a physician who earns his living by sniffing anuses.

Everything about the Whig speaker's claims is crazy. The Tories' purported claim about the Whigs is manifestly absurd, and the speaker's defensive attempt to find anatomical differences between English and Irish is deranged. After all (Swift implies), the differences in their health, their diet and prosperity are all too horribly self-evident. Not only is the speaker's investigation of excrement misguided – it is superfluous. And once again, the Whig speaker is unable to confront the reality of Dublin's street life, namely the "immense Number of human Excrements at the Doors and Steps of waste Houses, and at the Sides of every dead wall." Instead of recognizing impoverished natives, insanitary conditions and English neglect, the Whigs' "policy research" in Ireland takes the form of anal probes.

But in his determination to expose Tory malice and plotting, the pamphleteer glosses over the claim mentioned briefly at the start of the paragraph, that "these Heaps were laid there privately by British Fundamentalists, to make the World believe, that our Irish vulgar do daily eat and drink." (When in fact, Swift ironically points out, they are starving, and unlikely to produce excrement in any quantity at all.) But by rushing off to calculate whether they are English or Irish turds, the speaker fails to consider the implications of what is obviously a wry Tory joke. The Tories have been making trouble by rumoring mischievously that the streets of Dublin are blocked with Whiggish turds – which, in Swift's view, was more or less true. Swift's point is that, English or Irish, all shit looks the same – and Dublin is full of it. Beneath Swift's focal parody of a paranoid Whig speaker, Swift implies that Dublin is buried in excrement – it is a dumping ground for British waste-matter.

The scene is of course intended as an allegory of the state of Ireland: Dublin is saturated with surplus English imports, but stripped of its own resources by the Whig administration. Swift's point is that the Whigs will go to any lengths to make it look as though Ireland is flourishing – to give the Irish economy the appearance of prosperity, when really it is burdened by the detritus of English trade and commerce. Swift plays upon the fact that the most degraded surplus (Irish excrement) can have a symbolic value assigned to it that makes it look like something significant, worthy of examination and preservation.

The effect of Swift's satire is to strip the object of its professed significance – to leave mere material superfluity, mere remainder. The attack on his political enemies is devastating, as Swift converts political rhetoric back into excrement; he shows the Whigs' willful conversion of a grim practical reality into a site of imagined ideological warfare.

The inability to recognize filth for what it really is provides the satirical twist in Swift's political poem "Traulus" (1730), where excrement figures as slander directed at him by his political enemy. Here, the gratuitous filth smeared through Swift's poem enables him to articulate a perception that the linguistic abundance often characterizing praise can become indistinguishable from the overwrought rhetoric of abuse. The character of Traulus is Lord Allen, a Dublin Whig who attempted to have Swift prosecuted for his polemics against the English government in Ireland. Swift attacks Lord Allen violently because he sees him as a turn-coat – he had previously been Swift's friend and supporter. Traulus ("lisp-ing") rants wildly in a stream of worthless abuse, which, from the pen of an aggrieved Swift, is figured as a barrage of the turncoat's own ex-crement. Swift's charge in the poem is that excremental abuse takes the place of the equally mindless flow of political flattery that was hitherto laid at Swift's feet. Traulus is a flatterer turned critic, so mired in the voluminous production of slander and sycophancy that he can no longer distinguish between the two. In a description that suggests the curious affinity between insult and panegyric, Swift compares Traulus's hurling of abuse to a madman in Bedlam hospital who throws his feces at passers-by:

> Yet many a Wretch in Bedlam, knows,
> How to distinguish Friends from Foes;
> And tho' perhaps among the Rout,
> He wildly flings his Filth about,
> He still has Gratitude and Sap'ence,
> To spare the Folks that gave him Ha'pence
> Nor, in their Eyes at Random pisses,
> But turns aside like mad Ulysses:
> While Traulus all his Ordure scatters.
> To foul the Man he chiefly flatters. (ll. 30–9)

The jubilant imagery of this passage makes it clear that the language of waste often overlaps with that of value: the Rabelaisian hurling of excrement in the scene has the fulsome extravagance of celebration. The rhyme "among the *rout* / He wildly flings his *filth about*" conveys a scene of bonhomie and communal pleasure in the sharing of excrement; the deliberate closing rhyme "ordure scatters" and "chiefly flatters" shows how, in his anxiety to please, Traulus mistakenly confuses filth and flat-tery. Traulus's random pissing, which sets him apart from his mad brethren, marks him as one whose effusions cannot be directed or made satirically meaningful. The description of Traulus's uncontrolled filth-mongering (and, by implication, flattery), is set against the reassuring discipline of Swift's own lines, with the neat rhyming of pisses with Ulysses, of sap'ence with ha'pence. Swift's verse shows a mastery of jux-tapositions, the very capacity to draw fine distinctions that he suggests is missing from Traulus's own ravings. Although he describes excess,

Swift's writing is never formally incontinent. Swift uses the image of waste to pose the satirist's dilemma: how are the linguistic excesses which give satirical pleasure to be distinguished from, and elevated above, the rantings and railing which draw his satirical ire?

Swift argues ironically that, like a madman, Lord Allen confuses flattery with filth, to "foul the man he chiefly flatters." The point, of course, is that Allen has not confused the two – he knows that he is flinging abuse rather than praise at Swift. But Swift's ironic stance intentionally misrepresents Traulus's thought-processes. By arguing that Traulus's slanders are the act of a madman, Swift empties his opponent's libel of its political bite. This is possible precisely because of the peculiar symbolic overlap between the characteristics of plenitude and filth. The symbolic properties of effluence enable Swift to confect an account of his enemy's political dementia, claiming that the deluded Lord Allen can no longer distinguish between waste and value; filth looks to him the same as flattery. And at the same time, Swift can insinuate that the excesses of flattery have, themselves, an excremental quality (praise was never Swift's preferred mode).

But there is a final turn still to come. Paradoxically, Swift shows that it requires greater literary sophistication to confuse filth with flattery than to render them distinct. Swift's technical achievement here is to show that language can make wasteful abundance look like valuable plenitude. But you have to be as good a writer as Swift to manage this oscillation skillfully – to represent waste and value in parallel terms, ironically as a means of discriminating between them. Swift's madman in Bedlam is not up to the task, for in refusing to throw ordure at his benefactors he sees only that waste and value are distinct. It is laborious to unpack the complex ironies in Swift's joke that Traulus throws excrement by mistake for obsequious homage. This is precisely because crude mechanical labor is needed to pull apart the almost invisible oscillations between waste and value on which Swift's text turns. But undisturbed, the overlapping of radically different kinds of excess in the poem has a rationalizing, even a stabilizing effect on Swift's satiric voice.

The peculiar quality of filthy remainders, then, is that they can deceive the eye. Or at least, in the hands of a satirist like Swift, they can seem to do so. Refuse can be manipulated to look like a precious surplus. And the poetics of praise – deployed in the period to celebrate abundant prosperity – can be applied with disarming success to a lavish oversupply of filthy effluence. Conversely we recognize that those objects most highly prized can be stripped of their value to be represented as mere superfluity. This is how a skeptical attack on eighteenth-century optimism asserted itself; filth could make the celebration of value seem misguided. Most significantly, for writers as competitive as these, the image of the surplus could make other people's literary success look like dismal failure.

Pope and Grub Street

The problematic similitude between virtuosic satire and the scribblings of a hack: this was the issue Pope tackled in the *Dunciad* (1743), his copious, incontinent, brilliant satire on the London book trade. How was Pope to discriminate between the exuberant excesses of his satirical inventions and the copious effusions of the writings he disdained? The London of the *Dunciad* teems with a surplus of excrement and pollution – as if all the effluence in eighteenth-century writing had washed up to provide Pope with the setting he needed. In this excremental landscape the "dunce" writers whom Pope despises wallow pleasurably. Their taste for sewage confirms the excremental quality of their writings: copious, superfluous, unpleasant. But it is not only the Dunces who relish the filthy scene; Pope himself is attracted to it. Sewers energize the satirist and his enemies simultaneously. For the Dunces, this is because they mistake filth for cornucopia; for Pope, because he turns effluence into magical abundance again.

An over-supply of degraded matter is spread across every part of the *Dunciad*; it stands for Pope's perception of the corrupt, decaying world of Grub Street. The crudeness of the dunce-writers is complete: they urinate in the streets, slide about in puddles of excrement, swim through an open sewer, cover the streets of London with the garbage of their own unwanted writings. The poem is sprawling and dense, structured around a tale of the dramatist Colley Cibber's appointment as King of the Dunces by the presiding Goddess Dulness. Cibber's coronation is attended by a sequence of epic events that include triumphal games, a journey to the underworld, a series of prophetic visions and, finally, a theatrical apocalypse that destroys the whole created world of literature and culture. The final line of the *Dunciad* proclaims: "universal darkness buries all." But the pleasure of reading the poem comes from the fact that Pope's dunces are oblivious to the quality of their own filth and the extent of their degradation.

Indeed, part of Pope's joke is that he creates a radical juxtaposition between the exquisite neatness of his couplets and the ludicrous vulgarity of the dunces' behavior. He "tricks" the Dunces into unashamedly parading their crassness, while he writes with a sophistication that obscures the real content of the lines from unsophisticated readers. So at the beginning of book two it takes us a moment to realize that Pope's dunces are holding a pissing competition:

> First Osborne lean'd against his letter'd post;
> It rose, and labour'd to a curve at most.
> So Jove's bright bow displays its wat'ry round,
> (Sure sign, that no spectator shall be drown'd)
> A second effort brought but new disgrace,
> The wild Meander wash'd the Artist's face:
> Thus the small jett, which hasty hands unlock,
> Spirts in the gard'ner's eyes who turns the cock. (II: 171–8)

Pope uses the image of the pissing bookseller (Osborne) to describe his professional inadequacy: he labors weakly, and then succeeds only in spraying his own face. The "wild meander" and the "watery round" tell us what kind of writing attracts Osborne's attention. The brilliance of the passage lies in the way Pope uses the act of urination to generate two wholly new literary conceits. The curve of Osborne's urine reworks a Homeric description of the rainbow to create a metaphor for weakness rather than strength: like Jove's bow it offers protection, but only because it is too paltry to cause damage. Osborne's action thus parodies a grand classical epithet to generate a metaphor for literary impotence. And the pedestrian image of a faucet that sprays its user in the face is co-opted to produce an extraordinary account of writing that has been produced too quickly and carelessly. The conceit is utterly surprising, and exactly accurate. The dunces mistake their own urination for a triumphal game, while Pope transforms the figure of their bodily discharge into a virtuosic display of his own poetic skill.

A little later in the "games" sequence in book two, one of the foremost dunces, the bookseller Edmund Curll, races urgently toward the effigy of a mock-poet created by the goddess Dulness. As he rushes to seize the figure in a frenzy of misguided homage and admiration, he slips in an overflowing kennel, and becomes drenched in waste:

> Full in the middle way there stood a lake,
> Which Curl's Corinna chanc'd that morn to make:
> [. . .]
> Here fortun'd Curl to slide; loud shout the band,
> And Bernard! Bernard! rings thro' all the Strand. (II: 69–70, 73–4)

117

The excrement in which Curll collapses is composed of Pope's allegorical recreation of a real scandal. Curll had turned himself into an enemy after buying from a woman (who called herself "Corinna") a collection of Pope's private letters, which he then printed in 1729. In Pope's version of the story, Curll's unethical conduct has been allegorized into a septic puddle in which Curll predictably slips. The crowd turns against their favorite, and they cheer for the rival Lintot ("Bernard, Bernard"). The scene is intended as a mocking allegory of the struggle for literary pre-eminence in Grub Street: bad writers wade through the filth they have created, trying to overtake their fellow men-of-letters. But this is not the end of Pope's fable – nor the of the symbolic work done by excrement in the scene.

Curll springs to his feet again and beats his competitors back, winning the trophy though he is covered in sewage. It turns out that his drench in effluence has given Curll just the burst of power he needs:

> Renew'd by ordure's sympathetic force,
> As oil'd with magic juices for the course,
> Vig'rous he rises; from th'effluvia strong
> Imbibes new life, and scours and stinks along;
> Re-passes Lintot, vindicates the race,
> Nor heeds the brown dishonours of his face. (II: 103–8)

Curll takes the ordure he has inhaled for a magically restorative potion. And indeed it does appear to have "sympathetic force," since he "rises vigorously" and beats his rival Lintot to the prize. So filth, whether literal or allegorical, seems to generate success rather than shame. This is precisely Pope's point: the real energy and vigor of the book trade is derived from its continual production of literary effluence. In Grub Street, as in this passage, "effluvia" have a certain crude value. So much so, in fact, that the Dunces mistake their "brown dishonours" for marks of real triumph – they lack the discrimination to distinguish the two. The episode plays on the deceptive overlap between filth and splendor – marked as they are by a shared abundance – which causes the dunces to believe their writings have significance. But for Pope the imagery of effluence, or remaindered matter, allows him to distinguish crude popular celebrity from real literary value. He shows that in Grub Street the two can appear to be synonymous – and that the dunces are hopelessly unsophisticated, unable to see that hack scribbling is just so much literary garbage.

Since garbage can be made to look a lot like matter of real value, Pope has his chief-dunce Colley Cibber engage in an act of generous gift-giving that turns out merely to be a form of ritualized garbage disposal. In the first book of the poem, Cibber lights a commemorative pyre to the Goddess Dulness – in gratitude to her as his guide and protector in the writing of tedious drama. Cibber's tribute is attended with much pomp and ceremony, as he generously "bequeaths" his most prized writings to Dulness. In Cibber's eyes he is performing an act of truly luxurious expenditure, donating his own manuscripts to the Goddess:

> And thrice he lifted high the Birth-day brand,
> And thrice he dropt it from his quiv'ring hand;
> Then lights the structure, with averted eyes:
> The rowling smokes involve the sacrifice. (I: 245–8)

But as Cibber idiotically burns a pile of his own manuscripts, we recognize that his act of devotional generosity, of unconditional expenditure, is one and the same thing as the disposal of garbage. Cibber is doing Pope's job for him. In a gleeful "sacrificial burning" sequence the flames consign Cibber's plays to the dust-heap – just as Pope would have it:

> The op'ning clouds disclose each work by turn,
> Now flames the Cid, and now Perolla burns;
> Great Caesar roars, and hisses in the fires;
> King John in silence modestly expires (I: 249–52)

We have seen that material remnants are markers both of surplus and emptiness. In representations of unwanted matter, surplus paradoxically marks the place where value has been lost. So on the one hand, remainders are symptomatic of decay and degradation, and on the other hand they maintain a perverse affinity with abundance, with the valuable plenitude to which remnants always provide a shadow. When they are represented in literary texts, effluence and affluence can be made to look the same: unwanted remainders can be manipulated into looking like luxurious surplus – and commercial abundance can be turned back into degraded waste. This oscillation makes it possible for satirists like Dryden, Swift and Pope to show that narratives of gain can always be re-cast as in terms of loss – and to undermine the celebrations of prosperity and progress that threatened to dominate early eighteenth-century writing.

Sophie Gee

References and further reading

Allen, R. (1998) *The Moving Pageant: A Literary Source-Book on London Street Life*. London: Routledge.

Beier, A. L. and Finlay, R. (1986) *London 1500–1700: The Making of the Metropolis*. London and New York: Longman.

Boyle, F. (2000) *Swift as Nemesis: Modernity and its Satirist*. Stanford, Calif.: Stanford University Press.

Brown, L. (2001) *Fables of Modernity: Literature and Culture in the English Eighteenth Century*. Ithaca: Cornell University Press.

Brown, N. O. (1964) "The excremental vision," in E. L. Tuveson (ed.) *Swift, a Collection of Critical Essays*. Englewood Cliffs, NJ: Prentice-Hall.

Douglas, M. (1966) *Purity and Danger: An Analysis of Concepts of Pollution and Taboo*. New York: Praeger.

Earle, P. (1994) *A City Full of People: Men and Women of London 1650–1750*. London: Methuen.

Elias, N. (c.1994) *The Civilizing Process*, trans. Edmund Jephcott. Oxford and Cambridge, Mass.: Blackwell. (Original work published in English 1978. Oxford: Blackwell.)

Fabricant, C. (1999) "Speaking for the Irish nation: the Drapier, the Bishop and the problems of colonial representation," *English Literary History* 66(2): 337–72.

Johnson, S. (1781) "Life of Dryden," in *Lives of the Poets*, ed. G. B. Hill. Oxford: Clarendan Press, 1905.

Mandeville, B. (1714) *The Fable of the Bees, or, Private Vices, Public Benefits*. London.

Manley, L. (1995) *Literature and Culture in Early Modern London*. Cambridge and New York: Cambridge University Press.

Ogborn, M. (1998) *Spaces of Modernity: London's Geographies 1680–1780*. New York: Guilford Press.

Pollak, E. (1985) *The Poetics of Sexual Myth: Gender and Ideology in the Verse of Swift and Pope*. Chicago: University of Chicago Press.

Pope, A. (1963) *The Poems of Alexander Pope*, ed. J. Butt. London: Methuen.

Rawson, C. J. (1985) *Order From Confusion Sprung: Studies in Eighteenth-Century Literature from Swift to Cowper*. London and Boston: Allen and Unwin.

—— (2001) *God, Gulliver and Genocide: Barbarism and the European Imagination, 1492–1945*. Oxford and New York: Oxford University Press.

Rogers, P. (1972) *Grub Street: Studies in a Subculture*. London: Methuen.

Stallybrass, P. and White, A. (1986) *The Politics and Poetics of Transgression*. London: Methuen.

Twyning, J. (1998) *London Dispossessed: Literature and Social Space in the Early Modern City*. Basingstoke: Macmillan; New York: St Martin's Press.

Wall, C. (1998) *The Literary and Cultural Spaces of Restoration London*. Cambridge and New York: Cambridge University Press.

Chapter 6

The Novel

Novels in the World of Moving Goods

Deidre Shauna Lynch

In 1775 Georg Christoph Lichtenberg declared himself disappointed with the novels of his native Germany. He didn't blame German novelists for this record of underachievement. Instead, he faulted his compatriots' underdevelopment of their transportation systems. For Lichtenberg, England alone represented a home-base suitable for aspiring novelists, because England alone boasted a well-developed system of post roads and speedy mail and coaches. Novels set in England practically organized themselves. It was that easy, Lichtenberg claimed, for the novelists of that nation to get their characters in motion and in touch with one another. On the other hand, "a man who wants to write a German novel hardly knows how he'll get his characters together or the narrative knotted" (Lichtenberg 1775: 223; my translation).

The syllabus of novels Lichtenberg might have consulted is easy to reconstruct. It likely includes such familiar prototypes for the road movie as Henry Fielding's *Tom Jones* (1749) and Tobias Smollett's *Roderick Random* (1748). The journey taking Samuel Richardson's heroine Clarissa hugger-mugger from her father's house may also be on Lichtenberg's mind. (He complains that, given the state of the German roads, a German father could overtake a runaway daughter and forestall a would-be novelist's narrative altogether.) But I begin with Lichtenberg's somewhat tongue-in-cheek exercise in technological determinism because it also offers an *alternative* to those familiar accounts of the British novel's eighteenth-century genesis in which Fielding, Smollett, Richardson, along with their forerunner Defoe, have played leading roles: accounts that by and large have allied the advent of the genre with the progress of individualism and yoked the genre's development to a history of the self. "Über den deutschen Roman," composed after the author's visit to England, gets passionate about the transportation networks that conveyed individuals, goods, letters, and news across and around that country. Taught to value the early novel for the nascent "realism" that will give readers an insider's view of the depths of unique individuals, we are likely to find such enthusiasms puzzling.

Since the Romantic era, when it first was elevated as a type of literature and endowed with a canon and history of its own, the novel has been described as the genre that gives voice to private psychology. In novels, selfhood is supposed to find its authentic utterance. The critic William Hazlitt in an 1819 lecture on "the English novelists" had the genre's history begin with *Don Quixote* (1605) on the grounds that the fiction of Cervantes (a naturalized Englishman in Hazlitt's book) was the first in which the characters were "strictly individuals, [and] do not so much belong to, as form a class by themselves"; Cervantes's characters, Hazlitt added, were "never lost in the crowd" (1819: 216–17). When Ian Watt granted pride of place in *The Rise of the Novel* (1957) to *Robinson Crusoe* (1719), similar reasoning might well have guided his selection. There was, after all, little risk that Defoe's solitary castaway could end up indistinguishable in a crowd. And Watt might easily have said of Defoe's protagonists what Hazlitt had said of Cervantes's: their "actions and manners", he asserted, "do not arise out of the actions and manners of those around them, or the station of life in which they are placed, but out of the peculiar dispositions of the persons themselves" (1819: 217).

In fact, "individual" remains critics' term of choice for the people populating those fictions they call novels. Contemporary critics may be more inclined than their predecessors to construe the deep "individuality" of a Crusoe or a Clarissa as an ideological effect. They may consider novels' dramatizing of the misfit between the individual and social categories an ideological ruse that makes the form's realism that much more potent an instrument of social control. Much current scholarship on novels preserves, however, the venerable evaluative scheme, established over the course of the nineteenth century, in which works of fiction which are deemed insufficient in their attention to "the peculiar dispositions of the persons" either represent something more hide-bound or primitive than novels – that is, romances – or represent something more vulgar – that is, mass culture. Yet one encounters few intimations of that scheme when Lichtenberg discusses the modernity of eighteenth-century English fiction. There are few traces, either, of the polarities between "middle class" and "aristocratic," "progressive" and "conservative," and "individualism" and "tradition" that literary historians since the nineteenth century have used to chart English novels' eighteenth-century overthrow of romances. For Lichtenberg, the social division those polarities register is not the key that unlocks literary history. Social motion is. Lichtenberg associates novels with the mechanisms that keep society's wheels turning: with the new channels of communication and commercial exchange that, as many observers claimed, had enabled Hanoverian Britain to leave behind the seventeenth century's political turbulence and to become, by 1775, Europe's historical prototype of the stable state.

My essay seeks to reframe the history of novels by resituating eighteenth-century fictions in the world of moving goods evoked in Lichtenberg's essay. Lichtenberg is a representative figure in assessing novels' characters not so much as *individuals*, but rather, first and foremost, as transients who are either shuttled themselves from one location to another or whose correspondence is. As his example suggests, audiences in the eighteenth century might well have used their fiction to make a new kind of society and social life make sense. Through the arts of narration, novels could supply readers imaginative purchase on the to and fro of bodies in motion: modern bodies, unmoored from the traditional corporate identities associated with the Guilds, Church, and Court, and yet, in new ways, meeting as buyers and sellers, colliding as fellow travelers, and, thanks to print technology's capacity to bridge geographical and social distances, convening as a "public." To analyze their staging of social motion, my essay contends, is to realize that novels of this period were as much associated with an emergent idiom of transport, transaction, commercial traffic and social mixing as they were with an idiom for the representation of separate selves.

This corresponds to what the historian J. G. A. Pocock has said about the social psychology Britons developed as they learned, over the course of the eighteenth century, to live in a commercial society founded on the exchange of mobile property. The virtuous independence prized in the landed gentleman was in some measure effaced then, Pocock asserts, by the virtues ascribed to the man of trade, who did depend on others, who made his living by sympathetically and speculatively anticipating other people's desires, and who was adept accordingly at negotiating the "increasingly transactional universe" of his commercial society. Commerce functioned to enrich and refine human personality because it created the conditions for "multiplying relationships, with both things and persons" (Pocock 1985: 48–9). Pocock does not examine how their transactions with fictions similarly multiplied the relationships in which eighteenth-century people were involved. But this was another way, in addition to their depictions of social worlds in motion, in which novels of eighteenth-century Britain promoted what Pocock calls "modes of consciousness suited to a world of moving objects" (1985: 109). Her passions "moved" by her reading matter, even a solitary reader might participate in the transactional universe of modern sociability. She might feel as if she were reaching out and touching someone, as a telephone company might put it, even while she sat still.

In coordinating these bonds between real and imagined personages, novels confirmed their status as *moving writing* – a term I take as my organizing rubric throughout this essay. Nicely equivocal, this term directs attention, for a start, to how throughout the century novels were often understood in conjunction with new places of public assembly such as urban coffeehouses and parks, and alongside newspapers, missives travelling through the postal system, and the social sciences that were starting to be taught in the Scottish universities (see also Chapter 3 PUB-LIC AND PRIVATE). Novels too formed a part of the culture's new machinery of interconnectedness and intersubjectivity. In novels and through novels, civil societies were generated and regenerated as individual persons came (in the 1767 words of philosopher Adam Ferguson) to "move with the crowd" (quoted in Burchell 1991: 136). In 1704 Daniel Defoe wrote, exultantly, that, whereas "Preaching of Sermons is Speaking to a few of Mankind," "Printing of Books is Talking to the whole World" (Preface to *The Storm*). My use of the rubric "moving writing" in the last section of this essay is meant to register how often eighteenth-century people followed Defoe's lead when they assessed the novelty of their novels, the first literary form to emerge into cultural centrality in the medium of print, and the first to exploit the capacities for the long-distance communication of the passions and the catalyzing of communities that this medium provided.

But first, starting in the two sections that follow, I will use the rubric "moving writing" in another sense: to emphasize that eighteenth-century novels were themselves mobile property. They were objects that traveled. They were distinctive for the ease with which they could be dislodged from origins. During the boom-market decades of the last third of the century particularly, novels moved off the shelves of Britain's circulating libraries with a speed that betokened their emphatic marketability. But by then, in fact, the novel had for almost a hundred years been associated with a lucrative circulation that propelled books around the market and across social frontiers – and, as we shall see, across the geopolitical boundaries defining nations as well. In the eighteenth-century experience of the novel, these texts appear to be disporting themselves with all comers. They appear to partake of the promiscuity that the Marxist theorist Walter Benjamin ascribes to the commodity: a capacity for sympathy enabling it, Benjamin asserts, "to see in everyone the buyer in whose hand and house it wants to nestle" (1973: 55).

Perhaps the unease that could be aroused by fictions' promiscuous movement from hand to hand (as by their movement from land to land) explains the staying power of the contrasting, post-Romantic conception of the novel as the expression of the individual inner life. To reattach novels to an origin in this manner, to make them "expressive" of something lying too deep for words, to correlate their realism with the middle class's individualism, domesticity, and Protestant habits of introspection, and to thus make "the self . . . the final signified of the English novel," can be, in effect, means of taking the genre out of circulation (Warner 1998: 27). This understanding brings novels back *home*, removing them from eighteenth-century culture's places of exchange and assembly. It also reinforces assertions about the Englishness of the English novel. Within that post-Romantic critical framework, novels appear predisposed to domestic realism and the exploration of private spaces and psychological depths. They appear a "barrier" to "transculturation" rather than its "agent" (Aravamudan 1999: 10). I focus on moving writings and moving goods in the eighteenth century so as to restore to view an alternative set of possibilities.

Portability: Transports of the Novel

To describe the eighteenth-century novel not just as narrating motion (the adventures befalling characters on the road), but also as a moving object itself, is to notice again what period commentators noticed about their reading matter. Of course, for much of the eighteenth century the term "novel" lacked the definitional stability that it would eventually acquire in nineteenth-century literary histories and twentieth-century classrooms. Contemporaries of Defoe, Richardson, and Fielding may have agreed that these writers had broken with prevailing conventions, may have detected in the plausible feel of a work like *Crusoe* a new "Manner of . . . telling a Lie" that might "make it a Truth" (Gildon 1719a: 33), or may have acknowledged the novelty of the new species of writing inaugurated in Fielding's "comic epics." Still, Watt's canonical trio of "novelists" seldom anticipate Watt's own schemes for differentiating their modern novels from pre-modern romances (not surprisingly, since these three would have felt displeased at being assigned to the same genre, accounts of their joint contribution to that genre's "rise" notwithstanding). "Novel" is not a label any one of them selects for his works. Indeed, on the infrequent occasions when they ventured generalizations about the very diverse roster of fictions they encountered, their contemporaries appear to have been preoccupied with the shared physical format of the books that gave those fictions material form and with the distinctive tempo of the reading that those fictions elicited. Arguably, what was rising in the early eighteenth century, in early eighteenth-century eyes, was not so much a distinctively *novelistic* fiction as a distinctively *portable* fiction.

For the first half of the century, the term "novel" often indicated something about a narrative's length. For many commentators, that is, the distinction between "novel" and "romance" pivoted on questions of quantity (numbers of pages) rather than quality, on form rather than content. "Novel" often served then as a label for a "small tale" (as for Samuel Johnson in his 1755 *Dictionary* (Johnson 1755, s.v. "novel")), or a "little gallant history . . . a kind of abbreviation of a Romance" (as for Lord Chesterfield, in a letter written c.1740–1 (Williams 1970: 100)). Our experience of the century's novels is different, in part thanks to the accidents of canon-formation: for modern-day readers of behemoths such as *Tom Jones* or *Clarissa*, aghast at the time these canonical blockbusters demand, the word "small" does not spring readily to mind. But it should be noted that over the course of the century, even as more people agreed to distinguish the novel from the romance on the grounds that the former was more probable, and more attuned to familiar life, than the latter, "novel" retained its association with the "small": booksellers had, in the interval, taught the patrons of book shops and circulating libraries to correlate content with physical format. Increasingly, the roomier and costlier formats for publication were reserved by booksellers for discourses – divinity, for instance – making loftier cultural claims than fiction did. Readers could count, accordingly, on fictions reaching them in small packages, either as octavo-sized or duodecimo-sized volumes (about 5 × 8 inches or 3 × 6 inches). Fiction was by and large experienced as something one might secret in a pocket and carry on one's person (see Warner 1998: 133).

That enhanced portability made "novels" suitable for a newly busy world in which people and things had to travel light. (Even the behemoth works I mentioned above accommodated themselves to this world's demands: *Clarissa* originally comprised seven duodecimo volumes;

Tom Jones's saga was distributed across six.) After 1695, the lapsing of the last of the Licensing Acts the Crown had used to regulate the press ushered in a rapid expansion of the printing trades. Simultaneously, a series of highly entertaining political controversies between, variously, Whigs and Tories, High Church men and Low Church men, and the monarchs' rival favorites fired literate people's demand for reading matter: the age of public opinion had begun (see Chapter 3 PUBLIC AND PRIVATE). Shaped by these developments, the taste of the times, commentators agreed, involved not just an appetite for the freshest news delivered in regular, rapid installments (the first daily newspaper began in 1702), but also an appetite for fictions that would likewise be delivered according to an equally accelerated schedule. The consensus was that fictions in small format and fictions that might be rapidly written, produced, consumed, and replaced could best accommodate the demands of restive English readers. According to the preface to Delarivier Manley's *The Secret History of Queen Zarah* (a text devoted to leaking and to fictionalizing the latest Court scandals), *romances*, whose publication customarily demanded a "Prodigious Number of Volumes," had lately been "cry'd down" (Williams 1970: 33); "little histories" were nowadays "more agreeable to the Brisk and Impetuous Humour of the English," who "no sooner begin a Book, but they desire to see the End of it" (Williams 1970: 33). Sir Roger de Whimsey, the persona adopted by the writer Charles Gildon in his grab-bag of scandal, advice, and social portraiture, *The Post-Man Robb'd of his Mail* (1719b), partakes of that humor. Whimsey establishes his qualifications for authoring by asserting that "you will not find in my Study many Folios; . . . I deal all in Abridgements." He touts "this mighty Inclination of mine to [a] short Sort of Writing" (Gildon 1719b: xii; xiii).

Any history of the histories of novels needs to acknowledge how often early eighteenth-century novelists defined their projects by instancing such inclinations and how often those definitions depended on a contrast between modern speed and the ostensibly unhurried pace at which reading and writing had proceeded back in the seventeenth century. Take, for instance, Defoe's opening to *A Journal of the Plague Year* (1722), a narrative that is as much about the spread of information as the communication of disease. On his first page, the narrator of *A Journal* asserts that "We had no such thing as printed newspapers in those days to spread rumours and reports"; "things did not spread instantly over the whole nation, as they do now" (1722/2003: 3). Statements in this style – identifying innovation and acceleration – told readers what to expect from contemporary writing.

Until recently, novel studies tended to represent eighteenth-century fictions as the class property of a nascent "middle class": of newly literate, progressive people eager to move out of the ranks in which they were born and leave literary traditions behind them. Recent studies by Ros Ballaster and Kathryn King of how Tory women such as Manley and Jane Barker used fiction to undermine the Revolution settlement of 1688 and to model a female allegiance to the deposed Stuart kings have made such accounts less tenable. Nowadays we take seriously early eighteenth-century culture's proclivity for storylines that restore exiles to their birthrights. Old-fashioned romance plotting, it turns out, shaped many of the works we call novels. But the conclusions we might draw about the political charge of that romance plotting are complicated by the evidence that writers and booksellers of all political stripes agreed that the times demanded books built for speed.

There was a second way in which the eighteenth-century experience of the novel entailed an experience of portability. At the start of this period fiction typically presented itself as a well-traveled, globe-trotting sort of writing. Novels' Englishness was, precisely, neither here nor there. (That Englishness is, however, presupposed in *The Rise of the Novel*, where Watt, influentially, finds French novelists "too stylish to be authentic" (1957: 30).) Fiction represented its audience (according to a courtly formulation found in several seventeenth- and early eighteenth-century prefaces) as hosts who would offer foot-sore heroes and heroines hospitable havens and who would obtain their guests' stories in exchange. The "Beauties of Great Britain" to whom a 1694 English translation of *Amadis of Greece* is dedicated are told that "In your soft Arms and silken Laps [Amadis] hopes to find that Repose, he has so long in vain been seeking thro' so many . . . Adventures" (quoted in McMurran 2002: 69 n. 23). The dedication prefacing Delarivier Manley's *The New Atalantis* (1709) – a text identified on its title-page as an English translation of the third edition of a French translation of an Italian original – works similarly. It traces the chain of events that brought these Italian-speaking "adventures" on their "visit" to "the court of Great Britain" (Manley 1709/1991: 3).

Furthermore, from Pierre-Daniel Huet's 1670 treatise *Traité de l'Origine des romans* (English translation 1715) to Clara Reeve's and John Moore's surveys of the "progress of romance" (1785 and 1797 respectively), the literary historian's primary subject was global migration: the travelling done not simply by certain, particularly mobile books, but by the art of fictitious narrative more generally. Within this syncretic style of criticism, fictions of all varieties – fables, allegories, the "novels" of antiquity and the novels of eighteenth-century Europe – were seen as linked by their potential for "transmission from one part of the world to another and from one language to another" (McMurran 2002: 57; see Warner 1998: 20). However dissimilar, they were linked by a long history of gregarious border crossing.

A commonplace of eighteenth-century literary histories held that fiction, like spice, was a product native to the fertile soil of the Orient. That claim exploits (as do the immensely popular Oriental tales of the period) associations linking the East, mystery, leisure, and pleasure. But this identification of the Orient and imaginative narration was arguably shaped to an even greater extent by the venerable notion of the *translatio imperii et studii*. This paradigmatic understanding of how "empire" was transferred/translated over time and space represented "culture" as a process of cultivation that unfolded, east to west, through a sequence of military conquests and commercial and social exchanges. In this context, culture itself was a principle of *connection*.

This definition of "culture" suggests that the origins that have been so important to twentieth-century novel studies were, for earlier commentators, a less compelling topic than relocations. In a century in which French- and English-language books occupied the same cultural field, and in which books translated from French constituted a large segment of the British fiction market (claiming a market share hovering at between 15 and 30 percent until the French Revolution), translation and *translatio* alike shaped the reception of the texts we know as the British novels (McMurran 2002: 68 n. 7). (Of course, books whose authors, like Manley on the title page of *The New Atalantis*, mischievously presented themselves *as* translators enjoyed a sizeable market share as well.) And prior to the nationalization of literature, and before ideas about originality had made it necessary to differentiate between authoring a text and translating one, translation would not imply the notions of "loss" that dominate discussions of inter-cultural exchange at present (McMurran 2002: 57).

Indeed, the garrulous prefaces and dedications that frame many novels published in the Restoration and first few decades of the eighteenth century go out of their way to call attention to the circuitousness of the journeys that these stories have taken before finding a lodging with English readers. They thus *emphasize* how their national origins are likely to have got mislaid along the way. *The New Atalantis* is typical in flaunting its status as a (pseudo) translation of a (pseudo) translation. It advertises its distance from a source. That demotion of points of origin and promotion of international exchange also shape some of the moves Aphra

Behn makes in *Oroonoko, or, the Royal Slave* (1688). From the outset, Behn takes pains to link the text that she is bringing to market (a text she casts as news of the New World and as, in a double sense, something "novel") to a trade in exotica shipped out from the American colonies to England. Of particular note is the passage in which Behn's narrator describes how the English trade with the Indians for the "habits" (clothes) that these natives of Surinam fashion for themselves of feathers. In ending with the narrator's assertion that "I had a Set of these [feathers] presented to me, and I gave 'em to the King's Theatre and it was the Dress of the *Indian Queen*, infinitely admir'd by Persons of Quality; and was unimitable" (1688/1973: 2), this passage ends by unsettling the reader. Up to the moment at which we resolve the passage's ambiguity – and settle whether the Indian Queen in question is a Londoner or an American, a costumed character on the Restoration stage who "imitates" an Indian or an Indian herself – this syntax leaves us at sea, drifting between the Old World and the New. This sentence's story of moving goods, of clothes re-making the woman, models on a small scale how notions about national provenance end up bracketed when these novels take advantage of permeable frontiers.

Writing the Story of Writing

Following the eighteenth century, after the entity known as "the English novel" had come to be extracted from the vast diversity of fictional practices that had engaged early modern literary criticism, it became harder to write the novel's history as a cosmopolitan story of a genre set loose from its moorings. It became harder to trace the story, to draw on the preface to Manley's *Queen Zarah*, of how nation after nation used its ingenuity "in improving Foreign Inventions" to "Naturalize" fiction upon its soil (Williams 1970: 45). The explanatory force that the category of the nation came to exert in accounts of culture represents one reason that this is so (see Chapter 12 Criticism). Under this dispensation, culture, to be authentic, must be home-grown. Another reason is that since the nineteenth century, discussions of novels have frequently been shaped by a metaphorics of voice. Hippolyte Taine's *History of English Literature* (1879) describes the novel's emergence in terms casting the genre, not as the writing or imprint, but as the voice, of the people. This "severe emanation of the middle class[,] welled up," "amidst the splendid corruption of high life," Taine asserts, "like the voice of a people buried underground" (quoted in Warner 1998: 27). Much theorizing about the nature of the novel has featured this charismatic storyline of vocal liberation, as Dorothy Hale and Ivan Kreilkamp each observe. The novel's achievement has often been said to lie in the way in which its realism lets characters *speak* for themselves.

Yet to downplay their written status and project onto novels our fantasies of what it would be like to enjoy unmediated communication with other people risks some wishful thinking. The linkage connecting novels to spoken words (personal utterance) tethers meaning to a fixed, unitary origin. It gives meaning a pedigree, in ways that, historically, have supported essentialist notions of personal identity and of national character. Writing has, since Socrates' day, been defined by its propensity for going astray: writing is what gets dislodged from its original context and recontextualized in new locales. However, the voice, by contrast, seems inseparable from the natural body and a single subject. Prior to the era of sound recording, it seems to model an immunity to the forces of dislocation and commercialization that propel texts into an impersonal marketplace.

Novel studies' metaphorics of voice cannot, however, do justice to the self-consciousness so many eighteenth-century texts display whenever they think about the distinctive opportunities (say, for anonymous utterance or for communication at a distance) that writing affords. Products of an age when, as Ogborn and Withers suggest (see Chapter 1 TRADE, TRAVEL, AND EMPIRE), "Each trade was inscribed in and surrounded by a network of writing," eighteenth-century novels do such thinking often. They are literary artifacts that shrewdly confront their own textual nature. Here we might reconsider the author whom Taine's *English Literature* (Warner 1998: 27) identifies as the realist tradition's first mouthpiece for the "voice of [the] people": Defoe. His *Journal of the Plague Year* presents the city of London as a set of surfaces plastered over with reading matter. "[I]t would fill a book," the narrator, H. F., claims, "to set down" the "doctors' bills and papers of . . . fellows, quacking and tampering in physick" which he saw affixed at street corners and the "posts of houses" (1722/2003: 31). The enormity of the task notwithstanding, Defoe appears to have aspired to re-materialize all this writing on the walls, in the form of so much writing on his pages (see Figure 6.1).

He appears to have aspired, similarly, to use H. F.'s story of the plague to demonstrate that governing London or any political body also means governing writing. Hence H. F.'s interest in the weekly bills of mortality, which are written up in such a way, he observes, as to disguise the spread of the epidemic. Hence his interest in the inscriptions that are chalked on the doors of houses that have been visited by the contagion, and which, he observes, end up being forged by householders who wish to flout the magistrates' regulations.

In the zeal with which it transcribes those writings, *A Journal* confirms eighteenth-century fictions' readiness to make written text both their medium *and* their subject matter. Indeed, this reflexivity links the Defoe of *A Journal* to a host of contemporaries and successors. Jane Barker – who politically speaking represents Defoe's antithesis – is a contemporary especially worth considering. In Barker's last two published novels, we see her exploring the idea of language that is front and center in a culture shaped by the technology of movable type – the idea of language as a concatenation of discrete signs that are arrayed side-by-side on the page and that, so arrayed, add up to more than the sum of their parts. We see her using this idea as a resource with which to conceptualize how human beings come to "compose" a society. Barker's earlier novel, *Love Intrigues* (1713), presents itself as the record of the sad life-story that one woman, the betrayed Galesia, shares with another as they take their morning walk among the groves of St Germain-in-Laye (the seat of the deposed James II, whose exile in France Barker had shared during the 1690s). But an altogether *different* pretext explains the existence of *A Patch-Work Screen for Ladies* (1723) and *The Lining of the Patch Work Screen* (1726). Those novels collect the "pieces of Romances, Poems, Love-Letters, and the like" (Barker 1723/1997: 74) that are all that Galesia (a rootless wayfarer following her return to England) finds in her baggage when she looks for scraps to contribute to a screen her lady-patroness is stitching together. Those later texts originate, then, not in an act of oral storytelling, but in other, transcribed texts. And the author's art is associated accordingly less with invention or self-expression than with the task of selecting these second-hand "pieces," transcribing them into new contexts, and "rang[ing] and mix[ing]" them "in due Order" (p. 74). Barker implies that, by virtue of their hodge-podge qualities, her patchwork novels have the power to lay social schism to rest and to remake social contention as aesthetic pattern. As miscellanies that offer something to everyone, and that anyone in funds might buy, they draw a "Set of Ladies together," "Whigs and Tories, High-Church and Low-Church," whose "Sentiments are as differently matched as the patches" in the ladies' own sewing baskets (p. 52).

The patchwork novels do not disguise Barker's royalist nostalgia. But Barker's books also look ahead. They forecast, for instance, how, later in the century, novels in letters would likewise present themselves as the means by which a group might experience both its cohesion and its

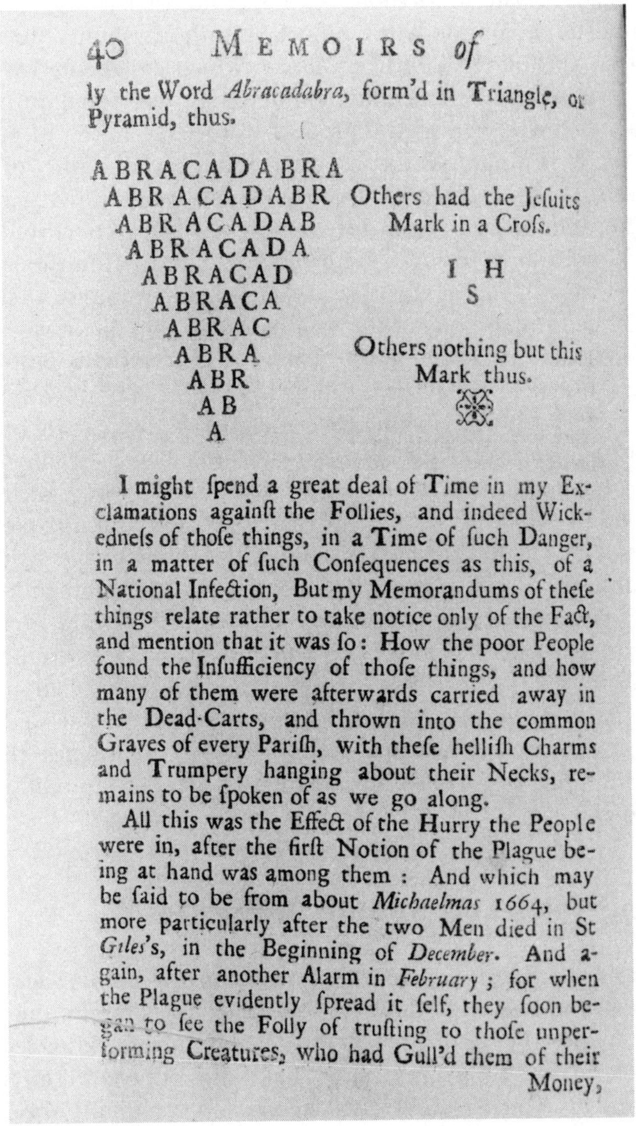

40   MEMOIRS *of*

ly the Word *Abracadabra*, form'd in Triangle, or
Pyramid, thus.

```
ABRACADABRA
ABRACADABR   Others had the Jesuits
ABRACADAB    Mark in a Crofs.
ABRACADA
ABRACAD         I  H
ABRACA            S
ABRAC
ABRA         Others nothing but this
ABR             Mark thus.
AB                 
A
```

I might fpend a great deal of Time in my Exclamations againft the Follies, and indeed Wick-
ednefs of thofe things, in a Time of fuch Danger,
in a matter of fuch Confequences as this, of a
National Infection, But my Memorandums of thefe
things relate rather to take notice only of the Fact,
and mention that it was fo: How the poor People
found the Infufficiency of thofe things, and how
many of them were afterwards carried away in
the Dead-Carts, and thrown into the common
Graves of every Parifh, with thefe hellifh Charms
and Trumpery hanging about their Necks, remains to be fpoken of as we go along.

All this was the Effect of the Hurry the People
were in, after the firft Notion of the Plague being at hand was among them : And which may
be faid to be from about *Michaelmas* 1664, but
more particularly after the two Men died in St
Giles's, in the Beginning of *December*. And a-
gain, after another Alarm in *February* ; for when
the Plague evidently fpread it felf, they foon began to fee the Folly of trufting to thofe unper-
forming Creatures, who had Gull'd them of their
Money,

Figure 6.1 Page 40 from the first edition (London 1722) of Daniel Defoe's
A Journal of the Plague Year. Registering Defoe's interest in communications
systems, the narrator here transcribes specimens of the typographical productions
of 1665. This recreation of the paper amulets Londoners wore to ward off the
plague simulates the very look of the letters forming the amulets' magic words.
Courtesy, The Lilly Library, Indiana University, Bloomington, Indiana.

variety. Barker's patchwork mode of composition anticipates, for instance, the pluralistic, accommodating model of authority built into the very form of an epistolary work like *Clarissa*, which designedly leaves it an open question whether meaning embodies an individual author's private intent or whether, as the product of the free-for-all of public debate, it registers a hard-won consensus among a community of readers. And, even though eighteenth-century Britons were known across Europe as an opinionated lot, it does appear that they concurred in very much liking to have feelings. With the popularization in the latter part of the century of moral theories of sympathetic response that located the sensitive human body at the foundation of civil life, novels became increasingly deft at exploiting the "cohesive fiction that we can actually feel one another's pain" (Lewis 1998: 104). Epistolary novels exploited this cohesive fiction by making each member of the reading public feel as though she were pooling her tears with those being shed by the other readers of a heroine's letters – both those readers who, as characters, reside within the book and, by an easy extension, those readers residing outside it. This technique for making the printed page a site of virtual communion and community is one ruse that eighteenth-century novelists developed so as "to disguise the phenomenology of a process that starts with one person writing and ends with one-by-one reading" (Hunter 1990: 238). In elaborating this ruse, epistolary fiction may be said to have demonstrated long ago a premise central to Benedict Anderson's account of modern nation-building, the premise that modern communities are *written* into being, that nations are manufactured from paper.

Moving Tales and Mobile Properties

Taking that demonstration seriously means giving up the idea that the circulation and commercialization of written texts betray the authenticity of an already existing people. Instead, it means acknowledging, in the very fact that writing goes astray, that it slips out of authorized hands, the means by which societies will be created. Certainly, the heroines at the center of the later eighteenth century's lachrymose cult of vulnerable femininity are menaced, the moment that they participate in the converse of the pen, by the possibility that their letters – which can be forged or stolen and copied and handed about – may expose them. (It is in this way that, stealing the show from the characters, letters themselves become the prime movers of plot.) When the heroine of a novel leaves a paper trail, she suffers. But it almost always happens that the same fiction that demonstrates the menace that a tell-tale correspondence poses to a young woman also *extends* that indiscretion about her private goings-on. After all, in so far as a printed text (as Defoe declared) represents a way of "talking to the whole World," it broadcasts those goings-on to all and sundry. But extending that indiscretion also means redeeming it: making private language public/published is, finally, according to the governing fiction of the genre, a means of securing the common weal. The heroine of Frances Brooke's 1777 *The Excursion* appears delightfully aware that this is the modus operandi of sentimental fiction. When Maria learns that she has indiscreetly written to a man who is engaged to be married to another, she weeps over the blow to her romantic hopes, but takes heart when it occurs to her that the "admirable writing" she had produced for the occasion need not be "thrown away": the narrator who rather archly recounts her adventures tells us that Maria "determined to insert the letter in her next novel" (1777/1997: 135–6).

There is a complementary story to be told here about the reflections on written language and its mechanical duplication that women writers inscribe within their works: reflections on how women, excluded en masse from the period's arenas of public oratory, physically vulnerable when visiting its sites of public assembly, might be enfranchised by print culture and thrive within the virtual, disembodied communities it engendered. As Ros Ballaster notes, commenting on the didactic strain in eighteenth-century Englishwomen's writings, the same fictions that school their heroines in the limits of their freedom often, as compensation, covertly document "the secret empowerment of women through a language free from the perils of the spoken word" (2000: 198). Apparently, women writers recognized early that print publication had altered the phenomenology of reading. This suggests a way of assessing, for instance, their preoccupation with characters who send anonymous letters and serve, under cover, as heroines' invisible monitors or with characters who lead an underground existence (like the many women, Haywood's eponymous *The British Recluse* (1726) included, who begin playing their parts in a novel's world only after they have feigned their own deaths). These figures might represent so many signs of female writers' recognition of the fact that, while the audience of mass print is out of range of the author's observation, the converse is also true: the author too eludes scrutiny. Writing is what communicates in the *absence* of an author. It follows that there may be little pay-off in searching for self-expression ("a female voice") within the works of eighteenth-century women. Ballaster proposes instead that we recognize that authorship is figured in works from Behn's to Austen's, not in personal terms, but as "the endless transaction, exchange, and dispossession of selfhood in the service of the public" (Ballaster 2000: 201; see also Gallagher 1994). "Selfhood" conceptualized like this resembles the moving goods circulating in the eighteenth-century marketplace, as well as the letters travelling along the post roads. It likewise represents the instrument of a kind of networking.

Attending to the story about writing encoded in eighteenth-century novels' stories about persons not only retrieves from the critical margins works by eighteenth-century women. It also, I've suggested, brings to the fore the social orientation of novels produced by both genders: the fact that the novelists' commitment to printed text represented a commitment to a medium that was perceived, wishfully or not, to be something more than an addition to the social stage; the fact that people ascribed to print – and especially printed fictions – the power to actively constitute social relations. One other way to examine how works of writing came to be credited for that social work is to consider the resemblance (an inauspicious one, if you correlate aesthetic value and formal unity) that links the novels of the eighteenth century to the chief contemporary form of patchwork, the anthology. Of course, epistolary novels, which collect choice pieces of writing by different hands and which declare themselves the works not of authors, but of editors, make that resemblance conspicuous. We might think here about how Richardson, self-declared "editor" of three "collections" of letters, assumed that anthologizing role in earnest when he compiled *A Collection of the Moral and Instructive Sentiments, Maxims, Cautions, and Reflexions contained in the histories of Pamela, Clarissa, and Sir Charles Grandison*: that 1755 publication rendered Richardson, for all intents and purposes, his own middleman, someone who had employed himself to mediate the relations between his self and the public. But even *Tom Jones*, a third-person narration that since Fielding's day has been celebrated for the perfect design of its plot, allies novel-writing with the keeping of a commonplace book dedicated to the transcribed words of others. That narrator defends his freedom to quote and declares the writings of the Ancients "a rich Common, where every Person . . . hath a free right to fatten his Muse" (Fielding 1749/1973: 474).

These examples suggest, as did the examples from Barker's patchwork earlier, just how enthusiastic eighteenth-century novelists were about the portability enabling written words to be conveyanced from book to book and about the materiality rendering those words collectibles that novelist-collectors might arrange as they pleased. They suggest, too, how little claim any one novel might have to be "itself" in this century, when, after all, tolerance for the episodic was higher than it is now. The boundaries of an eighteenth-century text could be very porous. But the open-door policy adopted by so many novelists might indicate, in addition, the *social* agenda that novels shared with the forerunners to the anthology, the eighteenth century's miscellanies and magazines. This agenda, which period miscellanies declared outright when they called themselves "asylums" or "hospitals" for "fugitives," or compared themselves to sites such as Hyde Park and the New Exchange, involves understanding the text as a place of social mixing, a virtual site of urban assembly (Benedict 1996: 11, 51). As they maximize print's capacities for juxtaposition and display, those producing texts in this mode sponsor the culture's conversation and conviviality. Barker and Defoe have already helped us see the aspects of the typographical climate turned to account by anthologists, novelists, and those who conflate the two roles. The page, like the book in which (in tandem with its fellows) it is bound, is to be understood as a scene in which discrete blocks of text rub elbows, and heterogeneous styles, topics, and even authors can mingle. Within these settings, difference may be both preserved and contained.

To trace how the eighteenth-century novel hosts such mingling and binding and undertakes this typographical management of difference is to see again how it set out to be a central player in the century's formation of a new sphere of civility. How would our readings change if we began to think of novels as both representing *and* providing those formative occasions of social motion that Lord Shaftesbury described in 1711: occasions when "we polish one another, and rub off our corners and rough sides by a sort of amicable collision" (1711/1999: 31)? In concluding I want to focus my remarks on that change on letters, since our discussions of their centrality to the fictional enterprise seldom refer to the period's new spaces of sociability, not even the space of the anthology. (This despite the fact that letters seem half-way toward being anthology pieces already – ready pickings for miscellany-makers.) Instead, novelists' love affair with the epistolary has been adduced as evidence of their commitment to accessing the inner lives of individuals. When Hazlitt's colleague at the *Edinburgh Review*, Francis Jeffrey, writes (in a passage that *The Rise of the Novel* quotes a century and a half later) that Richardson enables us to "slip, invisible, into the domestic privacy of [the] characters, and hear and see everything that is said and done among them," he helps initiate this account of how, thanks to novels, literature took an inward turn and how the letter provided the primary stylistic register for this new psychological realism (Watt 1957: 198). But as Jeffrey pursues this argument, the very letters he treats do a disappearing act. In his account, we do not read, but "hear and see." The mediating work of written language is wished away. His assumption is that the letter is a window yielding a view of an inner subjectivity. But this is to forget that a letter is from someone to someone *else*: its movement defines a transactional space (see Kay 1988: 10). Addressed to another, its meaning contingent not only on that other's reading but also on an earlier missive to which it replies or on the response that it anticipates, a letter might just as appropriately be seen as registering eighteenth-century Britain's interest in *relationship*. Letters are artifacts of individuals' mutual dependence. Go-betweens greasing the wheels of social intercourse, these moving writings which put people in touch with one another's feelings are also the vehicles of the "amicable collision" that for Shaftesbury was the essence of the civilizing process.

Engagement in the marketplace was, as Pocock has stressed, understood in comparable terms: "le doux commerce" was another resolver of differences. Indeed, while they describe the social benefits accruing from individuals' integration into the economic system, the era's writers on commerce rely on the same metaphors of circulation that the commentators on moving novels coined to describe how the passions were communicated fluidly from person to person. In their accounts of the workings of credit, economic writers dramatize the same acts of sympathetic imagination that are described by those vindicating the experience of fiction. For many a commentator, therefore, it seems fitting, not disturbing, to contemplate how letters of sentiment (fictitious and otherwise) and commodities alike traverse the nation and globe on the same post roads and shipping routes.

It seems right, too, that as lachrymose novels in letters peaked in popularity, in the wake of the publication, first, of *Clarissa* and, then, of J.-J. Rousseau's *Clarissa*-inspired *La Nouvelle Héloïse* (1761), they should be shadowed by a second set of stories of go-betweens. Throughout the century, but with special zeal from about 1760 to 1785, writers chose mobile, circulating *things* to fill the novelistic roles of first-person narrator and/or protagonist: a hackney coach, for instance, that discloses the secrets of the passengers it carries, or coins or banknotes that recount the adventures they undergo as they pass from hand to hand, or a lapdog brought from Bologna to London by a gentleman returning from the Grand Tour, who wants the pet to be "the Herald of Love wherever he goes" (Coventry 1751: 35) (see Figure 6.2).

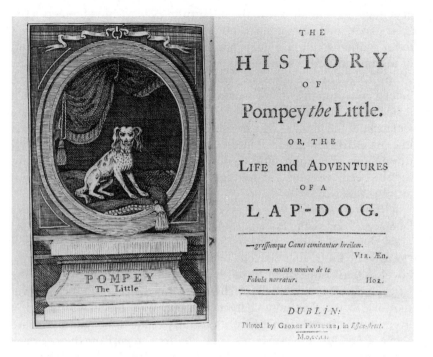

Figure 6.2 Frontispiece and title-page to the first Irish edition of Francis Coventry's *History of Pompey the Little* (1751). In the eighteenth century's popular "it-narratives," non-human commodities – in this case, a lap-dog – occupy the limelight and the humans who are novels' usual protagonists are sidelined to the shadows. Courtesy, The Lilly Library, Indiana University, Bloomington, Indiana.

We have seen Lichtenberg connect eighteenth-century novels to the transportation networks that facilitated the circulation of moving goods and marketable texts. It is testimony to the enthusiasm with which the novelists wrote *about* these networks on which they depended and *about* the systems of currency in which they participated, that they found out a way to personify them: hence the prosopopoeia that grants objects the power to talk about their peregrinations through the circuitry of the economy. Where we expect narrative to display characterological development, the process whereby individuals come to be all that they can be, these "it-narratives" are set up to dramatize the social agreements that get re-enacted by every act of buying and selling. The objects' journeys show how high society is inextricably connected to low. They dramatize, as well, the eighteenth-century conviction that value was created through circulation and that a state's economic prosperity depended on its multiplying the opportunities for its middle-men. (The "black coat" who narrates a 1760 novel of that title makes repeat trips to second-hand clothing stores and more than once falls into the hands of Monmouth Street's "new vamper[s] of old commodities" (*Adventures* 1760: 42)). The readiness to center fiction on moving goods – and, indeed, on property that repeatedly ceases to be *personal* but which instead (like the coat) resumes its habit of circulating – is not really a violation of the premise that novels ought to trade on subjects of *human* interest. Better to consider it testimony to the gusto with which the novel throughout the eighteenth century defined itself as a machine for social interconnection and reflected on the marketability permitting it to fill that role.

Jeffrey's *Edinburgh Review* essay, as we have seen, presented a preliminary version of the Romantic origins story that, side-lining those reflections, has ever since made it hard to consider a narrative that is "Related by Itself" (vs. "herself" or "himself") a novel at all. For Jeffrey, novels began rising when Richardson introduced his readers inside the letter-writing heroine's private chamber. But this account seems unresponsive to the politically charged plot trajectory that takes a Clarissa from imprisonment on her family's country estate to her glorious death above a London glove-maker's shop. Jeffrey's report on the origin of novels forgets that in *Clarissa*'s final volume, "her" "private" chamber (rented) abuts on the busy scene of exchange, open to all comers, that is the shop below stairs. In the letter concluding the work's third volume, Lovelace complains to his confidant that Clarissa's determination to remain her own woman represents a resistance to social existence itself, since "Mutual obligation is the very essence and soul of social and commercial life" (Richardson 1747–8/1985: 760). The manipulative Lovelace is, of course, an unattractive spokesman for the cohesive effects of "le doux commerce" and for the social passions fostered within modern commercial societies. But then *Clarissa* itself makes a point, notably, of denying its readers the chance to experience the autonomy and the detachment sought by its heroine. For the very form of this work – which forces us to read over Lovelace's shoulder and which all but finagles us, as we become increasingly intolerant of suspense, into anticipating Clarissa's rape as impatiently as that villain does – makes us feel that we have been placed in a position where we have no choice but to assent to readerly participation. We find ourselves complicit with the wrongs the heroine suffers. Having ceded control of our sentiments to Richardson's moving letters, we find, willy-nilly, queasily, that we are *involved*.

Through his affirmative depiction of his heroine's sense of integrity and privacy, Richardson may seem to have allied himself with the claims of the individual (as proper novelists, within the Romantic paradigm Jeffrey and Hazlitt helped create, are meant to do). But Richardson also emphasized, like Lovelace in the quotation above, the inevitability of relationship. Like Adam Ferguson, whose 1767 account of humans' propensity to "move with the crowd" helped establish the social sciences, this novelist too should be seen as an analyst of those intricate networks of modern traffic and trade – of commercial exchanges, ethical entanglements, and emotional ties – that by mid-century had made civil society seem a milieu where all had ended up implicated in the fate of each.

Acknowledgments

This essay owes much to the intelligence and insights of the graduate students who have pursued eighteenth-century studies at Indiana University and at the State University of New York at Buffalo: thanks in particular are due to Kyoko Takanashi, whose enthusiasm for eighteenth-century transportation technologies is contagious. I am grateful as well to Cynthia Wall, Janet Sorensen, Susan Staves, and Tom Keirstead for readings and to Christine Lehleiter for her assistance with Lichtenberg's German.

References and further reading

The Adventures of a Black Coat, Containing a Series of Remarkable Occurrences and Entertaining Incidents, That it was a Witness to in its Peregrinations through the Cities of London and Westminster, in Company with Variety of Characters. As related by Itself. (1760). London: J. Williams.

Anderson, B. (1991) *Imagined Communities: Reflections on the Origin and Spread of Nationalism.* London: Verso. (1st edn. 1987.)

Aravamudan, S. (1999) "In the wake of the novel," *Novel: A Forum on Fiction* 33: 5–31.

Ballaster, R. (2000) "Women and the rise of the novel: sexual prescripts," in V. Jones (ed.) *Women and Literature in Britain, 1700–1800* (pp. 197–216). Cambridge: Cambridge University Press.

Barker, J. (1723) *A Patch-Work Screen for the Ladies,* in C. S. Wilson (ed.) *The Galesia Trilogy and Selected Manuscript Poems.* New York: Oxford University Press, 1997.

Behn, A. (1688) *Oroonoko, or, The Royal Slave,* intr. Lore Metzger. New York: W. W. Norton, 1973.

Benedict, B. M. (1996) *Making the Modern Reader: Cultural Mediation in Early Modern Literary Anthologies*. Princeton: Princeton University Press.

Benjamin, W. (1973) *Charles Baudelaire: A Lyric Poet in the Era of Capitalism*, trans. H. Zohn. London: New Left Books.

Brooke, F. (1777) *The Excursion*, ed. P. R. Backscheider and H. D. Cotton. Lexington: University Press of Kentucky, 1997.

Brown, H. O. (1997) *Institutions of the English Novel: From Defoe to Scott*. Philadelphia: University of Pennsylvania Press.

Burchell, G. (1991) "Peculiar interests: civil society and governing 'the system of natural liberty'," in G. Burchell, C. Gordon, and P. Miller (eds.) *The Foucault Effect: Studies in Governmentality* (pp. 119–50). Chicago: University of Chicago Press.

Coventry, F. (1751) *The History of Pompey the Little: or, the Life and Adventures of a Lap-Dog*. London: M. Cooper.

Defoe, D. (1704) *The Storm: Or, a Collection of the Most Remarkable Casualties and Disasters which happen'd in the Late Dreadful Tempest*. London: G. Sawbridge, J. Nutt.

—— (1722) *A Journal of the Plague Year*, ed. C. Wall. Harmondsworth: Penguin, 2003.

Doody, M. A. (1996) *The True Story of the Novel*. New Brunswick, NJ: Rutgers University Press.

Fielding, H. (1749) *Tom Jones*, ed. S. Baker. New York: Norton, 1973.

Gallagher, C. (1994) *Nobody's Story: The Vanishing Acts of Women Writers in the Marketplace, 1670–1820*. Berkeley: University of California Press.

Gildon, C. (1719a) *An Epistle to D— D'Foe, The Reputed Author of Robinson Crusoe*, bound with idem., *The Life and Strange Surprizing Adventures of Mr. D—De F—* London: J. Roberts.

—— (1719b) *The Post-Man Robb'd of his Mail, or the Packet broke open*. London: Bettesworth and Rivington.

Hale, D. J. (1998) *Social Formalism: The Novel in Theory from Henry James to the Present*. Stanford, Calif.: Stanford University Press.

Hazlitt, W. (1819) "Of the English novelists," in W. Hazlitt, *Lectures on the English Comic Writers*. London: Taylor and Hessey.

Hunter, J. P. (1990) *Before Novels: The Cultural Contexts of Eighteenth-Century British Fiction*. New York: W. W. Norton.

Johnson, S. (1755) *A Dictionary of the English Language*. London: J. and P. Knapton.

Kay, C. (1988) *Political Constructions: Defoe, Richardson, and Sterne in Relation to Hobbes, Hume, and Burke*. Ithaca: Cornell University Press.

King, K. (2001) "The novel before novels," in D. Todd and C. Wall (eds.) *Eighteenth-Century Genre and Culture: Serious Reflections on Occasional Forms* (pp. 36–57). Newark: University of Delaware Press.

Kreilkamp, I. (forthcoming) *Voice and the Victorian Storyteller*. Cambridge: Cambridge University Press.

Lewis, J. E. (1998) " 'The Sorrow of Seeing the Queen,' 1714–1789," in J. E. Lewis, *Mary Queen of Scots: Romance and Nation* (pp. 103–21). London: Routledge.

Lichtenberg, G. (1775) "Über den deutschen roman," in K. Batt (ed.) *Lichtenberg: Aphorismen, Essays, Briefe* (pp. 223–7). Leipzig: Dieterich, 1970.

Lynch, D. S. (1998) *The Economy of Character: Novels, Market Culture, and the Business of Inner Meaning*. Chicago: University of Chicago Press.

Manley, D. (1709) *The New Atalantis*, ed. R. Ballaster. London: Penguin, 1991.

McKeon, M. (1987) *The Origins of the English Novel, 1600–1740*. Baltimore: Johns Hopkins University Press.

McMurran, M. H. (2002) "National or transnational? The eighteenth-century novel," in M. Cohen and C. Dever (eds.) *The Literary Channel: The International Invention of the Novel* (pp. 50–72). Princeton: Princeton University Press.

Pocock, J. G. A. (1985) *Virtue, Commerce, and History: Essays on Political Thought and History, Chiefly in the Eighteenth Century*. Cambridge: Cambridge University Press.

Price, L. (2000) *The Anthology and the Rise of the Novel: From Richardson to George Eliot*. Cambridge: Cambridge University Press.

Richardson, S. (1747–8) *Clarissa, or, The History of a Young Lady*, ed. A. Ross. Harmondsworth: Penguin, 1985.

Shaftesbury (1711) *Characteristics of Men, Manners, Opinions, Times*, ed. L. E. Klein. Cambridge: Cambridge University Press, 1999.

Siskin, C. (1997) *The Work of Writing: Literature and Social Change in Britain, 1700–1830*. Baltimore: Johns Hopkins University Press.

Warner, W. B. (1998) *Licensing Entertainment: The Elevation of Novel Reading in Britain, 1684–1750*. Berkeley: University of California Press.

Watt, I. (1957) *The Rise of the Novel*. Berkeley: University of California Press.

Williams, I. (ed.) (1970) *Novel and Romance, 1700–1800: A Documentary Record*. New York: Barnes and Noble.

Chapter 7

The Gothic

Moving in the World of Novels

Mark R. Blackwell

In a famous passage in Laurence Sterne's *A Sentimental Journey through France and Italy* (1768), Yorick enters an unoccupied carriage and, "finding it in tolerable harmony with my feelings," settles down to "write my journey." As he scribbles, the "see-saw" of the chaise in which he sits (a *Desobligeant*) begins to distract him, yet he writes on, excited by "the Novelty of my Vehicle." At last, interrupted by travelers who wonder why the stationary carriage is rocking, he informs them that the agitation of writing has produced its motion, and acknowledges that his preface would perhaps have been better if written in a *Vis a Vis*, a different sort of carriage producing a distinct experience of literary transport (1768/1967: 32–7). The scene calls attention to the rhythms of human experience, particularly the ups and downs of writing, and toys with the conceit that a book is a sort of vehicle whose capacity to transport its sedentary readers depends on its mechanics – namely, on its ability to resonate with its audience.

Sterne's reflections on the relationship between physical and literary transport were hardly unprecedented. In Part Four of *A Philosophical Enquiry into the Origin of our Ideas of the Sublime and Beautiful* (1757, 1759), Edmund Burke attempted to demonstrate "why the body is at all affected by the mind, or the mind by the body" (1757/1968: 129). Burke was particularly interested in the sublime, an experience of terror that causes delight. He explained this seeming paradox by speculating that the pain induced by the sublime contracts the muscles, forcing the body to exercise and thus rousing it from a "languid and inactive state" which might otherwise result in "[m]elancholy, dejection, despair, and often self-murder." The "surmounting of difficulties" inspired by the "labour" of sublime experience was thus a healthful tonic (p. 135). Burke's peculiar physiological theories of aesthetic transport were in the vanguard of contemporary medical opinion. Francis Fuller, Bernard Mandeville, James Carmichael Smyth, and other experts recommended swinging, jogging, and bouncing, as well as galloping and trotting on a horse, as cures for ailments ranging from consumption to depression. Various mechanisms, from swings to chamber horses, were designed for the purpose (Flynn 1990). In *De regimine mentis* (1763), Jerome Gaub even prescribed "Terror as a Therapeutic Agent," going so far as to hope for the invention of "a machine that will inspire extreme terror" (quoted in Flynn 1990: 162).

Such a machine was indeed devised in the eighteenth century, first appearing a mere year after Gaub's dream of an apparatus for inducing terror. The invention was the Gothic novel, a narrative vehicle with an unprecedented power to move its readers, and its appeal corroborated John and Anna Laetitia Aikin's claim that anyone who "could find out a new torture . . . would be . . . entitled to the applause of those who fabricate books of entertainment" (1773a: 192). Horace Walpole's *The Castle of Otranto* (1764), subtitled "A Gothic Story" in the 1765 second edition, initiated a fashion for such torture that crested during the 1790s with the work of the most influential and accomplished Gothic novelist, Ann Radcliffe (1764–1823). The distant forebears of suspense stories and horror movies, Radcliffe's fictions inspired the most important writers of the age to imitate, parody, or rail against the genre.

Attempts to explain the Gothic's vogue have proceeded apace ever since. The most noteworthy recent criticism views Gothic novels – especially Radcliffe's – as participants in ongoing debates about political and social reform spurred by the French Revolution. Such historically nuanced readings have thoughtfully countered the longstanding tendency of both critics and admirers to condescend to the genre as an amusing but vapid popular entertainment that moves its readers without taking them anywhere worthwhile. Yet they have too often colluded in ignoring the genre's narrative machinery, taking for granted its ability to provoke sensation. It remains "surprising just how little Radcliffe's works have received in the way of sustained analysis" (Johnson 1995: 76), though it is their capacity for manipulating readers' feelings, rather than their intervention in the period's political and social controversies, that has lately been slighted. This chapter explores the ability of Radcliffe's Gothic fiction to "exercise the sensibility" (Aikin 1773a: 211) by keeping the mind "on the stretch" (Aikin 1773b: 125) and considers period anxieties about the enormous popularity of such exercise.

The Gothic Art of Mechanical Reproduction

Sir Walter Scott praised the power of Radcliffe's adventures to "hurry the reader along with them," maintaining that "[t]he public were chiefly aroused . . . by the wonderful conduct of a story, in which the author so successfully called out the feelings of mystery and of awe, while chapter after chapter, and incident after incident, maintained the thrilling attraction of awakened curiosity and suspended interest" (1824/1968: 120, 124). Yet Radcliffe's ability to carry the public with her also provoked the censure of reviewers. Discussing *The Mysteries of Udolpho* (1794), Samuel Taylor Coleridge admitted that "curiosity is kept upon the stretch from page to page, and from volume to volume, and the secret, which the reader thinks himself every instant on the point of penetrating, flies like a phantom before him, and eludes his eagerness till the very last moment of protracted expectation." Echoing the Aikins' use of the term "stretch," Coleridge hints that Radcliffe's fiction provides a bracing mental exercise, yet complains that "[c]uriosity is raised far oftener than it is gratified; or rather, it is raised so high that no adequate gratification can be given it" (Coleridge 1794). Reviewing *The Italian* three years later, Coleridge was more dismissive, asserting that the "passion of terror" inspired by "the *modern romance*" was "excited by trick," and thus inevitably "would degenerate into repetition" (Coleridge 1798/1994: 56).

The redundancy of Coleridge's own language – "from page to page, and from volume to volume" – seems intended to mimic the numbing sameness into which Gothic narratives inevitably devolve, a sameness familiar to anyone who has watched myriad horror films in which creaking doors, dark passageways, labyrinthine castles, and dark-and-stormy-nights figure prominently. The problem of redundancy is acknowledged by Scott as well, though he contends that Radcliffe's achievement consists exactly in her power to create a durable narrative mechanism that sustains the reader's curiosity "chapter after chapter, and incident after incident": "The feelings of suspense and awful attention which she excites, are awakened by means of springs which lie open, indeed, to the first touch, but which are peculiarly liable to be worn out by repeated pressure" (1824/1968: 113). The Aikins also recognized the danger of "repeated pressure," noting that "sensibility does not increase with exercise . . . [O]ur habits increase, our emotions decrease, by repeated acts" (1773a: 211). Yet elsewhere they declare the capacity of "well-wrought scenes of artificial terror" to please despite readers' habituation to their conventions: "though we know before-hand what to expect, we enter into them with eagerness, in quest of a pleasure already experienced" (1773b: 125). Isabella Thorpe's promise to Catherine Morland in *Northanger Abbey* (1818) – "when you have finished Udolpho, we will read the Italian together, and I have made out a list of ten or twelve more of the same kind for you [that] . . . will last us some time" – substantiates the Aikins' contention that repeating "a pleasure already experienced" is exactly the point of suspenseful tales of terror. The redundant language of Catherine's reply to Isabella's projected reading list – "but are they all horrid, are you sure they are all horrid?" (Austen 1818/1969: 40) – intimates Austen's awareness that the genre's power consists in its capacity "to preserve [the reader's] mind in one uniform tone of sentiment, by presenting to it a long continued train of scenes and incidents, which harmonize with each other" (Anon. 1794: 279). Gothic fiction promises a pleasing, formulaic sameness, one that derives from a sustained pitch and – as with the *Vis a Vis* – a characteristic tempo.

Gothic romances are often set in a remote past, and Radcliffe's tales typically take place in a continental Europe imbued with superstition. Yet their appeal is insistently associated with the tempo of modernity, especially by faultfinding critics (Clery 1995: 10). An ever-greater number of fictions was being published and circulated in an ever-greater number of bookshops and libraries, rendering readers, in Clery's apt turn of phrase, "machines for reading" (p. 97). Texts were accessible and disposable as never before. One reviewer of Radcliffe's *The Italian* distinguished the "most excellent species of novel-writing" from the "modern romance," which is "perhaps more imposing than the former, on the first perusal: but . . . ceases to interest after it can no longer awaken our curiosity" (Anon. 1797: 282–3). In a world of extensive reading, however, where printed matter is readily available, second perusals are beside the point (Brewer 1997: 169–71). A taste for that literature of transport we have come to call "airplane reading" had emerged.

Wordsworth had another name for it in the Preface to *Lyrical Ballads* (1800): "this degrading thirst after outrageous stimulation." He blamed the modern condition for his contemporaries' increasing turn to "the application of gross and violent stimulants," noting in particular "the encreasing accumulation of men in cities, where the uniformity of their occupations produces a craving for extraordinary incident" – namely, the sort of incident found in the "frantic novels" of Radcliffe and her ilk (1800/1974: 128–30). In Wordsworth's view, the flatness and sameness of modern urban life drove readers to seek exactly the sort of exercise – involuntary motion rather than "voluntary exertion" – theorized by Burke and prescribed by medical experts. Coleridge later disparaged both circulating libraries and the kinds of exercise they promoted on similar grounds:

> [A]s to the devotees of the circulating libraries, I dare not compliment their *pass-time*, or rather *kill-time*, with the name of *reading*. Call it rather a sort of beggarly daydreaming, during which . . . the whole *materiel* and imagery of the doze is supplied *ab extra* by a sort of mental *camera obscura* manufactured at the printing office . . . We should therefore transfer this species of amusement . . . from the genus, *reading*, to that comprehensive class characterized by the power of reconciling the two contrary yet co-existing propensities of nature; namely, indulgence of sloth, and hatred of vacancy. In addition to novels and tales of chivalry in prose or rhyme, . . . this genus comprizes as its species, gaming, swinging, or swaying on a chair or gate. (1817/1983: vol. 1, 48–9n.)

Like Wordsworth, Coleridge associates novel reading practices and novel reading matter with torpor, sloth, mental vacancy. Unlike Wordsworth, Coleridge underscores not the outrageous stimulation afforded by modern fiction, but the mechanical and repetitive aspects of the pastime: its capacity to "manufacture" states of mind; its likeness to "swinging, or swaying on a chair or gate," back and forth, up and down; and its unlikely role as a monotonous remedy for boredom. However, scores of readers seem to have disagreed, finding in Gothic fiction's "almost limitless possibilities for painful infliction" a welcome "novelistic alternative to dullness" (Spacks 1995: 78–9) and enjoying "the strange luxury of artificial terror" such reading provided (Anon. 1794: 280). The narrator of Sophia Lee's *The Recess* (1786) remarks that we all begin life's journey ignorant of "the heights and depths through which we must labor; oppressed . . . and often overwhelmed with that most insupportable of all burthens, our own dissatisfied souls" (1786/2000: 10). Yet the laborious ups and downs of Gothic fiction offered readers a thrilling cure for the dissatisfactions of contemporary life.

Radcliffe's Public Transport System

Gothic novels are literary technologies designed to provoke particular responses in their readers. In Philip K. Dick's *Do Androids Dream of Electric*

Sheep? (1968), people inhabiting a futuristic world use a device called a mood organ to manipulate their emotional state. Gothic novels are mood organs in their own right. Consider, for a moment, a rollercoaster ride as a useful analogy for the experience of reading Gothic romances, and for the emotional ups and downs negotiated by their protagonists. The ride does not transport one to a physical location one is anxious to visit; rather, devotees seek a special kind of feeling, one for which a taxicab ride to the rollercoaster's terminus or an algorithm describing its mass, velocity, acceleration, and trajectory through space cannot substitute. Rollercoasters transport us, both physically and emotionally, by managing our experience of space and time – by carrying us up and down, conveying us faster and slower, and shaping our expectations about that motion.

Radcliffe likewise moved the public by controlling its experience of narrative time and space. Such narrative manipulation – and the feelings it generates – is the lasting legacy of her novels, whereas the resolution of her works' uncertainties dampens the anxious anticipation that distinguishes the genre. Hence Catherine Morland's conversation with Isabella Thorpe about *The Mysteries of Udolpho*'s incident of the "black veil":

> "Oh! I would not tell you what is behind the black veil for the world! Are you not wild to know?"
>
> "Oh! yes, quite; what can it be? – But do not tell me – I would not be told upon any account. I know it must be a skeleton. Oh! I am delighted with the book! I should like to spend my whole life in reading it." (Austen 1818/1969: 39–40)

Catherine's reluctance to have the mystery revealed, together with her desire to spend her whole life in reading Radcliffe's book, suggests that sustaining a mood of painfully delicious expectancy is the genre's hallmark. Well before John Keats's letter extolling *"Negative Capability,"* the ability of great writers to be "in uncertainties, Mysteries, doubts, without any irritable reaching after fact & reason," Radcliffe's fiction was teaching readers to embrace mystery and to rest content with forms of half-knowledge that are pleasing and affecting (Keats 1817/1958: 193–4).

Consider a single word: impend. Forms of the verb "impend" appear insistently in Radcliffe's fiction, typically in passages of landscape description which portray a cliff or a rocky outcropping as "impending":

> There appeared on a point of rock impending over the valley the reliques of a palace . . . (1790/1993: 125)

> Dark woods, intermingled with bold projections of rock, sometimes barren, and sometimes covered with the purple bloom of wild flowers, impended over the lake. (1791/1986: 247)

> These precipices were broken into cliffs, which, in some places, impended far above their base . . . (1797/1981: 90)

In these excerpts, the word means hanging over; indeed, Radcliffe often chooses an alternative phrasing which clarifies this denotation of the term, as when she describes a court "overhung by a rock" (1797/1981: 117) or "precipices, which sometimes overhung the road" (1791/1986: 240). However, "impend" can be used to express temporal imminence as well as a threatening physical proximity. Impending events are typically events we anticipate with dread, events whose prospect frightens us. Thus Adeline, the protagonist of *The Romance of the Forest*, "saw herself condemned to await in passive silence the impending destiny, infinitely more dreadful to her imagination than death itself" (1791/1986: 228). Here the word "impend" is closely related to the word "suspend": to hold undetermined, to defer or postpone, or to keep in a mood of expectation, to keep in *suspense*. When, in *A Sicilian Romance*, Radcliffe notes that the fate of her heroine "yet hung in perilous uncertainty" (1790/1993: 111), she is registering the fact that the narrative is holding readers in suspense, generating a peril-tinged mood of expectation by refusing to supply determinate answers. When Radcliffe uses "impend," its cousin "suspense" looms over us, together with semantically proximate substitutes such as "apprehension" and "anticipation," evoking the state of excited, anxious uncertainty which accompanies our intuition that something is about to occur, something at once expected and dreaded.

That state of excitement can of course be managed to good effect, as Walpole early recognized. In his preface to the second edition of *The Castle of Otranto*, he uses not "impend" or "suspend," but another cognate, "depend," when discussing his use of intervening comic scenes to slow the pace of the main plot and frustrate reader's expectations: "The very impatience a reader feels, while delayed by the coarse pleasantries of vulgar actors from arriving at the knowledge of the important catastrophe he expects, perhaps heightens, certainly proves that he has been artfully interested in, the depending event" (1764/1996: 10). Knowledge and catastrophe are pending in Walpole's work, but his aim is less to deliver the expected event – and thus satisfy his readers' desire to know – than to tease out his narrative by slowing the pace and digressing, luring his readers with unfulfilled promises of full disclosure, with half-knowledge that pleases them exactly by frustrating them.

Radcliffe teases readers in like fashion in *The Italian* (1797). Young lovers Ellena and Vivaldi suffer various misfortunes thanks to the interference of Vivaldi's status-conscious mother, the Marchesa, and her agent, Schedoni, a menacing monk with a dark past. Schedoni and the Marchesa have Ellena kidnapped and conducted to the monastery of San Stefano, where she is held against her will. Vivaldi and his servant, Paulo, manage to track Ellena down, and with the help of a sympathetic nun (in fact her long-lost mother), they make their escape. Yet even as they are hastening from the prison-like mountain retreat, fearful that they are being followed, Vivaldi, Ellena, and Paulo stop to "admire" the scenery (1797/1981: 158) and to engage in lengthy conversations about landscape aesthetics (pp. 158–63). The effect is peculiar. Students often complain that the scenes seem implausible, no more likely than escaped convicts pausing to stargaze and chat about astrophysics while the police are hot on their trail. Indeed, the slackened pace and unhurried intellectual speculation of these moments feels out of sync with the frenetic, headlong chase scenes that precede and often follow them.

Yet there is a logic to their inclusion. On the one hand, they serve the purpose of shifting narrative tempo, altering the cadence of the reader's experience less to release tension than to build it again, incrementally. On the other hand, such pauses, which almost always involve both landscape description and discussion of aesthetic philosophy, permit Radcliffe to comment indirectly on the aesthetic ideology of the novel itself. The bad guys in Radcliffe's work have goals for themselves and designs on others, plotting to get from point A to point B and move the story forward, while the good guys manifest a capacity to pause and enjoy nature – indeed, to partake in a communion with the outdoors and an identification with its sublime, overawing power that allows them at least temporary transcendence of their pressing concerns and thus establishes their moral and aesthetic superiority to their tormentors. Radcliffe produces narrative suspense that compels us to read for the plot, even using moments of descriptive arrest that frustrate our progress in order to stimulate our appetite for meaning. Yet at the same time, those moments of poetic elaboration that fail to advance the story – including both her famously pictorial descriptions of outdoor scenery and the poems that pepper her novels – encourage us to linger, hinting that we should not pursue the plot at all, but revel in a plotless natural world wherein true meaning and unmitigated pleasure reside. Matilda, the narrator of Sophia Lee's *The Recess*, muses,

> Methinks, while I expatiate on these trifles, time seems suspended, and
> the scene still living before me. The rich dew-drops, those jewels with which
> nature decks her bosom, glittering to the rays that wandered over the grass:
> the various animals that seemed to derive a daily existence from the re-
> turn of that glorious orb: the morning hymn of the winged creation – all
> united to awaken our gratitude, and humble us before the author of our
> being . . . I am tedious, and must have done with these puerilities, which
> yet on reflection yield the purest pleasures of our lives. (Lee 1786/2000:
> 12–13)

Nonetheless, the diegetic compulsion that drives us to find out how
the story ends is an embedded theme of much Gothic fiction. *The Castle
of Otranto* opens with a mysterious prophecy and an inexplicable event,
both of which point forward to the unfolding of the tale. *A Sicilian Romance*
begins with a description of magnificent ruins that inspired the narrator's "awe and curiosity" during a trip abroad, later recounting how his
curiosity was stoked by a friar's hints that a singular tale was connected
with the castle remains (1790/1993: 1). Even Radcliffe's epigraph to the
novel, "I could a tale unfold . . . ," provokes curiosity, intimating that a
story may be unravelled, but also communicating a reticence to disclose
and asserting a certain power of withholding. The ellipsis is a veil, hinting that something lurks concealed, something we may get a glimpse
of if only we press on a bit farther. Gothic fiction delights in such coy
appeals and half-promises, using them to cultivate a titillating obscurity
that "occasions a suspense of thought, and leaves the full meaning to
be guessed at" (Gerard 1759: 4).

Slowing Down to Read the Signs: Radcliffe's Dreadful Hieroglyphics

The provocation of a curiosity that cannot be satisfied is explored with
slightly different emphasis in some passages from *The Italian* that pit intelligibility against legibility. A simple example comes in a scene where
Vivaldi, unexpectedly seized by officers of the Inquisition, is called forth
to be interrogated. Having passed through a door over which hangs "an
inscription in Hebrew characters, traced in blood-colour" (1797/1981:
200), Vivaldi sees inquisitors seated at a table:

> A book, with some instruments of singular appearance, lay before him.
> Round the table were several unoccupied chairs, on the backs of which
> appeared figurative signs, at the upper end of the apartment, a gigantic

crucifix stretched nearly to the vaulted roof; and, at the lower end, suspended from an arch in the wall, was a dark curtain, but whether it veiled a window, or shrouded some object or person, necessary to the designs of the Inquisitor, there were little means of judging. (p. 201)

The threatening import of the Hebrew inscription is clear, but its denotation eludes both Vivaldi and the reader. Like the mysterious instruments and closed book on the table, like the signs on the chairs, and like the curtain that seems to conceal something important, the inscription intimates the existence of a meaning that it does not disclose, a meaning we have "little means of judging." Intelligibility impends, hovering just beyond the curtain, just behind an array of "dreadful hieroglyphic[s]" (p. 140) that we know to be legible, only not to us. Such figures of inscrutable, unreadable intelligibility serve as metaphors for the asymptotic experience of Radcliffe's fiction, which, through an effective form of figural and narrative calculus, carries us right to the limits of a meaning that is constantly approached but never quite reached.

A parallel sequence transpires in *The Romance of the Forest*. Adeline, the heroine, discovers a door hidden behind a tapestry hanging in her room. The door leads to another room, which in turn opens onto a suite of chambers, in the last of which she discovers a rusted dagger and a "small roll of paper": "She attempted to read it, but the part of the manuscript she looked at was so much obliterated, that she found this difficult, though what few words were legible impressed her with curiosity and terror" (1791/1986: 116). Adeline rushes back to her room, but before she can peruse the manuscript, she overhears snatches of a conversation. Believing the exchange to concern her future, she confronts one of the interlocutors, only to realize that the "words, unconnectedly as she heard them, imported little, and that her imagination had filled up the void in the sentences, so as to suggest the evil apprehended" (p. 121). Not until late the next day – several pages later – does Adeline return to the manuscript, only to be stymied by the guttering of her candle: "Adeline's light was now expiring in the socket, and the paleness of the ink, so feebly shone upon, baffled her efforts to discriminate the letters ... Thus compelled to suspend the inquiry ... she retired to her humble bed" (p. 128). Her obligations the next day render it impossible for her to scan the scroll until evening. This interrupted reading of the broken manuscript is interwoven with similarly frustrating encounters with the servant Peter, who, "mak[ing] a signal as if he had something to communicate," hastens away upon the arrival of La Motte, leaving Adeline "ruminating upon this signal, and the cautious manner in which Peter had given it" (p. 135). A later meeting with Peter is likewise interrupted before he can communicate any intelligence, "leaving Adeline in a state of alarm, curiosity, and vexation" (p. 138). When her sometime guardian La Motte complains that the manuscript " 'is so much obscured by time that it can scarcely be decyphered'" and dismisses it as "'a strange romantic story,'" he intimates the allegorical dimension of such scenes of failed reading, establishing an analogy between the strange romantic stories that Radcliffe's heroines attempt to decode and those that her readers hold in their hands.

Perhaps the best example of the figure of illegibility in Radcliffe's work comes during a tense escape sequence in *The Italian*. Vivaldi has promised to convey a note detailing an escape plan to Ellena in the monastery where she is being held captive. Having collected the note under duress, and having waited patiently to steal back to her cell in order to read it, suspense building all the while, Ellena finally returns:

> There, once more alone, . . . she sat down to read Vivaldi's billet, trying to command her impatience, and to understand the lines, over which her sight rapidly moved, when in the eagerness of turning over the paper, the lamp dropt from her trembling hand and expired. Her distress now nearly reached despair . . . Her only hope rested on Olivia's arrival before it might be too late to practice the instructions of Vivaldi, if, indeed, they were still practicable; and she listened with intense solicitude for an approaching footstep, while she yet held, ignorant of its contents, the billet, that probably would decide her fate. A thousand times she turned about the eventful paper, endeavoured to trace the lines with her fingers, and to guess their import, thus enveloped in mystery; while she experienced all the various torture that the consciousness of having in her very hand the information, on a timely knowledge of which her life, perhaps, depended, without being able to understand it, could inflict. (1797/1981: 132)

Olivia finally brings light, and Ellena at last can read, only to learn that a note she received over an hour ago urges her immediate flight (pp. 132–3). The image of a missive that one physically possesses but cannot read, a missive brimming with intelligence that is inaccessible, illegible, is powerfully evocative. It functions as an allegory for the tortuous experience of reading Gothic fiction, of feeling "enveloped in mystery" despite the fact that we ostensibly have the answer, the novel itself, in our clutches.

Our "torture" derives from moments of temporal suspension that are equivalent to those experienced by Ellena. As she waits impatiently for some means of reading the letter, so do we; as she agonizes about being rendered immobile, we do, too; and Radcliffe conveys that sense of inertia not merely at the level of what narratologists call the fabula – the order and pace of events as experienced, hypothetically, by Ellena – and not only at the level of the plot – the way in which the narrator extends, truncates, or re-orders the recounting of events in order to create certain effects for readers – but also at the level of syntax. Consider the final dependent clause of the passsage's last sentence: "while she experienced all the various torture that the consciousness of having in her very hand the information, on a timely knowledge of which her life, perhaps, depended, without being able to understand it, could inflict." The syntax is awkward, mostly because the word "torture" is followed by a relative clause ("that . . .") whose subject, "consciousness," is separated from its predicate, "could inflict," by an elaborate network of intervening prepositional phrases that defer syntactic closure. Radcliffe finds a means of enacting through syntactic suspension the very experience of delay and uncertainty that she is describing. Here is an instance of grammatical infelicity as aesthetic achievement.

Radcliffe and other talented Gothic writers adjust the cadence of their storytelling so as to manipulate their readers' feelings. When Radcliffe portrays Ferdinand in *A Sicilian Romance* as someone whose "imagination seized with avidity each appearance of mystery" (1790/1993: 36–7), she is describing her readers as well, whose irresistible desire to discover secrets is provoked by apparent mysteries that stir their imaginative thirst without slaking it. Gothic novels intimate that desirable information is imminent, then frustrate our progress toward that eagerly anticipated knowledge. Narrative and grammatical suspension are two formal means of decelerating the tempo of a story and accelerating our impatience to reach the looming crisis, the impending resolution; and various kinds of inscrutability and illegibility, often involving darkness or veiling, serve as means of justifying narrative suspension while also functioning as allegories of our thwarted desire to know what is at once tantalizingly within our reach and frustratingly beyond our grasp.

Acceleration and Narrative Curves

If one means of affecting readers is dilation, slowing the pace and extending the moment, another is abrupt immersion, furnishing too much information too quickly. If our figure for dilation is, say, slowly climbing to the apex of the rollercoaster's sine curve, our figure for this change of tempo is hurtling downward from that crest, always more quickly than we can prepare for. If our figure for dilation is the deliberate progress of the slasher-film protagonist down the basement stairs (always slowly, always with tension mounting), our figure for such narrative acceleration is the appearance of the hatchet-bearing psychopath sooner than expected.

Two examples of this phenomenon appear in *A Sicilian Romance*, and their occurrence in successive chapters suggests that Radcliffe is deliberately heightening the effects of narrative surprise through a pile-up of plot twists that increases our sense of narrative acceleration, our feeling that events are moving, not too slowly to satisfy our urge to know, but too quickly to comprehend. The first results from Radcliffe's manipulation of our conventional expectations about how parallel plots work. Radcliffe tweaks the laws of "meanwhile" through ellipsis, a narrative hole into which we step with wrenching consequences for our sense of narrative pace and linearity. The second depends on Radcliffe's capacity to confuse our sense of where exactly characters are located and of whether or not events are recounted sequentially. The situation is this: Julia, whose father is trying to compel her to marry a tyrannical older man, has escaped her family's Sicilian castle and taken refuge in a monastery. Like both her father and her intended, the monastery's abbot is a power-hungry paternal figure, so she flees the monastery with the help of her brother, Ferdinand, and boards a boat bound for Italy. Julia hopes, perhaps, to be reunited in Italy with young Hippolitus, the man she loves; she has just learned that Hippolitus, who appeared to have been fatally stabbed in an early effort to abscond with Julia, has been nursed back to health in Italy. Julia's boat trip is interrupted by a near fatal storm, and after finally being deposited on what may be the shores of Sicily, she and her brother are hospitably welcomed by the inhabitants of a villa. So ends chapter 12.

Chapter 13 introduces our "meanwhile." Instead of pursuing the story of Julia, Radcliffe reintroduces us to Hippolitus, so that we can be informed about what has happened since our last sight of him, stabbed and bloody, in chapter 3. The conventions of "meanwhile" lead us to believe either that the story of Hippolitus will be told until his plot and Julia's plot intersect, or that we will move back and forth – Hippolitus, Julia, Hippolitus, Julia – until these parallel plots are finally reconciled. The conventions also dictate, I would argue, that significant developments in one plot not be revealed in the other except by report (as when Ferdinand informs Julia that Hippolitus is still alive) or by a plot merge that is foreshadowed somehow (for example, were Hippolitus to cross to Sicily and happen upon a villa in the country, we might begin to suspect the events of the two plots to be dovetailing). We expect that the plots will cross at a recognizable time, or in a familiar place; otherwise, the narrator has some explaining to do, either because the story has been awkwardly recounted, or because we – that is, our narrative expectations – have been manipulated. In *A Sicilian Romance*, the latter is the case. Hippolitus returns to Sicily to search for Julia, wanders into the ruins of a monastery, discovers that it is overrun by murderous banditti, and in his efforts to sneak away, happens upon the body of a young woman who turns out to be Julia. Two sorts of unassimilable surprise result. First, we suffer a dislocation: Julia is not where we left her, nestled in the safety of a cozy villa. Second, we experience a sense of temporal disjunction: events have transpired in the Julia plot that have not been revealed to us, which means that we have lost a sense of temporal proportion and continuity. Perhaps five days have passed, perhaps five years – how can we be sure? Where are we, and when? Radcliffe has deliberately broken a narrative trust in order to produce an unsettling, dream-like sense that time and place are fluid and elastic, not measured and orderly. We are in the world of David Lynch movies, not of police procedurals.

Even as the close of chapter 13 soothes some of our narrative anxieties by explaining how Julia and her brother ended up in the moldering monastery, chapter 14 exacerbates our still nagging sense of disorientation. Having managed to escape the monastery by passing through dark vaults, iron doors, trapdoors, and subterranean passages, the reunited Julia and Hippolitus are chased by the duke who wants Julia as his bride, so they enter a serpentine cave in which Julia discovers a door. By now, readers are thoroughly lost. One threatening figure has blended into another – Julia's father, the duke, the abbot, the banditti – and one place has morphed into another – the castle of Mazzini resembles the St Augustin monastery, which is nearly indistinguishable from various other ruins, castles, and monasteries that the characters have encountered. Even the larger geographical setting may be uncertain for the inattentive first-time reader. Did Julia make it to Italy, or did she land on the coast of Sicily? Still, the dominant impression is one of motion, of characters' headlong career from one place to another. Hence the reader's surprise when Julia opens the bolted door in the recesses of the cave and finds herself in a locked room in her father's castle occupied by her mother, long presumed dead.

We are certainly confused about space at this point, having imagined that Julia was running farther and farther from home and having believed that the number of pages we had read – and adventures we had weathered – was some measure of the distance we had traveled with Julia. A like confusion comes in *The Romance of the Forest*, when Adeline's desperate flight from the clutches of the Marquis de Montalt carries her "through alleys and over lawns, without meeting with any thing like a boundary to the grounds" (1791/1986: 165), yet ultimately conveys her to a lighted recess occupied by the Marquis himself. What we took to be progress forward was in fact circular motion. In *A Sicilian Romance*, that circularity confounds our sense of time, too. We shift from anticipating the happy marriage of our young protagonists, Julia and Hippolitus, to unearthing the marital troubles – ancient history, as it were – of Julia's parents.

Yet our return to the castle and to the long buried crime of Julia's father feels less like circular motion than like travel through a wormhole that warps time and space, allowing us passage across years and miles in the turn of a page. The seeming illogic of this trajectory has a reasonable explanation, as it must in Radcliffe, yet what is meaningful about these unsettling final moments is less the resolution they provide than the uncanny surprise they afford. The discovery of the marchioness permits us to unravel the mystery of the story's events, yet what is most striking and memorable is not the provision of answers but the uncanny feeling generated by the way they are supplied. The remote recesses of a cave become the extremities of Julia's childhood home, a locale both familiar and strange. Julia encounters there someone who is both familiar – her beloved mother – and unfamiliar – a woman absent for years. The logical keystone of Radcliffe's plot, her narrative linchpin, is also its most mysterious event. This proximity of mystery to meaning, of nightmarish illogic to reasonable answers, of past to present and here to there, makes Radcliffe's Gothic novels tick, though the ticking is often like that of an unreliable watch, or the pace of Sterne's postillion (Sterne 1768/1967: 64–5) – sometimes too fast, sometimes too slow.

Ticking watches and their circling hands remind us that change and maddening sameness, progress and circularity are hard to distinguish in Gothic fiction. Most Gothic plots depict a heroine who must return to and acknowledge her family's obscured past in order to escape its power and make a fresh start (Clery 1995: 73). Ticking watches likewise remind us that the incremental increase of suspense and the threat of numbing repetition are inextricably intertwined, a lesson in narrative mechanics that the Edgar Allan Poe of "The Tell-Tale Heart" perhaps learned from Radcliffe. The legacy of Radcliffe's narrative machinations persists in genres of suspense and terror that continue to thrill the movie-going and novel-reading public. Yet Gothic fiction cannot simply be relegated to a world of popular entertainment it engendered. When we recollect the bait-and-switch technique of the "boy from Winander" passage in Book 5 of *The Prelude* (1805), which manipulates readers' feelings by encouraging them to confuse Wordsworth with a long-dead childhood friend, or remember the many moments in Book 7 when Wordsworth describes aspects of London – the "symbols" and "blazoned names" of the shops (l. 174), "'the face of everyone / That passes by me'" (ll. 597–8), a label upon the chest of a blind beggar (ll. 612–20), and the "undistinguishable world" of the city (l. 700) – as inscrutable texts which nonetheless intimate "[a]n under-sense of the greatest" things (l. 712), we feel the influence of Radcliffe's narrative experiments on the most ambitious and important works of her Romantic-era successors. Her impact on Wordsworth is perhaps plainest in the ups and downs of Book 6's Simplon Pass episode, in which "Effort, and expectation, and desire, / And something evermore about to be" (ll. 541–2) compensate for a mountain-climbing experience that fails to live up to Wordsworth's imaginings. As Wordsworth invokes imagination's power to anticipate impending events as a consolation for the disappointment of actual experience, we may well recall the capacity of swings and chamber horses to cure us of our *taedium vitae* – or the power of Gothic novels to move us without making us leave our seats.

References and further reading

Aikin, J. and Aikin, A. L. (1773a) "An enquiry into those kinds of distress which excite agreeable sensations," *Miscellaneous Pieces, in Prose* (pp. 190–214). London.

—— (1773b) "On the pleasure derived from objects of terror, with Sir Bertrand, a fragment," *Miscellaneous Pieces, in Prose* (pp. 119–37). London.

Anon. (1794) "Review of *The Mysteries of Udolpho*," *Monthly Review* 15: 278–83.

—— (1797) "Review of *The Italian*," *Monthly Review* 22: 282–4.

Austen, J. (1818) *Northanger Abbey*, in R. W. Chapman (ed.) *Northanger Abbey and Persuasion* (pp. 11–252), vol. 5 of *The Novels of Jane Austen*, 3rd edn. rev. Oxford: Oxford University Press, 1969.

Bal, M. (1997) *Narratology: Introduction to the Theory of Narrative*, 2nd edn. Toronto: University of Toronto Press.

Benedict, B. (1989) "Pictures of conformity: sentiment and structure in Ann Radcliffe's style," *Philological Quarterly* 18: 363–77.

Brewer, J. (1997) *The Pleasures of the Imagination: English Culture in the Eighteenth Century*. New York: Farrar, Straus and Giroux.

Burke, E. (1757, 1759) *A Philosophical Enquiry into the Origin of our Ideas of the Sublime and Beautiful*, ed. J. T. Boulton. Notre Dame: University of Notre Dame Press, 1968.

Castle, T. (1987) "The Spectralization of the other in *The Mysteries of Udolpho*," in F. Nussbaum and L. Brown (eds.) *The New 18th Century* (pp. 231–53). New York: Methuen.

Clery, E. J. (1995) *The Rise of Supernatural Fiction, 1762–1800*. Cambridge: Cambridge University Press.

[Coleridge, S. T.] (1794) "Review of *The Mysteries of Udolpho*," *The Critical Review* 11 (2nd series): 361–72.

Coleridge, S. T. (1798) "Review of *The Italian*," *The Critical Review* 23 (2nd series): 166–9, in D. D. Rogers (ed.) *The Critical Response to Ann Radcliffe* (p. 56). Westport: Greenwood Press, 1994.

—— (1817) *Biographia Literaria*, in J. Engell and W. J. Bate (eds.) *The Collected Works of Samuel Taylor Coleridge* 7, 2 vols. Princeton: Princeton University Press, 1983.

Durant, D. S. (1982) "Ann Radcliffe and the conservative gothic," *Studies in English Literature, 1500–1900* 22: 519–30.

Ellis, K. F. (1989) *The Contested Castle: Gothic Novels and the Subversion of Domestic Ideology*. Urbana: University of Illinois Press.

Ellis, M. (2000) *The History of Gothic Fiction*. Edinburgh: Edinburgh University Press.

Flynn, C. H. (1990) "Running out of matter: the body exercised in eighteenth-century fiction," in G. S. Rousseau (ed.) *The Languages of Psyche: Mind and Body in Enlightenment Thought* (pp. 147–85). Berkeley: University of California Press.

Gamer, M. (2000) *Romanticism and the Gothic: Genre, Reception, and Canon Formation*. Cambridge: Cambridge University Press.

Gerard, A. (1759) *An Essay on Taste*. London.

Haggerty, G. E. (1987) *Gothic Fiction/Gothic Form*. University Park: Pennsylvania State University Press.

Hoeveler, D. L. (1998) *Gothic Feminism: The Professionalization of Gender from Charlotte Smith to the Brontës*, University Park: Pennsylvania State University Press.

Howard, J. (1994) *Reading Gothic Fiction: A Bakhtinian Approach*. Oxford: Clarendon Press.

Johnson, C. L. (1995) *Equivocal Beings: Politics, Gender, and Sentimentality in the 1790s*. Chicago: University of Chicago Press.

Keats, J. (1817) "Letter of 21, 27(?) December to George and Tom Keats," in H. E. Rollins (ed.) *The Letters of John Keats* (vol. 1, pp. 191–4). Cambridge: Harvard University Press, 1958.

Kilgour, M. (1995) *The Rise of the Gothic Novel*. New York: Routledge.

Lee, S. (1786) *The Recess*, ed. April Alliston. Lexington: University Press of Kentucky, 2000.

Napier, E. R. (1987) *The Failure of the Gothic: Problems of Disjunction in an Eighteenth-Century Literary Form*. Oxford: Clarendon Press.

Poovey, M. (1979) "Ideology and *The Mysteries of Udolpho*," *Criticism* 21: 307–30.

Radcliffe, A. (1790) *A Sicilian Romance*, ed. A. Milbank. Oxford: Oxford University Press, 1993.

—— (1791) *The Romance of the Forest*, ed. C. Chard. Oxford: Oxford University Press, 1986.

—— (1794) *The Mysteries of Udolpho*, ed. B. Dobrée. Oxford: Oxford University Press, 1980.

—— (1797) *The Italian*, ed. F. Garber. Oxford: Oxford University Press, 1981.

Scott, W. (1824) "Ann Radcliffe," in *Sir Walter Scott On Novelists and Fiction*, ed. I. Williams (pp. 102–19). London: Routledge and Kegan Paul, 1968.

Sedgwick, E. K. (1980) *The Coherence of Gothic Conventions*. New York: Methuen, 1986.

Spacks, P. M. (1990) "Fathers and daughters: Ann Radcliffe," *Desire and Truth: Functions of Plot in Eighteenth-Century Novels* (pp. 147–74). Chicago: University of Chicago Press.

—— (1995) *Boredom: The Literary History of a State of Mind*. Chicago: University of Chicago Press.

Sterne, L. (1768) *A Sentimental Journey through France and Italy*, ed. G. Petrie. New York: Penguin, 1967.

Walpole, H. (1764) *The Castle of Otranto*, ed. W. S. Lewis. Oxford: Oxford University Press, 1996.

Watt, J. (1999) *Contesting the Gothic: Fiction, Genre, and Cultural Conflict, 1764– 1832*. Cambridge: Cambridge University Press.

Williams, A. (1995) *Art of Darkness: A Poetics of Gothic*. Chicago: University of Chicago Press.

Wordsworth, W. (1800) "Preface to *Lyrical Ballads*," in W. J. B. Owen and J. W. Smyser (eds.) *The Prose Works of William Wordsworth* (vol. 1, pp. 118–58). Oxford: Clarendon Press, 1974.

—— (1805) *The Prelude*, in J. Wordsworth, M. H. Abrams, and S. Gill (eds.) *The Prelude 1799, 1805, 1850*. New York: W. W. Norton, 1979.

Chapter 8

Gendering Texts

"The Abuse of Title Pages": Men Writing as Women

Susan Staves

Sophisticated eighteenth-century book buyers were, quite rightly, a suspicious lot. Print in the eighteenth century effectively severed the relation between an author and a text, opening up sometimes delightful, sometimes alarming possibilities for hoaxes, deceptions, and frauds. Two famous instances of deception were James McPherson's *Fragments of Ancient Poetry* (1760), supposedly by a third-century poet called Ossian, and Thomas Chatterton's poems, first produced between 1768 and 1770, but supposedly by a fifteenth-century poet called Thomas Rowley. Considering these, Paul Baines quite rightly argues that "forgery and plagiarism were not isolated side-shows but constitutive elements of [eighteenth-century] literary culture" (Baines 1999: 92–3). Famous living authors in this period often suffered from having spurious works foisted upon them, as Samuel Richardson, Henry Fielding, and Laurence Sterne all loudly complained. Even George Washington was attacked by a Tory enemy, John Randolph, who wrote and published *Letters from General Washington, to Several of his Friends in the Year 1776* (1778). In this chapter, I want first to consider briefly the general subject of spurious authorship, and then, in more detail, the particular case of male writers who appropriated the identities of living women on their title pages.

A print hoax like Swift's famous textual "killing" of Bickerstaff, the almanac maker, anticipating the consequences of its own revelation, was designed to teach readers salutary lessons about their own credulity; more common textual frauds were more simply intended to deceive. The eighteenth century was a great age of political writing in newspapers, in pamphlets, and in more weighty books. Like much eighteenth-century writing, most of this political writing was published anonymously or pseudonymously and much of it still has not been attributed to any author. Typically, the purported authors in political writing represented themselves as trustworthy and concerned for the public interest. In fact, the actual authors were very likely writing to advance some special interest. Politicians employed male secretaries to write for them and both politicians and commercial interests paid lobbyists not only to lobby for legislation favorable to them but also to put arguments favorable to their interests into print. Just as now political parties and commercial interests pay actors to appear in television advertisements as "real people" grappling with some real problem, so in the eighteenth century writers for special interests sometimes assumed very unreal "real" identities. Such practices were sufficiently familiar that Richard Brinsley Sheridan in his comedy *The Critic* (1781) has a character called Puff who plants all sorts of embellished and fictitious items in the newspapers, sometimes pretending to be someone who has personal experience relevant to a matter of public policy. At one point, the audience sees him looking at his notes for some "paragraph" he is about to send in: "Here is 'a CONSCIENTIOUS BAKER, on the Subject of the Army Bread;' . . . and promised for to-morrow" (p. 46).

Similarly, the eighteenth-century reader was often hard-pressed to discern whether purported authors of the enormous numbers of *Memoirs, Letters, Lives, Apologies,* and *Histories* that poured forth from the presses were the actual authors. Many, of course, were fictitious accounts of people who never existed, what we now call novels like Daniel Defoe's *Roxana The Fortunate Mistress: or, a History of the Life and Vast Variety of Fortunes of Mademoiselle de Beleau, afterwards call'd the Countess de Wintselsheim in Germany. Being the Person known by the Name of the Lady Roxana in the time of King Charles II* (1724). Some, like *The Memoirs of Mrs. Laetitia Pilkington, Wife to the Rev. Mr. Matth. Pilkington. Written by Herself . . .* (1748), were exactly what they claimed to be. Many of these books, however, were complicated mixtures, bearing some important relation both to journalism and life writing, on the one hand, and to fiction, on the other. As Lynda Thompson points out, these generic boundaries were very unstable.

It is not surprising, therefore, that one important aim of the new review magazines was to assist the relatively defenseless book purchaser to disentangle all this authorial deception. The original advertisement for *The Monthly Review* in 1749 declared: "the abuse of title pages is obviously come to such a pass, that few readers care to take in a book, any more than a servant, without a recommendation." On one level, the reviews hoped to offer consumers of books some protection from a kind of consumer fraud. More importantly, in an empiricist age when facts were thought to be important raw data for reasoning upon crucial matters of public policy and culture, they hoped to make a critical contribution to reducing the pollution of good data by spurious data. On some occasions, sometimes with the aid of inside information, sometimes by the sheer power of critical reasoning, the reviewers were able to discern would-be authorial deception. Often, they could only alert readers to the possibility of deception and suggest reasons for thinking a book genuine or spurious. Frequently, though, they were as deceived as the most naive book buyer. Sarah Scott, for instance, adopting the male pseudonym Henry Augustus Raymond, Esq. for her *History of Gustavus Vasa* (1761), fooled a reviewer who never suspected a woman had written the history. Occasionally, the reviews were in league with the deceivers and connived at deception.

As lived experience acquired increasing authority in the Enlightenment, writers were tempted to appropriate other people's experience, and, as the differences between male and female subjectivities were increasingly emphasized, women's experience seemed to have a specific authority that could tempt male writers to appropriate it. From a more commercial perspective, a text perceived as written by a woman was supposed to appeal to the growing market segment of female readers; it might also have novelty value, or, if the woman were famous or infamous, celebrity value. A good number of eighteenth-century male writers, from the most distinguished to desperate hacks, at one time or another – for a great range of reasons and with various degrees of sobriety and levity – on occasion published as women. Benjamin Franklin, for example, began his literary career in the 1720s with essays published in the *New-England Courant*. He wrote as the young widow Silence Dogood, advocated education for women, denounced hoop petticoats, and supported Defoe's proposal for a new kind of life insurance scheme that would help support widows. Christopher Smart, now more famous as a poet, from 1751 to 1753 wrote as Mrs Mary Midnight, a midwife, in his periodical *The Midwife; or, The Old Woman's Magazine*.

At mid-century, when some thought that women might be especially qualified to write essays and books of advice to women, two male writers, eschewing levity and maintaining sober female masks, promoted new ideas of delicate, modest femininity. John Hill, most remembered as a writer on botany, wrote two books for which he used the pseudonym, "The Hon. Juliana-Susannah Seymour": *The Conduct of a Married Life: Laid Down in a Series of Letters* . . . (1754) and *On the Management and Education of Children. A Series of Letters Written to a Neice* [sic] (1754). Hill makes explicit the claims that women possess a unique and valuable subjectivity, that women's writing has novelty value, and that women's articulation of their own experience has special value for other women:

> having been written by one of our Sex, [these letters] contain many Sentiments peculiar to us; and they are therefore useful in that they have something new. Men are the general Writers, and there pass many Things in our Hearts of which they know nothing. A Woman can best advise a Woman in Things which herself has experienced. . . . (*Management* 1754 vol. 2: 6)

Mrs Seymour lends the supposed authority of her female experience to strengthening the developing prohibition against female wit: "I never knew one of my own Sex, who had ever so small a Share of it, that did not make very bad Use of that" (*Management* 1754 vol. 2: 114). She also professes great shock at learning, from a gentleman, that the classic Greek and Latin texts are full of "Lewdness and Debauchery" and makes an early demand for strenuous expurgations to prevent boys from growing up to be adulterers or perhaps even sodomites.

More outrageously, William Kenrick, a prolific author described by the *Dictionary of National Biography* as "often drunk and violent," "a notorious libeller," published *The Whole Duty of Woman. By a Lady. Written at the Desire of a Noble Lord* (1753). This book went through an alarming number of editions in England, Ireland, and America. Kenrick's "Lady," adopting an oddly rhapsodic style, takes a very hard line on the propriety of separate spheres for men and women:

> It is not for thee, O woman, to undergo the perils of the deep, to dig in the hollow mines of the earth, to trace the dark springs of science, or to number the thick stars of the heavens. . . . Thy kingdom is in thine own house, and thy government the care of thy family. (*Whole Duty* 1753: 17–18)

A trifle coy in her advertisement to the reader, this "Lady" regrets the loss of her virgin innocence and stakes her claim to authority on sad "knowledge dearly bought by experience" (*Whole Duty* 1753: xi). Knowingly or not, Kenrick thus imitates a persona Eliza Haywood had used in her periodical *The Female Spectator* (1744–6). Kenrick's mask only momentarily wobbles in the advertisement when the author defends her

165

anonymity by saying that she does not want the value of her sentiments "to meet with less regard" because associated with a name "which on other occasions has been made so public." Enjoying his secret, the author remarks, "It is a reproach, too often justly, cast on writers of morality, that their names prefixed in the title-pages of their books, are little else than a confutation of the precepts that follow" (*Whole Duty* 1753: v). The name Kenrick hoped his reader might suspect as the name of the author was perhaps that of Constantia Phillips, the celebrity "courtesan," supposed author of the very popular *An Apology for the Conduct of Mrs. Teresia Constantia Phillips, more particularly that part of it which relates to her Marriage, with an eminent Dutch Merchant* (1748–49) and apparently the author of *A Letter humbly address'd to the Right Honourable, the Earl of Chesterfield. By Mrs. Teresia Constantia Muilman* (1750), offering advice to women. As contemporaries tried to reason about the subjects of gendered natures and about questions of disputed authorship, they were trapped in a hermeneutic circle where texts offered false evidence of gendered experience and capacity and attribution arguments often had to be based on preexisting beliefs about gender.

In the rest of this chapter, I want to concentrate on a special set of texts involving false authorial identities: those texts that to a contemporary purchaser in a bookseller's shop appeared to be written by a particular living woman, usually texts that had the woman's name on the title page as author, but which, in fact, were written by men. This is a smaller set of texts than the large set that purported to be written "By a Lady" or by a pseudonymous female author who did not exist. In some cases, the woman whose name appeared on the title page was a willing party to the deception. In other cases, the woman's name was pilfered. To pretend that someone else's work is yours is plagiarism and can be a legal offence, but to pretend that someone else wrote what you have written did not appear to violate common law or statute. Nevertheless, it could also be irritating, indeed, enraging, for a woman to be said to have written a work which she did not in fact write, especially if the words ascribed to her were words she would never have uttered. To put words into a woman's mouth when she does not want them there, and to force her to utter them in print, against her will, can be a kind of quasi-rape, a theft of her control over her identity. For the sake of discussion here, I want to group the false attributions to particular women into three categories: first, those produced by consensual relationships between the supposed female authors and men who served as ghostwriters; second, those produced by theft; and third, those "forced false attributions" motivated by a desire to attack the woman.

Consent

My first set of texts are those purporting to be written by a woman, but actually written at the request of the woman by a man or men over whom she exercised some control, men who expected to be rewarded for their literary labor. Just as great or notable men could find men to write for them, so women who wanted to offer defenses of their conduct might find collaborators and ghostwriters. The case of Sarah Churchill, Duchess of Marlborough, offers a well-documented example of a great woman who found male writers motivated by expectation of reward in the form of patronage and/or money to assist her to produce a text. *An Account of the Conduct of the Dowager Duchess of Marlborough, From her First Coming to Court to the year 1710. In a Letter from Herself to my Lord* – (1742) was not, in fact, written by the Duchess of Marlborough herself. This substantial book of 362 pages has sometimes been attributed to Nathaniel Hooke, but recent work by Henry Snyder and Frances Harris with the Blenheim papers offers a better understanding of its complex history. The Duchess was the object of considerable vilification and satire in the early eighteenth century when she was the favorite of Queen Anne. It is easy to understand how she could have been enraged by, for instance, Swift's suggestion in *Examiner* 16 that she was like a maid who had embezzled most of the money entrusted to her by her mistress. She was tempted to respond quite early with counter-narratives explaining the correctness of her behavior, but was inhibited by political considerations, by the awareness that dukes and more especially duchesses risked lowering themselves by entering into the world of print, and by her feeling that it was not proper for a woman to appear either as a politician or an author. "I don't like to be an Author," she wrote in a letter, "and I fancy somebody that has sense might turn [her fragments of narrative] in some way to make it useful without exposing me" (Harris 1982: 20).

At various points long before the publication of *An Account* in 1742, the Duchess of Marlborough had written unpublished accounts. After she was dismissed from Queen Anne's service, she "perceived how industriously Malice was employed, in inventing Calumnies to load me with," and thought to respond (*Account* 1742: 5). She also saved documents – including the letters to her from Queen Anne, which, despite the Queen's request, she refused to return – in part because she planned to print them as evidence with her narrative. Yet, according to Frances Harris, the Duchess was always aware of her limitations as a writer, particularly of her disorganization and repetitiousness:

"Consequently, although she supplied most of the material for the different versions of her vindication, she always employed a more experienced male collaborator to formalize the style and presentation" (Harris 1982: 15). Beginning in 1711, five different men were engaged to produce versions of *An Account*: Gilbert Burnet, Arthur Maynwaring, Whadcock Priest, Benjamin Hoadley, and finally, Nathaniel Hooke.

Some of these draft *Accounts* were first person, some third. The Duchess suggested to Maynwaring that he produce two separate texts: one a "paper of facts" of which she would appear the author and another "to come out upon that as if it came from somebody that had a mind to do Justice and to put things in a right light to the Publick" (Harris 1982: 15). The final decision that the printed *Account* appear written by the Duchess herself was, I think, made easier by the passage of time, by Hooke's expurgations, and by her recognition of the public's appetite for authentic historical memoirs.

Once published, *An Account* was promptly defended (by Fielding, for instance) and attacked. At least one attack insisted that the Duchess was not competent to have produced the *Account* herself. In *The Sarah-ad: or, a Flight for Fame. A Burlesque Poem in Three Canto's, in Hudibrastic Verse* (1742), she is made to say: "And this, because I write but badly, / And sometimes indeed spell most sadly, / I got a Clerk o' th'Inns o'Court / To write it down, and paid him for't" (*Sarah-ad* 1742: 8).

For a work to appear as written by a female aristocrat affected the rules of the game of criticism, as is evident in one of the more substantial rebuttals: *The Other Side of the Question: or, an Attempt to Rescue the Character of the Two Royal Sisters Q. Mary and Q. Anne, out of the hands of the D—r D— of— . . . By a Woman of Quality* (1742). The actual author of this was very far from being a "Woman of Quality." He was James Ralph, who began life as a merchant's clerk in Philadelphia, came to London in 1724 with Franklin, from thenceforth to become a busy London writer often favoring anonymity or psuedonymity. His journal *The Rembrancer* was so politically effective that, though he won no patronage by it, at least his targets, Henry Pelham and Thomas Pelham-Holles, Duke of Newcastle, paid him to stop printing it. Given the purported fact of the Duchess's authorship, not only does Ralph feel called upon to appear as "A Woman of Quality" himself, and to cast his attack on one Duchess as a defense of two ladies of yet higher quality, two Queens, but he also feels a need to defend the propriety of criticizing a lady. Addressing the Duchess, he warns: "be pleased to take into Consideration, that Authorship, as well as Love, sets all Mankind on a level; and that whoever draws a Pen is as liable to be called to an

Account for the Use made of it, as he that draws a Sword" (*Other Side* 1742: 2).

Other women, neither aristocratic nor rich, also were able to make consensual arrangements with male writers to write for them. Some women were able to capitalize on their celebrity and knowledge of their own "secret histories" to enter into exchange relationships with experienced male writers, sometimes based on a kind of profit sharing. We are told in Con Phillips's *Apology* that a bookseller approached her with an offer to find a person to write her story and to give her £1,000. The published *Apology* is narrated by a third-person male voice claiming that he is not "an *Author* by *Profession*," but simply a chivalrous gentleman who writes for an "unfortunate and distress'd Lady" (*Apology* vol. 1: 18). He suggests that she has a duty to counter unauthorized versions of her life already in circulation, promises to be impartial, and pledges to make her the beneficiary of any profits from the work. The narrative certainly seems to represent Phillips's point of view and interpolates many letters apparently written by her and others supposedly written by men. Phillips protected the copyright by registering it as her property and she capitalized on the market value of a scandalous woman's telling her own story by signing individual copies of the book to authenticate them, a tactic Laurence Sterne also resorted to in 1761 when he signed volume 5 of *Tristram Shandy* in hopes of distinguishing it from spurious competing texts. Lynda Thompson, however, argues plausibly that Phillips's male collaborator was Paul Whitehead, an opposition writer. It seems reasonable to regard this *Apology* as a collaborative work from which both parties expected to profit and did profit, although it is probably impossible to identify precisely authorship of particular passages and to disentangle all the elements of fact and fiction. A collaborative arrangement also seems the best explanation of the five volume *An Apology for the Life of George Anne Bellamy, late of Covent Garden Theatre, Written by Herself* (1785). This is genuinely an apology for the famous actress, very sympathetic, but seems to have been written by Alexander Bicknell, apparently with the cooperation of Bellamy. Bicknell published histories and novels under his own name, in one of which, published after Bellamy's death, he is described as the "editor" of Bellamy's *Apology*.

Theft

A second set of false attributions represents theft from a woman of her fame or notoriety by a male writer seeking to use it for his own profit.

The seventeenth-century French practice of stealing letters belonging to notable women and putting them into print as letters or parts of *Memoirs* was successfully engaged in by Curll in the early eighteenth century and continued by later English publishers (Altman 1986; Straus 1927). This practice demonstrated that there was a market for notable women's writing and prompted the manufacture of letters and memoirs to be attributed to notable women in cases where they had neglected to offer or even to write them themselves. As far as I know, and rather surprisingly, Curll never published such a purely invented volume, although he was capable of implying, without actually stating, that more famous authors had written works of the lesser known, as he implied that *The New Atalantis of the Year 1713* was the work of Delarivière Manley (Straus 1927/1970: 226). Tom Brown, a wit and younger friend of Aphra Behn, after her death included letters from "Aphra Behn" and "Anne Bracegirdle" in his *Letters from the Dead to the Living* (1702); at least two scholars have suspected him or Charles Gildon of being the authors of some of the "Behn" stories published for the first time in *The Histories and Novels of the late Ingenious Mrs. Behn* (1696) (Spencer 2000: 120–7). It is a sign of the value attached to the reputations of women writers like Charlotte Smith, Frances Burney, and Elizabeth Inchbald in the latter eighteenth century that we begin to see false attributions of novels to them, although these have not been studied carefully enough to be sure how much these false attributions derive from an intent to deceive and how much from accidents and mistakes.

In general, it would seem that writers who produce texts as theft need to produce texts in which their own identity is concealed, whereas writers who produce texts that attack their purported authors usually disguise themselves in ways meant to be seen through. This generalization, however, is an oversimplification of the boundary between theft and attack. Some of the writers of attack texts no doubt hoped that their advertisements and titles would lure purchasers hungry for inside knowledge about the purported woman author, even though they knew that once the texts were read with any degree of attention and intelligence, the purported authorship would be revealed as highly unlikely or impossible.

Love and Madness. A Story Too True. In a Series of Letters between Parties, whose Names would perhaps be mentioned, were they less known, or less lamented (1780) is worth considering here because it is unusually self-conscious about these matters. The book purports to be a compilation of the genuine letters of Martha Reay, the mistress of Lord Sandwich, and James Hackman, a Norfolk clergyman in love with her. It was published shortly after Hackman was convicted of shooting and killing Reay and surely was aimed in part at the same market as the pamphlets offering versions of the murder trial, defenses of Reay, and defenses of Hackman. The letters of both Reay and Hackman, however, were written by Sir Herbert Croft, an impecunious baronet and prolific writer, who also wrote the biographical account of Edward Young that appears in Johnson's *Lives of the Poets*, also published in 1780. The Hackman in *Love and Madness* assumes that Reay is interested in literary topics, including published letters and issues of verisimilitude, while he also regales her with true stories of murder and suicide.

Love and Madness teases the real reader so insistently with its awareness of the contemporary mania for printing genuine letters and memoirs and with the possibilities of deception that Croft seems more tempted by self-revelation than concerned to maintain the illusion that his text offers the genuine Reay and the genuine love-crazed Hackman. Hackman is made to express shock at the June 1777 execution of Dr William Dodd, also a clergyman, for forgery – an event proleptic of his own fate – and to decry how indifferent people, even women, have become to execution, how they can hear dying speeches and confessions cried up for sale in the streets "with as much indifference as they hear muffins and matches" (*Love and Madness* 1780: 106). The rush into print is so headlong that spurious texts appear in anticipation of events: "the printer always gets the start of the hangman, and many a man has bought his own dying speech on his return to Newgate by virtue of a reprieve" (p. 107). Condemned to death, "Hackman" writes his last letters to a friend and remarks, "Should the pen of fancy ever take the trouble to invent letters for me, I should not be suffered to write to you thus, because it would seem *unnatural*. Alas – they know not how gladly a wretch like me forgets himself" (p. 285).

That this textualized Hackman was actually so obsessed with Reay as to shoot her is made implausible, in part, by his inserting and discussing at length a set of letters purporting to be those of the poet Chatterton (who committed suicide in 1770), and Chatterton's sister. Hackman defends the authenticity of the Rowley poems, but also rails against the crudity of the talk about "deceit, imposture, and *forgery*" in the Chatterton debates: "For Chatterton's sake, the English language should add another word to its Dictionary; and should not suffer the same term to signify a crime for which a man suffers the most ignominious punishment, and the deception of ascribing a false antiquity of two or three centuries to compositions for which the author's name deserves to live for ever" (*Love and Madness* 1780: 138). Surprisingly, the letters Croft prints as written by Chatterton and Chatterton's sister actually were their letters; he was latter denounced by Southey for having, in effect, stolen the letters from Chatterton's mother and sister and deprived them of profits that should have been theirs.

While I find the letters of Reay and Hackman implausible as actual love letters and see *Love and Madness* as an interesting experiment in a teasing literary journalism, other readers have found the letters more convincing. An eighteenth-century reviewer wrote that it would take a "conjurer" to determine their authenticity, a nineteenth-century scholar argued that Croft must have had the actual letters before him and embellished them, and a distinguished twentieth-century critic found the book a successful novel about "mental and emotional disintegration delineated through a series of psychologically related allusions and fixations" (Lewis 1895: 457; Novak 1997: 192). Such disagreement, the possibility of plausible readings of the text as the authentic product of its purported author or authors, is typical of works in my second category of theft of the woman's name.

Quasi-Rape

Texts in my third category of "forced false attribution" are usually satiric. The women victims in these texts were even more likely than the women targeted for theft to be women considered to have violated the decorums proper to women: notable religious dissenters, political dissenters, and women guilty of sexual transgression. If such women had already spoken publicly or published texts, then they seemed still more tempting targets. Thus, Elizabeth Cellier, the Roman Catholic midwife tried for treason in the Meal Tub plot, acquitted, and then tried and convicted of libel for publishing her defense in *Malice Defeated* (1680), became the purported author of *Madam Celliers Answer to the Pope's Letter, dated from the Vatican, the 1st of August 1680* (1680). In this letter she is made to acknowledge that the Jesuits have been behind her actions and that they helped write her narrative. She offers the Pope "such a Mess of strengthening Jelly, as shall make Prick to mount his head aloft," and finally begs for a place, perhaps as "Midwife-General" to the "Pope's Seraglio" (*Celliers Answer* 1, 2, 4).

A more distinguished writer than Cellier, the historian and political writer Catharine Macaulay, drew fire principally because of her radical political views, although her second marriage gave a notable opening to those who disliked either her politics or her literary ambitions or both.

Richard Paul Jodrell wrote a particularly cruel, though not unfunny, epistle: *The Female Patriot: An Epistle From C—t—e M—c—y to the Reverend Dr. W—l—n. On her late Marriage. With Critical, Historical, and Philosophical Notes and Illustrations* (1779). I have found this catalogued as by Catharine Macaulay, although anyone reasonably familiar with Macaulay would have known that she neither could nor would have written it. The *Critical Review* had no difficulty spotting it as written "in the character of a certain female historian" (*Critical Review* 1779: 155). Jodrell was a graduate of Eton, of Oxford, and of Lincoln's Inn. In the 1790s he was elected to Parliament as a Tory; he presumably did not like Macaulay's politics. Many Englishmen did not approve of her support of the American rebels. Jodrell seizes the moment of Macaulay's second marriage, as a widow of 47, to James Graham, a medical man, aged 21. The news of the famous author of (at that point) five volumes of *The History of England* marrying a man so much younger than she was catnip to the caricaturists and satirists. Jodrell had gone after her in a Haymarket farce of July 1779 called *A Widow–No Widow*; there he cast her as a "Mrs. Sharp" trying to extort money from her gentlemen admirers. At the point of Macaulay's marriage to Graham in November 1779, rumor had it that Macaulay had written a letter to the Reverend Thomas Wilson, explaining her decision to make this second marriage. The elderly Wilson had so much admired Macaulay that he offered her a fête on her 46th birthday and had a statue of her as History erected in his local church. After her marriage to Graham, enraged, he decided she was a "modern Messalina" and a swindler; he also revoked a substantial legacy he had planned to give her and threatened to publish letters of hers in his possession, including the one explaining her reasons for marrying. That letter was never published, but someone other than Macaulay capitalized on the rumors of its existence to publish, in verse, *A Remarkable Moving Letter, which was Suggested by an Extraordinary Epistle Sent by her of Her Second Marriage to Her Clerical Admirer* (1779).

Like many male satirists who write as women, Jodrell imposes his idea of female nature as obsessively sexual; in this case, he imposes it on a woman whose own writings expressed no concern with sexuality, although her writing about history and politics violated decorums of femininity Jodrell aimed to enforce. Jodrell decides to imagine Macaulay writing to Wilson the morning after her wedding night. A long physical description of her new husband is accompanied by a sardonic note: "it is hoped this minute description by Catharine of the qualification of her Swain will be relished by every Reader of delicate taste, and particularly by the Ladies, those nice judges of personal merit in Men" (*Female*

173

Patriot 1779: 10–11). Echoing a famous scene in *The Dunciad* and probably also indulging in a little wish-fulfillment of his own, Jodrell makes Catharine sacrifice to Cupid by burning some of her favorite works of radical politics, including the works of Algernon Sydney, Wilkes's *North Briton*, and volumes of Benjamin Franklin, John Hancock, and Samuel Adams. Like Dido, Catharine is visited by the ghost of her first husband, reminding us that she has failed to uphold the highest standards of faithfulness and chastity. (This more modern ghost, however, urges Catharine to bear a line of patriots with her new husband.)

Women noted for their violations of sexual decorums were even more popular targets for attack than women who offended principally by their religious or political views. The possibilities of putting words into the mouths of favored mistresses of kings and princes particularly attracted male writers. Preferred forms for this were the dialogue, which offered the possibility of staging cat fights between female rivals, and the letter, in verse or prose. Among the royal mistresses thus forced to speak words not their own were Louise de Kéroualle, French mistress to Charles II, created by him Duchess of Portsmouth; Nell Gwynn, more popular as Charles II's English whore; Henrietta Howard, later Lady Suffolk, mistress to George II; Amalie Sophie Wallmoden, German mistress of George II, created by him Countess of Yarmouth; and Mary Robinson, mistress of the Prince of Wales.

Although as an unpublished dialogue it is not in my set of false attributions, an underlying dynamic of these texts in which royal mistresses are made to speak is exposed by John Wilmot, Earl of Rochester's "A Dialogue." Nell Gwynn and the Duchess of Portsmouth are imagined to be speaking in 1675, just as yet another rival for the King's favors, Hortensia Mancini, arrived from Italy:

> Nell.   When to the king I bid good morrow
> With tongue in mouth, and hand on tarse,
> Portsmouth may rent her cunt for sorrow,
> And Mazarin may kiss mine arse.
>
> Ports.   When England's monarch's on my belly
> With prick in cunt, though double crammed,
> Fart of mine arse for small whore Nelly,
> And great whore Mazarin be damned.

Some of the energy here comes from the exhilaration of exposing, behind the false and pretty decorums of representations like Pierre Mignard's court portrait of Louise de Kéroualle, the blunter realities of sex; some comes from the excitement (for men) of hearing women "talk dirty."

At the same time, this poem and similar texts express a jealousy toward women who have achieved such closeness to the sovereign and who have received favors – of all sorts – from him. The poet in fantasy puts himself in the speaking position of the favored one, boasting of favors, a position he feels, by right, ought more properly to belong to him. The satires against royal mistresses are most severe on foreign mistresses, who are, usually rightly enough, seen as diverting English wealth away from English subjects.

Rochester's "Dialogue" was not published and, of course, does not purport to be written by its speakers, but other texts were printed as though royal mistresses had written them. Only a naive reader could suppose that these were authentic documents rather than satires. In *A Letter from the Dutch. of Portsmouth to Madam Gwyn, on her Landing in France* (1682), the Duchess is made to assume a catty camaraderie with Nell Gwynn, offering a newsy account of her voyage across the channel to visit France, comments on the ladies of England, and cautionary advice that Nell had best marry quickly, "for you will find at my return, the Ebb will be so low, that the next Retrenchment must be upon the Whores" (*Portsmouth* 1682: 2). More fancifully, in a hit at the Duchess's ability to control patronage and a charge that she sometimes takes bribes without intending to perform, she is made to describe negotiations with Neptune, "*Charles*'s Vice-Admiral." Neptune offers fabulous jewels "if I would intercede to make him Admiral." She takes the jewels, but tells her confidant Nelly that she hopes to see her illegitimate son by Charles, the Duke of Richmond, made Admiral instead.

Nell is then made to reply in a separate publication, *Madam Gwins Answer to the Duchess of Portsmouth's Letter* (1682), ostensibly by a different publisher, although the typography and format appear suspiciously similar; this may be an early example of the booksellers' tactic of producing entertaining controversy by allowing the same writer to write on both sides of a question. As is usual in staged contests between these two, Nell gets the better of her rival. Nell patriotically complains about the Duchess's aspersions on the sexual appetites of English ladies. As befits her own low birth, she is made more overtly vulgar. She taunts the Duchess with the possibility that one of her illegitimate sons may enjoy favors the Duchess plans for hers: "You tell us of great things, that you are Big belli'd with hopes that your little Prince will Mount the Sea-*horse* and ride Admiral of the narrow *Seas*, but hold I have a little Lord that crept out of my cranny that may for ought I know prick your Bladder and let out that ambitious wind" (*Gwin's Answer* 1682: 3).

In the early decades of the eighteenth century, texts purportedly written by royal mistresses and other notable fallen women, while they retain some elements of the Restoration attacking satires, also are likely to show marked influence from both the Ovidian *Heroides* and the new perspectives of she-tragedy, and, consequently, to be more sympathetic (although not necessarily less sexist). Ovid's *Heroides*, verse epistles addressed by mythic, fictional, and historical women like Dido and Sappho to their absent lovers, were frequently translated and imitated. The brilliance of Pope's "Eloisa to Abelard" inspired further imitation; perhaps, also, Michael Drayton's earlier version of the *Heroides* in which classical personages were replaced by historical English women helped prepare the way for the further step of imagining living contemporary English women as authors.

Proponents of sharply contested positions on the nature of woman aimed to make their constructions persuasive by trying to match the evidence of particular women's behavior in the public, journalistic record with real or imagined presentations of what they claimed were the inner, private truths of the female mind, often using techniques borrowed from literary forms like the *Heroides* or she-tragedy. (See also Chapter 9 DRAMA.) Charles Beckingham in *Epistle from Calista to Altamont* (1729) takes facts from a criminal conversation trial. His *Epistle* purports to be the words of Lady Katherine Abergavenny, wife of William Nevill, 16th Lord Abergavenny, just divorced by her husband. His servants and a gentleman friend, hiding in the closet for the purpose, had discovered Lady Abergavenny *in flagrante* with Richard Lydell, a gentleman neighbor. The published account of the criminal conversation trial featured the usual servant testimony about tumbled bed linen, a bed heard "creaking," and kisses and intercourse viewed through keyholes. The high-minded moralizing of Lord Abergavenny's steward and his friend Mr Day during the discovery, as well as the immediate distress and repentance of the guilty ones, also testified to, offered less tawdry, more edifying moments. Turning away from older constructions of rapacious female sexuality and from comedy, Beckingham follows Nicholas Rowe's sentimental she-tragedy to make his flawed heroine plead woman's essential weakness as a partial excuse, as long as she also expresses self-loathing for the sexual crime. Like Rowe's Jane Shore or Calista, Beckingham's Calista demonstrates her worth by her willingness to die rather than live dishonored. Unlike the other women whose vices she satirizes (and whose names we are tempted to guess), Calista is at least repentant, and, therefore, relatively sympathetic:

> Let the *gay* WANTONS I've been bold to name,
> Triumph o'er Infamy, and conquer Shame,
> Not *Altamont!* is such *Calista*'s Soul,
> She knows her late Offence and knows it foul. (*Calista* 1729: 7–8)

Beckingham, however, does not allow his guilty speaker to offer more general complaints about the injustice of woman's lot, as Rowe does in Calista's famous soliloquy, "How hard is the condition of our sex, / Through ev'ry state of life the slaves of man!" or as Lady Mary Wortley Montagu does in *Epistle from Mrs Y[onge] to her Husband*, written in 1724 after another criminal conversation case, and almost entirely a denunciation of the sexual double standard. Once previously private female conduct became part of the public print record, as it did in criminal conversation trials or in scandal chronicles, writers felt compelled to address those records to make them conform to what they supposed were authentic constructions of womanhood.

While writers used the weapons of satire, usually associated with older constructions of woman as sexually rapacious or mercenary, throughout the eighteenth century, some of the mid- and late-eighteenth-century texts also show the legacy of the *Heroides* and of the more sentimental she-tragedy that Beckingham developed. Henrietta Howard, Countess of Suffolk and mistress to George II, was the purported author of *Female Honour: An Epistle to a Lady in Favour, From the Lady lately Kick'd-out* (1742), addressed to her successor as George's mistress, Amalie Sophie Wallmoden, Countess of Yarmouth. Unlike Nell Gwynn, the Countess of Suffolk was quite literate, indeed, famous for her wit in conversation and letters and could conceivably have written a reasonably stylish poem like this one to her rival. However, she was probably too decorous to have used a phrase like "kick'd out" in a title or to have published anything calling attention to her former life at any time, and certainly not after she had left the king and married the Hon. George Berkeley in 1735. Pope, Swift, and Arbuthnot all visited and corresponded with her and in her later years Horace Walpole adored listening to her stories. Indeed, she told Walpole that one of the letters published as by her had actually been dictated to her by Arbuthnot. It is to Walpole that we owe the oft-repeated observation: "She behaved with such extreme propriety that her friends affected to suppose that her relations with the king were merely platonic."

An Epistle from a Lady in Favour oscillates between jealousy over the exaltation of her foreign rival Yarmouth, regret at the loss of her own virtue, and philosophical observations on the transitoriness of pleasure and power:

> Of short Duration are a Woman's Joys,
> One Hour she charms, that Hour repeated, cloys. . . .
> By late Repentance taught, no Joy's sincere,
> There is no Station unalloy'd with Fear. (*Female Honour* 1742: 5, 12)

Although the "Countess" alludes to the likeness between the competition between her and her rival and the struggle in Nathaniel Lee's *Rival Queens*, with its "tragic Rants," and although she warns that one day Yarmouth may be supplanted by another British rival, her general tone is more meditative than furious. In fact, she ends by imagining the day in which the Duchess of Yarmouth will, as the Countess has, find a nobleman who will show her "No more a MISTRESS, but a virtuous WIFE" (*Female Honour* 1742: 12). Whoever the real author of this poem was seems divided between, on the one hand, satiric impulses to expose the immoral behavior of courtiers and the king and the hypocrisy of a society that allowed whores to turn into wives, and, on the other hand, a sympathetic identification with the attraction to power that leads women to become royal mistresses and the necessity of developing a capacity to accept the transience of favor. Although I do not think Swift wrote this poem, its attitudes resemble those expressed in his correspondence with the Countess of Suffolk.

One famous royal mistress and woman writer who did write and publish her own defense of her conduct was Mary Robinson, in 1779–81 mistress to Frederick, Prince of Wales. She was provoked into defense by attacks in the usual modes of the day, including satiric prints and at least two texts published as partly written by her, *Florizel to Perdita: with Perdita's Answer* (1781) and *Letters from Perdita to a certain Israelite and Answers to them* (1781). Robinson was known as Perdita because she was an actress appearing in that role in Shakespeare's *Winter's Tale* when the Prince first saw her. Her affair was unusual, as royal affairs went, in that the Prince corresponded with her for months before she consented to become his mistress. Only 18 at the time and apparently romantic, he borrowed another name from *The Winter's Tale* (in David Garrick's version, *Florizel and Perdita*) to sign his letters to her "Florizel." Mary Robinson, then 22, was already married to a man generally considered of bad character and certainly in substantial debt. In *The Memoirs of the Late Mrs Robinson. Written by Herself* (1801, the first part of which she does seem to have written later in her life) she reports that, before she meet the Prince, "I observed that Mr Robinson had frequent visitors of the Jewish tribe" with whom he met secretly (*Memoirs* 1801: 81). A satiric print of November 11, 1780 entitled "Florizel and Perdita" shows the Prince with his coronet falling off his head, Mary, and behind her, her husband, stag horns on his head, and in his hands a paper inscribed "Sir Peter Pimp." Many thought Mary Robinson's motives for this affair were more mercenary than lascivious. She seems to have argued to the Prince, in their correspondence, that if she became his mistress, she would have to abandon a lucrative stage career and implied that this might require monetary compensation. In addition to the usual sorts of presents royal mistresses got, she accepted from him a bond for £20,000 payable on his reaching the age of majority. She certainly kept the Prince's letters and realized their economic value to a publisher. After he discarded her, she threatened to publish the letters and, in exchange for desisting, extracted from the Prince's not very fond father, George III, £5,000, a sum the king called "undoubtedly . . . enormous" (George III, 1928: nos. 3396, 3377).

George III kept the authentic and expensive letters of Mary Robinson and the Prince out of print, but awareness of their existence incited the manufacture of less authentic, cheaper substitutes. Robinson's literacy had already been established with the publication in 1775 of a volume of her *Poems* and in 1771 *Captivity, A Poem; and Celedon and Lydia, A Tale*, written while she lived with her husband in debtors' prison.

Letters from Perdita to a certain Israelite, and his Answers to them appeared in 1781, containing what purported to be authentic letters written by Mary Robinson and a gentlemanly young Jewish businessman in love with her. The frontispiece offers a portrait of Robinson. An anonymous and hostile "editor" introduces the letters. Given that it is 1781, he makes much of his recognition of the supposed fact that "Women will exclaim against the Indelicacy of Publishing private letters, however obtained, and men, who have any Turn for Gallantry, always express a Disapprobation of such a Measure" (*Perdita* 1781: i). The Editor's principal excuse is that he feels obliged to expose a new species of swindling, now introduced by Mr and Mrs Robinson "into the Traffick of Love." He also claims that any obligation from gallantry not to publish Mrs Robinson's letters is cancelled by her having written and published *The Letters of Florizel and Perdita*, all of which, he claims (implausibly), she wrote herself. His brief and not entirely accurate account of Mary Robinson's life includes criticism of her published writings, of her poems as no more than a "very humble Imitation of Shenstone's," and the allegation that *Florizel and Perdita* and "all her compositions" have been "revised and bettered by some more correct and able pen" (*Perdita* 1781: 14–15).

The *Letters from Perdita* show "Mary Robinson" calculatingly playing her admirer for profit, stressing her financial distress and needs, while the young Jew is besotted with her but never entirely without suspicions. He declares: "Once in a gay happy Moment you said you loved me; it is well I do not believe you, for my Joy that would have heightened to Phrensy, is thereby kept with the proper limits of Moderation" (*Perdita* 1781: 21). Although his business in London interferes with his seeing her in Bristol, their affair has clearly been consummated when he writes: "what *Raptures* ineffable seize my *delighted imagination*, when I *recollect* the *delirious Transports* that throbbed to my very Soul, when that beauteous Form stood confessed in all the resistless power of *Nakedness*" (*Perdita* 1781: 28–9). Soon, however, her repeated demands for money and loans and her spending £200 in six weeks make him desperate and disillusioned. He complains, and refuses to provide more. She cuts him off most unsentimentally: "I find you have not answered my Draft. I do not wish an Acquaintance with any Man who professes so much Love, but who gives so little Proof of it" (*Perdita* 1781: 40).

The point of this exposé seems to be to suggest that Mary Robinson has had experience of bleeding men for money before she met the Prince and that she continues to be mercenary and calculating. I do not think the author is using the young Jewish gentleman to represent the Prince, and there is no evidence that Robinson had an affair with a young Jew. Despite the generally sympathetic character of the young Jew, the satiric point probably has more to do with exploiting anti-Semitism by showing her as "contaminated" by a having had intercourse with a Jew and as still more mercenary than a Jew. That the accusations of being calculating and mercenary stung is evident from her *Memoirs*, where she presents herself as sentimental and not much aware of financial matters. In the *Memoirs*, also, she regales readers with settlements offered her before she knew the Prince and insists that she spurned all such offers. Before her affair with the Prince, she claims, "I still had the consolation of an unsullied name"; during the correspondence with him, she contends in the *Memoirs*, she "disdained every sordid and interested thought" (*Memoirs* 1801: 141, 164). These contentions are almost certainly untrue.

Conclusion

From Margaret Fell in *Women's Speaking Justified* (1666) to Mary Robinson, women in the Restoration and eighteenth century had discovered that they might use printed pamphlets and books to make their own arguments and to tell their own stories. Yet, in the contest of stories that commercial print culture promoted, it was easy enough for others to create alternate versions of these stories, versions with varying degrees of plausibility. When a woman presented herself as a sympathetic character, her detractors could readily enough offer a *Shamela* to her *Pamela*. The fame of other women, like Nell Gwynn, who did not attempt to publish texts but who in other ways made themselves public characters on stage or at court, prompted appropriations of their identities. The reconstructed women appearing in the false attributions are insistently sexualized. This may not be surprising in the cases of the royal mistresses, yet the concern with women in terms of sexuality is obsessive. "Cellier" is made to say more about her vagina than about Roman Catholic theology or worship, "Macaulay" appears meditating on her wedding night not on the composition of her history, and even "Robinson" has nothing to say about acting. The difficulty – perhaps merely lack of interest – male writers had in imagining woman as having capacities other than sexual is also suggested by the persistence of the phrase "Written by Herself" in titles throughout the century, a phrase calling attention to a phenomenon that appeared anomalous.

We need to do more work on many texts claiming to be authentic lives, letters, or memoirs and to explore more carefully the persistent relationship between journalism and the novel. Not only are there many attribution problems associated with these texts, but our sorting of them is still crude. Several of the texts I have been working with, as well as more authentic letters and memoirs, appear in bibliographies of prose fiction and of novels; some texts, as we have seen, mix authentic documents and facts with elements of "fictionalized" treatments. While "True History" and "Genuine Memoirs," and even "Written by Herself," are phrases that persist in novel titles throughout the period, some of these texts are more accurately and usefully seen, not simply as novels, satires, or poems, but as topical journalism tied to publicly known fact. That we still share the Enlightenment concern about the relation between authors and title pages is evident in current controversies over the supposed memoirs of Asian women and Native Americans written by white men and the supposed holocaust memoirs not written by survivors.

References and further reading

Primary texts when quoted are cited in the text by abbreviated titles and are not listed below. Page references are to first editions.

Altman, J. G. (1986) "The letterbook as a literary institution, 1539–1789: Towards a cultural history of published correspondences in France," *Yale French Studies* 71: 17–62.

Baines, P. (1999) *The House of Forgery in Eighteenth-Century Britain*. Aldershot, Hants.: Ashgate.

Foxon, D. E. (1975) *English Verse 1701–1750: A Catalogue of Separately Printed Poems with Notes on Contemporary Collected Editions*, 2 vols. Cambridge: Cambridge University Press.

George III (1928) *The Correspondence of King George the Third from 1760 to Dec. 1783*, 6 vols., ed. The Hon. Sir John Fortescue. London: Macmillan and Company.

Griffin, R. (1999) "Anonymity and authorship," *New Literary History* 30, 877–93.

Hill, B. (1992) *The Republican Virago: The Life and Times of Catharine Macaulay, Historian*. Oxford: Oxford University Press.

Harris, F. (1982) "Accounts of the conduct of Sarah, Duchess of Marlborough, 1704–1742," *British Library Journal* 8: 7–35.

—— (1991) *A Passion for Government: The Life of Sarah, Duchess of Marlborough*. Oxford: Oxford University Press.

Lewis, E. H. (1895) "Are the Hackman Reay love-letters genuine?," *Modern Language Notes* 10(8): 454–63.

Lynch, J. (2002) "Samuel Johnson's 'Love of Truth' and literary fraud," *Studies in English Literature* 42: 60–78.

Novak, M. E. (1997) "The Sensibility of Sir Herbert Croft in *Love and Madness* and the 'Life of Edward Young,'" *Age of Johnson* 8: 189–207.

Raven, J. (1987) *British Fiction 1750–1770*. Newark: University of Delaware Press.

Raven, J., Forster, A., and Bending, S. (2000) *The English Novel, 1770–1829: A Bibliographical Survey of Prose Fiction Published in the British Isles. Volume 1, 1770–1799*. Oxford: Oxford University Press.

Snyder, H. L. (1965) "Daniel Defoe, the Duchess of Marlborough, and Advice to the Electors of Great Britain," *Huntington Library Quarterly* 29: 53–62.

Spencer, J. (2000) *Aphra Behn's Afterlife*. Oxford: Oxford University Press.

Stewart, S. (1991) *Crimes of Writing: Problems in the Containment of Representation*. New York: Oxford University Press.

Straus, R. (1927) *The Unspeakable Curll: Being Some Account of Edmund Curll, Bookseller. To which is added a full list of his Books*. New York: Augustus M. Kelley, 1970.

Thompson, L. M. (2000) *The "Scandalous Memoirists": Constantia Phillips, Laetitia Pilkington and the Shame of "Publick Fame"*. Manchester: Manchester University Press.

Woodmansee, M. and Jaszi, P. (eds.) (1994) *The Construction of Authorship: Textual Appropriation in Law and Literature*. Durham, NC: Duke University Press.

Chapter 9

Drama

Genre, Gender, Theater

John O'Brien

Consider the extraordinary satirical image "A Just View of the British Stage," published in December 1724 (Figure 9.1). The print (which has traditionally been assigned to William Hogarth, though it may be by someone else) appropriates the much-beloved contemporary genre of the rehearsal play, in which the audience is taken behind the scenes and shown the process of putting together a new production, to mock the current depraved state of the London theater. The triumvirate of actor-managers who ran the playhouse at Drury Lane – Robert Wilks, Colley Cibber, and Barton Booth – use puppets to work out a forthcoming production of *Scaramouche Jack Hall*, a piece that is apparently to be based on the life of a notorious house-breaker who had been executed in 1709. The puppets of Punch, Harlequin, and Scaramouche being manipulated by Wilks, Cibber, and Booth respectively refer to the current vogue for pantomimes, mixtures of continental *commedia dell'arte*, opera, dance, and farce that were performed as the afterpieces to five-act plays. Pantomime's extraordinary popularity with audiences often led these afterpieces to overshadow the dramatic works they followed and spurred a fevered competition between the two state-licensed London theaters (at Drury Lane and Lincoln's Inn Fields) to out-do one another with ever more elaborate, crowd-pleasing spectacles. *Scaramouche Jack Hall*, apparently intended to be one of these, existed only in the artist's imagination, but such a piece, even if only an object of fantasy, does not represent too much of a stretch; Drury Lane was at the moment of this print's publication just coming off a production of *Harlequin Sheppard*,

Figure 9.1 "A Just View of the British Stage," by William Hogarth (1724).
Reproduced by permission of The Huntingdon Library, San Marino, California.

a pantomime that exploited the current interest in the life and death of
the house-breaker and escape artist Jack Sheppard, who had been
executed only a few weeks before. The three ropes in the center of the
image that dangle over the heads of the managers thus forecast a
future "just" punishment for their own crime in pandering to the
public fascination with Sheppard rather than fulfilling their mission of
uplifting the audience.

More broadly, "A Just View of the British Stage" comprehends the
British stage's past, present, and future. The title refers to a text from
the comparatively recent past: the clergyman Jeremy Collier's *A Short
View of the Immorality, and Prophaneness of the English-Stage*, an anti-
theatrical screed whose publication in 1698 catalyzed already existing
animus toward the contemporary theater to set off a wave of reformist

literature, of which "A Just View of the British Stage" is a part. But the print reaches farther back, beyond Collier and the reformist wave of the *fin de siècle* to the Renaissance. On the left, the ghost of Ben Jonson rises through a trap door. A reminder of the English stage's glorious past, Jonson's ghost looks as if his rest has been disturbed by the clatter of modern stage-craft, as represented by the fallen statue, wine-flask, and dragon littering the stage. All of these are apparently the residue of a performance of *Harlequin Doctor Faustus*, the afterpiece, first produced in 1723, that had kicked off the fad for pantomime. On the picture's far right, playtexts of William Shakespeare's *Hamlet, Macbeth,* and *Julius Caesar,* as well as William Congreve's *The Way of the World,* are affixed to the wall over a privy; now merely toilet paper, these tattered embodiments of the English repertoire also, like Jonson, haunt the present state of a stage that has given itself over to spectacle, song, dance, and farce. An attack on the cynicism of the British theater's licensed custodians and their displacement of drama by spectacle, "A Just View of the British Stage" offers both a visual representation of the state of the theater at roughly the midpoint of the period covered by this volume and an account of how that institution had changed, an account that it casts as a story of decline. My goal in this chapter is to follow this image's lead and attempt to represent the Restoration and eighteenth-century British theater while also describing some of the ways in which the theater changed in that time. No account, of course, could ever hope to do full justice to the variety and range of the British theater over the course of almost a century and a half, and that is all the more true of an essay such as this one that must rely almost exclusively on only one of the constituent elements of what it is trying to describe, language. For the entity we refer to as the theater is a large and varied object of study, comprising a dramatic repertoire preserved in texts, to be sure, but also performance spaces, actors, dancers, audiences, and critics. This multiplicity, which never lets us forget that the theater is obviously a *social* institution, is also part of what makes the theater a compelling object of study; it accretes story, myth, legend, and custom. But historians have found that it proves notoriously difficult to conceptualize, describe, and account for how such complex forms of culture change over time. Should we understand change as innovation or transformation? narrate it as development or decline? assign change to the beneficial effects of reform or the baleful results of censorship? Should we attribute it in the first instance to human agents like authors, performers, or managers? Or should we rather look for more fundamental causes of change in intersubjective or impersonal factors like taste, the market, chance, or the almost infinitely complicated workings of history itself? The view of the Restoration and eighteenth-century British theater offered by this essay will come in large part through the lenses of genre and gender. These concepts had real effects; they helped structure the dramatic repertoire of the period and provided powerful categories through which theater-goers interpreted plays and felt the emotional impact of performances. But these categories are also defined in specific ways by each culture that uses them, and for that reason can be examined – the assumptions that support their articulation unearthed and subjected to critical inter-rogation. Viewed in this way, the Restoration and eighteenth-century British theater offers less a story of decline than one of continuous adapta-tion to a culture that was changing more quickly than its inhabitants could easily comprehend. Literary genre and human gender difference offered permanent, seemingly natural categories through which these changes could be managed: represented, but also contained, as the pres-sures of modernity prompted equally powerful desires to look to the past for authority and solace.

Neoclassical Theory and the Representative Character

From the first, the theater drew its models from older theatrical tradi-tions. The professional London theaters had been closed in 1642 and remained shut until late 1660, when new theaters licensed by royal patents opened under the management of William Davenant and Thomas Killigrew, two of Charles II's loyal courtiers who had spent much of the 1650s sharing his exile on the European continent. The vacuum in theatrical theory and practice was partly filled by returning to the Renaissance repertoire of Shakespeare, Jonson, Beaumont and Fletcher, and others, but many of these plays seemed antiquated, provincial, and rustic to tastes exposed to continental dramatic theory and stagecraft, so the English theater looked to antiquity. Dramatic theory of the late seventeenth and early eighteenth centuries was indebted to a neo-classical poetics based largely on an interpretation of Aristotle, one that English writers and critics adapted from the works of French writers such as René Rapin and François Hédelin, the abbé d'Aubignac. Neo-classical poetics offered a set of rules for the construction of plays, rules that were strongly ideological. I mean this in two senses. First, neoclassical principles often put theory over practice, structuring dramatic works in ways that frequently overrode previous theatrical practice and experience.

Thus, for example, playwrights were encouraged to follow the Aristotelian unities of time, place, and action, setting their works in a single place (or at least a single city), with events that took place in the same two-to-three hour span of time as that of the play itself (or at least in the 24 hours of a single day), and with one central plot line (or perhaps two plotlines that were tightly interwoven). My parenthetical remarks signal how dramatists attempted to push against the bounds of these restrictions, but the unities remained normative in spite of the fact that playwrights, critics, and audiences had plenty of examples of effective plays that violated them, such as the works of Shakespeare. His plays were extensively rewritten and adapted to meet the new standards of taste and propriety, purged of their irregularity and made to conform to neoclassical rules, their plots streamlined to obey the unities and their endings altered to create poetically just outcomes. Nahum Tate's 1682 *The History of King Lear*, in which Lear and Cordelia survive, was preferred on the stage throughout the period to Shakespeare's version in part because it proved the justness of what the critic John Dennis called "The Government of Providence," the wise supervision of the cosmos by a god who punishes the wicked and spares the good (1711/1939–43 vol. 2: 7).

It was only through following such principles that the theater could, it was believed, fulfill its mission to teach its audience lessons of morality and virtue. This is the second sense in which the drama's neoclassical principles were ideological: they were designed to instill moral principles, instructing the theater's spectators in proper behaviors for living in civil society. In a sense, theatergoers understood the drama to be fashioned according to much the same logic as that of the penal system that had sent Jack Sheppard to the gallows in November 1724: the logic of the example. Behind this logic was the belief, formulated powerfully by Aristotle, that humans are essentially imitative animals, that we instinctively wish to mimic whatever is placed before us. The theater, then, did not only portray the workings of desire in the form of love stories and narratives of political ambition, it was a form of desire in its own right. Herein lay the theater's power, which made it all the more important that the *right* examples – virtuous heroes and heroines who constituted good models of behavior; obviously ridiculous or reprehensible comic foils and villains who instructed us in what to avoid – be embodied on stage. Its strong association with desire, was also, of course, the theater's danger, as it was easy to imagine how the wrong kind of example might impress its spectators the wrong way, encouraging them to pursue dangerous or antisocial behaviors.

In theory, literary genre enabled the theater to channel desire in beneficial directions. Both dramatic theory and theatrical practice sharply distinguished comedy from tragedy, which were, as the critic and playwright Lewis Theobald put it, "Two Opposite *Glasses*, in which Mankind may see the true Figures they make in every important or trifling Circumstance of Life" (1717: 46). Each of these mirrors on its society was associated with a set of decorums. For example, comedy took place in the everyday world and was populated with recognizable characters in contemporary European societies, while tragedies were typically set in places that were alien by virtue of either time, space, or both, and featured noble, aristocratic or royal heroes and heroines. Comedy was spoken in the idiom of normal speech, while tragedy was normatively composed in verse; as late as 1753, by which point it had become possible to set tragedy in bourgeois contexts, Edward Moore's tragedy *The Gamester* was widely attacked for its being written in prose. But tragedy and comedy were not as completely severed from one another as these rules might make it seem. Both modes, for example, could coexist in a single play, as in John Dryden's *Love Triumphant; Or, Nature will Prevail* (1694) which was billed as a *"Tragi-Comedy."* Pantomime afterpieces like *Harlequin Sheppard*, immensely popular from the 1720s through the 1750s, typically interwove "comic" and "serious" sections, in part imitating, in part burlesquing the features of the two normative modes of mainpiece drama. As Peter Shepherd and Simon Womack put it, "the relation between the two significant genres is an *organized* one – they are distinct, but their distinctness is itself a form of connection, such that the identity of each is informed by the presence of the other" (Shepherd and Womack 1996: 140). Tragedies and comedies each presented examples of behavior that were all the more construable because they were underwritten by the generic identities made intelligible in such a system. Tragedy was supposed to offer positive examples, models of virtue that spectators could emulate. Comedy was supposed to offer negative examples, models of behavior so obviously *unlike* anything a spectator should want to imitate as to be actively repulsive.

A theory of spectatorial relations formed a corollary to this understanding of the decorums of genre. Actors expressed not only ideas but emotions, which were made intelligible to spectators by being construed according to a shared taxonomy of the passions – horror, fear, sorrow, astonishment, ravishment, and awe. Ideas were expressed in the first instance through words, but the passions were expressed through the body; each of these primary passions as well myriad secondary passions derived from their combinations was associated with a distinctive facial expression and set of bodily gestures. Characters in tragedy should be particularly intelligible, their virtues sufficiently marked and obvious that they constitute a clear template on which spectators could model themselves. The strong sensual bond between actor and spectator would ideally create a kind of spell in which spectators would become so absorbed in the performance that they would assimilate the virtues represented on stage. One of the best expressions of this occurs in Joseph Addison's *Cato* (1713), when Juba, a Numidian prince in love with the title character's daughter, is said to "copy out" Cato's bright example (1713/1978 vol. 1: 357). Juba models the ideal spectator of *Cato*, becoming the relay point in a chain of emulation that the play aims to create: we are to imitate Juba imitating Cato. Juba's adjective "bright" underscores the complete intelligibility of Cato's virtue, which is conceived as a visible pattern, a "character" in multiple senses: literary, ethical, typographic, and numismatic (Lynch 1998: 30). To copy Cato is to be "impressed" by the pattern that he presents to a subjectivity accessed most directly through the register of the visual in the manner of a die being stamped to produce a shiny new coin, or a sheet of paper being imprinted to produce the letters of a text (Shell 1978). The ideal spectator's mind is wholly absorbed by his engagement with the character of the tragic hero, whose virtue prompted the desire to emulate him and whose intelligibility rewarded that desire.

Comedy assumed that examples should be equally intelligible but repugnant. Rather than being attracted by a figure in comedy, the spectator should rather be revulsed, his absorption by the performance thoroughly broken by the negative force of the example that the playwright has presented. We should learn, that is, *not* to imitate Horner, the rake anti-hero of William Wycherley's *The Country Wife* (1675), and, perhaps more important, not to be as foolish as the men he cuckolds. Comedy offered models, not of virtue, but of human folly, models that should be so obviously ridiculous as to make imitation undesirable. It is not hard to see that this went against the grain of the assumption that the theater invariably prompted imitation. Hence anti-theatrical writers, who at times seemed to endow the theater with almost magic power, were particularly zealous to reform comedy. Collier and others believed that spectators were actually inclined to take their behavioral cues from the misbehaving casts of Restoration comedy, a claim that may have violated comedy's normative intentions, but that demonstrates the reformers' respect for the power of the theater's ability to prompt mimetic desire.

What comedy and tragedy shared was that both staged an exaggerated representation of reality. In order that their examples might readily be identified, marked, and taken as object lessons, dramatic works had them-selves to be striking; they were artificial in the good sense that they were clearly the product of craft and art rather than nature. The theater's par-ticipants – actors, playwrights, managers, critics, and audiences – never fully shed the belief that a performance was not so much a transparent window on the real as it was a stylized representation of its culture, a sensual emblem constructed through the interaction of language, spec-tacle, and the bodies of performers. As Dennis puts it, "A Man must come out of his ordinary state" in the theater, a transcendence to be accom-plished by presenting models for spectators' contemplation that were themselves extraordinary, related to the quotidian world from which audi-ences came and to which they would return, but at a sufficient remove from it to enable critical reflection (1698/1939–43 vol. 1: 149).

How is the relationship between actual persons and self-consciously artificial theatrical characters to be fashioned? Through what protocols were the real and its referents constructed? The theater frequently drew in other codes in which the relationship between a real thing and its representation were also articulated, most notably those derived from political theory. Seventeenth- and eighteenth-century writers never tired, for one thing, of drawing an analogy between the stage and the state, an analogy that cut deeper than the obvious fact that so much of its repertoire of serious drama in particular staged the actions of mon-archs, ministers, and warriors. Political theory was also used to describe the construction and function of individual characters. For instance, the epilogue to George Etherege's 1676 comedy *The Man of Mode; or, Sir Fopling Flutter*, written by John Dryden, calls on the rhetoric of parliamentary representation to describe how Fopling Flutter, the comic butt of the play, mirrors the audience back to itself. Stepping forth to address the audience, the actor who has just finished playing Sir Fopling observes that his character is not one of the "monstrous fools" typical of other plays, "nauseous harlequins" who derive more from the imaginations of their authors than from any social context familiar to the audience. Sir Fopling Flutter, by contrast, is "knight o'th'shire," who "represents" the "gallants" in the playhouse in the manner of a member of Par-liament (Etherege 1676/1966: 146). Dryden's reach for the rhetoric of political representation signals how important it is that the play's cast be understood to reflect back the mores of persons not only of its own moment, but of the very kinds of people who went to the theater. (See also Chapter 3 PUBLIC AND PRIVATE.) Hence his epilogue goes on to assert that Fopling's very costuming and gestures have derived from members of the pit itself: "One taught the toss, and one the new French wallow.

/ His sword-knot this; his cravat, this designed; / And this, the yard-long snake he twirls behind." Sir Fopling is a man of a mode in the very specific sense that he embodies the traits not only of men of his own moment but of the performance space that he shares with the fashionable denizens of the pit.

The Man of Mode became, as it happens, a crucial text in a debate over the nature of a representative character, a debate that helps identify some of the ways in which the nature of representativity changed in the course of the period. The debate was precipitated by Richard Steele's unconcealed desire to discredit the Restoration-era repertoire of satirical comedies in order to replace it with a kind of comedy structured on new, reformed principles. In *The Spectator* no. 65 (May 15, 1711), Steele attacked *The Man of Mode*, arguing that its rake-hero, Dorimant, was an inferior central character for a comedy because he was a poor representative of the figure of the "fine Gentleman," portrayed as "a direct Knave in his Designs, and a Clown in his Language" (1711/1965: 278–9). Dennis correctly understood Steele's argument to be about much more than just Dorimant or Etherege's play. At stake, as he put it in his essay "A Defense of Sir Fopling Flutter" (1722), was "the Nature of true Comedy," a question that turned on the nature of the representative character. Dennis sees Dorimant as a figure who is at once "allegorical and universal"; he both represents the specific traits of young men of his age (so much so that he was frequently taken to be a stand-in for the Earl of Rochester) and stands for the timeless character of the licentious young man (1722/1939–43 vol. 2: 243, 247). His representativity in effect doubled by the way that he incorporates both contemporary and transhistorical character traits, Dorimant for Dennis functions as the perfect comedic hero because he fulfills comedy's appointed role of teaching through "ridicule," exposing "Persons to our View whose Views we may shun and whose Follies we may despise; and by showing us what is done upon the Comick Stage, to show us what ought never be done upon the Stage of the World" (p. 245). Dennis realizes that Steele's attack on Dorimant is intended to undermine not only the prized place of *The Man of Mode* in the repertoire (where by 1711 it had become the representative Restoration play to early Augustan audiences, functioning, as Steele puts it, as "the pattern of genteel Comedy") but the long-accepted definition of comedy itself as the theatrical mode designed to reform its audience by offering negative examples who embodied character-traits to be avoided.

In this, Dennis is perceptive; Steele's intention is indeed to undercut ridicule as the means by which comedy achieves its goals. He proposes, in effect, that the heroes of comedy should now function as *positive* examples. The character that Steele offers to fulfill this program is Bevil, the hero of his last play, *The Conscious Lovers*, first produced in 1722. What Bevil represents, however, is not a composite of traits drawn from a segment of the audience in the manner of Sir Fopling Flutter. Rather, Bevil stands for an ideal of gentlemanly behavior, one that did not resemble any particular member of the audience, but was one to which all were to aspire. Significantly, this ideal was projected on a national scale, as is made clear by the play's prologue, composed by Steele's protégé Leonard Welsted (Chandler 2002). Dismissing the way that previous writers of comedies had excused their reliance on grimace, spectacle, domestic quarrels, and double-entendre by claiming that such features were simply "Copy'd from the Life," the prologue urges the audience to recognize that Steele's play is composed with higher aims in mind:

> Your Aid, most humbly sought, then *Britons* Lend,
> And Lib'ral Mirth, like Lib'ral Men, defend:
> No more let Ribaldry, with Licence writ,
> Usurp the Name of Eloquence or Wit . . .
> Redeem from long Contempt the Comic Name,
> And Judge Politely for your Country's Fame. (Steele 1722/1971: 304–5)

In the way that it offered examples for emulation rather than ridicule, and openly claimed to be doing so for the sake of promoting the nation's virtue, *The Conscious Lovers* might best be understood as comedy's appropriation of tragedy's salient features. In effect, Steele, who admitted to having been deeply affected by Collier's attack in his *Short View*, was performing a rescue operation on comedy by reconstituting it along the lines of tragic drama.

The Conscious Lovers came to be identified as a kind of landmark in the history of comedy, the starting-point of what came to be called "sentimental" comedy, a form that dominated comic drama for the next several decades. Sentimental comedy presented virtuous, rather than scandalous heroes and heroines, and typically aimed to provoke tears rather than laughter. The prologue to Edward Moore's 1748 comedy *The Foundling* sums up the form's goals:

> Intent to fix, and emulous to please
> The happy Sense of these politer Days,
> He forms a Model of a virtuous Sort,
> And gives you more of Moral than of Sport;
> He rather aims to draw the melting Sigh,

Or steal the pitying Tear from Beauty's Eye;
To touch the Strings, that humanize our Kind,
Man's sweetest Strain, the Musick of the Mind. (Moore 1748/1996: 140)

Moore's agenda was shared by enough other dramatists in the middle
years of the eighteenth century to make sentimental comedy into a recognizable form. The term sentimental comedy is even more problematic
than most generic labels. Its frequent dating to the first performance of
The Conscious Lovers occludes the many impulses that Steele shared with
playwrights like Colley Cibber and George Farquhar, each of whom
produced earlier plays with recognizably "sentimental" components, and
the term itself is too vague to be completely useful. Still, the emergence
of the category into public discourse is significant, as it identified a set
of shared values and expectations, linked them to a broader social movement of sentimentalism, and identified both of these as marking a
significant break with the past. Sentimental comedy, *The Foundling*'s prologue asserts, is "politer" than earlier comedies, by which it means the
satirical works of the Restoration theater. These now not only looked
scandalous and licentious, but archaic, old-fashioned, the residue of a
less civilized culture. Sentimental comedy reflected its own culture back
to itself by identifying that culture as polite, modern, a society reformed
away from the perceived excesses of the Restoration court.

By assimilating some of the key features of tragedy, eighteenth-
century comedy blurred the distinctions between the genres, or, perhaps
better, exposed how artificial those distinctions were in the first place.
The emergence of sentimental comedy as a recognizable if problematic
genre in its own right, however, helps identify the theater's historical
consciousness, the way that it distinguished the present from the past.
From the Restoration onwards, the British theater was informed with
a sense of its own history. Actors succeeded to roles in a familiar repertory, creating a genealogy of performance across the generations. And
the theater's past was now preserved in textual form as well, in printed
playtexts, collections, catalogues, and chronicles of the institution that
collectively helped create the British stage as an object of history. The
theater's evolution into an institution that was understood to be con-
tributing to the politeness of its society goes hand-in-hand with its historical consciousness, this ability to narrativize itself. (See also Chapter
12 CRITICISM.) But the advance of politeness, in and out of the theater,
did not come without a sense of loss. The comparative emptiness of a
sentimental hero like Bevil, his lack of specificity, enables him to embody abstract ideals that would appeal to a broad audience, but also marks

the disappearance of the face-to-face, close-knit culture in which a character like Sir Fopling Flutter, representing specific traits of the audience, had thrived. That loss was registered most fully, I want to argue, in serious drama, which, in the popular form known as the "she-tragedy," relied on another distinction in kind, that of gender difference, to articulate, indeed to mourn, the cultural changes brought about by the emergence of modernity.

Gender and Tragedy

Women have frequently been figured *as* spectacle, the object-to-be-looked-at and placed in the gaze of a spectator normatively imagined to be a man. The eighteenth-century theater is little different in this respect from other forms of cultural production like painting, photography, or film, where that spectatorial relationship has been theorized and articulated in great sophistication and detail (Mulvey 1988). As is well known, women performers were the signal innovation of the Restoration theater in Britain, the most obvious change from the stage practices of the Renaissance professional theaters. Actresses concretized and enhanced the erotics of the playhouse, and many contemporary accounts testify to the pleasure that theatergoers took in seeing actresses perform in familiar roles that had up to that point been played only by young men, as well as in new roles that were fashioned to exploit the possibilities offered by the presence of women. Dramatists frequently put women in trousers, in what were known as "breeches roles," as a way of better displaying the contours of women's bodies. While most of these roles are at least some degree motivated by the play's plots – Isabinda in Susanna Centlivre's comedy *Marplot* (1710) goes into breeches, for example, in order to spy on her husband – the spectacle of women is most frequently in *excess* of the narrative, creating an emotional or thematic surplus that cannot in the end be fully accounted for by the logic of the story. This is apparent, for example, in a serious drama such as Nicholas Rowe's *The Tragedy of Jane Shore* (1714), when the heroine's jilted husband rhapsodizes about his wife's beauty:

> Oh, that form!
> That angel-face on which my dotage hung!
> How I have gazed upon her, till my soul
> With very eagerness went forth towards her,
> And issued at my eyes. (1714/1974: 61)

Shore's speech describes the specular relationship that serious drama aimed to promote, the complete engagement of the observer with that upon which he gazes. Particularly in the genre that Rowe's epilogue to *Jane Shore* christened the "she-tragedy" (1714/1974: 75), the Restoration and eighteenth-century theater staged the spectacle of women, intensifying the visual pleasure of the playhouse as it exploited its most significant difference from the professional stages of the last age.

So-called she-tragedies represented probably the majority of the most frequently performed serious plays in the London playhouses from the early 1680s until at least the 1760s. Plays like Thomas Otway's *The Orphan* (1680), Joseph Banks's *The Unhappy Favourite* (1681), William Congreve's *The Mourning Bride* (1697), Rowe's *The Fair Penitent* (1703) and *Jane Shore*, Ambrose Philips's *The Distressed Mother* (1712), Edward Moore's *The Gamester* (1753), and John Home's *Douglas* (1758) among others, were staples of the repertory, staged year after year. They became the star vehicles for the most famous actresses of each generation, and were frequently more popular in their day than many of the plays of this period that are now anthologized, studied, and occasionally performed. Congreve's *The Mourning Bride*, rarely read and never performed now, may have been his most popular play in the eighteenth century, and was certainly more familiar to London audiences of the period than *The Way of the World* (1700), which is now generally regarded as his masterpiece. The proliferation and popularity of plays that are so alien to our sensibilities reminds us that, for all the things that we share with the eighteenth century, it is a profoundly different time from ours, which makes its cultural productions like these dramas all the more interesting for the way that they reveal features of the past that might be forgotten if we only paid attention to things that make us feel at home in it.

Like "sentimental comedy," the generic label "she-tragedy" is a coinage of the eighteenth century itself, and deserves to be treated with some caution. For one thing, it groups together plays that are different from one another in almost every other respect except for the way that they focus their spectators' attention on a suffering or grieving woman. This in fact seems to be part of the point of the label and of the plays themselves, which directed serious drama away from affairs of state to the domestic space, emphasizing crises in the family rather than in the nation at large. Such a recalibration of the object of tragedy from the domain of the state to that of the family is, indeed, frequently their professed goal; as the prologue to Rowe's *The Fair Penitent* puts it, the play that follows has been deliberately designed to eschew the typical tragic subject of the "fate of kings and empires" in order to direct its spectators' attention to "a melancholy tale of private woes" (1703/1969: 5). But this description far from exhausts the scope of she-tragedies, which are free to eschew royal subjects because they recognize that the locus of modern power is elsewhere, in the complicated and to some degree impersonal operations of political systems that do not have so spectacular and embodied a center as a king, emperor, or military conqueror. Not that it is Rowe's purpose here or elsewhere to use his plays to delineate the work of such systems in detail. Rather, the spectacle of feminine mourning that occupies the center of she-tragedies overwhelms the spectator's ability to disentangle the relations between adult men – social, generational, and political – that the plays ultimately reinforce. She-tragedies naturalize socially ordered structures of power and authority, making them seem to be the product of gender difference rather than constructions of their culture.

Rowe's *The Fair Penitent* is a good example of the way that the spectacle of a grieving woman serves to mask some of the consequences of the plot, the implications of the intergenerational politics between men that the play ultimately enacts. Rowe displaces politics with gendered spectacle; by focusing so much of our attention on his heroine's suffering, he occludes the complex political reorganization that is going on here, as a younger generation of men accedes to power. The story unfurls when it becomes known that the title character Calista has had a single sexual encounter with the rake Lothario; as soon as this fact, at one time held as a secret by Lothario and Calista alone, becomes public knowledge, the rest of the play's events – culminating in the deaths of Lothario (at the hands of Calista's fiancé Altamont) and of her father Sciolto (revenged by Lothario's cronies), and Calista's own suicide – follow with a kind of implacable necessity, one that the plot does not encourage its readers or spectators to question. The name Lothario would become synonymous with the rake-seducer, but his description of their one night of passion, when "The yielding fair one gave me perfect happiness" (p. 13), prompts the audience to consider her sexual desire for Lothario as the real lapse that leads to the play's consequences, the main or even sole cause of the disasters to come.

But the play's action cannot begin to account for its emotional impact, which is driven by Calista's overwhelming sense of shame and rage; shame at her belief that she really is responsible for the crises in the family and the community caused by her transgression, and rage at the patriarchal system that subordinates her and all women to the desires and interests of men (Johnson 1779/1903: 117). Calista's most powerful and most famous speech is uttered while she is alone on stage and addressed, not to her father, Lothario, or even Altamont, but to the audience:

How hard is the Condition of our Sex,
Thro' ev'ry State of Life the Slaves of Man?
In all the dear delightful Days of Youth
A rigid Father dictates to our Wills,
And deals out Pleasure with a scanty Hand;
To his, the Tyrant Husband's Reign succeeds
Proud with Opinion of superior Reason,
He holds Domestick Bus'ness and Devotion
All we are capable to know, and shuts us,
Like Cloyster'd Ideots, from the World's Acquaintance,
And all the Joys of Freedom; wherefore are we
Born with high Souls, but to assert our selves,
Shake off this vile Obedience they exact,
And claim an equal Empire o'er the World? (Rowe 1703/1969: 34)

Calista's anger is explicable given the extreme difficulties of her situation. But it is also in excess of the plot in the sense that it speaks more to the condition of women in general rather than just her own situation, which suggests that it must be here for something *else*. One thing her rage – expressed most eloquently here, but present throughout the play – does is to make it impossible to imagine how she could be reintegrated into the family structure, as it serves to mark the way that she is at war with aspects of her culture that are more fundamental than any events that might transpire in the play itself. The play takes pains to have both her father, Sciolto, and her fiancé, Altamont, ostentatiously forgive her (although the former leaves a dagger out for her with which to commit suicide). But mere penitence, it turns out, will not be sufficient to absolve her of her transgression, in spite of the play's title; she must and will die to expiate her sin, a solution to the problem she has created that she embraces as the only way to restore the honors of her father and fiancé. The play does not, however, even seem to want to accept this from her as a logical solution, in effect refusing to recognize her decision as anything other than a mark of insanity. Calista's intransigence is thus construable only as "madness" when she explicitly rejects religious authority, tossing away a book of meditations as merely "A trick that lazy, dull, luxurious gown-men" have produced (p. 62). Calista's rage against patriarchy and orthodox religion render her a locus of excessive emotion that must be contained in terms other than the demands of justice or the plot.

The emphasis on Calista's transgression and on her need to pay for it helps mask what the critic Vaska Tumir has rightly pointed to as the play's most significant structural moves, namely its substitution of horizontal bonds between men of the same generation (most notably that between Altamont and his friend Horatio) for the vertical authority of male scions, notably Sciolto, whose authority is unquestioned, professedly admired, but also brutally oppressive. Calista bears the play's burden of rebelling against but ultimately obeying the authority of fathers while upholding the rights of sons; as Tumir concisely puts it, *The Fair Penitent* "provides irreproachable authority for England's rejection of autocracy, while simultaneously retaining for its elite the Son's paternally approved right to rule" (Tumir 1990: 425). None of the younger men dares regard Sciolto in anything other than reverential terms, but it's also the case that they stand to benefit from his passing. The play prompts us to understand Calista as the cause of Sciolto's demise, her transgression making it impossible for him to live any longer. Considered this way, her crime is in many respects the best thing that could happen to men like Altamont and Horatio. It magically relieves them of the burden of the older generation while exempting them from culpability in its demise. Like many she-tragedies, *The Fair Penitent* recasts politics, in this case a shift in authority from an autocratic past to a more liberal present, as a domestic matter, a transfer of power from one generation of a family to the next, one whose costs are borne most acutely by women.

The displacement of complex political and social issues onto an emblem of grieving femininity signals some of the ways in which serious drama was changing, as well as how it was diverging from neoclassical standards. For although spectators were surely encouraged to admire and learn from virtue and fortitude in the face of suffering expressed by the heroines of these plays, they were not necessarily being held up as models to emulate. The emergence of she-tragedy, and the comparative decline after the 1670s of new plays featuring male heroes suggests that the neoclassical ideal of presenting exemplary heroes was increasingly at odds with the possibilities for heroic action in the culture. Even Addison's *Cato* also inspires doubts about Addison's confidence in the neoclassical model, the degree to which he really expects Cato to be capable of serving as an object of emulation. Juba's presence as the emulator-to-be-emulated might also be taken as a form of dramatic overkill, an attempt to buttress a model that no longer can be taken for granted. The play makes it clear that Cato is inimitable because his virtues are those of an era that is about to be overtaken. In exile with the last remnants of the Roman republic's senate, Cato is doomed from the start, as Octavian's army is poised to defeat him and thereby to usher in the empire. Cato is singular, the last example of a species of Roman republicanism that will now become an object of history rather than a code that can be reproduced in the present tense. There is no place for Cato in the world that Juba, or Addison's spectators, will have to inhabit, which suggests that the play itself can be read as an allegory about the advent of the modernity that some critics have taken to make tragedy impossible. In *The Death of Tragedy*, George Steiner points to Addison's play as a marker of the point at which authentic tragedy became impossible in the western theater: "the tragic poets, still in the grip of neo-classic conventions, would countenance no descent to the prosaic. Hence even their noblest efforts, Addison's *Cato* and Johnson's *Irene*, are cold, lifeless stuff . . . The gap between tragic drama and the vital centers of imaginative concern widened and were never again completely bridged" (Steiner 1961: 265). Deciding whether or not Steiner is right that authentic tragedy became impossible around about the middle of our period and has remained so is beyond the scope of this chapter, but what does seem clear is that Addison is aware that his central character prompts not only the desire for emulation but *nostalgia*, a kind of mourning for possibilities that are always on the verge of being extinguished. In this spirit, the prologue to John Home's *Douglas* (1758) observes that the "god-like race" that had once "sustain'd fair England's fame" lived in "ancient times," rendering the play that follows an exercise in time-traveling to a national past still capable of being a scene for heroic action (1758/1924: 27).

The nostalgia registered here and in so much serious drama of the period may have served other purposes as well. We might think of these plays as also mourning the shift in the theater's position within the culture, its separation from the church and the state. Writers of the late seventeenth century traced the origins of all theater to Greek rituals and the origins of the English theater to the middle ages, their historical inquiries motivated in part by the growing realization that the modern stage was no longer functioning as a place of ritual. This was one of Jeremy Collier's most urgent complaints; what made the English stage profane for Collier was not only the double-entendre that he identified in Restoration comedy, but, more important, the theater's scission from the church-state apparatus, its separation into an institution governed largely by its own norms rather than being put in the service of higher purposes. We might well see Collier's attack as self-interested, an attempt to bring the theater back under the purview of men like himself, traditionalists eager to turn the clock back. And we may also understand the theater's sacrifice of its ritual function as a kind of liberation, one that enabled the theater to deal with the issues of a disenchanted world, to represent the immediate concerns of its society rather than attempting to resolve cosmic questions. Still, the sense of loss, of the theater's diminishment, is palpable in texts such as "A Just View of the British Stage," the image with which I opened this chapter, and to which I now want to return. Above the stage set it represents, "A Just View" prints a banner with the motto "Vivitur Ingenio": literally "it is lived by genius," or, by implication, "we live by genius." The text (which may or may not have appeared above the actual stage at the Drury Lane Theater in this period) testifies to the high-mindedness of the institution and its managers, their professed abstraction from material concerns and economic self-interest. Given the print's obvious attack on the managers' greed and cynicism, the words are obviously intended to be read ironically. But in the context of the image's fixation on the gallows both as subject of the entertainments being remembered and rehearsed and managers' ultimate destination, the words also point unmistakably to the unwritten remainder of the motto: *cetera mortis erunt*, "the rest belongs to death." As viewers of this image, we are reminded that the theater stages the transit from life to death on a regular basis. We are for this reason called upon to do something that the theater managers conspicuously do not, to mourn the death of Jack Sheppard, whose life has been evacuated of any exemplary function and shaped into a vehicle for profit. As witnesses to this profanation of the British stage, we are also called upon to mourn the transformation of the theater from an institution that recognized its mission to uplift the audience to one that merely aimed to entertain it. Critics of the stage like Collier and the author of this image probably exaggerated the extent to which the theater of the past had lived up to its ideals and had fulfilled the ritual functions that they believed the modern theater to have abandoned. But we can take their disappointment and anger as testimony to the profundity of the change that the British theater underwent as it represented a culture undergoing the transition from past to present, from the last vestiges of feudalism and absolutism that characterized the late seventeenth century to the modernity that we can recognize as our own.

References and further reading

Addison, J. (1713) *The Miscellaneous Works of Joseph Addison*, 2 vols., ed. A. C. Guthkelch. Clair Shores, Mich.: Scholarly Press, 1978.

Chandler, J. (2002) "Moving accidents: the emergence of sentimental probability," in C. Jones and D. Wahrman (eds.) *The Age of Cultural Revolutions: Britain and France, 1750–1820* (pp. 137–70). Berkeley: University of California Press.

Dennis, J. (1698) "The usefulness of the stage," in *The Critical Works of John Dennis*, 2 vols., ed. E. N. Hooker. Baltimore: Johns Hopkins University Press, 1939–43.

—— (1711) "An essay on the genius and writings of Shakespear," in *The Critical Works of John Dennis*, 2 vols., ed. E. N. Hooker. Baltimore: Johns Hopkins University Press, 1939–43.

—— (1722) "A defense of Sir Fopling Flutter," in *The Critical Works of John Dennis*, 2 vols., ed. E. N. Hooker. Baltimore: Johns Hopkins University Press, 1939–43.

Etherege, G. (1676) *The Man of Mode*, ed. W. B. Carnochan. Lincoln: University of Nebraska Press, 1966.

Freeman, L. A. (2002) *Character's Theater: Genre and Identity on the Eighteenth-Century English Stage*. Philadelphia: University of Pennsylvania Press.

Home, J. (1758) "Douglas," in H. J. Tunney (ed.) *Home's Douglas*. Lawrence: University of Kansas Press, 1924.

Hume, R. D. (1976) *The Development of English Drama in the Late Seventeenth Century*. Oxford: Clarendon Press.

Johnson, S. (1779) "Life of Rowe," in *Lives of the Poets*. Troy, NY: Pafraets Book Company, 1903.

Lynch, D. S. (1998) *The Economy of Character: Novels, Market Culture, and the Business of Inner Meaning*. Chicago: University of Chicago Press.

Markley, R. (1988) *Two-Edg'd Weapons: Style and Ideology in the Comedies of Etherege, Wycherley, and Congreve*. Oxford: Clarendon Press.

Moore, E. (1748) *The Foundling, a Comedy* and (1753) *The Gamester, a Tragedy*, ed. A. Amberg. Newark: University of Delaware Press, 1996.

Mulvey, L. (1988) "Visual pleasure and narrative cinema," in C. Penley (ed.) *Feminism and Film Theory* (pp. 57–68). New York and London: Routledge.

Rowe, N. (1703) *The Fair Penitent*, ed. M. Goldstein. Lincoln: University of Nebraska Press, 1969.

—— (1714) *The Tragedy of Jane Shore*, ed. H. W. Pedicord. Lincoln: University of Nebraska Press, 1974.

Shell, M. (1978) *The Economy of Literature*. Baltimore: Johns Hopkins University Press.

Shepherd, S. and Womack, P. (1996) *English Drama: A Cultural History*. Oxford: Blackwell.

Steele, R. (1711) *The Spectator* no. 65 (May 15, 1711), in D. F. Bond (ed.) *The Spectator* (vol. 1). Oxford: Clarendon Press, 1965.

—— (1722) Prologue to *The Conscious Lovers*, in S. S. Kenny (ed.) *The Plays of Richard Steele*. Oxford: Clarendon Press, 1971.

Steiner, G. (1961) *The Death of Tragedy*. London: Faber and Faber.

Straub, K. (1992) *Sexual Suspects: Eighteenth-Century Players and Sexual Ideology*. Princeton, NJ: Princeton University Press.

Theobald, L. (1717) *The Censor*. London: Jonas Brown.

Tumir, V. (1990) "She-tragedy and its men: conflict and form in *The Orphan* and *The Fair Penitent*," *Studies in English Literature* 30: 411–28.

Chapter 10

Poetry

The Poetry of Occasions

J. Paul Hunter

Big Historical Generalizations, although sometimes helpful for quick orientations into unfamiliar times and places, can be in the long run a menace to pleasure. Three such BHGs stand between modern readers and the satisfactions offered by some of the best poetry of the eighteenth century, and before turning to the pleasures of the poems themselves I'd like to dispose of – or at least revise radically – the readerly expectations imposed by those generalizations. Poems from older historical periods sometimes need a footnote or two, but usually modern readers are better off if they don't bring too much historical baggage to the poems, especially if it involves wrong-headedness, misinformation, or misleading overviews.

One problematic generalization involves the century's interest in the past. Its admiration for the literary and intellectual classics of ancient Greece and Rome is everywhere in its texts and artifacts, and classical admiration is also embedded in countless cultural assumptions and institutions. And other pasts (Hebraic, Chinese, and the medieval past of Britain itself) repeatedly surface as sources of tradition, value, and guidance, so that attentive readers might be forgiven for thinking that the past was a preoccupation, virtually an obsession. The past *is* a crucial touchstone in eighteenth-century texts – as allusion, an inspiration, as a measure of the present – and the importance it assigns to historical perspective is crucial. But the past is not the *center* of attention; the main subject is always the present – its events, trends, problems, and occasions, current matters of many kinds.

A second generalization involves lyric in the eighteenth century, or rather the alleged lack of it. Look in the anthologies written for college classrooms or for general readers – the "canon" for short lyrical verse – and you find almost nothing from the eighteenth century, although examples from before Milton and after Blake are part of the acknow-ledged common store; it's hard to imagine an introductory course in poetry without Donne and Herrick, or Wordsworth and Keats, but very seldom there do students meet John Dryden or Alexander Pope or Mary Wortley Montagu. And there is nearly universal scholarly agreement that the eighteenth century had no talent for (or interest in) the lyrical. You are not expected to look for good lyrics in eighteenth-century England because the lyrical impulse was then supposed to be suppressed or unknown. Joshua Scodel, author of the most recent authoritative – and quite excellent – account of lyrics in the period, begins from the assumption that "The personal lyric . . . [as usually conceived] was not a major form between the early seventeenth-century flowering of the 'metaphysical' lyric and the lyric resurgence of the late eighteenth century and Romanticism" (Scodel 1998: 120), the basic working pattern of anthologists.

The third generalization is about generalization and generality itself: the century is said to practice (and specialize in) generalization at the expense of the particular, to look for the implication and principle rather than the specifics of ordinary observation, quotidian life, or actual human relationships. Samuel Johnson, for example, famously singled out, as if an ideal, Shakespeare's accomplishment as a "just representation of general nature" and pronounced that it is not the task of the poet to "number the streaks of the tulip" – that is, details and particularities in poetry do not matter (1765/1968: 61; 1759/1990: 43).

Each of these generalizations is about 40 percent true – that is, in all three cases, not quite a half-truth. Each is superficially accurate enough in its own way to be somewhat helpful when properly qualified, ex-plained, and applied: the past *is* important to eighteenth-century ways of thinking about standards and values (more important than to us) and the present does get measured against its several standards. And it is true that the lyric does *not* rate as high, with critics or poets, as longer, more elevated, and more "ambitious" forms such as epics and philo-sophical poems: poets believed that long poems held the key to their reputation and posterity, while usually regarding their shorter, more lyr-ical efforts as play or vacation from their vocation, a kind of informal break from the serious business of poetry. They sometimes (and later readers, often) treated these productions as "light" verse, that most triv-ializing and dismissive of literary categories into which poems can fade and disappear completely. And it is also true that eighteenth-century thinkers – philosophers, theologians, scientists, reformers, political and social analysts, architects, critics, and artists of many kinds – aspired to systematize thought and wished to find general truths that might even be universal, and they sought large certainties about principles across times and places, although their *hope* that it could be done is often stronger than their faith. The optimistic Enlightenment projects of the Continent never quite gained credence in more skeptical Britain, and in any case empirical modes, whatever end they had in view, required moments, examples, details, and accumulations rather than sweeping conclusions. Prose and poetry both lived in particulars.

This is not the place to explain fully the limitations of any of these three generalizations, but I want to suggest briefly how too literal an understanding of each one can limit our sensitivity to eighteenth-century poetic texts and to show how a close reading of the primary texts can refine our total sense of the period and (at the same time) lead to more rewarding readings of the texts themselves.

Assumptions

The past, for example, only gets its philosophical force from a prior preoccupation with the present, and so finally its impact in texts and artifacts (novels, plays, histories, buildings, statuary, gardens, and institutions) is mainly rhetorical. Eighteenth-century Britain was nearly, in fact, as obsessed with its present as we are with ours, and its poetry was far *more* centered on current events and contemporary situations. In part this was due to a perception that things had begun to move very fast, in a kind of "modern" and urban way (as opposed to the more leisurely ways of the rural past) and needed to be captured in words – represented, frozen, studied, and meditated upon. And poems (as well as prose treatises of many sorts) reflected a widespread cultural interest in discussing events of the moment – whatever was new, novel, surprising; anything being widely talked about. Conversation in London coffee houses centered obsessively on current matters; the so-called rise of the "public sphere" (see Chapter 3 PUBLIC AND PRIVATE) – in which growing percentages of the populace believed themselves knowledgeable about (and influential upon) happenings in the world – marked the cultural moment in Europe generally but more particularly in England. Foreign visitors throughout the century repeatedly were struck by the English lust for "news" – information, however garnered and however inaccurate – about matters of state and about economic and social trends more generally.

The past factored into this obsession mainly by providing comparison or contrast and potentially offering (it was hoped) both perspective and advice. Many decried the events and conditions of modernity and especially of urban growth, crowding, and degradation of human life and dignity; disease and violent crime were rampant and experienced to be even more so; life expectancy early in the century dropped precipitously, by about 25 percent, to under 30 years. Life in London – where an increasing percentage of English men and women lived – was getting crowded, publicly uncomfortable, and more and more dangerous; even those whose class and wealth provided generous living spaces found themselves endlessly jostled and threatened in the streets, and the insistent stench of open public sewers was intrusive on noses regardless of class. (See Chapter 5 THE SEWERS.) If England was noticeably moving into naval and commercial prominence and beginning to develop what turned into global recognition and then dominance, the price was continual war and insistent expense, while the government at home was developing a politics of corruption, intimidation, and cynicism. Many observers of the current scene veered between excitement and exhaustion; those in the remote countryside might enjoy relative immunity from the sense of conflict and uncertainty and too-rapid change, though personal awareness of London and urban and international matters increasingly penetrated towns and villages as travel became more popular (if not less arduous), and literacy and the power of print spread the sense of a troubled and intrusive present. There were good reasons to withdraw from the present, at least in one's own mind, but also compelling reasons to deal with it, at least intellectually; and the present/past nexus offered a convenient "literary" way to reflect on – and maybe judge – an obtrusive present that refused to retreat. Some observers (as in all ages) openly longed to live in earlier times or other places – nostalgia is pretty much what it used to be – but most of the interest in the past involved a quest for guidance or inspiration rather than escape; there was some antiquarianism for its own sake, but the main uses of the past arose from the everyday insistence of the present in ordinary life. It was the primary subject of public discourse. And (at that time) as in life, so in poetry.

If anthologists and teachers do not find much lyricism in the eighteenth century, the result mainly involves questions of what one is looking for. There are, it is true, few impulsive effusions, wild warblings, or impetuous shouts of cosmic triumph – little unbridled celebration that does not seem obligatory or strained or invented from nothing. If we look for the buoyant lyricism of the later Romantics, we will not find it, nor will we, except in the somewhat tired and effete imitations of the Cavalier poets in the Restoration, find much of the confident ebullience of Renaissance lyric. There was not enough cosmic confidence left to support the latter, and as yet not enough detached subjectivity to create the former. If one insists on defining lyric as purely harmonic in the sense of both mode and subject – so that the tone must be accepting, affirming, and even celebratory – there is (as Scodel suggests) little of that lyric to be found until quite late in the century, except perhaps for hymns that steadily gave expression, for true believers, to deep religious feeling and commitment. But the subjects and situations of lyric, especially those of traditional Renaissance lyric, are repeated and reexamined again and again for their honesty and applicability to modern life. Mostly, though, they are found wanting: friendship is to be treasured but where, oh where, can it be found? Romantic love is desirable but hard or impossible to achieve or sustain. And where are the ecstasies and fidelities of yesteryear? It is easier for eighteenth-century poets to see – and explore – limits, disappointments, derailments, breaches, ironies, trails of things going awry or away, and thus the lyricism of the period may not be what traditional readers expect or want or thrill to. But it can be revealing, canny, plaintive, subtle, and even satisfying in its way if one is willing to allow complication and surprise and disillusionment and loss into one's definition of lyric (Morris 2001: 225–48). To some readers, trained to expect narrower, more predictable, and more optimistic outcomes, that may seem more anti-lyric than lyric (the characteristic formal structures of the century were often more dependent on inversion than direct modeling), but it certainly occupies the same territory and offers readers just as distinctive pleasures – and a more sophisticated and sustainable view of life. For readers now, the main thing is to approach the lyricism of the eighteenth century on its own terms rather than from some essentialist or Platonic or earlier or later viewpoint so that it has a chance to work its own brand of magic, not that of another time or place or a different set of orthodoxies.

As for generality: the way to generalize, according to the eighteenth-century's best thinking, is to start from observations of the particular, even so small a particular as the streaks of a tulip, and try to reason outward or upward. Science was learning to do it, and philosophers – forsaking the familiar comfort of Aristotle and other authorities of the past or present – tried to work from empirical observation of the small and work cumulatively toward the larger (see Chapter 2 SCIENTIFIC

INVESTIGATIONS). Alexander Pope, for example, the most skilled poet of the century and also one of its boldest theorists and would-be philosophers, wanted in his boldest poem "to vindicate the ways of God to man," but he was insistent about methods and particulars; let us, he coached his readers, "expatiate free o'er all this scene of Man," exploring "where weeds and flow'rs promiscuous shoot":

> Together let us beat this ample field,
> Try what the open, what the covert yield:
> The latent tracts, the giddy heights explore
> Of all who blindly creep, or sightless soar;
> Eye Nature's walks, shoot Folly as it flies,
> And catch the Manners living as they rise (*Essay on Man* vol. 1: 9–14)

It is a walk, a hunt, an expedition, a trek through particulars. And that is what the poem does, Boyle- or Linnaeus- or Darwin-like: journey through noticeable particulars, in gardens, fields, and wildernesses, in search of abstraction and generalization, guiding our physical observations in order to order our minds. He craves generalization and aspires to it (his subject after all is humankind), but is himself devoted to the specific.

Public vs. Private

The poems I wish to discuss here all share a common feature: they center on some particular moment in present (or very recent) time that they wish to celebrate, lament, or otherwise preserve in memory for meditation and reflection. We usually call these poems, when we think of them collectively, "occasional" poems – poems written out of a particular temporal event that requires shared (or at least communicable) thinking. In traditional critical usage, the term "occasional" is often restricted to poems about *public* occasions or events that drive social conversation: wars, battles, treaties, activities of the royals, deaths of the famous, births in prominent families, anniversaries or memorials of some earlier major event that still stirs loyalty or dread. But here I want to extend the use of the term to include the thousands of contemporary poems about more *private* occasions as well – birthdays, meetings and partings of friends, journeys and arrivals, family events, small episodes in private life and other moments of shared experience that two or more people need to remember together – for these became the logical informal extension of the idea of verbally preserving occasions. Actually, the distinction is, in terms of tone and treatment, a fairly permeable one (as are most distinctions between public and private), for once the practice of poetically recording occasions became established (which it had by the mid-seventeenth century), poets habitually addressed the big moments in both the nation's life and in their own. Taken together, poems that grow out of public and private occasions constitute by far the most ubiquitous and popular class of poetry in eighteenth-century England.

Why occasional poetry is not more often discussed and more celebrated is a matter for speculation. One reason the term itself is not more familiar is that eighteenth-century critics, highly dependent on French neoclassicism, tended to label poems according to categories traceable to classical models: epic, georgic, pastoral or eclogue, elegy, epigram, satire, ode, lyric, etc. And there are certain benefits in these contemporary names because many poets consciously follow, although often at some distance, the conventions and expectations of these genres or poetic kinds. Poets in fact quite often certify their acceptance of the labels (and the whole idea of genres and of classical precedent) by including such defining terms in the title or subtitle of their work. Pope (and a host of other poets) began their careers, just as Virgil did, with *Pastorals* carefully titled to signal their youthful and innocent but ambitious apprenticeship to masters like Virgil or Theocritus; and a host of poem titles directly claim kinship with their sponsoring "kind." Lady Mary Wortley Montagu, for example, published *Town Eclogues*, signaling an intention to adapt the traditional rural setting of the form to polite urban life; John Gay wrote *Rural Sports: A Georgic*, and John Philips in a preface also identified his poem *Cider* as a descendent of Virgil's *Georgics*. Many tried to write epics, usually invoking the term "heroic poem" on the title page, and nearly everyone wrote label-conscious odes, elegies, and epigrams or epitaphs: William Collins, "Ode to Liberty" and "Ode on the Poetical Character"; Pope, "Elegy to the Memory of an Unfortunate Lady" and Thomas Gray, "An Elegy Written in a Country Churchyard"; Gay, "My Own Epitaph"; Pope, "Epigram. On One who made long Epitaphs" and "Epigram: Engraved on the Collar of a Dog which I gave to his Royal Highness."

The term "occasional poem," on the other hand, never quite achieved generic status with critics or in poem titles, largely because (although there were many classical precedents of poems constructed on and labeled by individual occasions, public and private) early neoclassical critics did not isolate it as a classic "kind." The term thus achieved its status largely in descriptive terms rather than taxonomic ones. No one then offered lists of occasional poems or attempted definitions, and literary handbooks even now usually settle for quite general accounts, a few examples, and often some patronizing comment; even the reliable M. H. Abrams cannot resist noting that some occasional poems "rise above" their occasion, implying that most are stuck in a limiting time and place. Some version of the term is sometimes present in titles of individual poems – "Occasion'd by some Verses of his Grace the Duke of Buckingham" (Pope) or "Lines Occasioned by the Burning of Some Letters" (Sarah Dixon) – and the practice of naming the time and place of a poem's originary event was widespread: "Ode on the Death of a Favourite Cat, Drowned in a Tub of Gold Fishes" (Gray) or "Alone in an Inn at Southampton, April the 25th, 1737" (Aaron Hill). Many poems obliquely define themselves as "occasional" by using the title to give quite a full account of the nature of the occasion: "To an Infant Expiring the Second Day of its Birth" (Hetty Wright) or "To the Rev. Mr – on his Drinking Sea-Water" (John Winstanley). The most common single title for volumes of verse – used in fact by most poets and booksellers when they collected a miscellaneous body of work – was *Poems on Several Occasions*. Literally hundreds of volumes bear that or a closely related title (*Poems on Particular Occasions*, etc.). The term obviously had currency if not prestige in common usage, but lacked utter precision and had the disadvantage (but also the advantage) of *blurring* some other formal distinctions; most elegies, epitaphs, and epigrams (and a lot of odes) obviously fit into the larger occasional category, and they both lose and gain something by being described in the more inclusive class.

A second reason for the neglect (or lesser prestige) of occasional poems has to do with present critical distrusts and suspicions, some of them quite deeply entrenched in habit and in literary history. One has to do with the obligatory nature of occasional poems, the fact that the poet seems to be culturally *required* to mark the moment. Public poems are more obviously subject to this objection than private ones: Pope does not *have* to write a poem to be inscribed on a dog's collar in the same sense that he believes he *must* celebrate, say, the Peace of Utrecht, and Hill would seem to be obliged to no one to record a singular moment of solitude. Public occasions, however, usually imply some social, political, or ideological statement or loyalty – and therefore an allegiance to some group or position, often involving national patriotism or pride or some version of identity politics; issues of sincerity and group thinking thus, for some readers, come into play.

But an even larger – although more vague – suspicion clings to the very idea of a poem based on an external event, anything that originates in the world of fact or quotidian life rather than in the mind or imagination where the muses are usually thought to operate. The eighteenth century – more social and less subjective than we are – was not as troubled as later ages by distinctions between those subjects that were available to prose and those to poetry: *every*thing was an appropriate subject for poetry at the start of the century – philosophy, science, ethics, work and play, large events and small, hard and disagreeable matters as well as pleasing ones. If you were making a complex argument, you were just about as likely to do it in verse as prose. Later ages, however, have privileged more the private, inner life as the proper province of poetry, and if we look, as most modern readers do, from that post-Romantic perspective at the domain or subjects of poetry, we are apt to be skeptical of any poem that takes its cue from an external event, public or private. Such events are likely to seem to us, out of the force of habit, "prosaic" and compromising to "true" poetic sensibility. But if we understand the nature of the "occasional poem" – indeed the mere fact of the category itself – we can see exactly how and where – virtually everywhere – poetry worked in the eighteenth century.

Public Targets

The idea of public obligation tends to operate in a top down-way, with those who are recognized as "major" poets or cultural figures being expected to approach and register particular occasions. Mostly the sense of obligation was unofficial, a matter of public expectation rather than legal requirement. Only the duly appointed poet laureate was actually required to perform such national duty. The laureate was seldom a really distinguished writer but usually a politically blessed one; he (always he, still) was obliged to write two official poems a year, both dictated by an occasion. One was for the monarch's "official" birthday (that is, a "declared" date of celebration of his/her life, not necessarily the anniversary of the birth itself); the other was for the birth of the new year. It was also generally understood that the laureate would take pen in hand fairly often to celebrate or lament other important public events – military victories or defeats, deaths of prominent figures and births in prominent families, coronations, publications of important books, etc. And in this regard other ambitious poets were expected to join him. At the end of the seventeenth century, for example, John Dryden as laureate (in this one case a distinguished one), wrote powerfully in defense of his king when rebellion threatened to topple him (*Absalom and Achitophel*) and wrote some of his very best poetry for specific occasions: *Alexander's Feast*, for example, was written to celebrate St Cecilia's Day (a day associated with the joys and power of music), and even before he was appointed laureate had lavishly celebrated Charles II's ascension to the throne (in "Astrea Redux" and "To His Sacred Majesty, a Panegyric on His Coronation") and written a long and powerful poem commemorating the series of awesome public events (fire, pestilence, war) of a single year: *Annus Mirabilis: The Year of Wonders, 1666*. As the Dryden example suggests, however, it was not necessarily "official" expectations that drove the poetry of occasions (the last three poems I have mentioned were written before he was appointed laureate), for all poets who aspired to major public recognition felt an obligation to address major events in verse, and usually such poems were published individually (as well as later collected in miscellanies or authorial editions) in showy and expensive formats (folios or large quartos). The Duke of Marlborough's great military victory over the French at Blenheim (1704) and the Treaty of Utrecht that followed (1713), to take just two examples, between them spawned more than a hundred separately published poems (Foxon 1975 vol. 2: 224–5, 264–5, 296). Events and current cultural trends – the times, its peaks and valleys, its happenings and directions, its subjects of conversation – occasioned a major part of the public poetic production of the time.

Most laureate verse and quite a lot of the less official but equally obligatory poetry of cultural celebration – like public panegyric more generally – deserves its bad reputation as predictable, formulaic, tired, repetitious, and dull. Jonathan Swift, only semi-ironically, claimed at the start of the eighteenth century that the materials of panegyric were running low, and it is of course a challenge – one that few poets of this or any other age could meet – to repeatedly praise the same authorized people and attitudes. When everyone is more or less required to celebrate, the quality of exuberance and credibility of praise tends to suffer quickly. Even very good, very creative poets tend, sooner or later, to capsize on the shoals of panegyric. Sincerity is a tough act to keep up, and the convention of sincerity soon wears thin and readily promotes skepticism or cynicism or just simple disbelief. Most poets in the century were best at turning the expectations of panegyric inside out and launching satirical attacks upon events and their "heroes"; lampoons, diatribes, satires, and mock poems of many kinds make up a major segment of the poetry of occasion in the century, far outnumbering poems of praise.

Still, trying to be original in a context of sameness was a challenge that some poets repeatedly met. Pope, for example, though not uniformly successful at genuine praise (and always better at satire and attack) nevertheless often rose to panegyrical challenges. In *Windsor Forest* (1713), for example, he took on the task of trying to make the makers of the Peace of Utrecht (and the queen and government of Robert Harley more generally) look good, and he turned the poem into a celebration of contemporary prosperity. Some readers then (and now) hated the poem for its sentiments of patriotism and complacency; others just as vehemently and mindlessly loved it for the same things. But what distinguishes it as an occasional poem is not in its "rising above" the occasion, but its tact in making the occasion understandable as a manifestation of nation, people, and history. The accomplishment lies not in transcending the time but in establishing the place of the event in the public consciousness, in making it culturally readable so that history could be understood through its lens. Pope accomplishes the task largely by painting present peace, harmony, and global commerce as naturally emerging from a British history that ultimately progresses from crude and barbaric origins through tempestuous challenges and then to its present moment of creative new beginning:

> What tears has *Albion* shed,
> Heav'ns what new Wounds, and how her old have bled?
> She saw her Sons with purple Deaths expire,
> Her sacred Domes involv'd in rolling Fire,
> A dreadful Series of Intestine Wars,
> Inglorious Triumphs, and dishonest Scars.
> At length great *ANNA* said – Let Discord cease!
> She said, the World obey'd and all was *Peace*!
> (*Windsor Forest* ll. 321–8)

This is propaganda, of course, a powerful political claim about Stuart rule that in the following year would end abruptly, but it is also very good poetry. Most poetry of the period was in service of some ideological position or social ideal and thus performed, for some group or other, a particular rhetorical role.

Windsor Forest is not altogether a typical poem of its kind; it celebrates a single moment but is not entirely of it. Pope did literally put it together for the occasion of the peace, but to do so he used some older poetic materials already on hand, passages he had written earlier about contemporary geography as a record of history, stitching together and revising lines he had written months earlier and worked on over a period of time, then molding them into a new text focused on happenings that made persuasive sense of the past. It is just as much a mistake to think that powerful occasions necessarily "inspire" great verse as that muses or moments of subjective epiphany do; sentiments sometimes are raised in power and persuasiveness because poets are genuinely moved and their motivation and articulateness elevated even as their powers of observation are sharpened and extended, but sometimes, too, time and reflection upon events works a more effective and lasting creative magic.

Like *Windsor Forest*, most poems of public praise (and virtually all satires) have a definable politics. Even moments of national celebration are usually cast in some specific political mold. It is revealing, for example, to compare the two most popular poetic treatments of Marlborough's victory at Blenheim, Joseph Addison's *The Campaign* and John Philips's *Bleinheim* [sic] (both 1705); Addison told the story from the Whig position, Philips for the Tory (among other things he insisted on calling the victorious general "Churchill" rather than using his title). Everyone at the time was prone to take a highly patriotic and nationalistic line against France – Thomas Tickell probably spoke for the times when he described the victory as "delivering all *Europe* from slavery" (Tickell 1722: x) – but each party had its own views on heroes and ultimately its own pantheon. It is cautionary, too, to remember how ideals change and heroism loses its luster. Marlborough's reputation fluctuated wildly in later years, and by his death in 1722, his popularity had suffered massively because of his perceived greed, represented by the construction overruns of Blenheim Palace, and also because of new political developments and issues. Here is how Swift "celebrated" his death in 1722:

"A Satirical Elegy On the Death of a late Famous General"

His Grace! Impossible! What dead!
Of old age too, and in his bed!
And could that Mighty Warrior fall?
And so inglorious, after all!
Well, since he's gone, no matter how,
The last loud trump must wake him now:
And, trust me, as the noise grows stronger,
He'd wish to sleep a little longer.
And could he be indeed so old
As by the news-papers we're told?
Threescore, I think, is pretty high;
'Twas time in conscience he should die.
This world he cumber'd long enough;
He burnt his candle to the snuff;
And that the reason, some folks think,
He left behind *so great a stink*. . . . (ll. 1–16)

Swift was operating from partisan views, of course, and not speaking for everyone. But public poetry takes, by definition, slippery and dangerous positions: times change quickly. The great power of occasional poetry lies not in getting a particular occasion "right" for all time, but in articulating a coherent view and offering, for some group or community, a persuasive consensus. The virtue lies in the way a single voice speaks for a particular moment, as well as of it – not by any means saying all or even saying Truth, but wrestling conscientiously with the burden of individual and collective interpretation.

Satire was most often effective when it was based in reality but demonstrably exaggerated and unfair. Praise normally worked best when restrained and tempered with realistic assessment. Dryden's stirring defense of his king, Charles II, in *Absalom and Achitophel* (1681) is often cited as a shining example of poetry's power to achieve successful effects in the real world, and it did help to shore up the royal cause at a critical moment of rebellion. Its satirical treatment of rebel leadership is pretty ruthless; Dryden works Biblical parallels with King David's enemies for devastating effects and, through historical allegory, paints a grim picture of his countrymen. The spoiled, fickle, and restless subjects ("Jews" = English) of David (Charles) are mutinous and the rebel leaders corrupt and terrifying:

> The Jews, a headstrong, moody, murmuring race
> As ever tried th' extent and stretch of grace,
> God's pampered people, whom, debauched with ease,
> No king could govern nor no god could please.
> [. . .]
> Some by their friends, more by themselves thought wise
> Opposed the power to which they could not rise.
> Some had in courts been great and, thrown from thence,
> Like fiends were hardened in impenitence.
> Some, by their monarch's fatal mercy grown,
> From pardoned rebels, kinsmen to the throne,
> Were raised in power and public office high:
> Strong bands, if bands ungrateful men could tie.
> Of these the false Achitophel was first:
> A name to all succeeding ages curst.
> For close designs and crooked counsel fit,
> Sagacious, bold, and turbulent of wit,
> Restless, unfixed in principle and place,
> In power unpleased, impatient of disgrace.
> *(Absalom and Achitophel* ll. 45–8; 142–55)

Charles, Dryden's "hero," is hardly perfect, and the poem in fact has a great deal of fun with the king's well known promiscuity and fathering of illegitimate progeny (the leader of the rebellion is in fact his illegitimate son, so he *has* to be dealt with in some plausibly imperfect way). But he in effect teases Charles about his reputation rather than berating or condemning him.

> In pious times, ere priestcraft did begin,
> Before polygamy was made a sin;
> When man on many multiplied his kind,
> Ere one to one was cursedly confined;
> When nature prompted and no law denied
> Promiscuous use of concubine and bride;
> Then Israel's monarch after Heaven's own heart,
> His vigorous warmth did variously impart
> To wives and slaves; and, wide as his command,
> Scattered his Maker's image through the land.
> (*Absalom and Achitophel* ll. 1–10)

A lot meaner things were possible. Pope, for example, portrayed his king (George II) in 1738 in similar factual terms, but less acceptably. His poem is an "imitation" of a Latin original by Horace, an encomium on the emperor Augustus, but Pope's version gets quite different effects from the Horatian praise of his leader's military exploits. George II was widely known to keep a German mistress, and his foreign-ness (he was German in lineage, spoke little English, and was reported to read no English or poetry at all) was a constant subject of ridicule. Pope's version turns on a pun ("arms") that works in English but not Latin, thereby being available to Pope's readers, but not presumably to the king:

> While You, great Patron of Mankind, sustain
> The balanc'd World, and open all the Main;
> Your Country, chief, in Arms abroad defend,
> At home, with Morals, Arts, and Laws amend;
> How shall the Muse, from such a Monarch, steal
> An hour, and not defraud the Publick Weal?
> ("First Epistle of the Second Book of Horace Imitated," ll. 1–6)

How indeed can a writer "steal" an hour from a king who can't or won't read poetry, and who can't tell arms from arms?

Another famous poem about kingship similarly trades on the issue of foreignness but to much different purpose. The immediate "occasion" of Defoe's *The True-Born Englishman* (1700) was the printing of another poem (*The Foreigner* by John Tutchin) that had attacked the Dutch background of then-king William III; the larger (or longer) "occasion" was the context of widespread xenophobia of the time (which, in the last three paragraphs alone, has been seen to involve three countries, France, Germany, and Holland). Defoe manipulated the prejudice to turn popular sentiment around, pointing out that all Englishmen were ultimately foreigners, descended from visitors and invaders, and that the mixture continues:

> In ev'ry Port they plant their fruitful Train,
> To get a Race of *True-Born Englishmen*:
> Whose Children will, when riper Years they see,
> Be as Ill-natur'd and as Proud as we:
> Call themselves *English*, Foreigners despise,
> Be surly like us all, and just as wise.
> Thus from a Mixture of all Kinds began
> That Het'rogeneous Thing, *An Englishman*.
> (*The True-Born Englishman. A Satyr* 1700: 19–20)

His poem has never achieved literary celebrity comparable to the work of Dryden or Pope, but in its time it had a powerful impact. It could even be argued that a whole category of prejudice was, for a while, driven out of the culture or at least popularly silenced. But the fact that Pope could, 38 years later, draw on a similar national prejudice reminds us of just how fleeting rhetorical victories over cultural habit may be.

The century's most celebrated single poem is probably Pope's *The Rape of the Lock* (1714), and from the beginning it traded publicly on knowledge of its occasion – the snipping off of a young woman's lock of hair by her shy but ardent suitor. The event led to alienation between the prominent families, and Pope wrote the poem, he said, to tease them toward reconciliation. The poem thus had a direct, public design – one with clear aims in the real world beyond the poem – but also sought (and attained) a wide readership well beyond the families or those who knew them. Literally millions of readers since then have shared knowledge of these events (or the poem's version of them), and so the poem has most of the attributes and presumed effects of the public poetry of occasions that I have been discussing. But there is also something different: the occasion itself was hardly a national or even public event and would have been totally unknown to most readers until they picked up the poem and saw its prefatory machinery that revealed the background. Readers therefore were being invited (or at least allowed) to invade the privacy of those involved, to have knowledge of their private lives, to ogle them and eavesdrop on their lives. This sense of invasion – of gaining private information not available to non-readers of the poem – offers something quite different from the poems we have looked at so far, and I now turn to poetry of private occasions which not only provides public windows into private life but flaunts and celebrates the fact of doing so.

Private Occasions

Poems about private occasions are often motivated similarly to those about public occasions; it is easy to see how an age expectant about poetic interpretation of the present modified practice to encompass the local, the personal, and even the trivial. But the effects tend to be quite different. The poetry of public occasions derives its cultural power from its ability to provide a communal voice of some sort and to find, or define, a particular reading community; it always speaks the view, and offers the vision, of some particular cultural group or subgroup. Sometimes the group is large; a poem may aspire (or pretend) to speak for all of Britain. More often, though, it involves some particular subset: Tories, Dissenters, women, landed gentry, merchants, Londoners, royalists, admirers of a particular person or set of opinions, supporters of a particular bill or position, or some other community of broad (but in some way limited and defined) scope. It sometimes aims to enlarge its constituency or enlighten beyond received opinion, but its effects depend primarily on locating agreed-on sentiments about a public issue and speaking those sentiments with clarity, persuasiveness, and often elegance. Poems on private occasions tend to seek an audience differently and provide quite a different effect. Often the ostensible readership involves an audience of one: the poet writes as if addressing another person involved in the occasion: "To Sir Godfrey Kneller, Occasion'd by L—y—s Picture," "Impromptu to a young Lady singing" and "An Answer to a Love Letter in Verse" (Montagu), "An Epistle from a Half-Pay Officer in the Country to his Friend in London" (Richardson Pack), "To Lucinda, visiting him in his Sickness" (James Heywood), "Written at Bath to a Young Lady, who had just before given me a Short Answer" (Mary Barber), "To a Coquet, disappointed of a Party of Pleasure" (Clara Reeve), "To a Young Lady who Commanded Me to write Satire" (John Oldmixon), "To the Honourable Robert Boyle" and "To one who said I must not Love" (Sarah Fyge Egerton), "To Mrs Mary Carne, when Philaster courted her" (Katherine Philips), "To a fair Lady playing with a Snake" (Edmund Waller). A lot of these poems are labeled "letters" or "epistles," and many others are written *as if* in epistolary style or as dialogues with another person.

Most of these poems are quite personal, but most were published during the poet's lifetime – meaning that the actual readership is quite different from just the addressee in the poem's title. Except for one reader, everyone else is, however, a kind of intruder or voyeur, and the effect is rather like opening someone else's mail. Many of these poems openly take the form of an epistle or letter (or pretend to be a conversation between poet and addressee), but others (what we might call addressee poems simply labeled "to" someone or other) offer virtually the same illicit pleasure of prying or being let into a secret. There is often a "you" named or implied, and most readers are not that "you." We might speculate on why poets would willingly give up their secrets in this way (and the answers are probably quite various), but what all such poems seem to have in common is the pretense of the intimate sharing of a moment against the actual fact of deliberate, calculated exposure.

Not that there is necessarily anything shameful or devious to expose. But there is usually something both personal and intimate, something two people share that no one else does – an observation, a feeling, an offguard discovery or revelation. Pope's "Epistle to Miss Blount, on her leaving the Town, after the Coronation," for example, calls up detail after detail of their shared friendship in London, teasing his friend about boredom and the rustic customs of her new life, and investing every memory with implied promises about future meetings and good times. This is not the pronouncing Pope in the role of public critic and nation's defender, but a witty, flirting, caring friend pretending to more sophistication and savoir-faire than he knows he has. There is nothing subversive about the airing of their shared moments, but the fact of the sharing both legitimates their near-intimacy and suggests how much more there is than public appearances can tell:

> As some fond virgin, whom her mother's care
> Drags from the town to wholsom country air,
> Just when she learns to roll a melting eye,
> And hear a spark, yet think no danger nigh;
> From the dear man unwilling she must sever,
> Yet takes one kiss before she parts for ever:
> Thus from the world fair *Zephalinda* flew,
> Saw others happy, and with sighs withdrew;
> Not that their pleasures caus'd her discontent,
> She sigh'd not that They stay'd but that She went.
>> She went, to plain-work, and to purling brooks,
> Old-fashion'd halls, dull aunts, and croaking rooks,
> She went from Op'ra, park, assembly, play,

To morning walks, and pray'rs three hours a day;
To pass her time 'twixt reading and Bohea,
To muse, and spill her solitary Tea,
Or o'er cold coffee trifle with the spoon,
Count the slow clock, and dine exact at noon;
Divert her eyes with pictures in the fire,
Hum half a tune, tell stories to the squire;
Up to her godly garret after sev'n,
There starve and pray, for that's the way to heav'n.

(*Epistle to Miss Blount* ll. 1–22)

Often such poems seem to share a secret or reminisce in a private way that, when made public, has an unusual tonal effect, one that often challenges conventional expectation or feeling. One of Swift's famous birthday poems to Stella, for example, is hardly flattering in any conventional way, but even its allusions to growing older and fatter suggest affection and honesty that belie what more complimentary poetry usually claims. The public sharing suggests a trust in the truth of a relationship that doesn't depend on flattery and lies and that certifies its own honesty and permanence:

Stella this Day is thirty four,
(We shan't dispute a Year or more)
However Stella, be not troubled
Although thy Size and Years are doubled,
Since first I saw Thee at Sixteen
The brightest Virgin on the Green,
So little is thy Form declin'd
Made up so largely in thy Mind.
Oh, would it please the Gods to split
Thy Beauty, Size, and Years, and Wit,
No Age could furnish out a Pair
Of Nymphs so gracefull, Wise and fair
With half the Lustre of Your Eyes,
With half your Wit, your Years and Size:
And then before it grew too late,
How should I beg of gentle Fate,
(That either Nymph might have her Swain,)
To split my Worship too in twain. ("On Stella's Birthday . . . 1718")

Poems of private occasions in fact often portray unusual, poignant, sensitive, and troubling situations and affections. The following poem, by Matthew Prior, takes some obvious risks involving imbalances of both age and class, but keeps a self-conscious eye on oddity, suspicion, and inappropriateness, finally disarming persistent anxieties with humor and absurdity. Here is the way it begins and ends:

"To a Child of Quality of Five Years Old, the Author Supposed Forty"

Lords, knights, and squires, the num'rous band
That wear the fair miss Mary's fetters,
Were summoned, by her high command,
       To show their passion by their letters.

My pen amongst the rest I took,
Lest those bright eyes that cannot read
Should dart their kindling fires, and look
       The pow'r they have to be obeyed.

Nor quality, nor reputation,
Forbid me yet my flame to tell,
Dear five years old befriends my passion,
       And I may write till she can spell.
[. . .]
For, as our diff'rent ages move,
       'Tis so ordained (would Fate but mend it!)
That I shall be past making love
When she begins to comprehend it. (ll. 1–12; 25–8)

Sometimes the revelations are quite intimate and surprising. Two famous Restoration poems – one by a man and one by a woman – both describe an episode involving love-making (or rather attempted love-making), and the details in the two poems are similar enough to suggest that one, fighting for gender perspective, consciously answers the other. The central event, in each case, involves male sexual dysfunction, impotency at the crucial moment. The Earl of Rochester calls his poem "The Imperfect Enjoyment"; Aphra Behn calls hers, with heavy irony, "The Disappointment." Both poems deal subjectively with the central moment, with predictably different gender responses, and both are sensitive, each in its own way, to the pathos of the situation, though the male poem seems more concerned with lost opportunity and generalized anger than with embarrassment about failure or personal responsibility.

We have no reason to think that the two poems record the same incident; in fact, we don't know if either poem is based on an actual occasion. But the two poems were published together, with Behn ostensibly "answering" Rochester, so that we have here a conscious comparison of reactions to a similar moment, implying major gender differences in response to sexual frustration. And both depend on a voyeuristic sense of our being included in the revelation, inappropriately though revealingly. Third-party observation is at the heart of the sense of loss here; something fully private when it happened – and awkward enough – is now fully and embarrassingly revealed to a whole community of readers who are faced with unaccustomed subjective responses, individuated at least at the gender level. We learn a lot about the unpredictability and lumpishness of clichéd private relationship and individual response and perhaps generalize it, but at some cost to our sense of propriety. Ecstasy foiled here seems somehow to stand for what happens to lyricism in the period: poets are best at capturing insufficiencies or disappointments or "almost"s or "not quite"s rather than successes that seem to satisfy and endure. Irony is often a crucial part of lyric in the period.

Quite a few poems of private occasion play with themes of ambivalent revelation. Here, for example, is an extraordinarily probing and poignant poem by Lady Mary Wortley Montagu; its title is in a sense as revealing as the poem itself.

"Written ex tempore in Company in a Glass Window the first year I was marry'd"

While Thirst of Power, and desire of Fame,
In every Age is every Woman's Aim;
Of Beauty Vain, of silly Toasters proud,
Fond of a Train, and happy in a Croud,
On every Fop bestowing a kind Glance,
Each Conquest owing to some loose Advance,
Affect to Fly, in hopes to be persu'd,
And think they're Virtuous, if not grossly Lewd:
Let this sure Maxim be my Virtue's Guide,
In part to blame she is, who has been try'd;
Too near he has approach'd, who is deny'd.

The disarming admission of culpability and conscious unconscious teasing is delicately managed; and so (through the title) is the public/private issue. Montagu did not publish the poem, so in one sense she kept the observation to herself. But her account of its construction ("in Company") betrays the reluctance/eagerness to articulate, confess, and go public: the "construction" of the poem is shared almost on stage at the

very moment of conception. The sharing of the subjective here takes
an unusual form of "publication," though shared reading in a coterie
or through manuscript circulation was not unusual and often has
important implications for poems that the author pretends to wish to
keep private (Love 1993; Ezell 1999).

There are also poems in which there is no other participant in the
private occasion and no particular implied reader – where nothing intimate or special has been shared before the fact of the poem. A poem
I have already mentioned, Hill's "Alone in an inn," is one example, but
there are many others where no second party is necessarily involved.
Titles provide both leading and misleading expectations: James Eyre
Weeks's "On the Great Fog in London, December 1762" unexpectedly
assumes a companion, for example, and Sara Fyge Egerton's "On my
leaving London, June the 29″" addresses itself to "Fate." But the compulsion to share with strangers often seems surprisingly important, as
if some kind of justification is to be gained through exposure, whether
or not someone else's privacy is compromised; often, it is enough to com-
promise one's own.

The Fictive

John Dolan has argued that occasional poems must have at their base
some real physical event that serves as referential basis – a "body" of
evidence – and anchors the "truth" of the poem (2000: 3ff), and that
may be so within a nineteenth-century aesthetic of authenticity. But
eighteenth-century poets liked to test their imaginations on "might-be"s
and outright fictions as well as in shifting the focus in ways that called
for imaginative intervention. A wonderful Mary Barber poem, "written
for my Son, and Spoken by Him at his First Putting on Breeches," in
which she pretends to write in her son's voice, may draw on a particular moment in the life of the son, but it self-consciously imagines the
son's thoughts and speech, putting words in his mouth that a small boy
would not use ("bewitches," "plague," "tyrant," "vanquished," "ligation"
– in effect ventriloquizing, giving him speech that he was not yet able
to create for himself. That kind of strategy was in fact quite common:
poets like to imagine themselves in different kinds of situations and different selves. One of Pope's most powerful poems, *Eloisa to Abelard* (1717),
for example, is written in the voice of a woman who lived centuries
before; her situation – she was a nun who fell in love with her priest-
teacher in twelfth-century France – didn't much resemble, at least on

the surface, Pope's own situation, but he used the poem not only to explore another age, another gender, and another consciousness, but also to vent his own frustrations. This is the way the poem ends, with Eloisa essentially projecting forward to Pope:

> And sure if fate some future Bard shall join
> In sad similitude of griefs to mine,
> Condemn'd whole years in absence to deplore,
> And image charms he must behold no more,
> Such if there be, who loves so long, so well;
> Let him our sad, our tender story tell;
> The well-sung woes will sooth my pensive ghost;
> He best can paint 'em, who shall feel 'em most. (ll. 359–66)

Similarly, Montagu projects herself into another consciousness, though an insistently contemporary one, in "Epistle from Mrs. Y[onge] to her Husband." The poet here provides Mrs. Yonge a voice that she did not have in real life; she was famously humiliated and divorced, a victim of the double standard, by her philandering and cruel husband:

> Think not this Paper comes with vain pretense
> To move your Pity, or to mourn th'offense.
> Too well I know that hard Obdurate Heart:
> No softening mercy there will take my part,
> Nor can a Woman's Arguments prevail.
>   [. . .]
>   Too, too severely Laws of Honour bind
> The Weak Submissive Sex of Woman-kind.
> If sighs have gained or force compelled our Hand,
> Deceived by Art, or urged by stern Command
> What ever Motive binds the fatal Tye,
> The Judging World expects our Constancy. (ll. 1–5; 9–14)

We may not always be sure here whether we are hearing Montagu's voice or Mrs Yonge's own: that is not a mistake, it is the art of the poem. The projection, here and in Pope's "Eloisa," consciously fictionalizes but retains the concrete particularity of the poetry of occasion based on fully experienced personal events. Here, as in other poems that reflect actual occasions or occasions we take to be actual, the effect depends on the exploration of highly specific situations, rendering them understandable to a listener-in, a reader who is allowed to intrude into a private matter for two purposes: first, to provide an interpretive audience, so that a private moment (often an unusual or atypical one) does not go unseen, unexamined, and misunderstood; and then, to offer the poem's tone a sense of simultaneous sympathy and violation. When lyricism itself, or a moment that aspires to it, goes awry, the window to the disappointment has to be at once clear and uncomfortable, with readers feeling just a bit uneasy in the eavesdropping discovery of fallings-short, just a little off balance: there is a kind of half-turn beyond lyric expectation. That accounts for, I think, the melancholy overlay of Prior's "To a Child of Quality" and for the uncomfortable pleasure in the wit of doubling in Swift's poem on Stella's birthday. We know the norm – what lyricism wants to do – and we are just allowed to glimpse it because we have pried into a private communication and seen that romance, and lyric revelation, is not quite what it seemed to be – and perhaps not quite accurate.

Occasional poetry did not bring out the best in all poets, and not all occasional poems are full of insights general or local, nor are all poems brilliantly original – or even charming. But the obligatory quality of public poems and the offhanded particularity of private ones can lull careless readers into missing a lot of poetic pleasures that the eighteenth century marked and explored very well.

References and further reading

Chalker, J. (1969) *The English Georgic: A Study in the Development of a Form*. London: Routledge and Kegan Paul.

Dolan, J. C. (2000) *Poetic Occasion from Milton to Wordsworth*. Basingstoke: Macmillan.

Doody, M. (1985) *The Daring Muse: Augustan Poetry Reconsidered*. Cambridge: Cambridge University Press.

Dowling, W. C. (1991) *The Epistolary Moment: The Poetics of the Eighteenth-Century Verse Epistle*. Princeton: Princeton University Press.

Ezell, M. J. M. (1999) *Social Authorship and the Advent of Print*. Baltimore: Johns Hopkins University Press.

Fairer, D. and Gerrard, C. (1999) *Eighteenth-Century Poetry, an Annotated Anthology*. Oxford: Blackwell.

Fowler, A. (1982) *Kinds of Literature: An Introduction to the Theory of Genres and Modes*. Oxford: Clarendon Press.

Foxon, D. F. (1975) *English Verse 1701–1750*, 2 vols. Cambridge: Cambridge University Press.

Hardison, O. B. (1962) *The Enduring Monument: A Study of the Idea of Praise in Renaissance Literary Theory and Practice*. Chapel Hill: University of North Carolina Press.

Johnson, S. (1759) *Rasselas,* in *Yale Edition of the Works of Samuel Johnson,* vol. 16, ed. G. Kolb. New Haven: Yale University Press, 1990.

—— (1765) "Preface to Shakespeare," in *Yale Edition of the Works of Samuel Johnson,* vol. 7, ed. A. Sherbo. New Haven: Yale University Press, 1968.

Lonsdale, R. (1984) *The New Oxford Book of Eighteenth-Century Verse.* Oxford: Oxford University Press.

—— (ed.) (1989) *Eighteenth-Century Women Poets: An Oxford Anthology.* Oxford: Oxford University Press.

Love, H. (1993) *Scribal Publication in Seventeenth-Century England.* Oxford: Clarendon Press.

Maddison, C. (1960) *Apollo and the Nine: A History of the Ode.* London: Routledge and Kegan Paul.

Messenger, A. (2001) *Pastoral Tradition and the Female Talent.* New York: AMS Press.

Morris, D. B. (2001) "A poetry of absence," in J. Sitter (ed.) *Cambridge Companion to Eighteenth-Century Poetry* (pp. 225–48). Cambridge: Cambridge University Press.

Rogers, P. (1978) *The Augustan Vision.* London: Methuen.

Rothstein, E. (1981) *Restoration and Eighteenth-Century Poetry, 1660–1780.* Boston and London: Routledge and Kegan Paul.

Sagano, M. Z. (1992) *The Poetics of the Occasion: Mellarme and the Poetry of Circumstance.* Stanford: Stanford University Press.

Scodel, J. (1998) "Lyric forms," in *The Cambridge Companion to English Literature 1650–1740,* ed. S. N. Zwicker (pp. 120–42). Cambridge: Cambridge University Press.

Sitter, J. (ed.) (2001) *The Cambridge Companion to Eighteenth-Century Poetry.* Cambridge: Cambridge University Press.

Spacks, P. M. (1967) *The Poetry of Vision: Five Eighteenth-Century Poets.* Cambridge, Mass.: Harvard University Press.

—— (1971) *An Argument of Images: The Poetry of Alexander Pope.* Cambridge, Mass.: Harvard University Press.

Sutherland, J. R. (1969) *English Literature of the Late Seventeenth-Century.* Oxford: Clarendon Press.

Tickell, T. (1722) "Preface" to *The Works of . . . Joseph Addison,* 4 vols. London: Jacob Tonson.

Chapter 11

Forms of Sublimity

The Garden, the Georgic, and the Nation

Rachel Crawford

Sublimity in eighteenth-century Britain is expressed in a variety of permutations, some familiar and some not. Longinus's ravishment and transport, Addison's unrestrained vistas, Burke's delightful horror, Thomas Whately's singularity and surprise, Kames's utility and moral worth, and most prominently, Kant's intellection of the human mind in comparison with which all diminishes, reveal the differing interpretations of what Kant defined as an aesthetic judgment. Despite Kant's influential theory, as Andrew Ashfield and Peter de Bolla point out, the sublime in Britain tends toward the pragmatic. As they show, "attention moves away from the obsessive drive to locate the sublime affect and effect towards the construction of a descriptive model which can account for the transactions between inner mental states and the qualities of objects in the world" (Ashfield and de Bolla 1996: 14). In differing negotiations between target audiences and ideal prospects, eighteenth-century British writers – authors of estate plans, poetry and architecture prefaces, horticultural and agricultural treatises – articulate a distinctive notion of the sublime that is simultaneously subjective and practical, aesthetic and political. In a further complication, the partition between the beautiful and the sublime so familiar to us through the carefully delineated categories of Burke, the politician, and Kant, the philosopher, is intricate and slippery in eighteenth-century usage, especially among gardeners and poets, but also among aestheticians such as Henry Home, Lord Kames. Imbued with utilitarian and moral objectives, the sublime could be appropriated for prospects in which beauty is not a separate taxonomic category, but slips into the sublime, bearing with it functional purposes. William Mason captures this pragmatic quality in "The English Garden" when he writes, *"Beauty* scorns to dwell / Where *Use* is exil'd" (Mason 1778–81: ll. 21–2). As these lines suggest, within the confined space of the garden distilled didacticism reveals itself as essentially sublime and poetic, beautiful and functional; moreover, beauty itself becomes one of the functions of sublimity. While it is true that sublimity during the first half of the century was inspired by Longinus's "instinctive" sublime in which the soul "takes a proud flight, and is filled with joy and vaunting, as though it had itself produced what it has heard" (Roberts 1935: 55), in Britain, a pragmatic element of the sublime existed in covert forms even when the ideal was the wide survey. As Stephen Switzer demonstrates in *Ichnographia Rustica* (1715), though the sublime landscape idealized the dissolution of visible boundaries over which the soul could scramble to take its flight, it enclosed hidden fields and kitchen gardens which were not alienated from the plough or rake (Switzer 1724: vol. 1: xxxvi; vol. 3: 48, 82). By 1770 the relationship between space and sublimity modified as the ideal of the boundless view faltered in response to national concerns over the control of boundaries. Finally, the constraints of war and smaller purses assisted in locating a combustive form of the aesthetic in the covert enclosures overlooked by the wide survey. Thus by the end of the century, the aesthetic of sublimity had not been lost but redefined – detached from the unchecked view of the landed proprietor and relocated in the confines of the kitchen or cottage garden.

The trajectory of the sublime through the century traces changes in which the soul is capable of finding imaginative flight despite its political and moral charge. Such exalted flight, the literature of the landscape reveals, could take place from within the contained garden as readily as from the wide survey. Thus the defining metaphors for the social ideals that accompanied this change were diminution, containment, and, especially, enclosure. Parliamentary enclosure (1760–1815), a land policy that legislated the hedging in of open agricultural fields, spawned debates that reached a heated polemic in the 1760s. These legislated enclosures set in motion a loss in ideological force, if not in actual practice, of the extensive view (Daniels 1993: 5); significantly, despite their antagonism, polemicists on both sides of the debates express a correlation between enclosed space and productivity. By the last quarter of the century, this correlation became a convention in landscape treatises that migrated to the confines of common gardens: places linked to contrivance, productivity, and compressed sublimity. Parliamentary enclosure, therefore, brings into focus the disquiet of space and an alternative sublimity in Britain's eighteenth century. Particularly fraught as a land policy, parliamentary enclosure was nevertheless caught up in a nexus of spatial codes that included imperial prospects, architecture, the welfare of laborers, British manliness, cultivated landscapes, and forms of poetry. Translated into metaphor, legislated enclosure thus makes visible the signifiers that altered the relationship between space and sublimity. Analyzed figuratively rather than socially or agriculturally, as they have been in the past, parliamentary enclosures are merely the most visible aspect of discursive practices that defined the evolution of all manner of forms in the eighteenth century.

Congruencies between landscape and poetry must be proved against a legitimate skepticism of explanatory relationships between such diverse forms as landscape and poetry. Longinus nudged his readers in this direction when he noted the application of the rhetorical sublime to powerful landscapes such as the Nile (Roberts 1899/1935: 135); Addison took Longinus's cue in the popular *Spectator* papers, the "Pleasures of the Imagination" (first series 1711–14, 535–82); Susan Stewart suggests "we can posit an isomorphism between changes in genre and changes in other modes of production" (Stewart 1993: 6). The isomorphism Stewart postulates – relationships between things drawn by virtue of their forms – is wise, but not entirely accurate in this case. The congruencies between landscape and poetry articulated here must be judged instead in terms of isomorphism's cousin, isomerism. Rather than focusing exclusively on form, isomerism considers different generic and material structures (for example, words and space) in terms of shared social proportion and weight whether or not they display different properties. Such relations are clearly revealed in texts that situate the concept of social space in the interstices between topographies and poetry, where practitioners of gardening or farming and poetic composition pilfer from each other's disciplines as they work to build consensus and authority for their respective trades. Isomeric relationships readily negate material differences between words and space in order to privilege social and theoretical congruencies.

The rhetoric of the parliamentary enclosure debates is symbolic in that it exposes the assumption that containment generates productivity. In this chapter I follow a line of inquiry in which the sublime affect is renegotiated within this symbolic rhetoric. I show how the representation of vernacular space, whether in topography or popular poetic forms such as georgic (remarkably long poems inspired by Virgil's versification of agricultural treatises) and the sonnet (a 14-line lyric form), configures the fears and desires of Britain in the midst of the loss of its first empire and economic changes that accompanied the French and Napoleonic wars. Vernacular space becomes a receptacle for a nation's self-idealized image. Because cultivated land retains conventional and therefore easily recognizable forms, it could be filled, like other forms, with the contents of an evolving social practice (Mintz 1993: 266). This means that land itself could be imbued with changing national ideals so long as it remained familiar – so long as it could be recognized in its vernacular forms. For this reason, an aesthetic such as the sublime could be adapted to ideal English space during these decades. Though ideal English space was represented first by the unhindered view and later by the restricted garden space, both expressed a linkage, sometimes fantasized, between enclosure and productivity (see Figure 11.1).

The Act of Union (1707) provided impetus for an idea of Britain that fashioned new parameters of nationhood and redirected native sensibilities to the land and its productive prospects. Because of this shaping act, the British, now enclosed on all sides by the sea, could fantasize a "Britannizable" world (Bayly 1989: 103). James Thomson, author of the most popular georgic of the century, exemplifies this sensibility in his phrase, "an equal wide survey," which defined a sublime of unlimited yet disinterested possibility (Thomson 1730: "Summer", l. 668). Such an idea would not have been possible without the sense of nationhood produced by the Union, which established connections between Britishness, commerce, agriculture, science, and literature.

English Georgic

In the eighteenth century English georgic, a Virgilian form that conceived of England as a global heartland, surfaced one year after the Act of Union with John Philips's *Cyder* (1708). Based on a Virgilian model but reshaped by Miltonic poetics, Philips's hybrid georgic communicated the production of English space central to British values. *Cyder*'s concluding reference to the peripheral colonial possibilities of an English metropole provides a microcosm of the dialectic between boundless views and confined internal spaces recommended by essays such as Addisons's and treatises such as Switzer's on kitchen gardens (1727). Weighted early in the century toward unrestrained prospects, a georgic dialectic evolved between two commonplaces: the wide survey and the equally sublime "cabinets for retirement . . . where the Mind may privately exult and breathe out those Seraphick thoughts and Strains" (Switzer 1724: I. xxxvi).

229

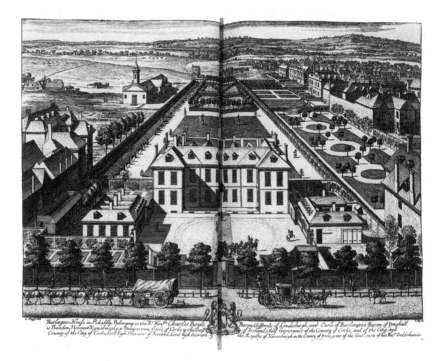

Figure 11.1 "Burlington House in Pickadilly," J. Kip and L. Knyff, *Britannia Illustrata, or Views of several of the Queens Palaces as also of the Principal Seats of the Nobility and Gentry of Great Britain* (London 1714, vol. 1: plate 29). This engraving depicts a controlled viewpoint that conceals the small formal gardens appended to houses of the town so that the eye will be drawn past the estate's formal gardens to the wide expanse beyond. Reproduced by permission of The Huntington Library, San Marino, California.

As these commonplaces suggest, though georgic poetry purported to provide practical instruction about farming in the pleasing form of verse, it was in fact profoundly conceptual. The English view in these poems is the ideological point of view and a wide spectrum of British folk could participate in the power and pleasure of its representation of English space. Although laboring poets such as Stephen Duck in *The Thresher's Labour* (1736) and Mary Collier in *The Woman's Labour* (1739) contested its concealment of labor, English georgic provided a powerful vision from its English perspective that promulgated a conception of English centrality and British potentiality that could be grasped by a heterogeneous population.

This was possible in part because georgic poetry offers an image of the world that issues from a single English center while it simultaneously promises an infinitely expanding space through which the mind darts in an exercise of subjective freedom. By means of this strategy visual space forms an isomeric relationship with mental space, while mental space fashions a temporal center which authenticates a sublime historical trajectory: a present which expands back into an archaic British past in order to validate an English present and forward to presume the eschaton of a British future. Englishness thus becomes a means of locating the heart of a present moment that is geographical and temporal, unified by an invisible point of view that represents the space of England at the same time that it produces British space (Anderson 1983). To borrow Henri Lefebvre's terms, the producing and produced space of English georgic works both as a representation of space and a representational space (Lefebvre 1991: 38–9). Iambic pentameter, characteristic of georgic, reinforces this point, since it was believed to represent the indigenous rhythm of the language, while the unrhymed line endings provided a verse equivalent of unfettered feet redolent of British liberty.

Georgic's sublime vistas take for granted the primacy in landscape of the ancient seats of landed gentry, a tradition that permeates loco-description – from the country house to the tourist viewpoints of the picturesque. Over the course of the century, many estate owners redesigned their grounds to fulfill the expectations of the concept of which they were in part constitutive. They transformed walled gardens into unimpeded views that obfuscated contained gardens and "cabinets," which lacked the representational power to define what it meant to be English in an expansionist discourse. Until the advent of the civil and military distresses of the 1770s such spaces were lost to view in the discursive although not the lived tradition of the culture: the continuous tradition of town and kitchen gardens are preserved solely in the records of nurserymen and observers. The kitchen garden, as J. C. Loudon would point out in the nineteenth century, was one of the commonest English sites: "Of private British gardens, the most numerous class of gardens, and those the most regularly distributed over the British Isles, are those of the country labourer, or what are usually denominated cottage-gardens" (Loudon 1835: 1225). The humble kitchen garden, not the great parks of the gentry, established the ideal of Englishness by the nineteenth century.

John Philips's *Cyder* and Richard Jago's *Edge-Hill* span the georgic decades and track the arc of sublimity in the eighteenth century. *Cyder* was important primarily for providing an ur-narrative that idealized native English character as issuing from the sheltering apple orchards of

Herefordshire in England's heartland. His poem recapitulates the essential georgic theme elaborated by Milton: that labor is the consequence of expulsion from a fruit garden; yet, for Philips, England becomes that garden, a benign world in which labor is a sweet delight (see Figure 11.2). Philips conceptualizes a poetic application for this theme that unites the three lands, England, Wales, and Scotland, out of which Britain was born. The soil is his earthy theme:

> What Soil the Apple loves, what Care is due
> To Orchats, timeliest when to press the Fruits,
> Thy Gift, *Pomona*, in *Miltonian* Verse
> Adventrous I presume to sing; of Verse
> Nor skill'd, nor studious: But my Native Soil
> Invites me, and the Theme as yet unsung. (*Cyder* I. 1–6)

The chiasmic positioning of *soil* in this initial verse paragraph resituates the subject of Milton's epic: where Milton places "the Fruit / Of that Forbidden Tree" within a theodicy, Philips relocates it in the world of horticulture (Milton 1957: I. 1–2); where Milton outlines a theater of cosmic proportions, Philips restricts himself to his own "Native Soil," suggesting the movement of his plot between the soil's role as an essential component for orchards and its wider symbolic status as the ground out of which Britain rises. The opening of *Cyder* recasts *Paradise Lost* in terms of its latent georgic possibilities at the same time that it extols English soil for nationalistic purposes. Indeed, the entire second book transforms the forbidden fruit into a British brew that will lubricate the world:

> where-e'er the *British* spread
> Triumphant Banners, or their Fame has reach'd
> Diffusive, to the utmost Bounds of this
> Wide Universe, *Silurian* Cyder borne
> Shall please all Tasts, and triumph o'er the Vine. (II. 665–9)

Philips's humor conveys the resolute message that Britain's rewards will be realized in the fermentation of the apple that caused the Fall; infused with cider's spirits, other races become Britannizable.

Once the connection between soil and nation had been identified, georgic form could be attached to other topics, thereby perpetuating and widening the terms within which its space and corresponding notions of the pragmatic sublime could be understood. Georgics thus sprang up devoted not only to the soil, but to aristocratic pleasures (John Gay's *Rural Sports* (1713), and William Somervile's *The Chace* (1735)), the beer industry (Christopher Smart's *The Hop-Garden* (1752)), the wool indus-

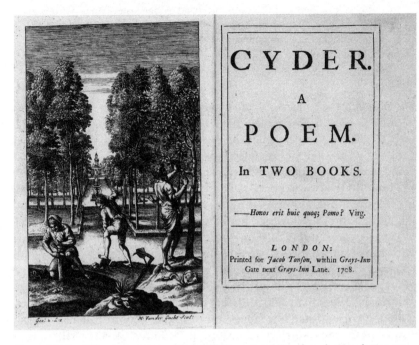

Figure 11.2 "Frontispiece," from John Philips, *Cyder* (London: for Jacob Tonson, 1708). This first edition frontispiece depicts an orchard arranged in parterres with a formal fountain and canal intersecting a scene foregrounded by georgic labor. Reproduced by permission of The Huntington Library, San Marino, California.

try (John Dyer's *The Fleece* (1757)), and the sugar industry, (James Grainger's *The Sugar-Cane* (1764)). James Thomson's *The Seasons* (collected edition 1730) stood in a class by itself: the stately march of his poem virtually neglects homely instruction and relocates georgic's ideological underpinnings by focusing on the effect of changing seasons on England's landscape. He thus emphasizes the sublime affect of cultivated soil. John Aikin defends Thomson's reinterpretation of the form: "If Virgil really designed to instruct the farmer by his Georgics, he might have done it much more effectually in plain prose" (Aikin 1777: 58). Although since ancient times some critics had elevated the utility of prose treatises over didactic poetry, Aikin's comment reveals a prevailing modern reading sensibility less inclined to be diverted by lengthy poetry, very likely, in fact, to be entertained by prose. In comments directed at an older school of critical opinion, he says concerning Thomson's descriptive technique,

Why not allow [georgic] the same privilege as her Sister-Muse, who is at liberty to employ her pencil on what parts of nature she most delights in, and may exhibit the rural landskip, without encumbering herself with the mechanism of a plough, or the oeconomy of the husbandman? (Aikin 1777: 57–8)

The Seasons came to be considered the greatest of English georgics in part because Thomson disregarded metaphrasis, the versification of technical manuals. This had a deep effect on poets who followed him. When James Grainger writes that he "preferred the way of description, wherever that could be done without hurting the subject," he alludes to the influence of Thomson over the form (Grainger 1764: vii). Richard Jago's *Edge-Hill* provides a fitting closure to the literary era when georgic was a predominant form by following, though with less sublimity, Thomson's lead.

Jago devotes three of *Edge-Hill*'s four books to surveys of Warwickshire's landed estates. He thus transforms the celebration of English soil into a topography engraved with the memorials of kings, lords, and gentry and rewrites local lore to underscore a soil marked by "paternal Worth, / No less than lineal Claim" (I. 219–20). The Roll-Rich Stones, a modest circle of standing stones, for example, are construed by "vulgar Fame" as ancient warriors "transform'd to Stone" (I. 531, 530). Jago's wiser lore reveals a "Fabric monumental, rais'd / By *Saxon* Hands, or by that *Danish* Chief / Rollo! the Builder in the Name imply'd." (I. 535–7).

The colloquial name preserves a narrative that inscribes Warwickshire soil with the text of its ancient history: conquerors who through time become absorbed into an indigenous Warwickshire patrilineage. He transforms conquest and seizure into benevolent signs of traditional social bonds. Jago's celebration of Britain emphasizes a local topography striated with the signs that encode its history. His redistribution of subject matter from crops rooted in the soil to an encoded surface provides a metaphor for a shift in perspective, from earthy depths to topographical surfaces: from viewing the form as the noblest means of celebrating national unity, character, and productivity in the most pleasing form, to viewing it as the encoded surface of a more solid substance. His georgic thus marks the beginning of a shift in sublime potential which he articulates in the third book of the poem.

Here Jago turns from his topographical survey to the metal industry that provides the tools that make georgic endeavor possible and celebrates Birmingham, "the first manufacturing town in the world" (Hopkins 1989: 26). This would have seemed odd in the forum of public

opinion since Birmingham was viewed as the locus for the manufacture of counterfeit products, from coinage to plated household goods or
cheap imitations of precious metals such as tutania or pinchbeck. The
legacy of this reputation remains in the OED's citations for "Birmingham" and its colloquial name "brummagem." There we find a continuing
record from the last quarter of the seventeenth century, when Birmingham "was noted . . . for the counterfeit groats made here, and from hence
dispersed all over the Kingdom," to 1843 when Southey invokes "a
Brummejam of the coarsest and clumsiest kind." Jago, like Birmingham's first historian, William Hutton (1781), strives to elevate the city's
national reputation by celebrating the vibrancy of its metal industries
and industriousness of its artisans:

> 'Tis Noise, and Hurry all! The thronged Street,
> The Close-piled Warehouse, and the busy Shop!
> With nimble Stroke the tinkling Hammers move;
> While slow, and weighty the vast Sledge descends,
> In solemn Base responsive, or apart,
> Or socially conjoin'd in tuneful Peal. (*Edge-Hill* III. 539–44)

Following Jago, Hutton, in one of the georgic metaphors that punc-
tuate histories of the coal and iron industries, attributes the industry and
invention of Birmingham's citizens to the profit motive: "It is easy to
give instances of people whose distinguishing characteristic was idleness,
but when they breathed the air of Birmingham, diligence became the
predominant feature. The view of profit, like the view of corn to the
hungry horse, excites to action" (Hutton 1781/1795: 85). In a riposte
to conventional belief, Jago and Hutton assert that such qualities define
an industry that prospers on novelty and technological innovation. The
picture of Birmingham provided by all of its local patriots provide an
image of the body politic teeming like Virgil's bees: one that compresses
industry within a confined and well-delineated space. The industrious
citizens of Birmingham epitomize Englishness; yet their hive of industry and ingenuity nestles in *Edge-Hill*'s extended descriptions of estates.
The wide survey encloses the compressed sublimity of Birmingham's
bustling industries.

Brummagem

Hutton's account suggests that Birmingham citizens are quintessentially
georgic in that they capitalize not on planting and tillage but on the

connection between the mineral products of the soil and the production of English values. The black soil's richness marks not its fertility but its use for manufacturing "the instruments of war and of husbandry, furniture for the kitchen, and tools for the whole system of carpentry" (Hutton 1781/1795: 24). Similarly, Jago's poem ignores the agricultural yield for which Warwickshire was famous – its cheeses, its meats, its corn – for coal mining and iron smelting, refining, and smithying. His georgic endeavor to supply an indigenous local history linked to Birmingham's mineral produce takes precedence, however, over accuracy. This is not unusual in georgic poetry. When Philips rejects amending the soil under apple trees in the first book of *Cyder* only to recommend it in the second he reveals that georgic "instruction" often cloaks a social principle; when he espouses Virgil's erroneous instructions for grafting, he does so not out of horticultural ignorance, but for political reasons. Similarly, Dyer's exacting description of Silurian sheep in *The Fleece* skews representation in favor of mythicized national ideals (Goodridge 1995). Despite the satisfying appearance of technical precision, carefully contrived errors may be incorporated into the verse. Error may therefore be viewed as a convention of georgic that serves a larger purpose – a commonplace that could be termed Virgilian misinformation. Jago pushes this convention to a limit, however, which provokes an examination of the tenuous balance between surfaces and depths, brummagem and authenticity.

Jago introduces two different kinds of misinformation into his poem. First, he permits ambiguities concerning the historic role of mineral coal in the iron founding process. This enables him to construct a local history of Birmingham's citizens linked to an ancient British industry. Second, he purveys technical information of a gentlemanly rather than a scientific sort – the kind that would have circulated in newspapers rather than instructional manuals. There is a good reason for this: no coal treatises were published in English between 1708 (which predates technology that dramatically altered the relationship between the coal and iron industries) and 1797, well after Jago's death (Flinn 1984: 3). In the absence of actual treatises, Jago simulates the instructional core of georgic poetry. The parallel between Jago's simulation and the reputation of Birmingham industries may be fortuitous, but calls attention to the presence of simulation at the heart of Jago's poem. Like Birmingham smiths' simulation of precious metals, Jago's simulation of georgic technique calls attention to the poem's surface rather than its substance, its brummagem. Most importantly, in an unconscious irony for English georgic, Jago celebrates Birmingham's arts of simulation as the substance of Englishness.

The concerns of social critics, both contemporary and modern, suggest important questions about the nature of simulation and what drives it. Typically critics assume that simulation entails imitation in common materials of objects originally made from rare and expensive materials; however, as the correlation in Birmingham between simulation and innovation suggests, common materials can create rather than imitate fashion. Such was the case with jewelry in the eighteenth century. As Samuel Timmins pointed out a century later, iron and steel jewelry were fashionable in their own right: the " 'toy trade' [small metal objects] of that age *represented and anticipated* the extent of the jewelry trades of the present time" (my emphasis; Timmins 1866: 216). In other words, fashions for precious metal jewelry imitated those of inferior metal products. Imitation and simulation are not synonymous; whereas imitation involves the reproduction of an original object, simulation obfuscates the difference between originals and reproductions (Baudrillard 1994). The arts of simulation scatter the memory of any original object; originality, though not invention, is drained of meaning and ingenuity takes precedence over genius. James Watt did not invent the steam engine or copy machine, but perfected them and brought them into use. The play of images provides further dimension to the toys of Birmingham industries, for Birmingham inventors played out the baffling relationship between imitation and genius, duplication and invention, conferring authority on surfaces rather than depth. As Jago and Hutton implicitly suggest, brummagem is a sign not of falsity but of native ingenuity.

Thus we return to the question of the real nature of georgic, especially since English georgic is both a simulation and a reinvention of a Virgilian form; an indicator of English ingenuity and a gauge of British substance; a vehicle of instruction and a tenor of sublimity. The product of several orders of simulation, English georgic simulates a Virgilian original, itself a poetic simulation of prose treatises. One of Virgil's primary sources, Varro's *De re rustica*, simulates a dialogue between two people. In like manner, georgic achieves its aims by means of a simulation of Miltonic verse and "our English georgic," Philips's *Cyder* (Dunster 1791: 6). The fact that Jago handles the form in ways so imitative of both its English manifestation and the Birmingham arts of simulation articulates the redistribution of value from georgic substance to georgic devices of ornamentation: from georgic consideration of depth to a preoccupation with legible surfaces. Yet, at its close, he returns his poem to the subject of Philips's poem: "A Garden's Cultivated Trees" (1767: IV. 228). In so doing, he amends the pagan Virgilian scene of georgic virtue by recollecting Milton's mythic tale of the fall from a dream of innocence. Here, fruit, rather than causing the fall of our youthful first parents, redeems the time. Despite this redemptive conclusion, however, Jago has turned the innocent produce of the soil in the happy realm of the rural swain to the legible surfaces of Warwickshire soil and sublime productivity of urban industry. Jago's simulation of English georgic is not simply a forward-looking celebration of modern technology and industrialization. Rather, within a traditionalist framework, his inquiry permits a redirection to artifice – a concern with surfaces – and its bond with the combustive potentiality of the sublime when hived within the enclosed space.

Lyric Enclosure

The most ordinary and yet most remarkable and enduring of these enclosed topographical spaces was the British kitchen garden, the prototype for the cottage garden so highly profiled by the British tourist industry today. The kitchen garden had always inhabited the British landscape in the lordly estate, the yards of ordinary people, or the market gardens that sprang up in London's neathouses the latter of which produced fruit, vegetables, herbs, and flowers year round for urban and suburban dwellers. Unlike the vistas celebrated in the evening ascents of georgic poetry, the kitchen garden was embedded in the countryside and suburbs, a site that was simultaneously enclosed and productive, and productive because it was enclosed. The extraordinary attention paid to its design in garden manuals bears out this conclusion: plans for kitchen gardens were intricately designed, even indistinguishable from those for the formal parterres (geometric plots of grass, flowers, and fragrant herbs often delineated by low hedges, in front of the public rooms of a great house) – only captions of plans reveal their differing purposes. Yet any member of a gentry household who visited local towns and villages would have seen the kitchen gardens attached to cottages: these, and not the open prospect, were the customary views of the vast majority of people. Coalminers, laborers, and artisans had some kind of garden, whether rented or owned, which they filled with vegetables, flowers, herbs, and fruit. As Loudon would later point out, these gardens were not places for merely keeping a pig or growing a few cabbages, but sites within which the ordinary person had "an opportunity of displaying his taste in its cultivation" (Loudon 1835: 1225). The kitchen garden preserved a sense of the bounded, domestic space, even when landscape treatises applauded extension as the emblematic British prospect (see Figure 11.3).

Throughout the eighteenth century, authors of garden manuals and landscape treatises maintained that contained space required its own set of aesthetic guidelines – it could not without absurdity simply miniaturize larger forms. The bounded space projected an aesthetic characterized by compression, delineation, and artifice that, though designed to be useful, was nonetheless acclaimed for its sublimity and productivity; not least, beauty was one of its products. The language of the sublimely beautiful, drawn primarily from the works of Spenser, Sidney, Shakespeare, and Milton, imparted poetry's pleasing grace to horticultural instruction; as importantly, references to England's vernacular poets placed instructional manuals within an authoritative English lineage. Manuals thus resorted to both georgic and lyric impulses, conforming to the profitability, industry, and instruction required by the former and to the artifice and sublime immediacy of the latter. In the continuous tradition and increasing visibility of the kitchen garden manual in the eighteenth century we can discern the aesthetic for contained space taking shape in the convergence of artifice and sublimity, an alteration in social values that provided the lesser lyric with the elevated status it maintains today. Contemporary poets and critics acknowledged this turning point in a proliferation of horticultural metaphors: Coleridge notes, "After a certain period, crowded with Poetry-counterfeiters, and illustrious with true Poets, there is formed for common use a vast garden of Language – all the shewy, and all the odorous Words, and Clusters of Words, are brought together" (Coleridge 1973: no. 4313); Wordsworth marks to the sonnet's "scanty plot of ground"; and Keats quotes Hunt's "Places of nestling green for poets made." The linguistic thefts practiced by horticulturists, poets, and critics underscore the fact that minor lyric, that small plot of poetic ground, was perceived not merely as a sensibility or expression of subjectivity, but as a formal *space* that generates a sublime yet functional content, an element of which is beauty. In drawing attention to artifice and sublimity, literary critics formulate a set of assumptions concerning lyric constriction isomeric with those established by the authors of landscape treatises earlier in the century.

Isomerism as expressed in the correspondence between artifice and sublimity has a direct connection with the British evolution of representational space. One of Switzer's successors, Thomas Whately, clarifies this: his *Observations on Modern Gardening* (1770), written at the cusp of the American War, signals a disquietude about unchecked prospects, which he regards as a dubious freedom. He exposes the dilemma introduced when space is defined only by extent. In this he follows Kames, who claims, "within certain limits, [grandeur and sublimity] produce their

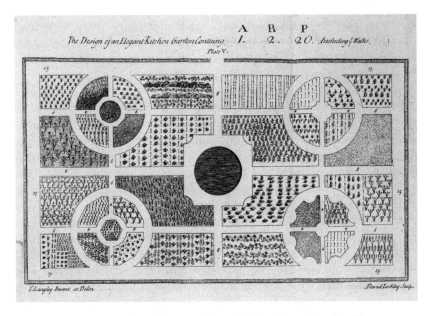

Figure 11.3 "Design of an Elegant Kitchen Garden," Batty Langley, *New Principles of Gardening* (1728). Langley's garden depicts the ideal marriage of use and beauty. The formal parterres are filled with recognizable plants, which, though highly stylized, would have been realized as a profusion of vegetables, herbs, and flowers. Reproduced by permission of The Huntington Library, San Marino, California.

strongest effects, which lessen by excess as well as by defect" (Kames 1765 vol. 1: 215). Consistent with Kames, Whately counsels that intelligible form resides in spaces that can be successfully delineated, and only then will these spaces be lent "ideal extent" by the imagination (Whatley 1770: 93). He maintains that the contained garden should be reserved for the prospect beneath our gaze and associates it with the virtues of productivity, frugality, and judicious restraint. We can see here the slippage by which "ideal extent" becomes a quality imposed by the mind rather than an attribute of the landscape. The soul transported by the contemplation of uncultivated nature in the end becomes the object of its own contemplation. The sublime is thus brought into the orbit of the singular rather than the boundless prospect:

> Singularity causes at least surprise, and surprise is allied to astonishment. These effects are not, however, attached merely to objects of enormous

size; they frequently are produced by a greatness of style and character, within such an extent as ordinary labour may modify, and the compass of a garden include. (Whately 1770: 21)

Without resorting to the word *sublime*, Whately brings the familiar concept into the terms of garden design. Style and character count more than an enlarged view and within the "narrow bounds" of the garden ordinary labor produces the effect that nature provides in "scenes licentiously wild" (Whately 1770: 14).

Artifice

Critical esteem for confined forms is determined in large part by the kind of value placed on artifice, considered here as the presentation of formal strategies in such a way that art stands in for nature – for artifice, which places art higher in the system of values than nature, is the hallmark of confined forms. Under the restriction of space concealment of design is not the object. Design forthrightly calls attention to itself and asserts itself *as* nature. Eighteenth-century garden manuals, however, locate a structural opposition less between nature and culture than between two categories of nature – cultivated nature and neglected nature. William Marshall astutely observes that "our idea of *natural* is not confined to *neglected* nature, but extends to *cultivated nature* – to nature *touched* by art, and rendered intelligible to human perception" (Marshall 1785: 587).

Artifice is more akin to Tasso's bower of Armida, a garden that "seemed to be the art of Nature herself; as though, in a fit of playfulness, she had imitated her imitator" (Hunt 1846 vol. 1: 453). It creates a productive confusion of origins between art and nature even as it privileges surfaces over substance. Artists thus kidnap nature in order to convert it into art's own highly ordered world. Literary critics considering the merits of lesser lyric in the later eighteenth century articulate the productive relationship between confinement and nature that Kames and Whately endorse: the smaller the space of the literary form the more artful it should appear. In her preface to the first collected edition of Collins's poetry, Anna Laetitia Barbauld observes that a minor ode, "like a delicate piece of silver filligree, receives in a manner all its value from the art and curiosity of the workmanship. Hence Lyric Poetry will very seldom bear translation, which is a kind of melting down of a Poem, and reducing it to the sterling value of the matter contained in it" (Collins

1797: v). For Barbauld, the "sterling value of the matter" constitutes the intrinsic value of the epic. Lyric poetry, by contrast, shifts value from substance to surface, from matter to manner. She elaborates, "The *sub-stratum*, if I may so express myself, or subject matter, which every composition must have, is, in a Poem of this kind, so extremely slender, that it requires not only art, but a certain artifice of construction, to work it up into a beautiful piece; and to judge of or relish such a composition requires a practised ear, and a taste formed by elegant reading" (Collins 1797: vi). Her defense of Collins's poetry opens a vista onto a historical moment when reading patterns are shifting from one sensibility to another. She exemplifies this point in her posture toward his poems, for though reluctant to fully endorse artifice, she demonstrates that lyric forms require not only a different reader sensibility than long poems, but a recognition of the formal strategies which distinguish them from traditionally more prestigious forms.

Poets borrow the formal requirements of the great ode, especially as practiced by Young and Gray, and apply its strophic principles to the far more compressed forms of the lesser lyric. By means of concentration, the intensity and immediacy fundamental to the sublime power of the great ode is recreated in a lesser poetic form. One strategy for producing this effect is to relieve images from their strict connections to each other by introducing bold transitions. The sonnet's volta is a contracted version of this device, as is the oxymoron, which distills transitions into their most rarified essence. The central strategy in these instances is to expunge words that hold merely syntactical places. Recognizing and censuring lyric strategies, Samuel Johnson comments, insightfully though disapprovingly: "Independent and unconnected sentiments flashing upon the mind in quick succession may for a time delight by their novelty, but they differ from systematical reasoning, as single notes from harmony, as glances of lightening from the radiance of the sun" (1969: 5.192). It was precisely this quality, Longinian in its sensibility, that nurtured the turn to a lyric sensibility; for if lightning could intermittently glance on the long reaches of epic and georgic poetry or in the strophic turns of a great ode, how much more sublime if those glances could be isolated, extracted, and made the substance of one brief but illuminating verse. It was almost inevitable, therefore, that critics would increasingly apply such techniques to minor lyric forms. John Ogilvie observed that lyric diction is "adapted with great accuracy to the sentiment, as it is generally concise, forcible, and expressive. Brevity of language ought indeed particularly to characterise this species of the Ode, in which the Poet writes from immediate feeling, and is intensely animated by his subject" (Ogilvie 1762: xxx–xxxi).

John Pinkerton exemplifies an increasing tendency to blur distinctions between the great ode and minor lyric forms when he falls into a vocabulary usually reserved for the former when discussing the poetics of the latter: "Above all, uncommon elegance in turns of language, and in transition, are so vital to this kind of lyric poetry in particular, that I will venture to say they constitute its very soul; a particular that none of our lyric writers, before Gray, at all attended to. His mode of expression is truly lyrical; and has a classic brevity and terseness, formerly unknown in English, save to Milton alone" (Pinkerton 1785: 34–5). Pinkerton's examples reveal the synaesthetic effect when phrases such as "liquid air of noon" are compressed to "liquid noon" (Pinkerton 1785: 35).

As such images suggest, lyric operates on the principle of extraction from an external context and expansion from within. Rather than plot time in the manner of epic, which presumes a narrative, or georgic poetry, which roughly follows the seasons of the year or periods of the day (but is more accurately organized by calculated digressions), the glassy hothouse of the lyric extracts a moment from an unspoken context and intensifies or essentializes it. What begins as a spatial metaphor becomes a metaphor for temporality. Time in such a form is conceived as both bounded and infinite (Cameron 1979: 204). Lyric space thus reorganizes sequentiality into simultaneity and discontinuity, the temporal order figured in the sonnet's volta. Such images map space onto time, exposing lyric's power to control time and open internal space. The bounded, well-delineated space, as Blake perceived, is the purchase from which eternity is earned.

Thus, as figures of containment are unlinked from figures of mental limitation, the containment of form is dealt with not by arguing that containment per se is beneficial, but by transforming containment into a sign of vastness and power. In particular, despite the fact that lyric is a self-reflexive form while garden manuals are instructive, both fabricate the idea of a self-enclosed world. In the case of lyric poetry this world whispers poetry's secrets into her own ear. In kitchen garden manuals the self-enclosed world is, like Milton's Eden, a horticultural plenum filled with diverse fruits and vegetables from the four corners of a Britannizable world. Most strikingly, lyric's self-reflexivity, its self-proclaimed enunciation of private emotion, is ironically designed for a highly public purpose. Inversely, the kitchen garden manual begins with the assumption that the speaker occupies a public forum; yet it presumes, as the etymology of the word "garden" suggests, a guarded and secluded space, one shielded from the eye of the passerby that shuts out the external prospect. As readers of the kitchen garden manual, we peer through the chink in the wall or break in the hedge. The allure in each case, so unlike the indifferent gaze over the wide prospect presumed by the aesthetic of the landscaped park or open forms of georgic and the great ode, is the allure of a bounded and excluded space which nevertheless reveals itself to the public domain.

References and further reading

Addison, J. and Steele, R. (1711–14) *The Spectator*, ed. D. F. Bond, vol. 3. Oxford: Clarendon Press, 1993.

Aikin, J. (1777) *An Essay on the Application of Natural History to Poetry*. London: J. Johnson.

Anderson, B. (1983) *Imagined Communities: Reflections on the Origin and Spread of Nationalism*. London: Verso.

Ashfield, A. and de Bolla, P. (1996) "Introduction" in *The Sublime: A Reader in British Eighteenth-Century Aesthetic Theory* (pp. 1–16). Cambridge: Cambridge University Press.

Barrell, J. (1972) *The Idea of Landscape and the Sense of Place 1730–1840: An Approach to the Poetry of John Clare*. Cambridge: Cambridge University Press.

—— (1983) *English Literature in History 1730–1840*. New York: St Martin's Press.

Baudrillard, J. (1994) "The precession of simulacra," in S. F. Glaser (trans.) *Simulacra and Simulation* (pp. 1–42). Ann Arbor: University of Michigan Press. (Original work published in 1981.)

Bayly, C. A. (1989) *Imperial Meridian: The British Empire and the World 1780–1830*. London: Longman.

Cameron, S. (1979) *Lyric Time: Dickinson and the Limits of Genre*. Baltimore: Johns Hopkins University Press.

Chalker, J. (1969) *The English Georgic, a Study in the Development of a Form*. London: Routledge and Kegan Paul.

Coleridge, S. T. (1973) *The Notebooks of Samuel Taylor Coleridge*, vol. 3 ed. K. Coburn. Bollingen Series 50. Princeton: Princeton University Press.

Colley, L. (1992) *Britons: Forging the Nation 1707–1837*. New Haven: Yale University Press.

Collins, W. (1797) *The Poetical Works of Mr. William Collins. With a Prefatory Essay, by Mrs. Barbauld*. London: Cadell and Davies.

Daniels, S. (1993) *Fields of Vision: Landscape Imagery and National Identity in England and the United States*. Cambridge: Cambridge University Press.

Duck, S. and Collier, M. (1736, 1739) *The Thresher's Labour: Stephen Duck and The Woman's Labour: Mary Collier*, ed. M. Ferguson. Los Angeles: University of California Press, 1985.

Dunster, C. (1791) *John Philips's Cider, a Poem in two Books. With Notes Provincial, Historical, and Classical by Charles Dunster*. London: Cadell.

Flinn, M. W. (1984) *The History of the British Coal Industry*, vol. 2: *1700–1830: The Industrial Revolution*. Oxford: Clarendon Press.

Goodridge, J. (1995) *Rural Life in Eighteenth-Century English Poetry*. Cambridge: Cambridge University Press.

Grainger, J. (1764) *The Sugar-Cane: A Poem in Four Books*. London: R. and J. Dodsley.

Hopkins, E. (1989) *Birmingham: The First Manufacturing Town in the World 1760–1840*. London: Weidenfeld and Nicolson.

Hunt, L. (1846) *Stories from the Italian Poets: with Lives of the Writers*, 2 vols. London: Chapman and Hall.

Hutton, W. (1781) *An History of Birmingham*, 3rd edn. Birmingham: Thomas Pearson, 1795.

Jago, R. (1767) *Edge-Hill, or the Rural Prospect Delineated and Moralized. A Poem in Four Books*. London: J. Dodsley.

Johnson, S. (1969) *The Rambler*, in W. J. Bate and A. B. Strauss (eds.) *The Yale Edition of the Works of Samuel Johnson*, vol. 5. New Haven: Yale University Press.

Kames, H. H., Lord (1765) *Elements of Criticism*, 3rd edn., 2 vols. Edinburgh: A. Millar, et al. (Original work published in 1762.)

Lefebvre, H. (1991) *The Production of Space*, trans. D. Nicholson-Smith. Oxford: Blackwell. (Original work published 1974.)

Loudon, J. C. (1835) *An Encyclopaedia of Gardening*. London: Longman, et al.

Marshall, W. (1785) *Planting and Ornamental Gardening: A Practical Treatise*. London: J. Dodsley.

Mason, W. (1778–81) *The English Garden: A Poem. 4 books*. London: J. Dodsley, et al.

Milton, J. (1957) *Paradise Lost*, in M. Y. Hughes (ed.) *Complete Poems and Major Prose* (pp. 207–469). Indianapolis: Odyssey Press.

Mintz, S. (1993) "The changing roles of food in the study of consumption," in J. Brewer and R. Porter (eds.) *Consumption and the World of Goods* (pp. 261–73). London: Routledge.

Ogilvie, J. (1762) *Poems on Several Subjects. To Which is Prefix'd, an Essay on the Lyric Poetry of the Ancients*. London.

Philips, J. (1927) *Cyder*, in M. G. L. Thomas (ed.) *The Poems of John Philips* (pp. 43–87). Oxford: Blackwell.

Pinkerton, J. [pseud. Robert Heron, Esq.] (1785) *Letters of Literature*. London: G. G. J. and J. Robinson.

Roberts, W. R. (1935) *On the Sublime*, in *Longinus on the Sublime: The Greek Text edited after the Paris Manuscript* (pp. 41–161), trans. W. R. Roberts. Cambridge: Cambridge University Press. (Original work published in 1899.)

Stewart, S. (1993) *On Longing: Narratives of the Miniature, the Gigantic, the Souvenir, the Collection*. Durham: Duke University Press.

Switzer, S. (1724) *Ichnographia Rustica: or, the Nobleman, Gentleman, and Gardener's Recreation*, 2nd edn., 3 vols. London: Thomas Woodward. (Original work published 1715.)

—— (1727) *The Practical Kitchen Gardiner*. London: T. Woodward.

Thomson, J. (1730) "Summer," in *The Seasons* (pp. 1–71). London: Millar.

Timmins, S. (1866) *The Resources, Products, and Industrial History of Birmingham and the Midland Hardware District*. London: Hardwicke.

Whately, T. (1770) *Observations on Modern Gardening, Illustrated by Descriptions*. London: Payne.

Williams, R. (1973) *The Country and the City*. New York: Oxford University Press.

Chapter 12

Criticism

Literary History and Literary Historicism

Mark Salber Phillips

> *It may, however, be observed, that in* civil *history, there is to be found a much greater uniformity than in the history of learning and science, and that the wars, negociations, and politics of one age resemble more those of another, than the taste, wit, and speculative principles.*
>
> David Hume, "Of eloquence" (1742)

> *Whoever has lived long enough to compare one race of men with that which has preceded it, will have observed a change, not only in the tastes and habitudes of common life, but in the fashion of their studies, and the course of their general reading. Books influence manners; and manners, in return, influence the taste for books.*
>
> Anna Laetitia Barbauld, Preface to *The Spectator* (1804)

> *From the romance we learn what they were; from history what they did; and were we to be deprived of one of these two kinds of information, it might well be made a question, which is most useful or interesting.*
>
> Walter Scott, "Southey's *Amadis of Gaul*" (1803)

Literary history enjoyed a decided surge of energy in the final decades of the eighteenth century and the first of the nineteenth. Admittedly, comprehensive narratives of national literature of the sort written by Warton or Hallam were still scarce, but a range of editorial, antiquarian, biographical, and entrepreneurial projects demonstrated a wide engagement with the English literary past. A number of circumstances encouraged this development, including the patriotism spurred by the struggles with France, the expansion of print production, the growth of the periodical press, and changes in the laws concerning copyright, leading to new conceptions of intellectual property. But along with these external conditions, students of the period have generally looked for an intrinsically literary cause. The clearest explanation that has emerged focuses on the idea of literature itself. Early modern times, it has been argued, possessed an idea of "letters," a wide and undiscriminating category that included many forms of learned writing, as well as poetry, drama, and fiction. Towards the end of the eighteenth century, however, this relaxed and eclectic *ancien régime* gave way to a more exclusive idea of "literature" considered as works of heightened imagination. For literary history, the argument proceeds, this was a decisive moment because it gave literary history its own proper object of study. "In the beginning," as David Bromwich puts it, "literature was just books," but around 1800 the term took on an evaluative function and came to be applied only to works of a certain quality of taste and creativity (Bromwich 1989: 2). In this way, "literature" acquired clearer features, and literary history became for the first time a distinctive and powerful form of literary study. In David Perkins's slightly different formulation (which typically stresses a Germanic and philosophical genealogy), "Hence it was and is usually said that literary history began in antiquarian works of the eighteenth century. Assimilating ideas of Herder and the Schlegels, the discipline soon became intellectually profound" (Perkins 1992: 1).

This explanation of the progress of literary history rests upon the assumption that literary history is self-evidently a form of *literary* study – hardly a remarkable view, it might be thought, but an important one to clarify because it underpins the consensus that the motives for change in literary-historical thought will have to be sought within the literary field. These assumptions are easy to justify in the context of the modern curriculum, where literary history plays no part in the training of historians, but is one of the fundamental components of literary study. Two centuries earlier, however, a different ordering of the arts still prevailed and in this setting our exclusive attention to the literary may well obscure connections between literary history and other bodies of writing, especially other forms of historical description that flourished in the same period.

I do not mean to argue that literary history is not about literature, only that in the long eighteenth century literary history answered to historical ends as well as critical ones. It follows that we need to be more alert than we have been to the *historiographical* context of literary-historical work: to the sort of historical sensibility, for example, that might draw readers to take as much interest in the lives of poets as of politicians, or to the sense of national history that looked back to the early seventeenth century not only as a time of growing parliamentary independence, but also (and for closely connected reasons) as the moment when the English language matured and English poetry found its proper voice.

To approach literary history from this direction evidently requires us to take a wider than usual view of the historiography of the age as well as of its literature (Phillips 2000; 2003a). Conventionally, history has been thought of in narrower terms – as a (more or less) monolithic body of writing whose essential features are defined by concern for the political nation. This does not mean that historians have neglected biography, memoir, histories of manners or the arts, philosophical history, local history, and the like. When history as such is under discussion, however, these "minor" or specialist genres are assumed to be subodinate forms with little power to affect the wider horizon of historical understanding.

There is no reason to picture history (any more than poetry or the novel) in unitary terms. A more flexible approach would give us a view of historical writing as a cluster of overlapping and competing genres that collectively make up a family of historiographical forms. Over time, as these genres respond to new needs or fashions, the result is not only a change to particular genres, but also a broader reconfiguration of historical thought (Phillips 2000; Phillips 2003b). In this context, the "minor" historical genres, far from being less important to the historical outlook of the time, are often the best indicators of the pressures exerted by new interests or audiences. Less burdened by ancient decorum, these "lesser" genres were freer to fashion new conventions of their own – often in explicit opposition to the established traditions of canonical histories – and could be expected to lead rather than follow in establishing new directions of historical writing.

If we examine the arguments made for literary history *c.*1800 in these terms, it becomes clear that among the things that distinguished literary history from other historical narratives was the access that the works and lives of authors seemed to offer to the thoughts and feelings of another time – in short to a kind of inwardness that to this day remains one of the elusive prizes of historical description. Unlike the conventional forms of political history which were firmly anchored in public events, an inward-looking literary narrative was not tied to any single location or subject matter. It was not the exclusive property of high poetic imagination – though the words of poets were often evoked to "body it forth"; it was not – at least in Britain – primarily identified with national spirit or racial gift. It was not even the property of exceptional individuals, except again insofar as they displayed a superior power to articulate what everyone felt. On the contrary, part of the attraction of literary history seems to have been its capacity to describe a very wide range of experiences, often of the most everyday sort.

This engagement with the everyday is crucial because it aligns literary history with the extraordinary enlargement of historical horizons that, in my view, is the most significant feature of the historical thought of the long eighteenth century (Phillips 2000; 2003a). Hume, Smith, Ferguson, and a host of others had broadened the scope of history in ways that made the exclusively public concerns of the classical tradition seem narrow and superficial. The result was a growing realization that historical change was not confined to the fall of kings or the rise of empires. On the contrary, it was increasingly apparent that a ceaseless historical current works its way through the most commonplace features of custom, manners, and language, with consequences that are all the more compelling because change in this form – though unspectacular compared to the great revolutions of political power – is silent, complex, and all-pervasive.

Here, I want to suggest, literary history held particular significance for the broader family of historical genres. As Hume had pointed out in a prescient passage (see the epigraph), the history of the arts, far more than the annals of public life, show us human experience in all its variability and change (Hume 1742/1987: 97). More than any other kind of historical description, in fact, literary historical enquiry gave access to this mobile inward world of ideas and feelings. For Britain, at least, the historicist insights yielded by this Humean history of taste and opinion seem as fundamental to the historical sensibility of modernity as anything announced by the "profounder" philosophy of Herder or the Schlegels. About historicism of this sort, however, historians have had very little to say – another artifact perhaps of the separation of literary history from other kinds of historical narrative.

The Versatility of Literary History

The attractions of literary history from an historiographical point of view were bound up with the close association between literature, manners, and what Hume called "opinion." In his *Specimens of the Early English Poets* (1803), for example, George Ellis cited manners as the chief reason for the popularity of travel narratives and argued that any reader would find still more to interest him in the poetry of his own ancestors

(Ellis 1803: 1–2). A later poetic anthology, Campbell's *Specimens* (1818), drew a similar response from Francis Jeffrey. Nothing, he wrote, could be more delightful than the chance to trace the progress of poetry through all its stages, "coloured as it is in every age by the manners of the times which produce it." Since poetry is "conversant with all that touches human feelings, concerns, and occupations," its character has been impressed "by every change in the moral and political condition of society." Much like the landscape itself, he concluded, poetry carries with it all the "traces" of all the amusements and pursuits of the people (Jeffrey 1846 vol. 2: 10–11).

Jeffrey, it is evident, does not point us to a single quality in poetry that would make it evocative of all that has passed. He does not say, for instance, that it is in the intensely imagined experience of the poet that the age finds its most concentrated expression. Instead, there seems to be a wider distribution of concerns bundling together but never fully uniting the social world of manners with the inward one of "all that touches human feeling." Even so, there is something useful in the thought that poetry provides a record of human experience as comprehensive as the changing shape of landscape itself – a kind of inner landscape perhaps, but one more subtle and responsive than even the land could be to all the accidents of human manners, morals, and occupations.

Poetry was not unique, however, in acting as a register of changing social experience. In another place, Jeffrey offered a long list of genres that, more effectively than "regular" history, conveyed a picture of manners and daily life. For earlier ages, these included chivalric romances, chronicles, Shakespeare and the comic dramatists, farces and comedies, polite essays, libels and satires, private letters, memoirs, and journals. In more recent times, social habits and manners were made known by satirical novels, caricature prints, newspapers, "and by various minute accounts (in the manner of Boswell's *Life of Johnson*) of the private life and conversation of distinguished individuals"(Jeffrey 1846 vol. 1: 478–9).

Literary historians put Jeffrey and Hazlitt in opposing camps, but on the matter of novels and the history of manners their views coincided. Among the attractions of the novel for Hazlitt was its close and realistic imitation of social life. In them, he wrote, we see "the very web and texture of society as it really exists." If poetry has something more divine in it, he added, the novel "savours more of humanity." Like Jeffrey, Hazlitt believed that there were aspects of historical understanding for which novels provided the best access. "As a record of past manners and opinions . . . such writings afford the best and fullest information." Nothing, for example, amongst the "authentic documents" of the period could match *Joseph Andrews* as an account of the "moral, political, and religious feeling" of the time of George II. "This work, indeed, I take to be a perfect piece of statistics in its kind" (1930–4 vol. 6: 106).

Scott too was strongly attracted to any form of literary and historical record that evoked the past in familiar terms: among them the medieval romance and its modern counterpart, the novel of manners. "The novels of Fielding and Richardson," he wrote in a review of Southey's *Amadis of Gaul*, "are even already become valuable, as a record of the English manners of the last generation. How much, then, should we prize the volumes which describe those of the era of the victors of Cressy and Poitiers" (1835 vol. 1: 3). Romances, he declared, give us an "intimate knowledge" of another time; they tell us what "our ancestors" thought, the language they used, "their sentiments, manners, and habits." Narratives of this sort were an essential supplement to regular history, but which in the end was most valuable, Scott hardly felt able to say (see the epigraph).

It is characteristic of arguments of this kind that they presume a conventional idea of History which then serves as a foil for the attractions of other, less formal and more intimate kinds of histories. This strategy particularly suited literary biography, a genre devoted to lives more notable for private thoughts than public actions. "No species of writing combines in it a greater degree of interest and instruction than Biography," Robert Bisset wrote in the "Life of Addison" with which he prefaced an edition of *The Spectator* (1799): "Our sympathy is most powerfully excited by the view of those situations and passions, which, by a small effort of the imagination, we can approximate to ourselves. Hence Biography often engages our attention and affections more deeply than History" (1799: vii–viii).

Literary biographers, like Bisset, argued strongly for the inseparability of biographical curiosity and the pleasures of reading. When we read the works of great writers, he insisted, we "anxiously" desire to know the histories of those from whom we have received so much pleasure and instruction. Godwin made the same point, but with greater passion and eloquence. "I know not how it is with other men," he wrote, "but for myself, I never felt within me the power to disjoin a great author from his work. When I read with delight the production of any human invention, I pass irresistibly on to learn as much as I am able, of the writer's personal dispositions, his temper, his actions, and the happy or unhappy fortunes he was destined to sustain" (1815: vi).

A writer's life might be presented in a variety of ways, but in a sentimental age, letters and other self-expressive documents held particular fascination. This was the reason that the great age of the epistolary novel also pioneered the collecting of letters as a method of literary biography. Both uses of epistolarity – the novelistic and the biographical – meet in Anna Laetitia Barbauld's edition of the correspondence of the novelist, Samuel Richardson. Barbauld admired Richardson's work and was also an acute analyst of the advantages and disadvantages of the epistolary method, but she seems to have been as much moved by the ordinary letters of his correspondents as by those that came from his fictional imagination. "Nothing," she wrote, "tends so strongly to place us in the midst of the generations that are past, as a perusal of their correspondence. To have their very letters, their very handwriting before our eyes, gives a more intimate feeling of their existence, than any other memorial of them" (1804a: ccx).

Much of what was recorded in Richardson's correspondence had little directly to do with authorship, and few of Richardson's interlocutors were, in fact, writers. Nonetheless there was something about literary lives that provoked this sort of sentimental interest. Even those whose connection with literature was no more than commercial somehow carried with them an extra measure of curiosity. Witness the way a *Blackwood's* reviewer greeted the publication of *The Life and Errors of John Dunton*, the autobiography of a London bookseller from the early years of the previous century. Despite all that had been preserved from this period, the reviewer noted, Dunton's "indefatigable self love" had succeeded in adding still more to our picture of those times. If only his example would not be lost on his successors, he added with a mix of facetiousness and truth: "There are no other traffickers, with whose minutest and most peculiar objects of interest so large a portion of readers must at all times be found to sympathize." The autobiography of any other tradesman would have no interest to anyone outside of his own particular calling. Yet what would be more amusing for "the great masses of the reading public in 1919 than a Sketch of the Life and Errors of William Blackwood, or Archibald Constable, or John Ballantyne, citizens of Edinburgh, – or of William Davies, or John Murray, citizens of London – written in true Duntonian fulness and freedom" (*Blackwood's* 1819: 24).

Revolutions in Taste and Traditions

Changing literary tastes meant that two epochs of English literary history were subject to a thorough revaluation around 1800: the Elizabethan and the Augustan ages. These reversals of reputation played a considerable part in stimulating literary-historical interests, but more than poetic taste alone was at stake in the new narrative of national literature that began to emerge.

Among the Augustans, Addison is perhaps the writer whose changing reception most clearly indicates the continuing connection between literary history and the question of manners. Throughout the eighteenth century Addison was admired as a master of style, but the appreciation was as much social as literary. Johnson, most notably, placed Addison in a genealogy of writers on manners that begins with Castiglione and della Casa – writers who now suffer neglect because they succeeded in effecting "that reformation which their authors intended." Before the appearance of the *Tatler* and *The Spectator*, however, "England had no masters of common life." There were no writers, that is, who wrote to instruct Englishmen in the smaller sorts of duties, nor did periodicals themselves (the instruments of this reformation) predate the Civil War (Johnson 1905 vol. 2: 92–3).

Johnson's hints at a narrative of the progress of manners are much more fully developed in a work of the first decade of the nineteenth century, Nathan Drake's *Essays, Biographical, Critical, and Historical, illustrative of the Tatler, Spectator, and Guardian* (1805). Drake, it is clear, was aware of the problem identified by Johnson, namely that the success of the reformers' efforts made their work seem less engaging to a modern reader. Accordingly, he needed to recreate the sense of difference without which he could make no case for his chosen authors. As Drake himself put it, his survey of literature and manners should impress the reader with an idea of the "value of the instruction which the periodical essay is calculated to afford; and will enable us, likewise, in a succeeding part of our work, clearly to ascertain to what amount we are indebted to these papers for the progress of civilization and the diffusion of learning and morality" (1805 vol. 1: 40). Inevitably, Johnson is one of those quoted to give authority to this picture of the sometime ignorance and incivility of the English; so, even more revealingly, is the *Spectator* itself – a nice example of the reciprocity of literary history and manners by which the literature of another age served to document its social history, while its social history became a context for understanding these same writings.

The sketches of the crudity of English manners drawn from such sources helped Drake to establish the temporal contrasts on which his "retrospect" relied. Not content, however, to leave the lines of historical recession implicit, he identified a series of epochs leading up to the stylistic and social achievements of the eighteenth-century periodical essayists.

In keeping with the new climate of appreciation for the older English writers, Drake credited the age of Elizabeth with awakening the strength of the language, but (perhaps because his subject was prose rather than dramatic verse) he stopped well short of the wholesale admiration with which his contemporaries were beginning to write about their Elizabethan and Jacobean forebears. For Drake, English writing only acquired a proper degree of clarity in the Restoration – a gift, he did not hesitate to say, of the Francophile tastes of the court (1805 vol. 2: 39). Still, much was wanting to give the language the full sense of "systematic correctness" as well as force and precision that it has since attained. This was the work of the period that began with the reign of Queen Anne, a time, Drake pointed out, when "national success and glory" had the effect of adding "fresh nerve and vigour" to literary and scientific pursuits (pp. 79–80).

A New National Narrative: Southey's *Specimens*

Drake was as capable as anyone of enlivening his history with patriotic sentiments, but his view of literary progress seems essentially unaffected by the intense Francophobia provoked by the French Revolution and the Napoleonic Wars. Within the same decade, however, a counter-narrative was establishing itself, fashioned by writers as disparate in their political commitments as well as their poetic tastes as Robert Southey and Francis Jeffrey. Their revision of the long-established outline of literary progress (of which Drake was a late exponent) not only presented a strikingly different view of the stages of national literature, but also gave literary history a more overt ideological presence.

A summary of the new narrative of national tradition – compact but essentially complete – is presented in Southey's Preface to *Specimens of the Later English Poets* (1807). Southey intended his collection as a continuation of Ellis's *Specimens*, but in paying this compliment to the older collection, he endowed the earlier volume with a new historical significance. Together, Southey asserted, in his most succinct statement of the new narrative, the two collections "will exhibit the rise, progress, decline and revival of our Poetry, and the fluctuations of our poetical taste, from the first growth of the English language to the present times" (1807 vol. 1: vi).

Southey's subject was explicitly "taste," but his terms were more historical than aesthetic. "The taste of the publick may better be estimated from indifferent Poets than from good ones," he wrote. The ordinary poet writes for his own time, the great one for posterity. "Cleveland and Cowley, who were both more popular than Milton, characterise their age more truly" (p. vi). Still, Southey's criteria inevitably were mixed, and he imposed a strong chronological divide at the Restoration. Before this time the selection is largely governed by a documentary purpose; afterwards, poetic merit becomes a larger factor – albeit for a revealing reason. "Those of later date must stand or fall by their own merits," Southey argued, "because the sources of information, since the introduction of newspapers, periodical essays, and magazines are so numerous." The value of poetry as social documentation, in other words, is reduced in later periods by the accumulation of those other kinds of record we have already seen noted by Jeffrey. "The Restoration is the great epoch in our annals, both civil and literary: a new order of things was then established, and we look back to the times beyond, as the Romans under the Empire, to the age of the Republick" (p. vii).

The division of the story at the Restoration, however, was more than a matter of scarcity and distance; the return of the Stuarts from Continental exile also marked the essential moment of decline, when a native English style gave way to foreign influence. Spurred by the energies of the Reformation, then checked in the reign of Mary, English poetry had burst into bloom under Elizabeth "with the sudden luxuriance of an Arctick summer" (Southey 1807 vol 1: xxi). In the strife of the Civil War, however, poetry had already begun to suffer, and the great age of the drama had left no successors. "The nation was too busy to be amused, and we had now imbibed the barbarizing superstition of Scotland" (p. xxv). At last, the Restoration gave the country back the tranquillity necessary for art, but unfortunately the return of Charles II proved still more damaging than civic strife had ever been. French tastes, Southey insisted, were imposed on the country of Chaucer, Spenser, Shakespeare, and Milton, and though the poets who followed might be praised for their versification, their wit, or their reasoning, these things "do not constitute poetry."

In short, Southey concluded, reversing the conventional terms of historical progress, the "time which elapsed from the days of Dryden to those of Pope, is the dark age of English poetry" (p. xxix). Pope, Southey writes dismissively, "was completely a Frenchman in his taste," and yet even in his own day a "Reformation" had begun. Thomson called the nation back to the study of nature, and the growing taste for Shakespeare gradually brought "our old writers" back to notice, helped along by the good work of Warton and especially of Percy's *Reliques of Ancient Poetry*. For Southey the latter was "the great literary epocha of the present reign" – hence perhaps even more than Ellis's *Specimens*, the true begetter of his own collection (p. xxxi).

For all its crudity of outline, Southey's schematization of British literary history seems too powerful to ignore. Not only did it call upon strong currents of anti-French sentiment and the talismanic name of Shakespeare, but it also captured the power of a completely plotted history. And indeed, within a very few years this narrative, or one quite similar, was adopted and elaborated by Jeffrey and others, becoming in many ways a conventional (and conventionally Whig) view of British literary tradition. In the immediate moment, however, the *Edinburgh* greeted the *Specimens* with unmitigated scorn – an attitude that, without doubt, was rooted in the journal's hostility to everything connected to the Lake poets, but one which, from the standpoint of literary history, may also be interesting on other grounds.

Southey's reviewer in the *Edinburgh* has been identified as Brougham, one of the mainstays of the journal. Brougham took his stand on the grounds of taste against those of history, seizing on Southey's view that earlier ages might be best represented by selections from their most popular poets. "It seems to be here directly announced, that the object of the compilation is not to collect a body of valuable poetry, but to afford a key to posterity to judge of the prevailing taste of the British public" ([Brougham] 1807: 32). In fact, Brougham argued, Southey's selections in themselves would offer no such opportunity, and he went on to suggest that "the gentle reader of the twentieth century" would have to go to the full expense of buying "the entire works" of Dryden, Thomson, Pope, Akenside, Gray, Cowper, and the rest to remedy what was missing. Brougham did not push the tension between history and taste so far as to deny altogether the interest of historical illustration, but he did insist on the primacy of aesthetic judgment. "If the curious reader should be distressed to know the state of public taste in his father's or his grandfather's time, he had assuredly better trust to the good than the bad poets of the age. . . . A few instances of neglected merit, no doubt, will occur; but if he wishes to know the taste of the period of Pope, let him read Pope, not Betterton" ([Brougham] 1807: 36).

What is most striking in all this is the absence of any recognition of the force of Southey's representation of national history. Brougham did not try to refute Southey's narrative or correct it in any way; instead, his review simply overlooks this dimension of Southey's collection as though it had no bearing on its value as a representation of the literary past. Perhaps Brougham simply did not recognize Southey's outline of literary history for what it was, but – thanks in part to his own journal and its editor, Francis Jeffrey – it would soon become more difficult to ignore the mutual entanglement of literary history and national tradition.

Jeffrey's Two Modes of Literary History

In the early years of the *Edinburgh*, it was far from obvious that literary history would emerge as an important concern. The *Review* – which under Jeffrey's editorship quickly emerged as the most influential journal of its day – addressed a broad intelligence in the country, and it was scornful of anything that smacked of merely antiquarian interest, including most literary-historical scholarship. All too typical is the tone of Hallam's review of Scott's edition of Dryden: having decried the work of Dryden's earlier editor, Edmond Malone, as "an eminent instance of that undistinguishing collection of rubbish, which the amateurs of black letter have principally introduced," he turned around and declared that the "painful drudgery" of Malone had left Scott little to do (Hallam 1808: 116).

Jeffrey himself frequently spoke against anything that seemed too antiquarian. In reviewing Douce's illustrations of Shakespeare, for example, he was willing to concede that the poet's annotators had been able to provide "little odds and ends of information as to the manners and tastes of our ancestors" and occasionally they were able to give a more correct idea of minor passages. "But this petty sort of antiquarianism probably is not the object of any one who takes up the volumes of Shakespeare; and the scanty elucidation which the poet now and then receives, makes us but poor amends for the quantity of trash which is obtruded upon us." Shakespeare's name, he complained, sanctifies everything connected to it, "and that miserable erudition" which belonged in the *Gentleman's Magazine* or "some county history" is in danger of seeming more worthy when it appears as an illustration of Shakespeare's writings (Jeffrey 1808: 449–50).

Another feature of the *Edinburgh* that seemed unlikely to invite an historical approach to literature was Jeffrey's notorious polemic against the "Lake poets" – an element of Jeffrey's reviewing that has very nearly monopolized the attention of literary scholars. "Poetry has this much, at least, in common with religion," he wrote in an early essay on Southey, "that its standards were fixed long ago, by certain inspired writers, whose authority it is no longer lawful to call in question" (Jeffrey 1802: 63). Yet, though Jeffrey continued to hold up the failings of modern poets against the standards of a higher canon of poetic achievement, in time the canon itself acquired an increasingly historical identity. Indeed, his need to consolidate his criticism of Wordsworth and Southey while remaining open to the achievements of other contemporaries seems to have propelled him towards the more refined and complexly historical view of English literature that becomes a marked feature of the *Review* in its second and third decade.

The new view of English literary history Jeffrey and other contributors began to articulate combined two separate but compatible programs. The first was a theory about the dilemmas of the modern poet seen as a late-born child of the muses (Bate 1970); the second was a narrative of the national literary tradition as it developed from Elizabethan to modern times, counterpointed against the temporary domination of French and classical models from the Restoration to the Augustans. This second strand in Jeffrey's literary history followed essentially the same outline that Southey had proposed in his *Specimens* – a narrative of the rise, fall, and re-emergence of Englishness. Jeffrey elaborated it in a number of essays, beginning with his 1811 review of the works of the Elizabethan dramatist John Ford. In 1813, James Mackintosh offered a similar account in an essay on the poetry of Samuel Rogers (Phillips 2000: 210–11), and Jeffrey himself returned to the subject in an important essay on Swift (1816) as well as in later writings on Campbell and Byron.

Jeffrey's commentary on the dilemma of the "after poets" took a relatively narrow form in his 1808 essay on Burns, where he focused on the psychology of poetic creation and comes close to adumbrating recent theories of the "anxiety of influence." Two years later, however, in an essay on Scott's "Lady of the Lake," Jeffrey provided a fuller discussion that reflects the continued influence of Hume's speculations on "The Rise and Progress of the Arts and Sciences." Here he moved beyond psychological dynamics to entertain a broader consideration of the position of the arts in an advanced state of society (Bate 1970). In this perspective, Jeffrey was less inclined to see belatedness as implying a simple loss of creativity. The age, in fact, was "unusually prolific of original poetry" (Jeffrey 1846 vol. 2: 237). The problem, rather, was that the steady progress of refinement in the arts had created an almost irremediable split between popular and refined tastes. The earliest poets, "may be said to have got possession of all the choice materials of their art." But "after-poets" cannot have this same sense of ease and are put to a variety of more self-conscious strategies – for some, a greater minuteness and fidelity in observing characters or objects, for others a more exacting analysis of a more limited vein of the emotions. The result has been that modern poetry has been "enriched with more exquisite pictures, and deeper and more sustained strains of the pathetic, than were known to the less elaborate artists of antiquity; at the same time that it has been defaced with more affectation, and loaded with far more intricacy" (p. 244).

This passage carries an obvious echo of his polemic against the Lake school – a preoccupation that had once seemed likely to inhibit any possibility of an historical approach to literature. But in this Humean speculation on the refinement of the arts we also find a place where the theory of belatedness converges with his narrative of national taste, where other, more ideological factors play an important part.

As we have already seen, Jeffrey was not the first to sketch the history of English poetry in terms of the suppression and revival of a native tradition. Much of the force of his account, however, comes from its success in combining a genealogy of successive schools of English verse with wider historical and ideological commitments. The result – only foreshadowed in Southey – was that the history of English poetry was subsumed in a compelling narrative of national tradition. Thus in his pivotal essay on Ford, Jeffrey argued that the English love of Shakespeare is not extravagant or willful, as foreign critics like to think; it is "merely the natural love which all men bear to those forms of excellence that are accommodated to their peculiar character." In attempting "to bespeak some share of favor" for those of Shakespeare's contemporaries who had suffered neglect in an era when French tastes had prevailed, "we are only enlarging that foundation of native genius on which alone any lasting superstructure can be raised, and invigorating that deep-rooted stock upon which all the perennial blossoms of our literature must still be engrafted" (Jeffrey 1846 vol. 2: 50).

It was not Hume who presided over this kind of writing, but Burke, and the contrast between the two approaches has as much to do with distance as with doctrine. No longer simply an abstract and universalizing inquiry into the nature of taste, this strand of Jeffrey's literary-historical thinking casts literature (broadly conceived) as the embodiment of the nation's spirit and presses the reader towards a new degree of involvement in its evolution. Nor – as the essayist "bespeaks our favor" for the neglected dramas of Jacobean England, or forms his repeated contrasts between the native and the foreign, the natural and the artificial – would it be possible to say where a purely literary history leaves off and a broadly national one begins.

It would be false to draw too strict a division between a Humean history of taste and opinion and a Burkean history of tradition. Elements of both mix in many of the histories of this time. (In this same essay, for example, Jeffrey speculates on the "deeper and more general causes" that spurred the invigorating effects of the Reformation and looks as much to Taylor, Bacon, and Hooker, as to any of the poets to define the greatness of the age.) But the Burkean strain is not only important in its own right; it also gives us a particularly clear example of a form of literary mediation of the past that points well beyond the confines of whiggish literary histories: I mean the way in which nineteenth-century writers and their audiences were drawn to literary sources when they wished to intensify their affective and ideological engagement with the past. What better way, after all, could there be to narrativize an essentially intangible history? How better to make the past of a nation *familiar* than through the thoughts, feelings, and experiences of its poets?

Just Books

Hume's argument that the wars and politics of different ages are far more alike than their "taste, wit, and speculative principles" is extremely suggestive of the role that a broadly conceived literary history might play amongst the genres of historical description (1742/1987: 97). For Hume, the question was both historical and philosophical, a matter of ascertaining the degree to which different arenas of experience were subject to systematic observation. Considered in this light, the variability of the arts presented the philosophical historian with some real difficulties. It could also be argued, however, that the very things that made opinion or the arts harder to regulate or explain also gave literary history a special value as a varied and subtle record of human experience. As Hume wrote in another essay, "The great variety of Taste, as well as of opinion, which prevails in the world, is too obvious not to have fallen under every one's observations" (p. 226).

By the beginning of the next century, Hume's abstractly stated observations found echoes in the thoughts of English men and women reflecting on nothing more abstruse than the way that reading fashions had shifted in their own lifetimes. "In my youth the world doted on Sterne!" wrote Isaac Disraeli. "Forty years ago, young men in their most facetious humours never failed to find the archetypes of society in the Shandy family – every good-natured soul was uncle Toby, every humorist was old Shandy, every child of Nature was Corporal Trim!" Now, however, Sterne had "passed away to the curious" (Disraeli n.d.: 333). Jeffrey made a similar observation about the decline in reputation of

Swift and the Augustans. "By far the most considerable change which has taken place in the world of letters in our days," Jeffrey observed, "is that by which the wits of Queen Anne's time have been gradually brought down from the supremacy which they had enjoyed." In his own student days, it seemed that anyone who had any pretension to education was familiar with their writings as well as their lives. "Allusions to them abounded in all popular discourses and all ambitious conversation; and they and their contemporaries were universally acknowledged as our great models of excellence" (1846 vol. 1: 159).

If Jeffrey remembered a time when "every young man was set to read Pope, Swift, and Addison," Barbauld recollected Addison's female audience as even more devoted. In 1804, Barbauld published an abridgement of *The Spectator*, an editorial task that gave her the opportunity to think back to her own first acquaintance with the work. In those days, she wrote, *The Spectator* was the favorite item in a young lady's library and probably the first book after the Bible she would have purchased. "Sir Roger de Coverley and the other characters of the club were 'familiar in our mouths as household names;' and every little circumstance related of them remained indelibly engraven on our memories. From the papers of Addison we imbibed our first relish for wit; from his criticism we formed our first standard of taste; and from his delineations we drew our first ideas of manners." It required little attention, she added, turning to the tastes of a new generation, to be convinced that this was no longer true for the young women of the present (Barbauld 1804b: iv).

Barbauld might have responded to the change in Addison's fortunes with simple nostalgia for another time. Instead, she sought a wider significance in these alterations of reading habits amongst the young and – like Hume, Johnson, or Drake – found it in the association of literature with manners and opinion. "Books," she wrote, "make a silent and gradual, but a sure change in our ideas and opinions; and as new authors are continually taking possession of the public mind, and old ones falling into disuse, new associations insensibly take place, and shed their influence unperceived over our taste, our manners, and our morals . . . This new infusion of taste and moral sentiments acts in its turn upon the relish for books" (1804b: 1). It is true, she added, that a great book will never truly disappear, since it will live on as a classic. Nonetheless, it will no longer be a book that everyone is expected to know, and to which everyone refers. It "loses the precious privilege of occupying the minds of youth; in short, it is withdrawn from the parlour-window, and laid upon the shelf in honourable repose" (p. iii).

The practice of literary history seemed calculated to produce such moments of retrospect or prospect, giving writers reason to evoke the manners of earlier ages or to imagine the responses of readers a hundred years on. In Barbauld's case, the task of selection and abridgment suggested the need to consider changes (social as well as literary) that had overtaken the books she had read in her youth. Barbauld was an attentive editor and she evidently made the most of what must largely have been a commercial proposition. Even so, her alertness to the historicity of reading was not simply a matter of personal sensitivity; it was also the product of an established habit of looking to the arts as a register of everyday and inward experience: the part of history that chronicled what Hume called "the variety of Taste and opinion" (1742/1987: 226) When Barbauld re-read *The Spectator* under the lamp of manners, it was only natural that she would reflect on the way time had brought changes "not only in the tastes and habitudes of common life, but in the fashion of their studies, and the course of their general reading. Books influence manners; and manners, in return, influence the taste for books" (1804b: 1).

To explore the reasons that readers like Barbauld found literary history a gateway to the sort of complex and self-conscious temporal experience evidenced in these remarks, we need to broaden our view of both the literary history and the historiography of the period. This requires something more than an effort to provide historical backgrounds to the history of literature; crucially, it also means considering literary histories in terms of their historiographical function and context In this regard, I have tried to suggest that if we want to understand how contemporary readers thought about books and authors as historical objects, it would be fruitful to consider the kinds of historical descriptions literary lives and literary texts made possible – including the various forms of affective and ideological engagement to which literature, more than histories of public life, promised access.

Note

This essay forms a part of a larger investigation of the construction of historical distance as a dimension of historical representation. For the sake of economy, I have left the theme largely implicit here, but a reader wanting a clearer understanding of what is meant by several references to "distance" might want to consult two recent essays, cited below, especially Phillips (2003a). My discussion of Jeffrey here in part follows that in Phillips (2003b). The present essay grows out of a series of seminar papers presented to the Research Centre of King's College, Cambridge. I want to thank King's College for the Visiting Fellowship that provided the occasion for these seminars. I am especially grateful to Simon Goldhill and Stefan Hoesel-Uhlig who organized the seminars, and to Simon Schaffer, Peter de Bolla, and Stefan Collini who were the principal respondents. I am also indebted to April London, whose parallel interest in literary historical writing in this period has done so much to encourage my own.

References and further reading

Barbauld, A. L. (1804a) *The Correspondence of Samuel Richardson, to which are prefixed a biographical account of the author, and observations on his writings.* London.

—— (1804b) *Selections from The Spectator, Tatler, Guardian, and Freeholder, with a preliminary essay.* London: J. Johnson.

Bate, W. J. (1970) *The Burden of the Past and the English Poet.* Cambridge, Mass.: Harvard University Press.

Bisset, R. (1799) *The Spectator, with Illustrative Notes, to which are prefixed the Lives of the Authors . . . with Critical Remarks on their Respective Writings. A New Edition.* London.

Blackwood's (1819) "Notices of reprints of curious old books: *The Life and Errors of John Dunton,*" 6: 24–32.

Bromwich, D. (1989) *A Choice of Inheritance; Self and Community from Edmund Burke to Robert Frost.* Cambridge, Mass.: Harvard University Press.

[Brougham], H. (1807) "Southey's *Specimens,*" *Edinburgh Review* 11: 32–6.

Drake, N. (1805) *Essays, Biographical, Critical, and Historical, Illustrative of the Tatler, Spectator, and Guardian,* 3 vols. London.

Disraeli, I. (n.d.) "Of Sterne," in Beaconsfield (ed.) *Literary Character of Men of Genius* (pp. 33–9). London: Frederick Warne.

Ellis, G. (1803) *Specimens of the Early English Poets,* 3 vols., 3rd edn. London.

Godwin, W. (1815) *The Lives of Edward and John Phillips, nephews and pupils of Milton, including Various Particulars of the Literary and Political History of their Times.* London: Longman.

Hallam, H. (1808) "Scott's Dryden," *Edinburgh Review* 13: 116–35.

Hazlitt, W. (1930–4) "Lectures on the English comic writers," in P. Howe (ed.) *Works* (p. 6). London: Dent.

Hume, D. (1742) *Essays, Moral, Political, and Literary,* ed. E. Miller. Indianapolis: Liberty Press, 1987.

Jeffrey, F. (1802) "Southey's *Thalaba,*" *Edinburgh Review* 1: 68–83.

—— (1808) "Douce's *Illustrations of Shakespeare, and of Antient Manners,*" *Edinburgh Review* 12: 449–68.

—— (1846) *Contributions to the Edinburgh Review,* 3 vols., 2nd edn. London: Longman.

Johnson, S. (1905) *Lives of the English Poets*, 3 vols., ed. G. Birkbeck Hill. Oxford: Oxford University Press.

Perkins, D. (1992) *Is Literary History Possible?* Baltimore: Johns Hopkins University Press.

Phillips, M. (2000) *Society and Sentiment: Genres of Historical Writing in Britain, 1740–1820*. Princeton: Princeton University Press.

—— (2003a) "Relocating inwardness: historical distance and the transition from Enlightenment to Romantic historiography," *Publications of the Modern Languages Association* 118: 436–49.

—— (2003b) "Histories, micro- and literary; problems of genre and distance," *New Literary History* 33: 211–29.

Scott, W. (1835) *Periodical Criticism of Sir Walter Scott*, 5 vols. Edinburgh.

Southey, R. (1807) *Specimens of the Later English Poets, with Preliminary Notices*, 3 vols. London: Longman, Hurst, Rees, and Orme.

Index

Titles of most primary sources are listed under the author's name. Secondary sources quoted, although not paraphrased or generally cited, are also included. Page numbers in bold indicate an illustration.

Abergavenny, Lady Katherine, 176
Abrams, M. H., 209
absolutism, 200
Academy of Ancient Music, 67
accounting, 15; book-keeping, 20
Act of Union, 1707, 229
actors, 163, 185, 189, 190, 194, 195;
  see also drama, theater, women
Adam, 36–8, 43, 45
Adamolatry, 53
Adams, Samuel, 174
Addison, Joseph, 6, 48, 81, 91, 226,
  229, 254, 262; The Campaign, 213;
  Cato, 189, 198–9; "The Pleasures
  of the Imagination," 228; The
  Spectator, 48, 51, 84, 228, 254;
  on the sublime, 226, 229; The
  Tatler, 254
Admiralty (British), 18, 21, 22
Adorno, Theodor W., 2
Africa, 13, 15, 18, 19
afterpieces, see drama

agriculture, 10; tropical, 15;
  agricultural treatises, 226
Aikin, John, 233; and Anna Laetitia,
  145–6
air pump, 53
Akenside, Mark, 257
Algeria, 85
allegory, 128
Allen, Lord, 114–15
Amadis of Greece, 128
Amazon, 19
America, 15, 165; see also Canada;
  North America; United States
American Revolution, 15
ancien régime, 248
ancients, 202; ancient decorums, 249
Anderson, Benedict, 134
Angel in the House, 2
animal spirits, 52
animals, 102
Anne, Queen, 75, 167, 168, 212,
  255, 262

anthologies, 203, 205
antiquarianism, 205, 247, 248
"apologies," *see* biography
Appleby, Joyce, 28
apprentices, 67, 70, 73
Aravamudan, Srinivas, 125
Arbuthnot, John, 177
Arcadia, 42
architecture, 10, 66, 204, 228;
   architects, 204; architectural
   plans, 93; architectural prefaces,
   226
aristocracy, aristocrats, 14, 42, 47,
   54, 64, 66, 72, 123, 168, 188, 232,
   234
Aristotelian scholasticism, *see*
   scholasticism
Aristotelian unities, *see* drama
Aristotle, 41, 187, 206
arithmetic, 13, 14
Armida, 241
Arnold, Matthew, 1, 9
art, 66, 67, 77, 101; artists, 15, 204,
   241; ordering of the arts, 248
artifice, 241; *see also* nature
artisans, 54, 238
Ashfield, Andrew, 226
Ashmole, Elias, 44
Ashmolean Museum, 44
Asia, 13
astronomy, 13, 14
Atlantic, 20
atomism, 36
attributions, *see* authorship
audience, 9, 47, 67, 183–5, 249;
   reading, *see* readers; spectatorial
   relations, 187–93
Augustans, 7, 10, 101, 102, 105, 107,
   191, 253, 254, 259, 262
Augustus, 215
Austen, Jane, *Northanger Abbey*,
   147, 150; *Pride and Prejudice*, 2,
   63, 65
Australia, 19, 29

authenticity, 8, 134, 169, 172, 181,
   222; in manufactures, 235; in
   travel narratives, 20
authorship, author, 4, 8, 52,
   135, 249; anonymous, 163;
   pseudonymous, 163, 164, 166;
   spurious, 162–81
autobiography, *see* biography

Bacon, Francis, 4, 26, 36, 37, 48, 261
Baines, Paul, 162
ballads, *see* poetry
Ballaster, Ros, 128, 135, 136
Banfield, Ann, 51
Banister, John, 67
Bank of England, 6, 59, 75
Banks, Joseph, 22; *The Unhappy
   Favourite*, 195
Barbauld, Anna Laetitia, 10, 241–2,
   247, 253, 262–3
Barber, Mary, "Written at Bath to a
   Young Lady, who had just before
   given me a Short Answer," 217;
   "Written for My Son, and Spoken
   by Him at His First Putting on
   Breeches," 222
Barker, Jane, 6, 7, 81, 128, 132, 134,
   137; *The Lining of the Patchwork
   Screen*, 86, 132; *Love Intrigues*, 132;
   A Patchwork Screen for the Ladies, 132
Battestin, Martin, 2
Beaumont and Fletcher, 186
beautiful, the, 10, 226–44
Beckingham, Charles, *Epistle from
   Calista to Altamont*, 176
Bedlam, 114
beer industry, 232
beggars, 6, 80–98, 103, 104, 105;
   literary, 6, 82–7; sentimentalized,
   97; stereotyped, 82–7; women, 6,
   80, 88–98
Behn, Aphra, 7, 170; "The
   Disappointment," 220–1;
   Oroonoko, 130

Bell, Maureen, 61
Bellamy, George Anne, 169
Bender, John, 59, 68
Bengal, 15
Benjamin, Walter, 125
Bentley, Richard, 49
Berkeley, George, the Hon., 177
Bickerstaff, Isaac, 162; *The Life . . . of Ambrose Gwinett*, 85
Bicknell, Alexander, *Apology for the Life of George Anne Bellamy*, 169
biography: "apologies," 163, 166, 169; biographies, 249; "histories," 163; journals, 251; letters, 163, 170, 181, 251, 252, 253; "lives," 163, 181; memoirs, 163, 170, 181, 249, 251
Birmingham, 10, 53, 234–8
Bisset, Robert, "Life of Addison," 252
Black Guard, 85
Blackwood's, 253
Blake, William, 97, 203, 243
Blenheim, Battle of, 211, 213
Bligh, William, 4, 21
Bodleian Library, 44
Bolingbroke, *see* St John, Henry
Bolla, Peter de, 226
Bologna, 138
books, 124, 125, 137, 262; book trade, 116–19; book buyers, 162; booksellers, 166
Booth, Barton, 183
Boswell, James, *The Life of Johnson*, 251
Bougainville, Louis Antoine, 18
boundedness, *see* enclosure
bourgeois public sphere, *see* public sphere
bourgeois society, bourgeoisie, 6, 59, 64, 65, 67
Boyle, Robert, 39, 40, 41, 44, 47; *Occasional Reflections*, 40; *Skeptical Chymist*, 43

Boyle Lectures, 47, 49
Bracegirdle, Anne, 170
Bracey, Robert, 2
Braddon, Lawrence, *Regular-Government and Judicious Employment of the Poor*, 92
Britain, *see* Great Britain
British Museum, 53
Britton, Thomas, 67
Brome, Alexander, *Bumm-Fodder*, 105–7
Bromwich, David, 11, 248
Brooke, Frances, 7, 135; *The Excursion*, 135
Brougham, H., 257
Brown, Laura, 2, 11
Brown, Norman O., 101
Brown, Tom, 46; *Letters from the Dead to the Living*, 170
"Brummagem," 235–8
Burke, Edmund, 8, 25, 148, 226, 260, 261; *A Philosophical Enquiry into the Origin of our Ideas of the Sublime and Beautiful*, 144–5; *Reflections on the Revolution in France*, 74
burlesque, 108
Burnet, Gilbert, 168
Burney, Frances, 170
Burns, Robert, 259
Byron, George Gordon, Lord, 259

cabinets, 231
Calcutta, 19
Cambridge, 48, 60
Campbell, Jill, 11
Campbell, Thomas, 259; *Specimens*, 251
Canada, 135
canon, literary, 203
capitalism, 4
Carew, Bampfylda, 6, 81, 86
Caribbean, 15
caricatures, 251
carriages, 144; *Vis a Vis*, 144, 147

cartography, 16, 23, 24, 25; mapmakers, 24
Cassini surveys, 24
Castiglioni, 254
Catholics, 105, 111
Cavalier poets, *see* poetry
Cellier, Elizabeth, 171, 181; *Malice Defeated*, 172
censorship, 6, 58
Centlivre, Susanna, *Marplot*, 194
Cervantes, *Don Quixote*, 122
chamber horses, 145, 159
chamber pots, 7, 102, 103
character, *see* drama; novels
charity, 81, 94
Charles II, 4, 13, 37, 46, 75, 174–5, 186, 214–15, 256; restoration of, *see* Restoration of monarchy
Charleton, Walter, 38
Chatterton, Thomas, 162; *Rowley Poems*, 162, 171–2
Chaucer, Geoffrey, 256
Chesterfield, Earl of, *see* Stanhope, Philip
children, beggars, 88–9, 91–4
China, ancient, 202
Christie, O. F., 1
chronicles, 251
Church, 9, 123; church-state apparatus, 199; High, 127; Low, 127
Churchill, John, Duke of Marlborough, 211, 213
Churchill, Sarah, Duchess of Marlborough, *An Account of the Conduct of the Dowager Duchess of Marlborough*, 167
churchwardens, 96
Cibber, Colley, 116, 119, 183, 193
circulating libraries, 124, 148
Civil War, 7, 51, 64, 105, 256
class, 2, 11, 30, 62–8, 93; *see also* aristocracy; artisans; beggars; gentry; merchants; middle classes;

nobility; paupers; the poor; traders; upper classes; workers
Cleveland, John, 256
clubs, 71–3, 82
coaches, 121, 138
coalminers, 238
Cody, Lisa, 94
coffee houses, 25, 69–73, 204; pamphlets, 71, 73; women and, 69–74
Coleridge, Samuel Taylor, 146, 148, 239
Collier, Jeremy, *A Short View of the Immorality, and Prophaneness of the English-Stage*, 184, 192, 199, 200
Collier, Mary, *The Woman's Labour*, 230
Collins, William, 241–2; "Ode to Liberty," 208; "Ode on the Poetical Character," 208
colonialism, 2, 229
comedy, *see* drama
commedia dell'arte, *see* drama
commerce, 15, 16, 18, 123
commercial directories, 15
commodities, 125, 138
concerts, 67
concordia discors, 6, 51
conduct books, 164–5
Congreve, William, *The Mourning Bride*, 195; *The Way of the World*, 185, 195
consumerism, 2, 15
containment, *see* enclosure
Cook, James, 4, 16, 22
Cooper, Anthony Ashley, Earl of Shaftesbury, 137
Copernicus, 36
copyright, 169, 247
Corporation of the Poor, 91
counterfeit, *see* authenticity; "Brummagem"
country houses, 2, 66
Court, 123

Coventry, Francis, 81, 84, 138;
    Pompey the Little, 83, **139**
Cowley, Abraham, 256
Cowper, William, 257
craftsmen, see artisans
crime, 205
Critical Review, 173
critics, 185, 204, 241–2
Croft, Herbert, Sir, 171–2; *Love and
    Madness*, 170–2
Cromwell, Oliver, 15, 27, 37, 60
cultural studies, 2
culture, 8; popular, 122
Cupid, 174
curiosity, 146, 152
Curll, Edmund, 117–18, 170
Cust, Richard, 71
custom, 250

d'Alembert, Jean Le Rond,
    Encyclopédie, 25
dance, 183
Davenant, Charles, 27
David, King, 214
decay, 101–19
Defoe, Daniel, 7, 32, 61, 81, 121,
    122, 125, 135, 137; *Colonel Jack*,
    85; *Compleat Mendicant*, 84–5, 92;
    Essay on the South-Sea Trade, 18;
    A Journal of the Plague Year, 127,
    131, 132, **133**; *Robinson Crusoe*,
    14, 29–32, 122, 125; *Roxana*, 163;
    Shortest Way with the Dissenters, 61;
    The Storm, 124; *A Tour thro' the
    Whole Island of Great Britain*, 25;
    The True-Born Englishman, 215–16
della Casa, Giovanni, 254
Dening, Greg, 21
Denmark, 24
Dennis, John, 187, 190, 191
Desaguliers, Jean Theophilus, 51;
    *Newtonian System of the World the
    Best Pattern of Government*, 50
Descartes, René, 51

descriptions: ethnographical, 20;
    "eye-witness," 21; geographical,
    14, 18, 20; historical, 249;
    landscape, 149; statistical, 14
Dick, Philip K., *Do Androids Dream of
    Electric Sheep?*, 148–9
Dickens, Charles, 97
Dickinson, H. T., 68
Dickson, P. G. M., *The Financial
    Revolution*, 76
dictionaries, geographical, *see*
    geography books
didacticism, 227
Diderot, Denis, 18; *Encyclopédie*, 25
Dido, 174, 176
discourse, indirect, 51, 52; "rational-
    critical," 59, 60, 70
disease, 205
Disraeli, Isaac, 261
dissenters, 217
Dixon, Sarah, "Lines Occasioned by
    the Burning of Some Letters," 209
Dodd, William, 171
Dolan, John, 222
domesticity, 125
Donne, John, 203
Douce, Francis, 258
Drake, Nathan, *Essays Biographical,
    Critical, and Historical*, 254–5, 262
drama: afterpieces, 183, 188;
    breeches roles, 194; character, 189;
    comedy, 188–94, 251; *commedia
    dell'arte*, 183; farce, 183, 251;
    pantomime, 183, 188; plays, 204;
    playwrights, 187, 190; reform
    literature, 184, 189–93; rehearsal
    play, 183; Restoration comedy,
    189–92; sentimental comedy, 176,
    192–3; she-tragedy, 176, 194–9;
    spectatorial relations, 188–93;
    stagecraft, 186; texts, 193; theory,
    186; tragedy, 188–9, 194–9;
    unities, 187; *see also* theaters
Drayton, Michael, 176

Drury, Robert, 29
Drury Lane Theatre, 183, 200
Dryden, John, 1, 7, 9, 101, 104, 119, 190, 203, 216, 256, 258; *Absalom and Achitophel*, 210–11, 214–15; *Alexander's Feast*, 211; *Annus Mirabilis*, 211; "Astrea Redux," 211; *Love Triumphant*, 188; *MacFlecknoe*, 101–5; "To His Sacred Majesty, a Pengyric on His Coronation," 211
Dublin, 108, 111–13
Duck, Stephen, *The Thresher's Labour*, 230
Dunton, John, *The Life and Errors of John Dunton*, 253
Dyer, John, *The Fleece*, 233, 236

East India Company, 15
Eden, 4, 36, 243
Edinburgh Review, 137, 140, 257, 258
editors, 136
effluence, 7, 101–19
Egerton, Sarah Fyge, "On my leaving London," 222; "To one who said I must not Love," 217; "To the Honourable Robert Boyle," 217
Egypt, 24
electricity, 53
elite, *see* aristocracy; gentry; middle classes; nobility; upper classes
Elizabeth I, 256; *see also* Renaissance
Elizabethan, *see* Renaissance
Ellis, George, *Specimens of the Early English Poets*, 250, 255
Ellis, Markman, 76
empire, 13, 14, 15, 16, 18, 19, 24
Empson, William, 42
enclosure, 10, 227, 228; acts, 2, 227–8; concepts of containment, 231, 238
England, 1, 16, 51, 54, 64, 66, 67, 70, 71, 95, 101, 103, 106, 121, 130, 165, 175, 204, 226–44

English language, 106, 129, 215, 249
Englishness, 231, 236, 249, 254, 259
Enlightenment, 2, 11, 20, 24, 25, 76, 164, 181, 204; anti-Enlightenment, 93
epic, *see* poetry
"epistles," *see* biography; poetry
epistolarity, 253; epistolary novels, *see* novels
Erickson, E. L., 68
essays, 251
estate plans, 10, 226
estates, landed, 234; *see also* aristocracy; gentry; nobility
Etherege, Sir George, *The Man of Mode*, 190–1
Europe, 13, 14, 15, 16, 19, 24, 59, 123, 129, 134, 147, 186, 188, 204
Evans, Tanya, 94
Evelyn, John, 37
exchanges, 25
Exclusion Bill, 71
excrement, 101–19
"excremental vision," 101
experimental philosophy, 4, 19, 36–54

fables, 128
fabula, 155
farce, *see* drama
Farquhar, George, 193
fashion, 15
Fawkes, Francis, "Elogy on Sir Isaac Newton," 49
Fell, Margaret, *Women's Speaking Justified*, 180
Female Honour: An Epistle to a Lady in Favour, 177–8
feminist theory, 2, 68
Ferguson, Adam, 124, 141, 249
feudalism, 200
Fielding, Henry, 81, 121, 125, 136, 162, 168; *Joseph Andrews*, 252; *Shamela*, 181; *Tom Jones*, 86, 121, 126, 127, 136

film, 194; filmgoers, 159; horror,
146, 156
filth, 101–19
Fleet Ditch, 104
Fleet River, 104
Florida, 15
Florizel to Perdita, 178–9
Ford, John, 259
Fordham, H. G., 3
forgery, 171
Foucault, Michel, 93
Fox, Charles James, 1, 61, 68
France, 24, 51, 75, 175, 211,
216, 247; Blenheim, 211, 213;
Francophobia, 255, 257;
French language, 129; French
neoclassicism, 186–7, 208; French
novelists, 128; French publishing
practices, 170; French taste, 256;
Napoleonic Wars, 229, 255; *see also*
French Revolution
Franklin, Benjamin, 164, 168, 174
frauds, textual, 163
Frederick, Prince of Wales, 174, 178
free indirect discourse, *see* discourse
freemen, 63
French Revolution, 145, 255
friendship, 206
Fuller, Francis, 145

Galileo, 38, 45
gardens, 10, 66, 204; cottage, 227,
238; English, 227; formal, **230**;
horticultural treatises, 226; kitchen,
10, 227, 228, 231, 238; manuals,
238–44, **240**; neathouses, 238;
parterres, 238; walled, 231
Garrick, David, *Florizel and Perdita*,
178
Gaub, Jerome, *De regimine mentis*, 145
Gay, John, 6, 81, 82, 84, 103;
Beggar's Opera, 82; "My Own
Epitaph," 208; *Rural Sports: A
Georgic*, 208, 232; *Trivia*, 103

gazetteers, *see* geography books
gender, 8, 9, 11, 162–81, 186, 194–8
generalizations, 202, 203, 207
generals, 203, 207; *see also*
particulars; poetry
genre, 9, 122, 186, 208, 249, 251;
see also allegory; burlesque; drama;
fables; historiography; journals;
novels; parody; poetry; satire
gentleman, 4, 19, 43, 47, 67, 123
Gentleman's Magazine, 258
gentry, 65, 217, 234
geography, 4, 6, 25; and fiction,
28–32; geography books, 14, 15,
16, 19, 26, 27; special, 26
geology, 19
geometry, 13, 14
George II, 50, 174, 177, 215, 252
George III, 179
georgic, *see* poetry
Germany, 24, 121, 215, 216; literary
influence, 248; novelists, 121;
roads, 7, 121
ghost writers, 163
Gildon, Charles, 7, 125; *The Histories
and Novels of . . . Mrs. Behn*, 170; *The
Post-Man Robb'd of his Mail*, 127
Girouard, Mark, 65–6
Glanvill, Joseph, 38
Glasgow, 19
Glorious Revolution, *see* Revolution
of 1688
Godwin, William, 252
Goldsmith, Oliver, 97
Gordon, Patrick, *Geography
Anatomiz'd*, 26
Gordon, Thomas, *Cato's Letters*, 63,
68
Gosse, Edmund, 1
Gothic, *see* novel
Graham, James, 173
Grainger, James, 234; *The Sugar-Cane*,
233, 234
Grand Tour, 14, 138

gravity, 41, 49, 50, 51, 52, 53
Gray, Thomas, 242, 243, 257; "Ode
  on the Death of a Favourite Cat,"
  209
Great Britain, 13, 14, 18, 26, 58, 66,
  69, 123, 124, 138, 204, 217,
  226–44, 249
Great Fire, 16
Great Plague, 103
Great Southern Continent, 18
Greece, 202; Greek rituals, 199
Gresham College, 27, 37
Grew, Nehemiah, 53
Grub Street, 2, 116–19
guilds, 123
Guthrie, William, *New Geographical,
  Historical, and Commercial Grammar,*
  26
Gwynn, Nell, 174–5, 177, 181
gypsies, 86

Habermas, Jürgen, 6, 58–77
Hackman, James, 170–2
hacks, 102, 116, 164
Hakluyt, Richard, *Principall
  Navigations,* 23
Hale, Dorothy, 131
Hallam, Henry, 247, 258
halls, medieval, 66
Hancock, John, 174
Hanoverian succession, 75
Harlequin, 183
Harlequin Doctor Faustus, 185
Harlequin Sheppard, 183, 188
Harley, Robert, 61, 212
Harrington, James, "Modell of the
  Common-Wealth of Oceana,"
  62–3
Harris, Frances, 167, 168
Hartlib circle, 27
Hasbach, *Die parlamentarische
  Kabinettsregierung,* 75
Hawkesworth, John, 22
Hawksmoor, Nicholas, 91, 92

Haywood, Eliza, *The British Recluse,*
  135; *The Female Spectator,* 165
Hazlitt, William, 122, 141, 251
Hédelin, François, abbé d'Aubignac,
  186
heiresses, 68; *see also* women
Herder, Johann Gottfried von, 248,
  250
Herefordshire, 232
Hermes Trismegistus, 40
Herrick, Robert, 203
Heywood, James, "To Lucinda,
  visiting him in his Sickness," 217
Hill, Aaron, "Alone in an Inn at
  Southampton," 209
Hill, John, 164; *The Conduct of
  a Married Life,* 165; *On the
  Management and Education of
  Children,* 165
historians, 248–50
historiography, 10, 247–63
history, 9, 204, 247–63; literary, 10,
  247–63; local, 249; national, 248,
  255–8; philosophical, 249; *see also*
  natural history
"histories," *see* biography
Hoadley, Benjamin, 168
hoaxes, literary, 162
Hobbes, Thomas, 27, 51
Hogarth, William, "A Just View of
  the British Stage," 183–5, **184**, 200
Holland, 15, 215, 216
Holmes, Geoffrey, *British Politics in the
  Age of Anne,* 76
Holocaust, 8
Home, Henry, Lord Kames, 226,
  239–41
Home, John, *Douglas,* 195, 199
Hooke, Nathaniel, 167, 168
Hooke, Robert, 4, 37, 38, 39, 44, 45,
  46, 48, 54; *Micrographia,* 38, 46
Hooker, Richard, 261
Horace, 215
Horkheimer, Max, 2

horticulture, *see* gardens
hospitals, 81, 91, 137; Bedlam, 114;
  Foundling Hospital, 91, 92, 94, 96;
  geriatric wards, 94; Guy's, 96;
  lying-in, 94; Magdalen Hospital,
  92, 94; St Bartholomew's, 95;
  St Thomas's, 95; Westminster
  Hospital, 91, 96
houses, 66; *see also* country houses
Howard, Henrietta, Lady Suffolk,
  174, 177–8
Huet, Pierre-Daniel, *Traité de l'Origine
  des romans*, 128
Hughes, John, "The Ecstasy," 49
Hume, David, 250, 259, 260, 261,
  262, 263; "Of Eloquence," 247,
  263
Hume, Robert D., 67
Hunt, Leigh, 239, 241
Hutton, William, 235–6
hydrography, 16

iambic pentameter, 231
ideology, 11
illiteracy, 43, 44
imperialism, 4, 228, 229
implied reader, *see* readers
Inchbald, Elizabeth, 170
India, 15, 24
Indies, 15
individualism, 122, 123, 125
industrialization, industrialist, 2, 4,
  54
industry, 15, 232–8
institutions, 6, 81, 82, 91, 204;
  specialized, 93; theater as social,
  185, 199; *see also* hospitals;
  parishes; workhouses
intellectual property, 247
intellectuals, 70
Interregnum, 7, 37, 105
Ireland, 27, 95, 111–13, 165
isomerism, 228, 239
isomorphism, 228

it-narratives, 139
Italy, 24

Jacobite Rebellion, 24
Jacobites, 111
Jago, Richard, *Edge-Hill*, 231, 234–5,
  236, 238
Jamaica, 15
Jeffrey, Francis, 137, 138, 140, 141,
  251, 255, 257, 258–61, 262
jewelry, 237
Jews, representations of, 178–80,
  214; Hebraic past, 202
Jodrell, Richard Paul, *The Female
  Patriot*, 173–4
Johnson, Samuel, 2, 48, 126, 203,
  242, 254, 262; Boswell's *Life*, 251;
  Dictionary, 126; *Irene*, 199; *Lives of
  the Poets*, 171; *Rambler*, 48; *Rasselas*,
  203
Jonson, Ben, 185, 186
journals, 21, 29, 30, 58, 93;
  journalism, 181
Junius, 74

Kame, Lord, *see* Home, Henry
Kant, Immanuel, 226
Keats, John, 149, 203, 239
kennels, 103, 117
Kenrick, William, *The Whole Duty of
  Woman*, 165–6
Kéroualle, Louise de, Duchess of
  Portsmouth, 174–5
Killigrew, Thomas, 186
King, Kathryn, 128
King, William, 81; *The Beggar Woman*, 87
Kip, J. and L. Knyff, "Burlington
  House in Pickadilly," **230**
Kit-Kat Club, 72
Kreilkamp, Ivan, 131

labor, 37; alienated, 54; laborers,
  228, 238; "laboring poets," 230;
  rational/intellectual, 41, 42

Labrador, 15
Lake poets, 258, 260; *see also* Coleridge; Southey; Wordsworth
Landau, Norma, 65
landed gentry, landed elite, landowner, *see* aristocracy; gentry; nobility
landscapes, 103, 228; landscape treatises, 227, 238, 239
Langley, Batty, "Design of an Elegant Kitchen Garden," **240**
Lapérouse, Jean-François, 18
Latin, 215
laystalls, 103
Lee, Nathaniel, *The Rival Queens*, 178
Lee, Sophia, *The Recess*, 148, 151–2
Lefebvre, Henri, 231
Leibniz, Gottfried Wilhelm, 48
A Letter from the Dutch. of Portsmouth to Madam Gwyn, 175
Letters from Perdita to a certain Israelite, 178–9
Letters of Florizel and Perdita, 179
"letters" (belles lettres), 248; *see also* biography; poetry
libel, 58, 251
liberty, 231; of the press, *see* press
Licensing Act, 58, 127
Lichtenberg, Georg Christoph, 7, 121–3, 139
life expectancy, 205
literacy, 2; *see also* illiteracy
literary history, 10, 128, 129, 247–63
"literary sphere," 69–74
literature, 66, 77, 82; impact on social policy, 93
"lives," *see* biography
Locke, John, 42; *Two Treatises of Government*, 69
log-books, 21
London, 3, 15, 16, 23, 46, 59, 60, 67, 71, 82, 102, 108, 138, 168, 217; Tudor-Stuart, 102; *see also* beggars; clubs; coffee houses; concerts; societies; stage; streets; theaters
London Corresponding Society, 72
Longinus, 226, 227, 228, 242
longitude, 21
Loudon, J. C., 231, 238
love, 206
Lucretius, 45
Lunar Society of Birmingham, 53
Lydell, Richard, 176
lyric, *see* poetry

Macaulay, Catharine, 172–4, 181
machines, 4, 7, 8
Mackenzie, Henry, 6, 81; *The Man of Feeling*, 53, 83
Mackintosh, James, 259
Macky, John, *A Journey through England*, 72
McPherson, James, *Fragments of Ancient Poetry*, 162
mad houses, 91
Madagascar, 29
Madam Celliers Answer to the Pope's Letter, 172
Madam Gwins Answer, 175
madness, 52
mail, 121
Malone, Edmond, 258
Malthus, Thomas, 28
managers, 185
Mancini, Hortensia, 174
Mandeville, Bernard, 145; *Fable of the Bees*, 51, 107
Manley, Delarivier, 7, 128; *The New Atalantis*, 128, 129, 170; *The Secret History of Queen Zarah*, 127, 130
manliness, 228
manners, 249, 250, 251, 254, 262
manuals, garden, *see* gardens
Maori, 22
mapmaking, *see* cartography
maps and mapping, 14, 15, 16, 18, 19, 23, 24, 25, 29

Marie Antoinette, 74
Marine Society, 92, 96
market, 7, 8, 19, 124, 129, 164, 171, 185
Marlborough, Duke and Duchess of, *see* Churchill, John; Churchill, Sarah
Marra, John, 22
marriage, 2; companionate, 2; of convenience, 2
Marriott, Matthew, 91
Marshall, William, 241
Martin, Matthew, 87–9; *Letter . . . on the State of Mendacity*, 87
Marvell, Andrew, 46; *Last Instructions to a Painter*, 45
Marxism, Marxist theory, 2, 64, 65, 76, 125
Mary I, 256
Mary II, Queen, 168
Mason, William, "The English Garden," 227
mass culture, *see* popular culture
mathematics, 48
Matthews, John, *Vox Populi, Vox Dei*, 61
Maynwaring, Arthur, 168
Meal Tub Plot, 172
mechanical arts, 41
mechanical philosophy, 43
medievalism, 202
meeting rooms, 25
memoirs, *see* biography
men, beggars, 6, 80–98; posing as women writers, 8, 164–81
Mendacity Enquiry Office, 87
mercantilism, 15
merchants, 15, 19, 20, 217; merchant companies, 21; merchants' guides, 15
metal industry, 234
metaphrasis, 234
micrography, 4
microscope, 4, 45

middle classes, "middling sort," 66, 93, 94, 123, 128
Mignard, Pierre, 174
migrants, 28; Irish, 89
military, 9, 15, 24, 27; academies, 25
Milton, John, 6, 37, 40, 43, 229, 231, 239, 243, 256; *Of Education*, 37; *Paradise Lost*, 37, 40, 45, 232, 237–8; *Paradise Regained*, 40
Mingay, G. E., 64; *English Landed Society in the Eighteenth Century*, 76
modernity, 200, 204
Moll, Herman, 29
monarchy, 13, 15, 51; monarchical birthday, 210
Montagu, Lady Mary Wortley, 203; "An Answer to a Love Letter in Verse," 217; *Epistle from Mrs Yonge to her Husband*, 177, 223; "Impromptu to a young Lady singing," 217; "To Sir Godfrey Kneller," 217; *Town Eclogues*, 208; "Written ex tempore in Company in a Glass Window," 221–2
Monthly Review, 164
Moore, Edward, *The Foundling*, 192, 193; *The Gamester*, 188, 195
Moore, John, 128
morality, in drama, 187–93; morals, 251
Moray, Robert, 37
Morgan, Thomas, 52
Morse, Jedidiah, *American Universal Geography*, 26
Moses, 43
motion, 121–41
"moving writing," 124, 138
music, musicians, 66, 67, 101

Napoleonic Wars, 229, 255
narrative strategies: curiosity, 146, 152; digression, 150; formula, 147; intelligibility, 153, 155; plot, 158; setting, 157; storytelling, 155;

suspense, 146, 150; tempo (or pace), 147, 149, 150, 151, 155–6; terror, 146
nationalism, national identity, 10, 13, 229, 232, 234, 243, 249
Native Americans, 8, 24
natural history, 23, 41
natural philosophy, 27, 44, 206
nature, cultivated, 241
navigation, 13, 14, 16, 21; navigators, 24
Navy (British), officers, 21
Needham, Marchamont, 62
neoclassicism, 9, 186–94, 199, 208
Neptune, 175
New Historicist theory, 2
New Jerusalem, 4, 54
New World, 130
New Zealand, 18
news, 205; newspapers, 58, 127, 163, 251
Newton, Sir Isaac, 4, 41, 48, 49, 50, 52; *Opticks*, 48, 49, 50; *Principia Mathematica*, 48, 53
Noah, 40
nobility, 66, 72, 234; *see also* aristocracy
North, Roger, 49
North America, 13, 14, 15, 24, 85, 86
Northwest Passage, 18
nostalgia, 199
novelists, 28, 121
novels, 2, 4, 7, 66, 121–41, 204, 251; of antiquity, 129; epistolary, 134; Gothic, 8, 144–59; rise of the, 2, 76; romance, 122, 126, 127, 128; *see also* narrative strategies; satire
Nussbaum, Felicity, 11

observers, 39
occasional poetry, *see* poetry
occasions, public, 9
ode, *see* poetry

Ogborn, Miles, 131
Ogilby, John, 3, 4, 13, 16, 19; *Africa*, 16; *America*, 16; *Atlas Chinensis*, 16; *Atlas Japannensis*, 16; *Britannia*, 3, **5**, 16, 25; *Embassy to China*, 16
Ogilvie, John, 242–3
Old World, 130
Oldenburg, Henry, 40, 43
Oldmixon, John, "To a Young Lady who Commanded Me to write Satire," 217
opera, 183
optics, 45
Orient, 129; oriental tales, 129
original sin, 37
Orpheus, 40
Osborne (bookseller), 117
Ossian, *see* McPherson, James
Otway, Thomas, *The Orphan*, 195
Ovid, *Heroides*, 176, 177
Oxford, 27, 37, 60

Pacific, 18, 21
Pack, Richardson, "An Epistle from a Half-Pay Officer," 217
Paine, Thomas, *Rights of Man*, 61, 68
painting, 194
pamphlets, 58, 60, 61, 71, 163; coffee-house, 71, 73; murder trials, 171; political, 105; social reform, 98
panegyric, *see* poetry
pantomimes, *see* drama
Paracelsus, 44
Paradise, 36
parish officers, 94
parish settlements, *see* settlements
parishes, casualty, 95; St Clement Danes, 95; St Dionysius Backchurch, 95; St Martin in the Fields, 80, 95
parliamentary enclosures, *see* enclosures
parody, 110

particulars, 203, 207; *see also* generals; poetry

party (political), 58; *see also* Tories; Whigs

passions, 138, 188

past/present, 202, 204–5, 207, 247, 250

Pateman, C., 68

patriotism, 247

paupers, 6, 81, 93, 96; agency of, 98

Pelham, Henry, 168

Pelham-Holles, Thomas, Duke of Newcastle, 168

"people," 62

Pepys, Samuel, 46, 67

Percy, Thomas, *Reliques of Ancient Poetry*, 256

performers, 185, 194; *see also* actors; drama; theatre; women

periodical press, 247

Perkins, David, 248

Petty, William, 27

Philadelphia, 168

Philips, John, *Bleinheim*, 213; *Cyder*, 208, 229, 231–3, **233**, 237

Philips, Katherine, "To Mrs Mary Carne," 217

Phillips, Ambrose, *The Distressed Mother*, 195

Phillips, Constantia, *An Apology for the Conduct of Mrs. Teresia Constantia Phillips*, 166, 169

philosophers, 204

philosophy, moral, 28; natural, *see* natural philosophy

photography, 194

physiology, 8

Pilkington, Laetitia, *The Memoirs of Mrs. Laetitia Pilkington*, 163

Pincus, Steven, 73, 76

Pinkerton, John, 243

pirates, 85

pissing, 114, 117

Pitt, William (the Younger), 1, 62

Plato, 40; Platonism, 206

plays, *see* drama

pleasure, 9, 11, 202, 224, 232

Plot, Robert, 44

Pocock, J. G. A., 123, 124, 138

Poe, Edgar Allan, "The Tell-Tale Heart," 158

Poems on Several Occasions, 209

poet laureate, 210

poetry, poems, 1, 4, 259; on affairs of state, 58; audience, 217, 218–22, 244; ballads, 82, 105; Cavalier poets, 206; classical precedents, 208; diatribes, 211; eclogues, 208; elegy, 208, 209; epic, 45, 203, 208, 242, 243; epigram, 208, 209; "epistles," 217, 218; epitaph, 209; georgic, 10, 208, 228, 229–35; ideological, 209; lampoons, 211; "letters," 217, 218; "light" verse, 203; lyric, 10, 108–10, 203, 205–6, 208, 238–41, 242, 243; mock poems, 211; occasional, 9, 202–24; ode, 10, 208, 209, 241–4; panegyric, 211; pastoral, 208; philosophical, 203; private, 217–24; public, 207–17; satire, 208, 211, 214; sonnet, 109

poets, 1, 52, 249

"polite," 6, 101, 193; essays, 251

political analysts, 204

political arithmetic, 14, 27, 28; economy, 14, 28; theory, 190

politicians, 163

politics, 4, 9; "political" public sphere, 70

poor, the, 80–98; agency of, 93–8

Poovey, Mary, 28

Pope, Alexander, 1, 6, 7, 9, 47, 49, 102, 104, 107, 116–19, 177, 203, 216, 262; *Dunciad*, 52, 104, 116–19, 174, 208, 211, 256, 257; "Elegy to the Memory of an Unfortunate Lady," 208; *Eloisa to*

Abelard, 176, 222–3; "Epigram:
Engraved on the Collar of a
Dog which I gave to his Royal
Highness," 208, 209; "Epigram:
On One who made long Epitaphs,"
208; "Epistle to Miss Blount, on
her leaving the Town," 218–19;
Essay on Man, 47, 207; "First
Epistle of the Second Book of
Horace Imitated," 215; "Occasion'd
by some Verses of his Grace the
Duke of Buckingham," 209;
Pastorals, 208; *The Rape of the Lock*,
216; *Windsor-Forest*, 209, 212–13
popular culture, 122
postcolonial theory, 2
poverty, 6, 81, 93, 112
Poverty Bay, 22
power, 10, 21, 54, 82, 250
present, *see* past/present
press, 58, 60; liberty (or freedom) of,
59, 60, 74
Priest, Whadcock, 168
Priestley, Joseph, 53
print, 136; circulation, 26; culture,
180; production, 247; technology,
123
Printing Act, 58, 59, 74
printing houses, presses, 60
Prior, Matthew, "To a Child of
Quality of Five Years Old, the
Author Supposed Forty," 220, 224
privacy, private spaces, 9, 10, 125;
private life, 210; *see also* public
sphere
productivity, 229, 234
projectors, 81
property, 7, 69, 124, 128;
intellectual, 247
prose, 1
prospects, 10, 228, 229, 238, 240
prostitution, prostitutes, 2, 94
Protestantism, Protestants, 36, 125
psychoanalytic theory, 2

psychology, 122, 123, 125
public opinion, 73
public spaces, 7, 25
public sphere, 2, 6, 10, 25, 58–77,
123, 204; literary, 69–74, 123; and
private sphere, 68–74; women
and, 68–9, 73
publishers, 170; *see also* books:
booksellers
Punch, 183
Puritans, 105
Pythagoras, 40

Rabelais, 114
race, 2, 11, 30
Radcliffe, Ann, 8, 144–59; *The Italian*,
146, 147, 150, 151, 152–3, 154–5;
The Mysteries of Udolpho, 146, 149;
The Romance of the Forest, 150,
153–4, 158; A *Sicilian Romance*,
149, 150, 152, 155, 156–8
Ralph, James, *The Other Side of the
Question*, 168; *The Remembrancer*,
168
Randolph, John, *Letters from General
Washington*, 162
rank, 62
Raphael (Archangel), 43
Rapin, René, 186
Ray, John, *Historia Generalis
Plantarum*, 48
Raymond, Henry Augustus, *see* Scott,
Sarah
readers, readership, 66, 73, 124, 159,
218, 250; implied reader, 218–22;
reading practices, 148; reader
response, 148, 155; women, 70,
73, 135, 164
realism, 122
reason, 1, 9, 30, 37, 62, 73, 77, 101
Reay, Martha, 170–2
Reeve, Clara, 128; "To a Coquet,
disappointed of a Party of
Pleasure," 217

reform, 1; reformers, 204
Reformation, 256, 261
rehearsal play, *see* drama
religion, 4, 36, 38, 105
A Remarkable Moving Letter, 173
Renaissance, 9, 10, 23, 25, 185, 186, 206, 253, 255, 259, 260
Republicans, 105
Restoration, 255, 256, 259
Restoration comedy, *see* drama
Restoration of monarchy, 37, 60
reviews, 164
revolution, 1
Revolution of 1688, 50, 59, 64, 67, 75, 76, 128
Richardson, Samuel, 125, 136, 141, 162, 252, 253; *Clarissa,* 121, 122, 126, 134, 138, 140; *A Collection of the Moral and Instructive Sentiments,* 136; *Pamela,* 181
Richetti, John, 11
roadmaps, 3
roads, German, 7, 121
Robinson, Mary, 174, 178–80, 181; *Captivity, a Poem; and Celedon and Lydia, A Tale,* 179; *Memoirs of the Late Mrs Robinson,* 178–9; *Poems,* 179
Rochester, Earl of, *see* Wilmot, John
Rogers, Samuel, 259
romance novel, *see* novel
romances, chivalric, 251
Romanticism, Romantic period, 9, 122, 140, 141, 159
Rota Club, 72
Rousseau, G. S., 52
Rousseau, Jean-Jacques, *La Nouvelle Héloïse,* 138
Rowe, Nicholas, 176; *The Fair Penitent,* 195–8; *The Tragedy of Jane Shore,* 194–5
Rowley, Thomas, *see* Chatterton, Thomas

Royal Society, 4, 18, 23, 37, 38, 43, 48, 53; *Philosophical Transactions,* 39, 53
Royalists, 105, 132, 217; *see also* Cavalier poets
Rump Parliament, 106
rural, 204

The Sarah-ad, 168
St John, Henry (Viscount Bolingbroke), 61
Saintsbury, George, 2
Salmon, Thomas, *Modern Gazetteer,* 26; *New Geographical and Historical Grammar,* 26
Sappho, 176
satire, satirists, 105, 116, 173, 177, 193, 208, 211, 214, 251; *see also* biography; novel; poetry
Scaramouche, 183
Scaramouche Jack Hall, 183
Schlegel, August Wilhem von, and Friedrich von, 248, 250
scholars, 43
scholasticism, schoolmen, 14, 42, 44
science and literature, 45–54
scientific method, 19, 206
scientists, 204; *see also* natural philosophy
Scodel, Joshua, 203, 206
Scotland, 24, 124; Military Survey of, 24
Scott, Sarah, *History of Gustavus Vasa,* 164
Scott, Sir Walter, 8, 146, 247, 252; "Lady of the Lake," 259
selfhood, 122, 136
Sellers, John, *The Coasting Pilot,* **17**
sensibility, 145, 146, 210
sensory experience, 36
sentimental comedy, *see* drama
sentimentalism, 252
servants, 14, 63, 66, 69, 70, 73, 94, 176

settlements (parish), 80, 88, 89, 94
Seven Years War, 15
sewage, sewers, 7, 101, 103–4, 106, 205
sex, sexuality, 2; of beggars, 87; sexual equality, 2
Seymour, Juliana-Susannah, *see* Hill, John
Shadwell, Thomas, 101–3, 105
Shaftesbury, Lord, *see* Cooper, Anthony Ashley
Shakespeare, William, 109, 186, 187, 239, 256, 257, 260; Douce's illustrations, 258; *Hamlet*, 185; *Julius Caesar*, 185; *Macbeth*, 185; *The Winter's Tale*, 178
Shapin, Steven, 20
Shenstone, William, 179
Shepherd, Peter, 188
Sheppard, Jack, 184, 187, 200
Sheridan, Richard Brinsley, *The Critic*, 163
she-tragedy, *see* drama
ships, 21; shipping routes, 16
shopkeepers, 19
Sidney, Sir Philip, 239
Siena, Kevin, 94
slavery, 19; anti-slavery, 19
Smart, Christopher, *The Hop-Garden*, 232; *The Midwife*, 164
Smith, Adam, 28
Smollett, Tobias, 121; *Humphry Clinker*, 53
Smyth, James Carmichael, 145
Snyder, Henry, 167
social policy, 93, 97
societies, private, 67, 71
Society for the Promotion of Christian Knowledge, 91
Society of Arts, 53
sociologists, 204
Socrates, 131
Solkin, David, 76
Somervile, William, *The Chace*, 232

South Seas, 18
Southey, Robert, 235; *Amadis of Gaul*, 247, 252; *Specimens of the Later English Poets*, 255–8, 259, 260
space: conceptual, 227; contained, 238–9, 241; English, 229; as God's sensorium, 50; interstellar, 45; narrative, 149, 157, 158; social, 228; and time, 243; vernacular, 228, 229; *see also* enclosure; prospects
Spacks, Patricia Meyer, 148
Spain, 15, 85
The Spectator, 48, 51, 71, 72, 84, 252, 254, 262, 263
spectators, *see* audience
Spenser, Edmund, 239, 256
Sprat, Thomas, 4, 36, 37, 39, 43, 50
stage, 2; women on, 2; *see also* theater
Stamp Act, 60
Stanhope, Philip, Earl of Chesterfield, 126
state, 9, 24; affairs of, 58; analogy to stage, 190
state of nature, 51
Stationers' Register, 59
statistics, 14, 28, 88, 89
status, 62
steam engine, 237
Steele, Sir Richard, 6, 48, 91; *The Conscious Lovers*, 192–3; *The Spectator*, 48, 51, 84, 191
Steiner, George, *The Death of Tragedy*, 199
Stephen, Leslie, 1
Sterne, Laurence, 162; *A Sentimental Journey*, 144, 158; *Tristram Shandy*, 169, 261
Stewart, Susan, 228
Stone, Lawrence, 64
Strachey, Lytton, 2
streets, 6, 80–98, 101–19
Strype, John, *Survey of London*, 84

Stukeley, William, 41
subjectivity, 124
sublime, the, 10, 144–5, 226–44
sugar industry, 233
Surinam, 130
survey, *see* prospects
surveyors, 24
surveys: Cassini, 24; Down, 27;
   Military Survey of Scotland, 24,
   Ordnance, 24
Swift, Jonathan, 6, 7, 81, 102, 103,
   105, 107, 108–16, 162, 211, 259,
   262; *Conduct of the Allies*, 70, 74,
   177; *An Examination of Certain
   Abuses*, 111–13; *The Examiner*, 167;
   Gulliver's Travels, 4, 14, 29, **30**, 46,
   86; "The Lady's Dressing Room,"
   108–10; "A Satirical Elegy On the
   Death of a late Famous General,"
   213; "On Stella's Birthday . . .
   1718," 219, 224; "Traulus,"
   113–15
swings, 145, 159
Switzer, Stephen, 229, 239;
   Ichnographia Rustica, 227
Sydney, Algernon, 174

Taine, Hippolyte, *History of English
   Literature*, 130
Tasmania, 29
Tasso, Torquato, 241
taste, 101, 185
Tate, Nahum, *The History of King Lear*,
   187
taxation, 16
Taylor, William, 261
teachers, 205
telescope, 4, 38, 45
terror, 8
Thackeray, William, 97
Thames, 102, 104
theaters, 9, 66; "court," 66; Drury
   Lane, 183, 200; licensed, 183, 186;
   Lincoln's Inn Fields, 183; London,

67, 183, 186; modern, 200;
   "public," 66; *see also* actors; drama;
   neoclassicism
Theobald, Lewis, 188
theodicy, 36, 37
theologians, 204
things, 123, 126, 138; *see also* it-
   narratives
Thompson, E. P., 64, 76
Thompson, Lynda, 163, 169
Thomson, James, 47, 48, 52, 257;
   The Seasons, 47, 48, 52, 229, 233–4
Tickell, Thomas, 213
time, narrative, 149; and space, 243;
   see also narrative strategies
Timmins, Samuel, 237
title pages, 8, 164
Toland, John, 62; *The Militia
   Reform'd*, 63
topographies, 228, 234, 238
Tories, 58, 111–15, 127, 128, 162,
   172, 213, 217
tourist industry, 238
trade, 13, 14, 15, 20, 25, 83, 105,
   123, 130
traders, tradesmen, 2, 24, 28, 43, 66
tradition, 123
translatio, 129
translation, 129
transport, 7
travel, 13, 14, 18, 126; narratives,
   14, 18, 19, 20, 250
travelers, 123
treatises, *see* agriculture: agricultural
   treatises; gardens: horticultural
   treatises; landscapes: landscape
   treatises
Treaty of Utrecht, 211, 212
Trenchard, Sir John, *Cato's Letters*, 63,
   68; *A Short History of Standing
   Armies in England*, 75
Trevelyan, G. M., *English Social
   History*, 65, 66
Tudor, *see* Renaissance

Tumir, Vaska, 197
Tutchin, John, *The Foreigner*, 215

United States, 26
universities, 25, 44; Scottish, 124
upper classes, 86, 93; *see also*
    aristocracy; gentry; nobility
urban, 204, 205
Utrecht, *see* Treaty of Utrecht

Vancouver Island, 18
Varro, Marcus Terentius, *De re rustica*,
    237
Virgil, 229, 236; *Georgics*, 208, 228,
    229
virtuosi, 39, 41, 43, 46
voyages, 14, 20, 21
voyeurism, 218

Wales, 16
Wales, William, 22
Waller, Edmund, "To a fair Lady
    playing with a Snake," 217
Waller, Richard, 44
Wallmoden, Amalie Sophie, Countess
    of Yarmouth, 174, 177, 215
Walpole, Horace, 177; *The Castle of
    Otranto*, 145, 150, 152
Walpole, Robert, 61, 111
war, 227; civil, *see* Civil War; First
    World, *see* World War I; Glorious
    Revolution, *see* Revolution of 1688;
    of Independence, American, *see*
    American Revolution; Napoleonic,
    see Napoleonic Wars; Second
    World, *see* World War II; Seven
    Years, *see* Seven Years War
Ward, Edward (Ned), 6, 46, 82, 84,
    103; *History of London Clubs*, 82;
    London Spy, 46, 47, 103
Warton, William, 247, 256
Warwickshire, 234, 236, 238
Washington, George, 162
waste, 7, 101–19

Watt, Ian, 7, 76, 125; *The Rise of the
    Novel*, 76, 122, 128, 137, 138
Watt, James, 237
wealth, 2, 62
Weeks, James Eyre, "On the Great
    Fog in London," 222
Welsted, Leonard, 192
West Indies, 85
Whately, Thomas, 226; *Observations
    on Modern Gardening*, 239–41
Whigs, 58, 102, 111–15, 127, 213, 257
Whytt, Robert, 52
widows, 68; *see also* women
Wilkes, John, 74; *Essay on Woman*,
    61; *North Briton*, 61, 174
Wilks, Robert, 183
William III, 75, 215–16
Willoughby, Francis, *Historia Piscium*,
    48
Wilmot, John, Earl of Rochester,
    174–5, 191; "The Imperfect
    Enjoyment," 220–1
Wilson, Kathleen, 72
Wilson, Thomas, Rev., 173
Winstanley, John, "To the Rev. Mr –
    on his Drinking Sea-Water," 209
wit, 2
Withers, Charles, 131
Wollstonecraft, Mary, 68
Womack, Simon, 188
women, 2, 8, 69, 136, 217; actresses,
    194–5; aristocratic, 168; Asian, 8,
    181; beggars, 6, 80, 88–98; and
    coffee houses, 69–74; excluded
    from concerts, 67; false attributions
    to, 162–81; illegitimate births, 94;
    lying-in hospitals, 94; and
    marriage, 2, 68; as mercenary, 180;
    as mistresses, 174–6; and the
    "private" sphere, 68–9; and
    property, 68; prostitutes, 94; public
    sphere, 68–9, 135; readers, 8, 70,
    164; sexual equality, 2; as sexually
    rapacious, 173, 177; on stage, 2;

women (*cont.*):
  subjectivity, 164; in trade, 2;
  working mothers, 94; writers, 135,
  162–81; *see also* authorship;
  heiresses; widows
Woodward, John, 26; *Brief Instructions
  for Making Observations*, 23
wool industry, 232–3
Wordsworth, William, 97, 203, 239,
  259; Preface to *Lyrical Ballads*,
  147–8; *The Prelude*, 159
workers, 54
workhouses, 80, 81, 90, 91, 93, 94,
  96; London workhouse, 84;

medical provisions in, 94; St Luke's
  Chelsea, 94
World War I, 2
World War II, 2
"world writing," 4, 14
Wright, Hetty, "To an Infant
  Expiring the Second Day of its
  Birth," 209
Wycherley, William, *The Country Wife*,
  189

York, archiepiscopal see of, 60
Young, Edward, 242; *Night Thoughts*,
  52, 171